Speculative Fictions

---

*Family Money*
Jeffory A. Clymer

*America's England*
Christopher Hanlon

*Writing the Rebellion*
Philip Gould

*Living Oil*
Stephanie LeMenager

*Antipodean America*
Paul Giles

*Making Noise, Making News*
Mary Chapman

*Territories of Empire*
Andy Doolen

*Propaganda 1776*
Russ Castronovo

*Playing in the White*
Stephanie Li

*Literature in the Making*
Nancy Glazener

*Surveyors of Customs*
Joel Pfister

*The Moral Economies of
American Authorship*
Susan M. Ryan

*After Critique*
Mitchum Huehls

*Unscripted America*
Sarah Rivett

*Forms of Dictatorship*
Jennifer Harford Vargas

*Anxieties of Experience*
Jeffrey Lawrence

*White Writers,
Race Matters*
Gregory S. Jay

*The Civil War Dead and
American Modernity*
Ian Finseth

*The Puritan Cosmopolis*
Nan Goodman

*Realist Poetics in
American Culture,
1866–1900*
Elizabeth Renker

*The Center of the World*
June Howard

*History, Abolition, and the
Ever-Present Now in
Antebellum American
Writing*
Jeffrey Insko

# Speculative Fictions

## EXPLAINING THE ECONOMY IN THE EARLY UNITED STATES

Elizabeth Hewitt

Ohio State University

Great Clarendon Street, Oxford, OX2 6DP,
United Kingdom

Oxford University Press is a department of the University of Oxford.
It furthers the University's objective of excellence in research, scholarship,
and education by publishing worldwide. Oxford is a registered trade mark of
Oxford University Press in the UK and in certain other countries

First published 2020
First published in paperback 2022

Published in the United States of America by Oxford University Press
198 Madison Avenue, New York, NY 10016, United States of America

British Library Cataloguing in Publication Data
Data available

Library of Congress Cataloging in Publication Data
Data available

ISBN 978-0-19-885913-0 (Hbk.)
ISBN 978-0-19-287138-1 (Pbk.)

*For Eli and Gideon*

## { ACKNOWLEDGMENTS }

I have accrued many debts over the long period in which this book developed, of which these acknowledgements can provide only an inadequate tally. I am grateful to colleagues near and far who generously fielded questions, entertained arguments, read drafts, and improved my thinking in all sorts of other ways. Thank you in particular to Kate Adams, Philip Barnard, David Brewer, Alan Farmer, Molly Farrell, Duncan Faherty, Fritz Fleischmann, Theresa Strouth Gaul, Mark Kamrath, Drew Jones, Frank Kelleter, Leslie Lockett, Sandra Macpherson, Brian McHale, Sean O'Sullivan, Matthew Pethers, Elizabeth Renker, Jake Risinger, Clare Simmons, Lisa Voigt, Roxann Wheeler, Andreá Williams, Susan Williams, and Luke Wilson. At Ohio State University, I have been privileged to have worked under three chairs who were especially important to me. I was hired by Jim Phelan whose intellectual and personal generosity is second to none. Valerie Lee provided encouragement and wisdom that still sustains me. And Robyn Warhol quite literally made this book happen by providing the necessary time in which to bring it to completion. I also want to thank Oliver Scheiding at Johannes Gutenberg University, Mainz, for sponsoring my Fulbright Fellowship that allowed me to teach and present early versions of this book. I am grateful to so many of my undergraduate and graduate students at Ohio State: their wisdom and goodness makes me optimistic about our collective futures. I am especially happy to have had the opportunity to work with, and learn from, Lindsay Dicuirci, Andrew Kopec, and Kristina Garvin.

I am deeply grateful to Oxford University Press, especially Jacqueline Norton, Aimee Wright, Thomas Wells, Katie Bishop, Fiona Tatham, and Vigneshraj Durairaj for their care and attention. Oxford also shepherded the manuscript to anonymous readers whose comments and suggestions were invaluable to me. I cannot even begin to express my gratitude to Gordon Hutner whose good counsel, kindness, and editorship never ceases to amaze.

I have the good fortune to be attached to those who make my world better in all sorts of ways. Two extraordinary women, Marlene Longenecker and Natsu Ifill, died before I was able to finish this book, but they still inspire me. I learned about the world from my students at Columbus Refugee and Immigration Services. Drs. Leslie Kearns, Muna Aldiab, and Paige Turner made me healthier. Lynn Singleton has given me music and friendship. Susan Gardner and Bruce Brooks have made my world more beautiful. Kiki and Capote have sat in my lap and walked with me when I really needed it. My first teachers, Jack Hewitt and Myrna Hewitt, have loved me the longest, and their pride remains vital nourishment. Aman Garcha, Danielle Demko, and their splendid daughters, Violet and Vivian, have always given me joy and delight—not to mention food, drinks, and jokes. My dear friends Michael Trask and Stephen Trask are my treasure. It is foolish to even try to put into prose what I feel about Jared Gardner who has been my best friend for over thirty years now. He has read this manuscript more times than I like to admit, but more crucially, he has loved me. He is also my co-author in the manufacture of our very best work, Eli Gardner and Gideon Hewitt. All grown up now, they are already making the world so much better and brighter.

# { TABLE OF CONTENTS }

Conclusion: Explaining the Economy in the
Twenty-First Century                                               258

# { LIST OF FIGURES }

# { Introduction }

## HAMILTON'S COUNTRY

This book began as a quest to answer what seemed a relatively simple question: why is Alexander Hamilton absent from most narratives about American literary history? The *Norton Anthology of American Literature* only reprints Hamilton's "Federalist 1," the *Heath Anthology of American Literature* replaces this with Hamilton's "Federalist 6," and the *Bedford Anthology of American Literature* contains no writing by Hamilton. Yet all three volumes include substantial excerpts from Thomas Jefferson, James Madison, and John Adams. Jefferson is referenced by numerous essays in Sacvan Bercovitch's *Cambridge History of American Literature*, but Hamilton is not mentioned at all. A search for *Notes on the State of Virginia* in the MLA International Bibliography reveals seventy-three scholarly citations to Thomas Jefferson's text. Conversely, the same search for the subject heading "Report on Public Credit" reveals a single entry written by a historian; a search for "Report on Manufactures" likewise reveals only one essay, this time by an economist; and there is nothing to be found under the search for the subject "Report on a National Bank." Yet Hamilton's Reports are certainly no less "literary" than Jefferson's *Notes*. After all, none of these works are belletristic. Each exemplifies the impeccable, if longwinded, style of the eighteenth-century politician, and each text accompanies its narrative prose with extensive political arithmetic in the form of charts, tables, and inventories. So why has Jefferson's prose so captivated generations of literary historians, while Hamilton's work has been largely ignored?

The question becomes even more perplexing when we reflect on the strange paradox that even as the first Secretary of the Treasury's writing much more substantially shaped the trajectory of American socio-economic development, it is the Jeffersonian story that has

*Speculative Fictions: Explaining the Economy in the Early United States.* Elizabeth Hewitt, Oxford University Press (2020).
© Elizabeth Hewitt.
DOI: 10.1093/oso/9780198859130.001.0001

defined a national mythos that envisions the rise of finance and commercial capitalism as a betrayal of the nation's democratic ideals. We might consider two examples from the twentieth century. First, Franklin Delano Roosevelt, whose responses to the fiscal calamities of the Great Depression so resembled Hamilton's that Paul Samuelson explicitly links the two men in his 1948 economic textbook. Yet Roosevelt modeled his political persona after Jefferson. It was Roosevelt who pushed for the construction of the Jefferson Memorial and, when it opened, he lauded the third president for "establishing the practical operation of the American Government as a democracy and not an autocracy."[1] The unnamed autocratic counterpart, for Roosevelt, was Alexander Hamilton, an opinion he derived from his devoted reading of Claude G. Bowers's *Jefferson and Hamilton: A Struggle for Democracy in America* (1925), the only book that Roosevelt ever reviewed, and a work that firmly established the perception of Hamilton as elitist anti-democrat.[2] Second, let us consider Ronald Reagan, who tripled Federal debt to 2.7 trillion dollars during his eight years in office, thereby following Hamilton's faith in the power of debt, but who nevertheless identified Thomas Jefferson as the spiritual prophet of his "Economic Bill of Rights," declaring, "We're still Jefferson's children."[3] The crucial point to draw is that we have two twentieth-century American presidents, from two different political parties and ideological positions, both of whom adopt fiscal policies inherited directly from the first Secretary of Treasury; yet both refuse this lineage, thereby confirming George Will's quip, "we honor Jefferson, but live in Hamilton's country."[4] Hamilton's country, in this formulation, is one ruled by financialization, commercialization, and industrialization—the product of the Secretary of Treasury's advocacy on behalf of public credit, a national bank, and manufacturing. And so Hamilton is recognized as the proverbial architect of an institutional infrastructure whereby the United States matures into an economic superpower. But he has been cast, even by those who relish the position of the United States as economic powerhouse, in the role of villain in a populist national history that sees the rise of finance and commercial capitalism as a betrayal of democracy. Clearly, then, one reason Hamilton has been relegated to the margins of American literary culture is that, unlike Jefferson, he has been associated with the very institutions that are said to disfigure both culture and democracy.

This mythos became something of a scholarly consensus in the early part of the twentieth century with the publication of Charles Beard's *Economic Interpretation of the Constitution* (1913). Beard argued that the Constitution had to be understood as resulting from a conflict between different economic interests: on one side were "personality" men who wanted to promote commerce, banking, and finance, and on the other were farmers and planters who wanted a government dedicated to the protection of property. Hamilton, according to Beard, was the "colossal genius of the new system" that developed when the economic interests of "personality" ultimately prevailed.[5] The argument was foundational to Bowers's study of early national politics that was so influential for Roosevelt. Beard's work was likewise a crucial influence on early studies of American literature, including Vernon L. Parrington's *Main Currents in American Thought* (1929). Parrington devotes a section of his book to Alexander Hamilton—one that he provocatively titles, "The Leviathan State." He writes, "Of the disciplined forces that put to rout the disorganized party of agrarianism, the intellectual leader was Alexander Hamilton."[6] Parrington titles the section on Thomas Jefferson "Agrarian Democrat," and in so doing represents the partisan conflict as one between a tyrannical king and a ragtag collection of farmer democrats.[7]

Beard's thesis was largely overturned by the mid-twentieth century as many historians insisted he had overstated the importance of economic interests in determining delegate responses to Constitutional framing, and that other political and social issues had a much greater impact in shaping the positions of the Constitutional delegates.[8] But his legacy has been much more durable in Americanist literary scholarship, whose narratives remain profoundly Beardian. As Eric Slauter observes, "New accounts of class conflict and democratization return to the terrain first plowed by progressives like . . . Charles Beard a century ago."[9] Indeed, the most familiar history of American literary development depicts a transition from the republican potential of eighteenth-century literature to the liberal entrenchment of nineteenth-century romanticism. Ed White explains that this conventional literary history is at heart an "economistic explanation of nineteenth-century literature [that] perpetuates an approach most influentially formulated in the early literary histories of the Progressives."[10] And so, even though our literary histories no longer celebrate Jefferson as a radical democrat, they do sustain crucial antinomies that grow from this Progressivist soil, including assumptions about the fundamental contradiction between financialization and democracy and between economics and cultural production.[11] And the field of early American literary studies has been especially committed to the belief that early republican literature occupies a space anterior to the corruptions of the capitalist engine that Hamilton built. As White nicely summarizes, "If economic liberalism called forth romanticism, no similar economic determinant explains the earlier republican writing, which is rather explained in terms of the vaguely organic consensus of social and political values, not economic conditions."[12] Given this commitment to a non-economic reading of early national literature, Hamilton's absence from literary criticism becomes much less surprising.[13]

While we associate the critical ethos I describe above with early twentieth-century Progressivism, it has its roots in the 1790s. Parrington's portrait of an autocratic Hamilton vanquishing the political ambitions of simple farmers rehearses a story that, as we will see, was told throughout the first decades of the United States. This is precisely the tale spun by an eighteenth-century Republican Congressman who condemns Federalist financial policy for allowing "the proud speculator to roll along in his gilded chariot, while the hardy veteran, who had fought and bled for your liberties, was left to toil for his support, or to beg his bread from door to door."[14] There are two crucial components to the fantastical story. The first is the characterization of the protagonists as Manichean opposites: villainous financier and heroic veteran. The second is that the plot emphasizes a simple economic causality: the speculator's profiteering comes directly from the veteran's pocket. This characterization and plotting are typical of the stories told about Hamilton's financial policies throughout the 1790s, and both narrative components are crucial to the longevity of Jeffersonian rhetoric.

Indeed, quite remarkably both strategies continue into our current century. We can see both at work, for example, in the political cartoon shown in Figure 0.1 published in 2009, in the midst of the Great Recession.

The eighteenth-century veteran has become a twenty-first-century laid-off worker—both men are beggars. The speculator riding his gilded coach has transformed into a more contemporary allegory for Wall Street: Rich Uncle Pennybags (aka Mr. Monopoly). Uncle Pennybags clutches the man's losses in his hand in the form of the

0.1 *Mike Luckovich, October 15, 2009*

"bonus" he collected as a member of the 1 percent. Despite, then, the enormous changes to the American economy between the eighteenth century and the twenty-first, the representation of the greedy speculator mercilessly stealing from a humble man remains the same.

What also remains is the articulation of deep anger about the inequities of capitalism, even as the protest signals a deep commitment to its laws. After all, the poor man's sign reads: "Financial meltdown cost me my job, my home, my insurance, my 401K, my marriage." His suffering takes the form of lost property (an income, a house, a retirement plan, a wife)—but much of this property necessarily has its origins in the stock market and instruments of credit. Similarly, at the end of the eighteenth century Hamilton's opponents attacked his fiscal policies as predatory and evil, even as they also embraced the essential tenet of economic liberalism: the protection of private property. Indeed, those on each side of the partisan divide held very similar fundamental assumptions about their economic world. They agreed in a "doctrine of the universal economy," which held that goods had been distributed unevenly across the world thereby making market commerce the necessary means by which various nations could acquire such goods.[15] They understood the protection of private property as the justification for government and they had faith that this same economic self-interest allowed the commercial market to function. They believed that wealth did not consist of money and also that the prices of all goods and labor correlated with monetary supply. Despite, then, the vitriol of their rhetoric, the members of the early national political-economic elite accepted the foundational premises of market capitalism: the invisible hand proposition, the theory of comparative advantage, and the quantity theory of money.[16] They each recognized that the national and global economy were elaborate systems, and they felt an urgency to bring explanatory order to this complexity.

But the nature of their explanatory projects was fundamentally different. For Hamilton, the imperative was to reproduce in his explanations the complex interdependencies and vicissitudes of the market by narrating manifold speculative plots. In his financial proposals, we encounter narratives that emphasize contingent causality and strive to reproduce mimetically the wide terrain of possible economic consequences in which any individual might be implicated. Planning for the economic future, in this regard, seems less a science than a record of suppositions—a collection of speculative fictions. For Jefferson and his fellows, by contrast, the ambition was to provide for readers the very regularity and simplicity that the new economic world had already begun to shatter with its increasingly specialized labor market and mediated supply chains. And the Jeffersonians not only challenged Hamilton's advocacy of public credit, banking, and manufacturing, but they also associated his suppositional explanatory style with financial malfeasance. Following a well-rehearsed Augustan rhetoric that linked economic chicanery with linguistic misrepresentation, they attacked both Hamiltonian policy and rhetoric. And they conversely declared their own explanatory project as dedicated to transparency and simplicity: they aimed to show just how easy it was to trace the movement of capital. *Speculative Fictions* thus approaches the political conflict of the United States' first decade as an economic dispute that can profitably be investigated through a study of literary form: an analysis of the narrative structures by which writers on both sides of the partisan divide attempted to bring coherence to what the economist Jacob Viner describes as "the wilderness of economic phenomena."[17]

In turning to the fiscal debates of the 1790s, I follow a critical tradition of approaching early national literature with special attention to the partisan feuds of that first generation of American politics.[18] But where we have traditionally focused on the political language of this battle—about discrepant understandings of representation, authority, virtue, citizenship—I emphasize the economic conflict that provided the fuel for this partisan fire. Hamiltonians imagined public credit as a public good because they saw the infusion of capital and governmental control over monetary supply and finance as beneficial to economic growth and prosperity. They believed American wealth would come from cheap credit and a flourishing manufacturing and commercial base. Jefferson's party, conversely, saw transferable debt as a public ill because it placed individuals and states on vulnerable economic footing, and they maintained that financialization was only productive of illusory—or paper—wealth. American prosperity would instead be found in the aggregated bounty of small-scale agricultural enterprises. This is the basic outline of the economic conflict that organized the two sides of a debate that "shaped the political life of the new republic in its opening years."[19] And there is voluminous historical literature that seeks to test the veracity of this portrait of early American economics by putting pressure on Hamilton's commitments to national finance and by questioning Jefferson's dedication to the yeomen farmer.[20] My project, however, is not to calibrate the discrepancies between political ideology and economic practice. *Speculative Fictions* is not about the early American economy per se, but about how early American writers *explained* this economy to their fellow citizens. In this way I seek to recast the economic feud between the two parties as a literary debate about the best way to narrate and describe the movement of global capital.

When we approach early republican literature with this emphasis on explanation, we can avoid the familiar critical tendency to read backwards into literary history a future conflict between economic and imaginative writing. I take the terms "economic" and "imaginative" from Mary Poovey, who provides a history of the bifurcation of the two genres in the context of British literature, a division that she locates at the turn of the nineteenth century.[21] My archive draws from precisely this period in which the disciplinary division was being formed. I thus presume no crucial differences between, for example, Hamilton's Report on a National Bank and Judith Sargent Murray's *The Gleaner*. There are certainly generic distinctions between these texts. Hamilton writes to compel his legislative audience to support his fiscal proposal, while Murray tries to sell her literary wares by pleasing and provoking her readers; Hamilton writes a bureaucratic report, while Murray writes periodical essays. But both authors approach their literary tasks with a similar agenda: to explain and represent the complexities of the modern economic world. Literary scholars, however, have typically approached the intersection between economics and literature of the period by stressing an anachronistic generic distinction. We consider the ways that poetry, novels, travel writing, and drama accommodated citizens to life under capitalism by making its systems seem familiar and natural, or alternatively we propose that imaginative literature offered an alternative to the rising dominance of the "cash nexus."[22] Because we always already assume this generic antagonism, we are inclined to read fiction as the heroic knight, gallantly resisting the dominations of capitalism, or as the vanquished hero, ultimately capitulating and lending cultural power to this form of economic production.

This book shifts our attention away from ideology, instead attending to the formal differences that exist between the narratives by which various authors tried to describe the emerging capitalist economy to their only recently postcolonial readers in the United States. Economic science would increasingly come to rely on mathematical formulas to articulate the causal relationships existing between numerous economic variables. But authors also rely on semantics and syntax to make the wilderness of economic contingency cohere, and in the American fiscal debates of the 1790s we can read two very different narrative strategies by which various writers articulated the mechanics of commerce and finance. From the Hamiltonians, we read emphases on the individual's inability to apprehend the full extent of an economic system of which he or she is only a small, contingent part. From the Jeffersonians, we see a synthetic model that locates the individual as the center with which to stabilize and plot this open system.

I use the term "system" because this is the word Adam Smith invokes to describe the intellectual project of political economy at the end of the eighteenth century. And as we will see, those on both sides of the economic debates of the 1790s will copiously cite from Smith's *Wealth of Nations* (1776). Smith's writing also gives expression to the competing allure of *both* the Hamiltonian and Jeffersonian explanatory models. Smith, after all, provides the archetypal critique of the economic "man of system [who] seems to imagine that he can arrange the different members of a great society with as much ease as the hand arranges the different pieces upon a chess-board," but he also posits his own analysis as an example of precisely such a system.[23]

We see something similar in one of Smith's early meditations on philosophical explanation—on how writers set out to "represent[] the invisible chains which bind together...disjoined objects, [and] endeavour[] to introduce order into this chaos of jarring and discordant appearances."[24] It is in this essay, "History of Astronomy" (c. 1750), where his lens focuses on large-scale systems both celestial and human, that Smith first uses the phrase, "invisible hand."[25] Smith identifies the experience of "wonder" as the sensation in the mind that occurs when our imagination is disrupted by a "gap or interval" in a habitual sequence of events or ideas, and he provides examples of such wonder in both astronomical and economic registers. We feel it when we see a solar eclipse because we do not expect the sun to go dark before dusk.[26] We also feel it in the "work-houses of the most common artizans; such as dyers, brewers, distillers," as we marvel at the magic of production—at how commodities "present themselves in an order that seems to us very strange and wonder-ful."[27] Smith theorizes that science is motivated by encountering the "wonder" of such complicated systems. In the face of this amaze-ment, authors strive to produce narratives that "enable the imagina-tion to pass as smoothly, and with as little embarrassment [over these gaps] as along the most regular, familiar, and coherent appearances of nature."[28] Smith thus provides an outline of the two kinds of ex-planatory narratives I study in this book. One will elicit from its readers experiential "wonder" as it elucidates the network of micro-level exchanges that make up the economic wilderness. The other will provide imaginative solace as it illustrates economic complexity as an inherently "simple machine."[29]

Smith's conceptualization of these explanatory methods is echoed in significant ways by Charles Brockden Brown in an essay that has often been identified as a crucial artistic manifesto for understand-ing early American fiction, "The Difference between History and Romance" (1800). For Brown, the generic distinction between his-tory and romance does not reside in the question of facticity—it is not, he explains, that one "dealt in fiction, and the other in truth."[30] The crux of the difference, as Stephen Shapiro summarizes it, is their "explanatory potential."[31] The romancer is afforded license to conjecture the remote causes and effects that precede and extend from any individual action or process. Brown's romancer experiences "wonder" because he recognizes that any single "voluntary action...[is] not only connected with cause and effect," but itself constitutes a "series of motives and incidents subordinate and successive to each other." Thus the "most simple and brief [action]...is capable of being analized into a thousand subdivisions."[32]

My first chapter proposes Alexander Hamilton as just such a romancer, arguing that his major fiscal reports deliberately set out to explain and describe the remote and complex causality of the new nation's location in a global economy.[33] It may seem strange that I identify a man whose writing codified the highly organized and regulated political and economic systems of the Federalist Party as exemplary of a narrative project designed to illustrate the irregularities and contingencies of finance and commerce. Yet, as we will see, even as Hamilton's policies strive to bring order to the new nation's finances, he defends these policies by telling stories about the economy that mimetically represent the necessary unmanageability of market forces. We might therefore observe some evident similarities between what I am describing as Hamilton's approach to economic analysis and the contemporary methodology called actor-network theory, which likewise strives to describe the network of interdependent relations constituting an economy. Hamilton is, of course, a policy maker and not a theorist; yet his justifications for fiscal policy yield a theory of economic interdependence that looks forward to the work of Bruno Latour, Michel Callon, and especially Mark Granovetter.[34] Hamilton's descriptions of economic life neither argue for the preeminence of *homo economicus* nor *homo sociologicus*: the individual neither fully commands her economic world nor is she entirely subjected to the economic institutions in which she operates. A careful reading of Hamilton's work will highlight this mutually constitutive structure, or what Callon describes as the "morphology of the relations in which [economic actors] are involved."[35]

I begin Chapter 1 by looking specifically at the assumptions Hamilton makes about economic causality in his first proposal to extinguish the national debt. Hamilton and his supporters tell tales about debt and risk that depict economic exchange as entwined into a tapestry of events that dwarf individual action and motivation. Then reading Hamilton in relationship to the economic thinkers most crucial to him—especially David Hume and Malachy

Postlethwayt—I propose that we can see beyond the stereotypical rendering of Federalist Finance as the bogeyman that strangled American democratic possibility. I also argue that Hamilton's understanding of narrative implication is crucial to the partisan feuds surrounding the constitutionality of the Bank of the United States. At issue is not only disputes about the role of banks in shaping national finance, but also a contest over the stories we tell about this economy.

The second chapter shifts attention to Hamilton's opponents, focusing on political economic writing by Thomas Jefferson, George Logan, and John Taylor of Caroline. All three men are linked to literary and economic traditions associated with agriculturalism: pastoralism and physiocracy, the eighteenth-century French economic school that theorized land as the exclusive source of national wealth. Yet I posit that the Jeffersonian disposition towards pastoral poetics and physiocratic economic theory is less a consequence of an emphasis on agricultural production than an appreciation for the formal structure of simplification that is elemental to both pastoralism and physiocracy. The charm of the pastoral was not only the rural milieu but the fact that the life of the shepherd distilled and epitomized a vast social system. So too the appeal of French physiocrats—especially work by François Quesnay and Pierre Du Pont de Nemours—lay in the fact that their scientific method represented the economic traffic between landowner, manufacturer, and rural laborer as a simple allegory. The Jeffersonian explanatory narratives followed this model, and as they protested Federalist economic policy as authoritarian and manipulative, they turned their hands to a portrait of the nation's economy as simple machine.

The economic conflicts of the 1790s thus not only rehearsed arguments about national fiscal policy, but presented two different methods by which audiences could acquire economic literacy. And while our modern economy was shaped by Hamilton's policies, the Jeffersonian model of explanation prevailed in the realm of both economics and literature. As neoclassical political economic theory developed in the nineteenth century, it dedicated itself increasingly to synthetic and abstract models of explanation. Even before the disciplinary ascendency of mathematics in the marginal revolution initiated in the second half of the nineteenth century by William S. Jevons, Carl Menger, and Léon Walras, neoclassical economists saw their task not to explain economic irregularities but to provide the general

theories that could locate the common denominator behind seemingly heterogeneous economic effects. Much earlier in the century,
Jefferson articulates his predilection for this approach to economic
science in his translation of Antoine Louis Claude Destutt de Tracy's
*A Treatise of Political Economy* (1817), which Jefferson celebrates for
its stylistic simplicity and methodological efficiency. He commends
the superiority of Tracy's work over Smith's *Wealth of Nations,* insisting that while the latter is "prolix and tedious," Tracy writes with
"brevity, perspicuity," and offers "cogency of logic" and a "rigorous
enchainment of ideas."[36]

And by mid-nineteenth century similar criteria are used to evaluate
imaginative writing. As many historians of the novel have suggested,
the "mature" novel is celebrated for the coherence of its plot, the regularity of the narrative, the integrity of the characters who neatly
stand at the middle of the plot, and the harmonious representation
of matters both private and public.[37] According to such criteria, earlier American narrative fiction is understood as marred by its meandering plots, huge casts of characters, stylistic irregularities, and the
clumsy navigation of private and public registers that make it, like
Jefferson's assessment of *Wealth of Nations,* "prolix and tedious."
Which is to say, as much as we understand the nineteenth century as
marking a disciplinary fork in the road separating economic and
imaginative writing, we should also see that these respective forms
are both motivated, as Georg Lukacs once observed about the novel,
by a need to "think in terms of totality" precisely because the
"extensive totality of life is no longer directly given."[38] And so regardless of whether a reader turned to an economic treatise or a
domestic novel, the formal structure that explicated their economic
world followed the same imperative towards abstraction and simplification. This is why, perhaps, in his own meditations on the limitations
of the novel, Walter Benjamin observes the irony of our contemporary condition in which human beings have lost the "ability to
exchange experiences" even as we live in a world that is entirely
determined by exchange.[39]

But just because the dominant plots by which nineteenth-century
writers came to explain economic exchange were organized around
individuals—as either exemplary economic agents or as psychologi-
cally realistic characters—does not mean that this was the only way
to represent a capitalist economy. Likewise, just because capitalist
economies have naturalized a representational system that expresses

the equivalence of any alienable object (including labor) in a standard denomination called money, this does not mean that the stories we tell about capitalism had to follow suit. And so in Chapters 3 and 4, I consider how other genres from the late eighteenth century engaged in an explanatory method dedicated to narrative dispersal. They told the stories of various actors along extensive supply chains; they documented the numerous moments where actors and commodities intersected along these supply chains; they recorded the countless variables that determined value. They showed their readers, as Brown observed, how even the briefest encounter is "capable of being analized into a thousand subdivisions." In recovering these speculative fictions, I argue, we can also rediscover a better way to understand the ever more complicated and mediated structures of twenty-first-century finance and capital.

My third chapter turns to three writers whose work exemplifies such narrative dissemination: Philip Freneau, Judith Sargent Murray, and Charles Brockden Brown. All three wrote poetry, fiction, and non-fiction prose, incorporating this generic versatility into their periodical essays, a genre that was crucial to their respective literary careers. I suggest that each author turned to the periodical essay as the imaginative form best suited to represent socio-economic relations under capitalism. Or more precisely, each conceived of the formal structure of the periodical essay as the one most capable of reproducing the complex movement of commodified goods and labor. This argument flies in the face of conventional scholarly wisdom, which identifies the novel as the literary genre dedicated to recording the cataclysmic economic changes of the eighteenth century. In fact, two of Brown's novels—*Arthur Mervyn* and *Ormond*—are frequently read as portraits of the emerging capitalist economy of the United States.[40] Yet Brown and Murray actually theorize the periodical essay as superior to the novel in its ability to represent and explain socio-economic relations under capitalism, precisely because its plotless structure allows for the articulation of the multiple nodes of contact that lie between the component parts of a modern economy. And so they crafted into their formal projects the crucial recognition George Eliot would make almost a century later in her masterpiece of literary realism: "the fragment of a life, however typical, is not the sample of an even web."[41]

My fourth chapter turns to an eighteenth-century literary genre that also registers the numerous coordinates of a capitalist economy shaping an individual life: Black Atlantic captivity narratives. This is not, however, how the genre has typically been read: slave narratives, after all, are necessarily plotted around narratives of economic self-possession, and they give expression to life in a labor system that classical political economists understood as antithetical to the virtues of the free market. I suggest that if we shift our focus away from autobiography, we will register that such narratives also describe the enormous scale and complexity of capital markets. It is precisely because the ex-slave had occupied so many economic roles—commodity, money, debt, credit, consumer, producer, rent, profit—that he was uniquely able to articulate the invisible chains that linked goods and people across the globe. Focusing on the narratives of James Albert Ukawsaw Gronniosaw, Venture Smith, and Boyrereau Brinch, I argue that each used their experiences along the long commodity chains that linked Europe, Africa, Asia, and the Americas to explain the economics of both chattel slavery and the free market. And when we move away from an interpretive framework that evaluates the narrator's success in relation to the relative degree of autonomy he secures, we encounter an explanatory project designed to illuminate the mutualism between capitalism and chattel slavery and thus also to revise an essential argument of classical political economic thought.

This book thus argues that we should understand the writing of Freneau, Brown, Murray, Gronniosaw, Smith, and Brinch, as explanatory projects designed to inculcate economic literacy among the nation's citizens. As we will see, concerns about the consequences of economic illiteracy were as urgent at the end of the eighteenth century as they are in the twenty-first. Then, as now, we read lamentations that the American citizenry lacked a clear understanding of their location in an economic system that linked them to numerous unseen peoples, institutions, and nations. And then, as now, commentators on various ends of the political spectrum worried that this ignorance would cause individuals, institutions, and nations to make deleterious economic and political choices. For classical political economists, this nescience can cause individuals to take dangerous risks because they have faith in markets they do not understand. But this selfsame lack of comprehension can also yield a faithlessness that results in an abdication of the market to the individual's own fiscal detriment. If these assessments of the dangers of economic illiteracy are in the service of liberal boosterism, then it is also the case, of course, that Marxist economists make similar appeals to the need to comprehend capital markets. As Immanuel Wallerstein explains it, the central feature of all capital exchange is that profit emerges from the inequitable distribution of wealth and the "remarkable" feature of "capitalism as a historical system was the way in which this unequal exchange could be hidden."[42]

One paradox I mean to reveal in this book is that many of the early American writers who established themselves as spokespersons *against* the turn towards financialization employed literary strategies that actually served to hide, or mystify, the inequalities they ostensibly wished to illuminate. *Speculative Fictions* thus challenges the supposition that financial capitalism is best understood through simplification and abstraction. When Jefferson praises a fellow Democratic-Republican for explaining the nation's finances in such a way that "any farmer can understand them," he expresses his conviction that this tactic will make economic injustice visible to the citizenry. But the very fact that twenty-first-century oligarchs still use Jefferson's explanatory model while advocating on behalf of systems designed to obscure the inequities of capital reveals the deep dangers of the strategy. Returning to the eighteenth century, we can rediscover speculative fictions that provided other ways to explain the plethora of capitalism, narratives that might provide contemporary readers and writers with better tools for mapping the economic systems that entwine us. In an essay on twentieth-century science fiction, Fredric Jameson famously wrote, "Someone once said that it is easier to imagine the end of the world than to imagine the end of capitalism. We can now revise that and witness the attempt to imagine capitalism by way of imagining the end of the world." For Jameson, science fiction possesses a "secret method" that allows its authors to "break[] out of the windless present," out of the "Moebius strip of late capitalism," and follow "one thread, any thread, through to its predictable end."[43] This book argues that the "secret method" of authors like Hamilton, Brown, Murray, and Gronniosaw was to spin suppositious futures through numerous threads. While their speculative projects were designed to imagine the future and not the end of capitalism, their methods, I argue, still have much to teach us about our economic world.

{ 1 }

# Hamilton and the Complex Stories
# of Public Credit

In his analysis of the partisan disputes of the early United States, historian Stephen Knott suggests that while Thomas Jefferson was the "poet of the American founding," Alexander Hamilton engaged in the prosaic details of nation building.[1] The force of the distinction between poetry and prose seems to hinge on aesthetics: Jefferson is the beautiful visionary and Hamilton the unimaginative bureaucratic. Jefferson's America is a bucolic agrarian land and Hamilton's is the industrialized financial state. Yet, even if we admit that the topics of Hamilton's famous three reports—public credit, the national bank, and American manufacturing—seem neither beautiful nor sublime, we must acknowledge that this work, which has formed the foundation of American economic policy for over 200 years, was profoundly speculative—imaginatively projecting into the future with remarkable acuity. Perhaps this is why only thirty years after Hamilton's death, Daniel Webster would say of him,

> He smote the rock of the national resources, and abundant streams of revenue gushed forth. He touched the dead corpse of the Public Credit, and it sprang upon its feet. The fabled birth of Minerva, from the brain of Jove, was hardly more sudden or more perfect than the financial system of the United States, as it burst forth from the conceptions of Alexander Hamilton.[2]

Webster's rapture is directed particularly at the Secretary of Treasury's first Report on Public Credit, in which Hamilton outlined the detailed plan whereby the United States would refund their many debtors. Webster metaphorizes Hamilton's proposals as acts of divinity to acknowledge the prodigious speed in which Hamilton wrote his Report and to recall the seeming intractability of the new nation's finances circa 1789.

*Speculative Fictions: Explaining the Economy in the Early United States.* Elizabeth Hewitt, Oxford University Press (2020).
© Elizabeth Hewitt.
DOI: 10.1093/oso/9780198859130.001.0001

Hamilton's Report on Public Credit provided an intricate description of the heterogeneous array of instruments that had financed the Revolutionary War: the certificates of different maturities and interest rates distributed and traded between various state and federal institutions. Charged with bringing coherence to this financial mess, not to mention credibility to a nation that owed millions of dollars to both foreign and domestic creditors, Hamilton set out to explain the myriad causes and effects of any proposed financial policy. In making the case for public credit, his self-imposed mandate was to rationalize what almost all believed to be a fundamentally chaotic system of accounting and to justify what many believed to be an inherently dangerous system of funded public debt. At the same time, he needed to deflect suspicions that his explanations about the necessity for public credit constituted a larger scheme designed to defraud the populace and saddle the nation with even greater fiscal burdens. Hamilton largely failed at this second task, and this failure is one significant residue of his legacy: his writing may have articulated the premises of many foundational institutions of modern American capitalism, but he was never able to offer a literary strategy that could ameliorate the suspicions of his critics. This chapter will detail the literary form that Hamilton's economic writing took and also explain why it was so vulnerable to formal critique.

Hamilton seems to have recognized his predicament even before he begins drafting the Report. Writing the Marquis de Lafayette in 1789 to beg his patience for the repayment of the huge debt owed to France, Hamilton confesses his anxiety about his recent appointment as Secretary of Treasury: "In undertaking the task, I hazard much."[3] He begins the text of his Report likewise by describing the "no small degree" of anxiety he experiences as he measures the "difficulty of the task" (531). This is perhaps why Hamilton chooses to open with an appeal to natural law and a tidy tale about the moral obligations of debtors. Even as his long document is replete with explanations, statistics, and detailed accounting of debts and mechanisms for repayment through a variety of interest repayment plans, he also announces that "any attempt to enumerate the complicated variety of mischiefs in the whole system of the social œconomy" was futile and constituted "an improper intrusion on [the House's] time and patience" (532). He thus begins his proposal not by drawing out the intricacies of the nation's debt, but by telling a very simple story that stresses the analogy between the indebted nation and the personal debtor: "States, like individuals, who observe their engagements are respected and trusted: while the reverse is the fate of those, who pursue an opposite conduct" (532).

Hamilton begins with this simple allegory of the nation as an individual for numerous strategic reasons. He wants to diminish the significance of the confusing status of outstanding debts, and he likewise wants to deemphasize the complexity of his own proposal. And because Hamilton knew that there was suspicion of the science of finance, he opens not by appealing to a specialized vocabulary to describe the wealth of nations, but rather to the familiar terms used to characterize the wealth of individuals. Hamilton narrates this familiar tale in an effort to promote his belief in the necessity of public credit and to bolster his own credibility. He turns to a homily with an easy moral (the man who repays his creditors is trusted) and deploys a simple figure (the simile) to present his argument for public credit in a literary mode that transparently explains its symbolic assumptions. The United States is like the individual merchant who must repay outstanding debts lest his character as reliable businessman crumble and he subsequently fail. He trusts that his audience will appreciate the simile and therefore also trust his proposal to refinance the public debt. Faith is not merely, as Hamilton says, "the basis of public credit" (533), but also what he asks from his readers, as he suggests when he appeals both to "the immutable principles of moral obligation" and the patriotic calculation that asserts the national debt is quite literally "the price of liberty" (533). With this assumption of general consent, Hamilton can succinctly proclaim, "A general belief, accordingly, prevails, that the credit of the United States will quickly be established on the firm foundation of an effectual provision for the existing debt" (534). His description of this prevailing "general belief" points to the finesse of his paradoxical mandate, which is that the nation's credit will be buoyed not just by repaying debt, but by circulating more of it.

By hinging his policy recommendations on what he characterizes as a universally held belief that, as a young nation founded in revolution, the United States has to prove its fiscal responsibility so as to justify the confidence of their creditors and to "increase[e] respectability of the American name" (534), Hamilton postpones the more treacherous discussion of the "provisions" necessary to reinforce this financial reputation. Likewise by framing his argument in terms of the manifold social benefits that are secured by a position of strong public credit, Hamilton tells a story that works to obscure public credit's dialectic implication in public debt—that you cannot have one without the other. He attempts something similar when he proposes that credit bonds can function as currency—that so long as creditors have faith in their redemption, these bonds can function as money in the marketplace, effectively pumping capital into the cash-starved American economy. Hamilton posits the monetary function of public debt as a "well known fact," even though it was regularly disputed by his opponents, because it was the linchpin of his argument about the public good that derives from public credit. Further Hamilton argues that having debt circulate as if it were specie benefits citizens at *all* ranks since by increasing money supply, trade and economic growth in both "agriculture and manufactures" is augmented, which causes interest rates to drop, thereby helping both the farmer and the merchant, the poor as well as the landed.

Hamilton's logic thus assumes that public credit has positive benefits even for those individuals who cannot comprehend how they are incorporated into the larger commercial world. He also implicitly suggests that those who conceive of public credit as necessarily plutocratic fail to understand how commerce works. His opponents do not see the long and indirect causal chains that link manifold economic participants in a global credit economy. Inevitably, however, as Hamilton describes the intricate components of commerce and finance, his allegorical parable of the reliable debtor proves increasingly inadequate to the task at hand. Thus in describing the many social benefits that accrue from circulating public credit, Hamilton necessarily moves away from the simple story with which he began. The crucial paradox, however, is that even as the simple formulas and stories misconceive the economy, they nonetheless retain their allure and power. After all, if the key to public credit is confidence, then this demands that participants at least *believe* they understand how value is determined.

The citizenry's nescience about value—how it is realized in commodities and money—becomes a critical problem as Hamilton plunges into the details of his proposal. Although he begins by insisting that the intricacies of the new science of finance are insignificant to the larger case he wants to make, Hamilton was appointed Secretary of the Treasury, and made responsible for devising a solution to the nation's debt, precisely because he was one of the few citizens who had financial expertise. Hamilton's difficult charge was formally to represent finance as the extensive and multifarious system it was, and at the same time to render this heterogeneity systematic and comprehensible. And this is why, as we will see, his Report was both praised and condemned for its stylistic complexity. For those who supported it, the Report on Public Credit was read as a clear exegesis of a complicated plan. His opponents quite differently argued that both his Report and the financial plan it outlined constituted an ingenious and chimerical logic designed to obscure the truth.

Hamilton's anxious premonitions about the reception of his Report were fulfilled almost immediately when, before it was even presented to the House of Representatives, speculations as to the document's recommendations set off a firestorm throughout the nation. Controversy even surrounded the format by which it would be presented to Congress. When Hamilton's friend, and New Jersey representative, Elias Boudinot made the case for Hamilton to deliver his Report orally, explaining, "gentlemen would not be able clearly to comprehend so intricate a subject without oral illustration," some Representatives worried about the "propriety" of allowing "oral communications from the Head of such an important Department."[4] Similarly anxious about oral delivery, but emphasizing the document's complexity, other representatives demanded that it should find its expression with the "permanency of writing." Elbridge Gerry (another supporter of the bill) explained that no man "on this floor [should] suppose himself capable of comprehending and combining the parts of a general system, calculated to produce such a grand effect" because the "human mind" would be unable to retain "objects so extensive and multifarious upon a mere oral communication."[5] Fisher Ames likewise argued that its complexity made oral presentation problematic, suggesting that the Report ought to be delivered in print, as only "in this shape they would obtain a degree of permanency favorable to the responsibility of the officer, while, at the same time, they would be less liable to be misunderstood."[6]

Gerry, Boudinot, and Ames supported the proposal, and admired it for its intricacy, but they conceive of two entirely different strategies for mitigating the potential dangers the complexity might pose to its acceptance by Congress. For Boudinot, Hamilton's physical presence and "oral illustration" would be a useful corrective to the topic's abstraction and the intricacy of the refinancing proposals: the embodied author, Hamilton, would be able to secure meaning and value as he presented and explained his speculative text to Congress. Gerry and Ames conversely locate stable value not with Hamilton's voice, but with the ability for the printed text to represent and contain a "general system." Gerry insists that the individual "human mind," which constitutes only a small cog in the machinery of commerce and finance, is incapable of an accurate conception of the system. Notably, Gerry's argument on behalf of textual reproduction is predicated on the same claim about narrative complexity on which Hamiltonian finance is based. Like Hamilton, Gerry describes national finance as an economic structure in which individuals are incapable of comprehending their location in the vast system into which they are imbricated. Not only is the individual person unable to conceive the whole, but this same individual is only significant insofar as he or she is a part of a larger economic system and dependent on other economic individuals. Thus, although Hamilton's Report begins with a simple little story about individual debt, its narrative structure militates against the importance of any one person's economic decisions and this narrative logic is also a crucial justification for Hamilton's financial policies.

In the end, the fifty-one-page report was delivered to Congress both ways: it was presented orally, although not by Hamilton, who was not permitted to read the document in person; and it was also decided that the Report should be printed for members. Within a week of its presentation on January 14, 1790, *The Gazette of the United States* had published a "summary report" outlining the three major positions of Hamiltonian policy: a commitment to repaying both principle and interest on the outstanding debt; a refusal to discriminate between original and subsequent debt holders; and a decision to assume all outstanding individual state debts.[7] By the beginning of February, the full text of the Report had been published in newspapers around the country and the full-blown media war surrounding Hamilton's plan had begun. One Federalist writer records, "The subject of the Secretary's Report engrosses the public attention universally: It is the topic in all companies."[8] The extensive circulation of the proposal was controversial because conjecture as to whether Congress would enact Hamilton's proposals had considerable effect on the speculative valuation of the outstanding paper debt. Stories abound of Congressional public galleries filled to the rafters with interested spectators and speculators eager to discover how Congress would act. Two weeks after the initial report was presented, in response to suggestions that discussion of the proposal be delayed until May, Theodore Sedgwick pointed to the crowded galleries as proof of the need for all due speed. Here is an exemplary case of the ways that financial texts—like literary ones—depend on the credulity of their readers to make meaning and value.[9] For Sedgwick, who supported Hamilton's plan, the crowds of potential speculators, waiting to learn whether the paper they would buy would increase in value with the Federal government's commitment to repayment, confirmed how an extensive system of faith and confidence was fundamental to fiscal solvency.[10]

Hamilton's opponents, conversely, saw the frenzy of interest surrounding the Report as confirmation that speculation in public credit was a violation of both virtue and productive labor. And thus they notably and strategically made no distinction between the Report and the acts of speculation that might follow from it. It was not merely that that they assumed Congressional passage of Hamilton's proposals would render the all but worthless paper re-deemable at par, but they also assumed that news of the Report and Congressional deliberations were being secretly passed on to wealthy men who would profit from their privileged knowledge of Hamilton's plans. Paradigmatic, for example, is the frequently vituperative Senator William Maclay, who records in his journal: "'Tis said a committee of speculators in certificates could not have formed it more for their advantage."[11] Maclay implies that Hamilton was circulating a manu-script draft of the Report before its delivery to Congress so as to enable his friends and colleagues to make considerable profit from the legislation about to be advanced.[12]

Both sides recognized that in the world of finance, information is an instrumental component of value and therefore also profit taking. And therein lies the significance of the accusation made by so many of Hamilton's opponents that the funding system was complex and purposefully designed to obfuscate its consequences. They not only accused Hamilton of advocating for a scheme designed to aid specu-lators at the expense of citizens, but they also claimed that the Report's language and structure were deliberately designed to con-fuse all but the most financial savvy individuals. Maclay writes, "There is an obstinacy, a perverse peevishness, a selfishness which shuts him up from all free communication."[13] While his advocates would praise Hamilton for being able to fathom what was otherwise incomprehensible to those schooled in older models of economic theory, his opponents charged him with using his ostensible expertise to engage literary sleights-of-hand as the means to foist a fundamentally dangerous financial system on the nation. Hamilton, they claimed, indulged the specialized language of finance so as to confuse citizens who understood the debt certificates in simple terms—as promissory notes for service to the nation.

The invective directed at Hamilton came from different factions, but the most outspoken were those who argued on behalf of a policy of debt discrimination. These critics maintained that the original debt holders who had earlier sold the debt certificates for pennies on the dollar (or, more accurately, three shillings on the pound) because they assumed the debt would never be honored by the state or national governments, were still creditors—and deserved to be compensated by any proposed repayment plan. They further argued that speculators—those who had purchased this debt cheaply and now stood to make a substantial profit on the paper if Hamilton's plan passed—were perpetrating fraud by circulating debts as currency. They thus argued that a discrimination, or distinction, should be made on the repayment at par: original creditors should receive full value, but later purchasers should only receive the price at which they purchased the debt. Opposition to Hamilton also came from those who maintained that Hamilton's redemption plan itself constituted repudiation, since he proposed a reduced interest rate on the outstanding securities.

Crucially, however, while opposition came from different perspectives of political ideology and policy, one feature they shared was a critique of Hamilton's use of language. Despite the diverse character of these appraisals, all his critics posited an analogy between Hamiltonian finance and his rhetorical practices. They argued that just as Hamilton does not say what he means, as he employs abstruse prose, and as he engages in a loose construction of the Constitution, so too does his financial plan depend on a fallacious and alchemical transformation of debt into public credit, and public credit into money.

## David Hume's Plausible Fictions

The key texts and writers attributed with influencing Hamilton's writing on public credit are well known and include classical political economists like David Hume, James Steuart, and Adam Smith, as well as more policy-oriented texts including the Bank of England charter and writings on finance by the French Finance Minister Jacques Necker. These works not only theorized human consumption, exchange, and production as a new science, but also aimed to narrate the emerging science of economics. For example, describing Hume's monetary theory, Margaret Schabas writes, "the advent and rise of commerce and trade for Hume is a complicated tale of the interplay of human trust and deception."[14] It is therefore imperative that we understand the burgeoning science of political economy as a narrative exercise: its writers sought to tell the "complicated tales" necessary to explain how price was related to monetary supply, to describe the relative costs of labor, land, and capital, to reckon the correlations between interest rate and money supply, to explain the relationship between national wealth and agricultural production, and, more generally, to articulate the numerous other relationships that constituted the modern economy. Indeed, we might even understand Hume's repudiation of mercantilism as essentially a narrative project: the belief that the quantity of gold or silver in the nation's coffers comprised its wealth was based on a decidedly simple story, a veritable fairy-tale about value in which wealth is neatly symbolized by the gold coin stored in a national treasure chest. An explanation of a global capitalist system that must account for representational wealth and for the perpetual movement of commodities exchanged through heterogeneous currencies requires something more sophisticated than an allegorical pot of gold.

In telling his own story, Hamilton was deeply influenced by Hume. Stanley Elkins and Eric L. McKitrick are unequivocal in describing the intellectual relationship: "the affinity of [Hamilton's] thoughts, paragraph by paragraph, to those of Hume is striking."[15] They propose that Hume was of considerable importance because Hamilton had a strong affinity for Hume's belief that commerce engendered cultural development. Hume is also significant to my own analysis of Hamilton's narrative of American finance because Hume specifically meditates on the significance of literary style to economic explanation. Hume begins, for example, "Of Commerce" (1752) by describing the essential difference between "shallow" and "abstruse" thinkers. Depicting the latter as a rare commodity, and valued precisely because they offer analysis that cannot be learned "from every coffee-house conversation," Hume castigates those who censure refined thinkers simply because they offer analysis "beyond their own weak conceptions."[16] Identifying his own moral philosophy with the science of the "general," he describes the imperative to "enlarge" one's views so as to "comprehend under them an infinite number of individuals, and include a whole science in a single theorem."[17] Yet Hume also acknowledges that it is not "easy for the bulk of mankind" to see the subtle connections between the particular cases that constitute the general: "Every judgment or conclusion, with them, is particular."[18] Although Hume explains that he provides this meditation as an introduction to his writing on "commerce, luxury, money, interest, &c.," in an effort to forestall accusations that his analysis will "seem too refin'd and subtle for such vulgar subjects," he nevertheless also recognizes that when it comes to "politics, trade, œconomy, or any business in life," it may perhaps be better to err on the side of superficiality, since the more intricate and refined are the associations of reason, the more likely there is to be a "strong presumption of falsehood."[19] Hume thus describes the vexing paradox in which the study of commerce requires sophisticated thought and yet also renders itself vulnerable to charges of fraud or sophistry precisely because it engages such subtle and "abstruse" analysis.

Hume notes a similar paradox in his description of the narrow line that likewise must be navigated between excessive refinement and excessive simplicity in prose styling. In "Of Simplicity and Refinement in Writing" (1752), he warns against the dangers of excessive ornamentation, including "uncommon expressions, flashes of wit, pointed similes, and epigrammatic turns," characterizing their disfiguring possibility as something akin to the viewer who, "in surveying a gothic building," becomes so "distracted by the multiplicity of ornaments" that he "loses the whole."[20] What is striking about these observations is that Hume begins his interrogation of style in this essay on literary writing by warning against the very rarity of and comprehensive attention to subtle details that he praises in his observations about economic analysis. However, just as in "Of Commerce," wherein Hume described the potential dangers that characterized refinement in economic analysis, so too here does he warn against both excessive simplicity and complexity, confessing that ascertaining when writing strays too far in either direction is difficult, "if not impossible."[21] Hume's observations do not merely point to a similarity between economic and literary style, but also indicate the similar dangers entailed by excessive refinement in both literary writing and economic analysis, which is the "presumption of falsehood." Thus, Hume explains that all writers ought to be "more on [their] guard against the excess of refinement than that of simplicity," because "ordinary readers" are easily duped and stylistic rococo threatens to "pervert the taste of the young and inconsiderate."[22]

This concern about the "strong presumption of falsehood" entailed by ornate style and complex narrative seems likewise to inform Hume's conviction against public credit and in favor of a monetary policy in which paper instruments were secured by metallic currency. Hume understood money as a "fictitious" medium of exchange—as a symbol that secured intercourse between financial participants; and he explicitly compared commercial and linguistic systems, explaining that just as "languages are gradually established by human conventions," so too "do gold and silver become the common measures of exchange."[23] Hume's analogy also makes clear that that he does not make a fundamental distinction between metal and paper money: they are equally fictitious insofar as they merely serve as an agreed upon medium of exchange. But Hume nonetheless argues for specie backing and against using public credit as circulating media of exchange. His anxieties about paper currency and an expanding public debt funded by government securities are not a consequence of a belief that these instruments do not harness real value since his writing consistently describes paper vehicles as an essential tool in modern commerce. The problem, rather, is that non-metallic currency involves narratives potentially so confounding they undermine faith, or what economists sometime call, higher-order beliefs.[24] When Hume characterizes the arguments for public credit as similar to the "trials of wit amongst rhetoricians," he is both pointing to what he sees as the specious logic on the part of public credit's advocates *and* he is explaining with great precision why public credit fails.[25] Because its advocates make their case by way of "puzzling" stories, they necessarily undermine credit's credibility.

Crucially, then, we must locate Hume's political economy in terms of his larger philosophical conviction in plausible fictions—in his understanding that temporal progress, the continuity of objects, and personal identity all depend on feints of imagination. Consider, for example, Hume's explanation of how we come to believe in the "continu'd existence of all sensible objects." He writes, "this propensity arises from some lively impression of the memory, it bestows a vivacity on that fiction; or in other words, make us believe the continu'd existence of body."[26] Explaining Hume's fictions, Annette Baier writes, "Fictions are plausible stories we tell ourselves to organize our experience."[27] C. George Caffentzis explains that Hume makes a distinction between such plausible fictions and what he calls "artificial fictions"—those stories that are not universally believed and wherein belief "involves conscious deception."[28] This distinction, for Caffentzis, is the key to understanding the discrepancy between Hume's acceptance of the pragmatic use of paper currency and his deep skepticism about its public benefits. While metallic money is "rooted in a deeper, conventional layer of social life that arises from a sense of common interest," paper money involves self-conscious deception that strains at the credulity of its participants.[29]

The ambivalence in Hume's position towards paper money and public credit is crucial to debates about financing American public debt in 1790 for two reasons. First, Hume's authority was invoked by those both arguing for and against public credit. Indeed, one remarkable aspect about these debates is that Hume, Smith, and Steuart are cited by those on both sides of the fiscal fence in support of their respective arguments.[30] Second, Hume's analysis of the different degrees of imaginative credulity required by different vehicles of commercial exchange reveals the centrality of narrative style to the field of commerce. Hamilton's charge was to write the policy and supporting documents that would describe and illuminate the myriad and subtle tissues weaving together the plausible fictions on which the United States' economy would be based without threatening the citizenry's faith—a threat that always loomed because of the presumption of falsehood implied by both the abstruseness of his documents and the fiction of paper currency. At issue was not merely familiar accusations against paper currency, of which a transferable and circulating public credit was only one instance, but a more extensive anxiety that in adopting Hamilton's financial policies the nation's citizens were also choosing a fiction by which they were systematically organizing their lives.

## Fictions in the Report on Public Credit

Given the response to all three of Hamilton's proposals, it would seem that Hamilton did not heed Hume's warning especially well. And we might even locate a particular moment in the Report on

Public Credit where Hamilton makes the fatal narrative error in acknowledging that there is no "unanimity of sentiment" (537) as to the funding of the domestic debt. The contentious issue with which Hamilton begins is his conviction that there should be no discrimination made between original holders of governmental securities holders and subsequent purchasers. Hamilton knew that if and when Congress approved his proposal to fund the public debt, the old certificates, which had depreciated substantially since their initial entrance into the market, would return back to par value. In many ways, this was precisely what he desired, since it would prove that markets would follow confidence, and thus confirmed the basic logic on which his Report was founded: that the nation's financial position would be strengthened by its committed promise to repay debt by establishing new instruments of credit. Yet this positive consequence was also a public relations nightmare. Many veterans had been paid with these certificates, but these same creditors, out of financial necessity or because they imagined that they would never be repaid, had sold these securities at highly reduced market prices. Although Hamilton's plan would kindle the market in this old debt, the creditors who had previously sold their certificates gained nothing from the suddenly appreciating prices. Not surprisingly much of the anger directed at the report focused around this issue.

At first, it appears that Hamilton plans to respond to the critique by taking a similar tactic to that which began the Report—that he will appeal to first principles, essentially making an argument that admits of no dissent. Thus, while he describes his "deference" to the other position and he acknowledges the unfortunate scenario that emerges from his policy (in which the person to whom the debt was originally owed receives only three shillings to the pound, while the subsequent purchaser who paid only three shillings will be redeemed the face value of the debt), he nonetheless declares any policy of discrimination to be "inconsistent with justice" and a "breach of contract" (538). In this appeal to the inviolability of contract law, Hamilton makes an argument premised on liberal jurisprudence: because "every buyer … stands exactly in the place of the seller, [and] has the same right with him to the identical sum expressed in the security … his claim cannot be disputed, without manifest injustice" (538). The conventional reading of this argumentative move on Hamilton's part is that it reveals his deep commitment to a political liberalism founded in principles of contract and property rights. For example, Ron Chernow says that what is notable about Hamilton's refusal to entertain the possibility of discrimination is that he did not appeal to the practical obstacles of, for example, ascertaining original owners and sale prices. Instead, according to Chernow, Hamilton "established the legal and moral basis of securities trading in America."[31] Robert Wright similarly lauds Hamilton for not "try[ing] to sort out all the details as a simple administrative mind might."[32] And it is certainly the case that Hamilton's argument is based on his basic belief in the inviolability of contracts. But, as the Report continues, it moves away from abstract principles about property rights and the hypothetical equity of contracts, and more into the kinds of details that Chernow and Wright insist he largely ignores.

The Report rejects discrimination on the basis of two very different kinds of arguments. On one hand, Hamilton disputes a policy of discrimination by saying that it violates the premise of free contract and the transferability of public securities, which is the armature from which he is constructing his system of American finance. Public credit can only be a "blessing" if potential investors have confidence that the paper debt they buy can be transferred and redeemed. On the other hand, Hamilton argues that discrimination is illegitimate insofar as it misconceives of the formal structure that economic relations take. That is, he moves further away from claims about equity and increasingly into an analysis of the narrative complexity of financial transactions, arguing that this complexity is itself the reason why a policy of discrimination is unacceptable.

While recognizing that some original bond holders "sold from necessity," thereby nodding towards the potential inequity of these financial transactions, Hamilton also says that "it does not follow, that this was the case with all of them" (539). Here Hamilton subtly revises the terms of his analysis: discrimination is not anathema because it legalizes a breach in contract, but because it misunderstands and misrepresents the fundamentally contingent and incalculable variety that characterizes financial transactions. To demonstrate his point, Hamilton proceeds to speculate on the wide array of possible motivations sellers might have had to compel them to transfer their bonds, as well as the huge number of possible consequences from any single transaction. His speculation takes the form of a series of interrogatives, all of which seem to disallow a singular explanation or answer:

> It may well be supposed, that some of them [sold]...either through want of confidence in an eventual provision, or from the allurements of some profitable speculation. How shall these different classes be

discriminated from each other? How shall it be ascertained...that the money, which the original holder obtained for his security, was not more beneficial to him, than if he had held it to the present time, to avail himself of the provision which shall be made? How shall it be known, whether if the purchaser had employed his money in some other way, he would not be in a better situation, than by having applied it in the purchase of securities, though he should now receive their full amount? (539)

Employing the anaphora ("how shall?"), Hamilton turns both theoretical and speculative, and his questions imagine the myriad of possible storylines that might descend from any one transaction. While it might be the case that a poor veteran sold his continentals to a predatory speculator in order to buy bread for his dying wife (and such tragic tales frequently were offered in opposition to Hamilton's plan), it is also the case that this selfsame veteran might have taken the monies from selling his continentals and purchased land, from which he potentially could have made a considerable profit. Moreover, perhaps the speculator who purchased his securities might himself have had to decide whether to buy the credit certificate (with the hopes that he would make a profit sufficient to save his dying wife), and had he made another investment perhaps he might have fared better. Hamilton's use of the interrogative mode allows for precisely these kinds of narrative conjectures: indeed by asking questions instead of outlining the possible plotlines, Hamilton indicates the infinite number of possible ways the story of each individual transaction could have gone.

In this way, Hamilton emphasizes what he sees as the misconception of discrimination: that the myriad cases of debt all involved the same essential story. His opponents, he suggests, falsely imagine that the story of debt follows an unequivocal plot in which an individual bond holder sells at a loss to a wealthy speculator who profits from the misery of the original owner. Hamilton muses that while this may have been the denouement of any one transaction, it was foolhardy to speculate that such was the scenario for all the millions of dollars of debt that had accrued since the conclusion of the war. Hamilton insists that no one plot can capture the myriad of transactions of which this single exchange is only one strand, and his questions instead propose that any drama about financial exchange must be embedded in a longer and more elaborate tale—one capable of containing a series of interconnected causes, effects, outcomes and motivations. There are various reasons for sales and purchases: the monies spent and saved, profits gained and lost, involve infinite plot trajectories, which themselves ripple out in any number of possible consequences. Such stories are woven together as a chain of speculations, which is why Hamilton insists on the interrogative voice ("How shall it be ascertained" or "how shall it be known"). These questions imply that speculation is not the prerogative of stockjobbers alone: even the victims and losers of particular financial exchanges engage in speculation. They too strive to balance economic risks and gains. "It may well be imagined," he muses, that there were some original owners who sold their certificates and then purchased others "as an indemnity for their first loss" on the secondary market (539). Thus, Hamilton concludes his interrogative possibilities: "Questions of this sort, on a close inspection, multiply themselves without end" (539).

Hamilton attacks a policy that would discriminate between original and subsequent buyers not because of the bureaucratic difficulty of locating these transactions, but because such a policy miscomprehends the complex plot structure of the economic world. Those who argue on behalf of discrimination see each debt transaction as generic—as establishing the essential conditions, characters, and terms for all that follow—and thus they cannot even begin to fathom the manifold consequences that emerge from the policy for which they are advocating. And it is not merely the assumption that each economic exchange is fundamentally similar to the others that signifies a certain logical and narrative incapacity; it is also the fact that Hamilton's opponents tell stories of rapacious speculation that excise individual transactions from the social networks in which they are necessarily implicated. The significance of a bond between creditors, according to Hamilton, is not limited to these individuals (or even the persons immediately tied to them like widows and children); it rather spreads in rhizomatic fashion into relations between incalculable other persons, their nations, companies, governments, and families. By centering their attention on isolated and individual exchanges of goods and services for paper, and by transforming the heterogeneous variety of such exchanges into one potboiler tale of exploitative larceny, his opponents, he suggests, use sentimental oversimplification to misrepresent the economic relationships they depict.

I am arguing that Hamilton's critique is not just one of policy—in which he is accusing his opponents of making choices that will undermine public credit—but also an aesthetic critique of his opponents' ability to offer a mimetic representation of the modern economic world. He accuses his opponents of something like narrative caricature—of simplifying and reducing the complexity of the economic world they pretend to describe. To prove the point he provides his own little tale as a demonstration of the "capricious operation" caused by debt discrimination. Let us imagine, Hamilton proposes, "two persons, who may be supposed two years ago to have purchased, each, securities at three shillings in the pound, and one of them to retain those bought by him...the other to have parted with those bought by him, within a month past, at nine shillings" (540). A policy of discrimination, Hamilton continues, would reward the first purchaser who "had most confidence in the government" with six fewer shillings (plus interest) than the second purchaser, who "had less confidence" (540). Hamilton rehearses this counterstory of inequity so as to reveal the limitations of a policy of discrimination to capture the "immense" (540) range of individual transactions that constituted American credit. "To discriminate the merits of these several descriptions of creditors," Hamilton argues, "would be a task equally unnecessary and invidious" (542).

Hamilton designs his tale to reveal the limitations of his opponents' narrative imagination, but his illustration also points to the dangers that inhere because credit markets are built on such immense and precarious systems of interdependent belief. Hamilton thus seeks to explain why discrimination erodes a major advantage of public debt, which is the ability to circulate as a fiction shared by all readers. Discrimination, he says, depreciates the "quality" (540) of the public debt. According to Hamilton, were the nation to adopt a policy that adjusted redeemable value according to when the owner purchased the debt, it would necessarily undermine the credibility, and therefore worth, of the certificates themselves. Unless the market has faith in the exchangeability (and meaningfulness) of debt, then its value is necessarily depreciated. And Hamilton thus tries to counter the opposition by anticipating that one consequence of discrimination will be to lower the value of the certificates owned by original debt holders.

But even as Hamilton acknowledges that debt pricing will fluctuate and that his opponents misrepresent the cacophony of economic exchange, he also adamantly assumes that there is some shared meaning on which value has been communicated, and that this meaning will continue to be communicated in perpetuity. Recognizing the volatility and interdependence of credit markets, Hamilton's policy tries to ground a credible fiction in the centralized authority of the Federal government. The Report acknowledges that his proposal can control neither the numerous events that precede any economic transaction nor the countless consequences that descend causally from it: matters of contract, Hamilton says, can only ever involve "probabilities" (552). And yet, even while acknowledging that no financial policy can capture the complexity of the macroeconomic world, he offers his Report to stabilize the language in which these probabilities might be written.

It is this literary strategy of consolidation and unification with which contemporary readers are most likely to associate Hamilton's writing. Whether we see Federalism's "unifying simplicity" in positive terms, or negatively as a "frontal assault on the reader's deliberative position," literary critics have linked Hamilton's party with a kind of linguistic authoritarianism.[33] And certainly, as we will see, Hamilton's proposals on behalf of public credit, a national bank, and national excise taxes were read by his opponents as tyrannical assaults on deliberative democracy. But this assessment does not register the other literary style that Hamilton's economic writing adopts as he sets out to explain the financial revolution in which the young nation finds itself. This style has primarily been read as a symptom of Hamilton's logorrhea, his seemingly constitutional inability to "talk less."[34] I suggest that we read this tendency towards prolixity as a purposeful strategy designed to reproduce—to mimetically represent—the "fluctuation and insecurity" (535) of the economic world in which any single economic transaction can cause consequences that catapult onto the global stage. The sheer length and verbosity of Hamilton's reports expresses his belief that a centralized authority needs to be in control of the hazardous credit economy, but also a recognition of the unfathomable scale of this economy.

## Organizing Commerce

Hamilton's narrative project was deeply informed not only by his reading of Hume, but also by his study of a decidedly non-narrative text: Malachy Postlethwayt's *Universal Dictionary of Trade and Commerce* (1751). Hamilton's interest in Postlethwayt is well documented by numerous historians and biographers, and the *Dictionary* is widely understood to be crucial to Hamilton's autodidactic education in economics and finance. We know, for example, that while captain of the New York Artillery Company, Hamilton recorded copious notes from the *Dictionary* in the back of his Pay Book. It is this early devotion to the *Dictionary* that leads Chernow to propose that it was "probably the first book that Hamilton absorbed."[35] E. P. Panagopoulos describes the text as "the most important document yet discovered showing background and immediate sources of some of Hamilton's principle writings, especially in his Reports."[36]

Today, Postlethwayt's limited reputation is primarily through his writings concerning the slave trade. As an official for the Royal African Company in the 1740s, Postlethwayt had argued that Caribbean sugar, tobacco, rice, and rum production were the key elements of British economic power, and the only way to sustain this wealth was through the slave labor of Africans: "The more likewise our Plantations abound in *Negroes*...[the] more Land become[s] cultivated, and both *better* and greater *Variety* of *Plantation Commodities* [will] be produced."[37] A decade later, his position changed, and he wrote on behalf of an expanding trade with African nations that did not involve chattel slavery.[38] It was his *Dictionary*, however, for which he was best known during the eighteenth and nineteenth centuries. The two-volume *Dictionary* was itself a loose translation of Jacques Savary's *Dictionnaire universel de commerce* (1723), the first European encyclopedic dictionary of commerce and trade. Karl Marx gives us a clue to the significance of the *Dictionary* when he cites it in *Capital*, comparing Postlethwayt's reputation to that of John Ramsay McCulloch, the leading Scottish economist of the mid-nineteenth century.[39] Even Joseph Schumpeter, who calls Postlethwayt's reputation "an instance of the interesting phenomenon of the survival of names associated with substandard performance," nonetheless acknowledges the significance of the book when he remarks that it was found on the desks of most commercial men in the late-eighteenth and early-nineteenth centuries.[40]

Most scholars assume the significance of the *Dictionary* to Hamilton was as an instructional text: they propose that Hamilton trained himself in the manifold topics of global commerce through the various entries that Postlethwayt provides. Yet reading through the *Dictionary* reveals a substantial incongruity between many of Postlethwayt's manifest claims and Hamilton's own. For example, unlike Postlethwayt, whose entries in the *Dictionary* are on behalf of the African slave trade, Hamilton rejected its expansion.[41] Perhaps more crucially in the context of Hamilton's Report on Public Credit, Postlethwayt's *Dictionary* articulated a strong argument in opposition to public credit.[42] In his entry on "Public Credit," Postlethwayt employs John Trenchard's screed from 1722 against the "pickpockets, stock-jobbers, and bubble-mongers" who prey on "helpless women and orphans."[43] Similarly Postlethwayt begins his article on "Funds" by expressly stating that it is a "term adopted by the monied men...to signify the several taxes that have been laid upon merchandizes, either by way of duties of custom or excise...to supply the exigencies of the state."[44] As he continues, he makes clear the didactic purpose of this entry, which is to deride those proponents of public debt for arguing "an enormous debt is a blessing, as it is the fountain of public credit."[45] Significantly, then, Postlethwayt ridicules the very phrase Hamilton uses in the Report on Public Credit, and for which Hamilton would become notorious throughout the 1790s: "the proper funding of the present debt, will render it a national blessing" (569).[46] In later editions, Postlethwayt explicitly blames England's mismanagement of her public debt for the rupture with her North American colonies, an argument that contradicts Hamilton's praise of the British debt system as symptomatic of her sustained economic power.

I mention the differences between the two writers not to dispute Postlethwayt's influence on Hamilton, but to suggest that Hamilton's primary interest in Postlethwayt was less in the substance or content of the *Dictionary*, than it was on the text's *formal* structure—as a work of economics that eschewed narrative argument in favor of copious articulation of the myriad component parts of commercial relations. To put it succinctly, if somewhat paradoxically, Hamilton was less interested in the details that Postlethwayt provided than in the fact that Postlethwayt provided so many details. This concern with form was also of crucial importance to Postlethwayt himself, as he emphasizes almost obsessively in his many prefaces. The first of these, subtitled "Of Perusing this Work to the Best Advantage," signals Postlethwayt's recognition that he needs to help his reader make sense of the alphabetically arranged text. Describing a tension that we also see at work in Hamilton's Report, Postlethwayt acknowledges that economics is a science based on "fundamental axioms and principles," but also that these principles need to be understood as they are practiced in the real "state of the trade."[47] Postlethwayt, thus, directs his readers to understand his *Dictionary* in terms of this "double light" that will reveal both general axioms and particular practices. He parses the interpretive strategy required by this "double light" when he explains the tension between the *Dictionary*'s alphabetical organization, which would seem to offer a model of reading dedicated to the particular—in which users would look up words and terms as they needed them—and his other aspiration for the work, which is to provide a systematic and general study of commerce.

To this latter end, he provides a variety of different methods by which his readers can make sense of the "connected light" of the individual topics and entries. For example, he explains that one individual entry is "Trade," but that a much more nuanced and expansive definition of the term will emerge by not merely reading the entry under the letter T. In order to understand the far-reaching and fundamental "maxims" the book is making about trade, Postlethwayt insists, his audience will need to read the entries on Credit, Debt, Funds, and Monied-Interest, among others.[48] Only in stitching together these individual essays will the reader be able to understand the fundamental relationship between national trade and sound credit. Postlethwayt further makes clear that this exegesis of trade is only one example, and he goes on to offer thirty-two others. He advises his readers that they would be wise to follow this scheme for all other topics found in the *Dictionary*, because only by adopting this reading strategy will his readers be able to apprehend "the tenor and spirit of the Work in general."[49] Postlethwayt cautions his audience against reading the *Dictionary* start to finish and against reading it piecemeal: the meaning of his book—and of the topics of trade and commerce—is to be found through the infinite number of paths one takes through its pages, several of which he scripts and outlines for his readers.

Hamilton's notes from his own reading of the *Dictionary*, which are recorded in the back of his Pay Book, reveal his own struggles with how to organize his encounter with the sheer volume of information located in Postlethwayt's text. His notes occupy about 112 pages at the end of the Pay Book (the front of which was a record of expenses and accounts of the Artillery Company).[50] The extant notes begin with the recording of small passages from the entries "Fisheries" and "Glass," thus suggesting that Hamilton may have organized his reading around particular industries and commodity goods.[51] But this attention on goods shifts as Hamilton then copies from the *Dictionary*'s entry on "Greece." We might assume that he is proceeding vaguely alphabetically (he turns to Greece after Glass, skipping the long entry on Gold), except that Hamilton then returns back to "A," recording a series of observations on "Anatolia," or what he calls, "Asia Minor." Hamilton writes: "Asia Minor. Pamphylia produces a great number of goats whose hair make excellent camblets" and "Greece is a fertile country…Macedonia has rich mines of gold. Achaia produces rice, cotton, tobacco. Greece in general has plenty of corn wine and oil—several parts produce silk—its wool is coarse and bad."[52] Perhaps, then, Hamilton begins by imagining his reading could be organized around the category of commodity goods, but then realizes that such commodities can better be understood as the objects of production and trade from various geographical locations. One way of reading his notes, then, is to see Hamilton's examination of the *Dictionary* in terms of political geography. This supposition is corroborated by the fact that as we trace the pathway of his transcriptions and summaries of various sections from the *Dictionary*, we see him follow geographic paths, almost as if he is narratively demonstrating both the necessity and difficulty of moving goods across the globe. For example, Hamilton's notes migrate us from Asia Minor, with its "High Chain of Mountains in Capaocia" and their stores of "silver copper iron allum etc.," to "Britain," from which he records several pages in his Pay Book.

It is probably not surprising that Hamilton records such copious notes from Postlethwayt's long "Britain" entry given that he is taking them in the midst of a war against the same nation—a war in no small measure caused by conflicts surrounding trade and commerce. And Hamilton might have been especially interested in Postlethwayt's emphasis on Britain's "inland circulating commerce" and its "connection and dependency on each other, and on our plantations in America."[53] We can easily imagine that Hamilton would be especially keen to record the details of this connection and dependency. Notably, however, in his extensive transcriptions of Postlethwayt's long lists, Hamilton is exclusively focused on British domestic goods. He does not transcribe any of the *Dictionary*'s record of products that come from the "continent of America" or the "island colonies."[54] Instead, Hamilton focuses his attention on Postlethwayt's consideration of

England's internal coal trade, which Hamilton describes as "an immence trade [that] employs near 1500 sail of shipping and seamen," an enterprise that Postlethwayt remarks is "one of the most valuable branches of our home commerce, as it gives bread to an infinite number of people, independent of any foreign correspondence."[55]

We might ask why Hamilton, writing from the battlefields of the American war for independence, chooses to focus his inquiry on the domestic production of England and not on her commerce with America. One explanation could be that Hamilton is considering the ways that a domestic economy of his then only theoretical American nation could "give bread to an infinite number of people," and that he is speculating on the possibility of a self-sufficient American economy. This fantasy of economic isolation, however, is undermined by Hamilton's continued encounter with the *Dictionary*, and as his notes continue, his gnomic shorthand gives clear expression to the impossibility of autarky.

In their spare minimalism—especially when contrasted with Hamilton's characteristic compositional style—there is something almost poetic about these Pay Book notes:

These and several other branches of coasting trade for corn fish cyder glass etc. are computed to employ 100,000 persons.

The Hardware manufactures Birmingham and Sheffield—the latter employees 40,000 people.

The woolen manufactors employs a million of people—the consumption at home amounts to a million sterlings per ann.

Their fisheries a large branch—consist of herring Pilchards mackerel oysters, Lobsters—Salmon taken in the Severn.

Scotland produces grain which it sends partly to Spain Holland Norway—for trees of an immense size—a great number of black cattle—wool which goes chiefly to England.[56]

In several short sentences, Hamilton gives expression to the many component parts of British commerce. Beginning by noting the diversity of goods, both raw and manufactured, employed in coastal trade, Hamilton secures the connection between a wide variety of goods and the people who labor to deliver them. This consideration of human labor is stitched, in the second sentence, to manufacturing, and this migrates us from the coast to inland England. The third sentence extends the chain between commodity and human labor by introducing money: it attaches the labor of the one million employed in English woolen manufacturing to the one million sterling spent by English consumers to purchase them. Hamilton then returns to the waterways—and the topic with which he began—fishery, an industry that Postelthwayt declares as "not the least important articles of our commerce." Hamilton follows Postlethwayt's train of thought when he turns to Scotland, since the Scottish cod trade is the segue that leads Postlethwayt from fishery to Scotland. Hamilton does not record what Postlethwayt does, which is that Scotland has relatively unproductive soil, instead repeating his observations about the country's considerable export trade of grain, timber, and black wool to Spain, Holland, Norway, and England. And so in a matter of five sentences Hamilton's notes have navigated into the waters of international commerce.

Postlethwayt's entry on Britain visually documents the difficulty of explaining the heterogeneous topics that fall under global traffic. At the outset of his discussion of "the import from the colonies," Postlethwayt enumerates the significant goods that are traded between the metropole and her colonies.[57] But the list by itself is insufficient, and so he is obliged in each case to offer a cross reference—a kind of hyperlink—to the separate entries that are directly and tangentially related: to other geographical spaces ("Newfoundland," "New England," "Carolina," "Bermuda Islands," "Africa"); to other institutions ("Hudson's-Bay Company," "East India Company"); to other industries and goods ("Skins," "Fisheries," "Asphaltum"); and to other economic topics ("Balance of Trade," "Exchange," "Money," and "Coin"). The cross-referencing in the *Dictionary* makes visually explicit the immense intellectual and imaginative scope of global trade: it requires knowledge of political geography, of details about the goods that are traded and manufactured, of information about the institutions critical to the production and trading of said goods, and of the emerging theories of political economy. Hamilton's notes do not exactly capture this encyclopedic cross-referencing, but they offer something of the effect with his abbreviated sentences that offer little snapshots of the intersections between any two countries and a commodity: "The [Irish] trade a great deal with Flanders and the low countries especially for butter tallow and leather"; or "Among other articles exported to Germany [from England] are tobacco ginger sugar"; or "Hamburg and Germany has a ballance against England— they furnish her with large quantities of linen."[58]

After his notes on "Britain," Hamilton does not follow a clear path. He copies first from "Cash," and then "France," "Austria," "Austrian Netherlands," "Bohemia," "Hungary," "America," "British America," "Asia," "China," "Asia Minor Islands," "Funds," "Labor," "Egypt," "Amiantus," "Asbestos," "Florence," "Venice," "Azores Islands," "Canary Islands," "Landed Interest," "Money," "Labour," "People," "Spain," "Spanish America," "Portugal," and "Russia." This seemingly haphazard pathway, not to mention the heterogeneous facts that Hamilton records, might seem to indicate a random engagement with the *Dictionary*: that in the face of the many details to be found in the volume and the infinite number of paths through which one might approach them, Hamilton is simply overwhelmed. Such an eventuality was a distinct worry for Postlethwayt and explains why he included two separate prefaces outlining several ways his audience might organize their analysis of his book. He writes in the second of these prefaces, entitled "Of the Usefullness of this Work: With the General Contents More Particularly Delineated," that he fears the dictionary form may distort the "harmony and congruity" of that which he means to represent.[59] Postlethwayt assumes that although the dictionary form is the best way to convey the variety that characterizes the economic world, it might also misrepresent its topic by severing it into discrete and seemingly unrelated parts. Thus he rather plaintively writes, "Could the mere contents of this useful work be represented, though in the plainest and artless manner, it would stand in need of no other recommendation." The problem, he explains, is that "so various, so extensive, and so universal, is the matter therein contained, that it is scarce possible to convey a just idea thereof in a narrower compass than what is proposed to comprehend the whole."[60] Here Postlethwayt succinctly describes his formal conundrum, which is that although the dictionary is an ideal mode with which to offer thick descriptions of the array of topics that constitute the commercial world, this formal structure necessarily atomizes its parts, thereby obscuring the essential interconnections. As a writer who has taken upon himself to represent accurately the comprehensive orbit of modern global commerce, Postlethwayt understands that representing these interrelations is of critical significance.

Other economic writers from the period encountered a similar formal conundrum. While recognizing the suitability of the dictionary form to describe the scope and variety of commercial topics, they also registered the necessary incoherence of the dictionary's alphabetical structure. We see something similar, for example, in Richard Rolt's *Dictionary of Trade and Commerce* (1756). Rolt's text, which took a substantial amount of its own material from Postlethwayt, was also an important economic text of the late eighteenth century, and we know that Hamilton read it as well. In fact, Panagopoulos argues that sometimes it is impossible to discern whether Hamilton's Pay Book notes are derived from Rolt or Postlethwayt. Like Postlethwayt, Rolt begins his *Dictionary* with a preface, but instead of writing his own, he enlists Samuel Johnson to introduce his book. Johnson, who had completed his dictionary only a year earlier, declares the dictionary form to be the perfect genre with which to describe and represent commercial trade. Johnson announces that dictionaries are unsuitable for "systematical and coherent" disciplines like arithmetic and geometry, because the form has the potential to "confound" the intrinsic order of these sciences. But, because "[economic science] comprises innumerable particulars unconnected with each other, among which there is no reason why any should be first or last, better than is furnished by the letters that compose their names," the dictionary form is ideal.[61] Johnson thus establishes economics as a subject that eludes any systematic method more sophisticated than alphabetization. Yet as the introduction continues, Johnson seems to agree with Postlethwayt that the dictionary form also has the potential to undermine what is so crucial about the study of economics, which is the relationship between its innumerable particulars. Johnson announces, for example, that commerce is a subject "necessarily...so miscellaneous and unconnected as not to be easily reducible to heads." Consequently, he advertises that Rolt's dictionary strives to "treat of traffick as a science, and to make that regular and systematical which has hitherto been to a great degree fortuitous and conjectural."[62] The strategy of reading that Johnson proposes is much less intricate than that outlined by Postlethwayt. He merely provides a taxonomy of topics into which Rolt has distributed the dictionary's "parts": "the *materials*, the *places*, and the *means* of traffick."[63] Yet even this minimal structure highlights the crucial elements that Hamilton's notes follow: to tell any story of commercial traffic requires the concatenation of geographical "places," the "materials" harvested, trapped, mined, or manufactured, and the "means" by which these materials are delivered, consumed, exchanged, or otherwise transformed into value.

These mid-eighteenth-century dictionaries reveal something crucial about the early study of global capitalism, which is the inharmonious demand for both a systematic method that allows for explanation of economic exchange and a descriptive method that can give accurate expression to the vast array of microscopic particulars that compose economic exchange. The details offered by Postlethwayt, Rolt, and Hamilton are overwhelming and chaotic: they are, as Johnson puts it, "so minute as not easily to be noted."[64] But it is also the case that commerce consists of nothing more than these infinitesimal details, each of which has implications and consequences on the others. Postlethwayt's frenetic instructions as to how to read his dictionary illustrates his conviction that that every single individual entry in the dictionary and every commercial topic is linked to any number of other commercial topics and dictionary entries. The economist must view the commercial world as a matrix of these interconnected parts and also connect these topics into singular narratives.

This formal problem is precisely what Hamilton faced in the writing of his own Reports. And we see in his notes on Postlethwayt, his early recognition of the chaotic relationship between commerce's discrete components. As such, when Hamilton records that "Tenedos is famed for its excellent Muscadine wines," that "Upper Egypt among other things produces Rice," that Florence "produces abundance of wines citrons lemons oranges olives etc," he does so not because these particular facts were essential to his work as artillery captain, nor would they have been significant even if Hamilton had miraculously been able to predict his ultimate role as Treasury Secretary.[65] He records these particulars because they signify what is crucial to commerce as a whole: that trade consists of nothing more than these small facts, each of which are implicated in chains of cause and effect that refuse simple and linear narrative explanation.


## Incredible Stories


Hamilton's Report on Public Credit attempts to register the heterogeneity of American foreign and domestic debt: to recognize that the aggregate amount of the debt, $54,124,464.56, is a product of an immense number of economic transactions. But the Report also marks Hamilton's attempt to transform the variegated stories of this debt into a narrative that is, as Samuel Johnson put it, "regular and systematical." The simple story that Hamilton wants to tell is that the United States is a reliable creditor, and this is why he begins with the standard analogy by which politicians tell this tale: that governments should behave "like individuals" and repay their debts (532). But although Hamilton begins with this assertion, much of what follows in the Report repudiates this assumption. The individual, precisely because she only has one body with which to consume and labor, and one body with which to buy and spend, cannot serve as an adequate metonymy for global traffic. Yet if the Report maintains that one person's actions are an ineffective basis on which to theorize the economic situation of the nation, then it also recognizes that economics, as a field of study, can only proceed on the basis of the patterns of individual human actors.

This paradox, in which the market is said to transcend the trivial desires of individuals while simultaneously being composed of these desires, perhaps can help us fathom the significance of a crucial sentence from the Report, "Probabilities are always a rational ground of contract" (552). Hamilton here justifies one of the central premises of his Report, which is that his plan to refinance American debt will ultimately result in lowered debt costs, because of falling interest rates. This is the fundamental "probability" on which Hamilton builds his proposal, but this speculation itself depends on the aggregate effects of individual human confidence. In other words, Hamilton says that his plan will work because it will make credit cheaper, but credit will only become cheaper if purchasers have faith that his plan will work. "Opinion," Hamilton explains, "is the soul of [credit]" and is also influenced by "appearances, as well as realities" (560). Much depends on influencing this opinion and on speculating how best to induce this confidence from potential purchasers of American debt. Hamilton's solution is to tell stories that will appeal to a variety of individual consumers: he can secure opinion by providing numerous "options to the creditors." This is why Hamilton offers a myriad of possible "inducements" to convince debt holders to exchange their certificates for new public credit: Hamilton hopes that "different tempers will be governed by different views of the subject" (560). Hamilton constructs his menu of options with the belief that individual buyers will differently calculate risk depending on their experiences and tempers: some individuals will want to purchase debt and land, some will want debt at variously deferred interest rates, and some might opt for Hamilton's proposed tontine. Yet if his Report countenances these individual economic sentiments, it also tries to manage them: his proposal for public credit is ultimately intent on crafting a single story about the sturdy credibility of the new nation. He designs his fiscal plan to smooth these "different tempers" into a steady current of American confidence.

It is perhaps for this reason that his critics cast Hamilton and his supporters so often as fast-talking confidence men: "no terms are sufficiently strong to reprobate the measures of those false patriots and writers, who abusing the credulity of the people...make use of their confidence only to deceive them."[66] They declare Hamiltonian fiscal language as designed to change the value of both words and monetary instruments, legitimizing their alchemical transformations through appeals to the "science" of political economy and the complexity of their prose. The explanatory abstruseness, they claim, is solely designed to "beguile" the nation's citizens.[67] One critic, for example, describes the "length and minuteness" of Hamilton's Report as a ruse designed to overcomplicate the subject and deviously convince readers that the secretary "is better versed in [the subject] than any other person."[68] Another describes Hamilton's "long reports on finance" as "inveloped in darkness and mystery"—as conveyed in prose willfully crafted to "fatigue[] the memory, confound the judgment, and force his readers into such a labyrinth of error, that the clue of decision has not length enough to reach the extensive mazes of a wandering imagination."[69]

Similar accusations are at the center of a widely reprinted exchange between the pro-Hamilton "The Observer" and his interlocutor "The Independent Observer." The "Observer" was the author of eighteen essays on finance and banking that were originally published in Hartford's *The American Mercury* and reprinted in full in the Federalist *Gazette of the United States,* as well as sporadically in a host of other newspapers.[70] The essays argue on behalf of Hamilton's public credit proposal, accusing his critics of having a benighted understanding of "the arts of finance." So long as "popular prejudices" prevail, the Observer writes, the nation's leaders will never become more sophisticated in their knowledge of economics and the nation will never advance.[71] But clearly recognizing the dangers of overemphasizing the complex structures and language of economic science, the Observer also addresses himself to "American Farmers" and insists that Hamilton's agenda is to shed "order and light" on the subject of public finance. Indeed, he claims that the beauty of Hamilton's proposal against discrimination and for state assumption is that it constitutes a "plain and honest plan."[72] In so doing, he strives to distinguish Hamilton's Report from speculative profiteering: he maintains that speculators have "endangered the people" by obfuscating the rules of finance. He also identifies financial illiteracy with the susceptibility to fall under debt: "the man that must borrow his neighbors wits to manage his own affairs, must soon borrow money to pay his debt."[73] The essays thus posit that the citizen who accedes to the terms of Hamilton's Report secures not only the financial benefits of the new funding scheme, but also a kind of intellectual credibility.

Other writers, however, provide very different assessments of Hamiltonian stylistic tendencies. Not engaged in a "plain and honest plan," Hamilton is crafting "schemes" and a "stile" that are based on "erroneous" calculations, "sophistical" arguments, and proceeding from "false premises."[74] Further describing this style, another critic writes that the Report, "instead of being expressed in the language of plain sense, is introduced by a most elaborate oration," is "couched in the flowery language of the schools," and "deals largely in sophistical arguments."[75] As if to emphasize the contrast, those arguing against the Hamiltonian funding system defend their own style as transparently simple and based on self-evident law and natural language. The "Citizen of Philadelphia," for example, maintains that his opposition to Hamilton is predicated on the most rudimentary knowledge: "any boy at school or maid in a kitchen" is able to understand that the government failed its creditors and that justice cannot be secured until they are paid.[76] Another writer similarly asserts the moral simplicity of the problem regarding debt discrimination: "Ask a boy whom you meet in the street, whether it be just and equitable that one man, through the neglect of government, should lose three-fourths or seven-eighths of his property, and another get it—and then, that he who so lost it, should be taxed by government, to pay for what he lost? You would not wait long for the answer NO."[77]

It is in these terms that we can best understand why arguments against the Report were so often written by pseudonymous "farmers," "citizens," or "soldiers." The authors of the opposition fashion themselves as the ordinary citizens who provided food, shelter, money, and animals to the American cause, thereby adopting the personas of creditors said to morally deserve the repayment that

Hamilton's plan would offer. Many of these authors also begin their commentary with disclaimers or apologias for their "plain" speech, either implicitly or explicitly contrasting their simple prose with the recondite language of modern finance used by the speculators seeking to defraud them. A "Friend to Substantial Justice" begins by styling himself as a "plain man who wishes abler pens were employed" for his cause before lambasting the Hamiltonian plan as a "fraud" perpetrated by the speculators trying to convince "the poor ignorant soldiery that the public was not equal to the purchase of all they undertook."[78]

"A Farmer" offers a similar critique, expressing a wish that "some abler hand would take up the subject," precisely because Hamilton is so "artful" in his strategies to defraud American farmers. Accusing Hamilton of linguistic alchemy, he writes that the Report is designed to "preserve those magic words—*public credit*."[79] Another "Farmer" similarly argues, "the words [public credit] are mere jingle, calculated only to catch weak people."[80] While this jingle can captivate the simple minded, the Farmer predicts that "there is a time coming when the pen of history will detect and expose the folly of argument in favor of the proposed funding system." This pen, he hopes, will reveal the "injustice and oppression [that are] coloured over with fine words" by Hamilton's report.[81]

This same "Farmer" stresses the illicit misrepresentation involved in Hamilton's funding scheme when he compares the Department of Treasury to a "girl, who comes forward in a white sheet to do penance for a second bastard, without asking pardon of God and the congregation for her first breach of chastity."[82] Allegorizing the various instruments of credit (IOUs, continentals, debt certificates) that were offered during the Revolutionary war as the "first breach of chastity," the second, and more damnable transgression is the Hamiltonian plan to redeem the certificates without "mak[ing] up the losses sustained by widows and orphans by their paper money."[83] Harkening back to an Augustan portrait of Lady Credit, the author represents public credit not only as a fallen woman, but as one who tries magically to restore her virginity (the "white sheet").[84] This allegorical Lady Credit is not like Daniel Defoe's raped by stockjobbers, but instead feigns virginity even as she seduces. The same Farmer employs a similar metaphor when he describes those who argue against discrimination as "gamblers and prostitutes, who never suffer themselves to be called by those scandalous names, but cover their crimes with some more delicate appellation."[85] Here he not only defames the Hamiltonians as gamblers and prostitutes, but also locates their turpitude in their tendency towards symbolic misrepresentation. We might note, however, that our plainspoken Farmer is the one employing elaborate figures of speech that turn credit into adulterous women and Federalist politicians into gamblers and prostitutes. Which is to say, the Farmer seems to be trading in the very symbolic currency he indicts. Yet he implicitly distinguishes his own artful language from that of his political enemies by way of his position as "Farmer," establishing himself in a vocation that ostensibly can make wealth without the mediation of paper.

We see a similar critique of Hamiltonian misrepresentation by another essayist who accuses Hamiltonian finance of being popish. This author writes that the Report on Public Credit is "so much at variance with the principles he has stated as the source from which they are derived that...they appear as incompatible as the doctrine of transubstantiation is with reason and common sense."[86] In this elaborate figure, the Secretary of the Treasury is the priest who magically transforms old money into new. The author, by contrast, represents himself as the commonsensical Protestant who reveals the hocus-pocus both of Hamilton's literary style and his financial policy. Whatever the metaphor, the insult is the same: Hamilton's crime is located in the flourishes of his pen that fraudulently pretend to vindicate American credit, even as they are circulating American debt.

Another "Farmer" proposes that he can easily can cut through the artifice of high finance by explicating "the present danger of the farmers of America by a very simple simile." He proceeds to draw an allegory that compares Congress to a neighbor who blocks up the roads and waterways leading to a recently purchased mill, rendering the mill and surrounding property worthless.[87] According to his simile, if Congress adopts the Secretary's report, then the government "would be that quarrelsome and mischievous neighbor to every farmer and landholder in the United States." The force of his comparison rests on the notion that just as the hypothetical neighbor renders personal property useless by blocking access to the water that provides power, so too has the government rendered personal property (continentals and/or debt certificates received as payment during the war) useless by stopping payment. His "simple simile," therefore, tries to capture some of the complexity of financial relations, which is that damaging effects occur along long causal chains. The neighbor who has blocked the waterway has not literally touched the mill owner's property, and yet his actions have caused harm nonetheless. Yet the analogy also elides a crucial difference between the two financial scenarios: while the fictional mill owner still possesses the title to his property, the debt holder imagined in the scenario sold his long ago. If he were still in possession of it, then he too could profit from Hamilton's proposed refunding plan. In this regard, the simile would have been more accurate were it to describe a scenario in which the mill owner, no longer having access to a working mill because his meddlesome neighbor has damned up the stream, had sold it cheaply to the neighbor, who then sold the mill for twice what he paid for it. I belabor this exegesis only to show that the Farmer's chosen figure emphasizes not so much the straightforward similitude between vehicle and tenor as the knotty distinction, the inability of his "simple simile" to capture fully how public credit functions as a system of value.

Perhaps this explains why in his second essay, this Farmer changes his literary tactic, concluding his letter with a sentimental tale of "a reduced officer [in] his old regimental coat addressing the Congress."[88] Begging payment for his relinquished credit notes, he receives the scornful reply of "an American speculator and English broker": "By our opposition to you we helped to keep down the value of your certificates, and when the *peace* came, and all danger and risk were over, we bought up the greatest part of them for 26 in the pound...As to paying the balance to your soldiers who fought your battles, they have no right to it. They don't know the use of money."[89] Here the Farmer makes two significant rhetorical moves that are repeated consistently in the disputes surrounding public credit. First, he renders a portrait of an avaricious and anti-patriotic (and frequently British) speculator justifying his exploitation of veterans because of their economic nescience: "They don't know the use of money." Second, he compels a sympathetic audience with the melodramatic narrative of the evil speculator and the pathetic veteran.

### Real Value, Real Bodies

One of the most prolific of writers who developed this particular literary strategy was Pelatiah Webster, who sometimes wrote under the penname of "A Citizen of Philadelphia," but also put on the garb of expertise, writing as "The Financier." This latter pseudonym better describes his real occupation since he was one of the premier experts on finance and economy in the early United States.[90] Unlike many who opposed Hamilton's plan to redeem the public debt, Webster acknowledges that finance and commerce are subjects extremely "difficult and intricate," also concluding, "A good financier is as rare as a phoenix."[91] But Webster characterizes himself as having more than the requisite financial knowledge to enter into the debate, and in the preface to his collection of essays on finance, money, and banking, he asserts that he is particularly well suited to the task by virtue of his "literary way" and his expertise in "mercantile business." Moreover, although acknowledging that his writing will prove occasionally "abstruse," he also maintains that it will "afford some gratification and amusement to speculative people."[92]

Despite what would seem to be both an occupational and geographical propensity towards Federalist financial policy, Webster was an outspoken supporter of discrimination. His pamphlet, "A Plea for Poor Soldiers" (1790), proposed that original certificate holders should be paid the balance between what they sold their securities for and their nominal value.[93] His plan was ultimately the one James Madison would adopt in opposition to Hamilton, but Webster suggested it long before Madison joined the fray. Webster is somewhat different than many other anti-Hamiltonians who wrote on behalf of discrimination (including Madison) in that he framed his argument as both a moral and financial imperative. For example, not only does he stage the debate as an allegorical battle between a greedy speculator and a selfless veteran, but he also works to situate his argument on the same terrain as Hamilton: he claims that his plan is ultimately best for the nation's public credit. Explaining that the initial securities given to soldiers constitute a contract that has not been repaid because the soldiers did not receive nominal value for their sold securities, he argues that the issue hinges on how to understand the meaning of the instruments given to the soldiers in payment of their debts. He asserts that these "public certificates" should be understood neither as negotiable notes nor as bills of exchange. Unlike these kinds of monetary instruments whose value fluctuates according to the desires and confidences of market participants, the public certificates are stable symbolic placeholders for a debt that cannot be discounted or renegotiated. Webster states, "the real public creditors, whose cause I am pleading, *have not yet been paid;* this is as plain as that 20*s. is more than* 2*s.* 6*d*."[94] Although Webster here describes currency, which can only ever be a vehicle of exchange, his language invokes a notion of exchange (both monetary and linguistic) as having a permanent and real value. His words, like numbers, will "plainly" reveal an arithmetic fact: that twenty shillings is greater than two shilling, six pence. In these terms, Webster argues, the nation is in arrears, having failed to restore the face value of the debt to the original creditors. In making this latter claim, Webster replicates Hamilton's logic in the Report, which is to emphasize the inviolable principles of contract. For Hamilton, the United States can only prove its political and economic legitimacy by repaying its debts and fulfilling the obligations of its economic contracts. Webster tries to literalize Hamilton's argument, insisting that unless the original creditors receive the face value of their certificates (whether or not they sold them to a secondary buyer), the new nation is betraying the principles of contract: "Their demand is founded on the most solemn contract of Congress, who had good right to make such contract, which binds the honor, the morality, and the justice of the country, and nothing but payment can discharge the country from the guilt of injustice, and violation and truth most solemnly plighted to them."[95]

Webster constructs his opposition as a political-economic engagement with Hamilton, but he also argues that there is no significant distinction between fiscal responsibilities and emotional ones. He therefore describes those who argue against discrimination as emotionally bankrupt: there are "some men (*horribile dictu*) who can rise up with a front as hard as an anvil" to deny the claims of the original debtors.[96] He accordingly demands that just as the Federal government has an economic obligation to repay the face value to original creditors, so too does it have a moral obligation to experience literally, or reenact, the adversity of these original creditors:

> With a heart melted in sympathy with the sufferings of my country's deliverers, with a sublimated sense of the importance, as well as sacred nature, of the justice and judgment of our nation, I most devoutly implore...that these sovereign and sacred virtues may dwell, not only in our supreme councils, but in the heart of every member who shall give his vote in the decision of this most capital and interesting cause which I am pleading.[97]

His writing sets out to cultivate a sympathetic vibration between the hearts of the creditors and the hearts of the congressmen who will vote on the public debt proposal. And he represents this sentimental bond in much the same way as he describes the fiscal exchange between nation and creditor—as a literal and fixed exchange: his heart feels the suffering of the original creditors, and through his own writing, the "heart of every member" of Congress will feel the same. His text thus functions as both the stable currency and sentimental current that will correct what Webster sees as both Hamiltonian representational fraud and heartlessness. As soon as his audience learns the true story about public debt, their sentiments will find their proper channel, culminating in "general pity for the soldiers" and an unequivocal consensus that they have "been injured and ill used."[98] Thus, even as he acknowledges that the "heart-moving and unparalleled distresses of very many thousands of these worthy patriots" is not in and of itself sufficient to "alter the stipulations of contract," he nonetheless asserts, "no government ought to be callous to their influence or hardened into an insensibility of their force."[99] Once the legislators feel right (to use Harriet Beecher Stowe's language from *Uncle Tom's Cabin*), they will abide by the naturally just and true terms of the financial contract. Webster expresses concern, however, that the corruptive language of his opponents will derail the natural pathos that should emerge: their "whole harangue," he opines, is "ever so well-dressed and polished… [that it] must wound the natural feelings of the humane mind."[100] Here Webster not only familiarly characterizes the Hamiltonian argument as linguistically fraudulent, but he also renders their speech acts as capable of inflicting physical and emotional violence.

Webster's accusation of bodily violence is taken up by other writers eager to craft Hamiltonian finance not only as sexually scandalous and as Catholic, but also as viciously predatory. On the congressional floor, Georgia Representative James Jackson rehearsed his own story of the "gallant veteran" and "his virtuous and tender wife," now endangered by "rapacious wolves," "savages" and "speculators."[101] Jackson's racist language, which equates speculators, American Indians, and wolves, is not especially surprising, since by 1790 American writers were well-versed in such allegories. What is notable, however, is the way that Jackson's story works to literalize what otherwise seems to be merely a metaphoric comparison between the three villains. The gallant veteran, "deprived of [his] limbs" in the

Revolution, is further "devoured" by the wolfish speculators, and their "insatiable avarice" has also driven the veteran and his family into the wilderness where they are "exposed to the arms of savages." Although Jackson is deploying figural language, his story tries to stabilize its symbolic economy by literalizing the villainy of wolves, Indians, and speculators.

We see something similar by another essayist who accuses both Hamilton and financial speculators of "monopolizing the public Securities from the poor Soldiers," and in so doing of "stab[bing] to the vitals, and giv[ing] the mortal wound, to our public faith and credit."[102] The author's dramatic styling is somewhat unusual because the victims sustaining these stab wounds include both actual soldiers and an allegorical public credit. In this way, the author (who signs himself "An Advocate for Public Credit") describes the moral injustice done to real individuals and to an abstract economic concept. He conflates the two so as to relay a tale that compels sympathy for those who never received the nominal value for their credit securities, and this sympathy is therefore necessarily tied to provisions for faith in public credit. According to the moral formula this essayist provides, whether one profits from the Hamiltonian plan, or merely accedes to it, he causes injury to the bodies of individuals and the nation. And appropriately enough, a bodily response is the only appropriate response to this injury: "Strange gentlemen, indeed, if you are real friends to justice, and the public credit, that in all your zeal, you should never drop one tear of pity, nor exhibit one compassionate thought of mercy, for so many thousands of good people, who were invited and urged to put their trust and confidence in those impracticable promises of the Continental Currency."[103] The citizen who does not cry real tears cannot be a real friend to either justice or credit. In both the sentimental and credit economies this author describes, he insists on literalism—on the face value of both debt certificates and tears.

Given the significance of literality to these debates about economic contracts, it is perhaps not surprising that we often encounter allusions to William Shakespeare's *Merchant of Venice*. One pamphlet that protests Hamilton's proposed interest reduction concludes with the passage: "It must not be, there is no power in Venice / Can alter a decree established... And many an error, by the same example, / Will creep into the state; It cannot be."[104] The cited line is spoken by Portia when she seems to affiliate herself with Shylock's adamant appeal to the letter of the law. Her argument here is essentially the same as that which Hamilton makes in his Report: the legitimacy of a nation depends on the credibility of its contracts. To violate the absolute terms of a contract would be to establish a legal precedence that would also undermine the authority of the state. Were Shylock not to receive his flesh, or were the United States not to pay the original terms of the interest payment, "error" will necessarily "creep into the state." When the pamphleteer adopts this position, therefore, he effectively accuses Hamilton of betraying the terms of contract: he thus seems to cast Hamilton into the role of Bassanio, as appellant to mercy and equity, and himself in the role of Shylock.[105] Not surprisingly, however, the pamphlet's author does not follow through on the logical implications of his allusion to *Merchant of Venice*, and he instead restates Portia's argument by citing James Steuart: "When Great Britain borrows money on the public faith, the rate of interest is always stipulated, and these stipulations must be religiously fulfilled, or credit will be at an end."[106]

The reason for this shift in textual references is easily explained when we consider the ubiquity of anti-Semitism deployed against Hamilton's financial proposals. Speculators who purchased the debt certificates on the secondary market were often described as Shylock-like villains hungry for flesh. One author suggests, for example, that every member of Congress should "lay his hand on his heart" and declare that "he was no speculator, and that he did not come forward to claim for *himself* the price of the blood, or of a limb, or of the life of a poor soldier."[107] Another correspondent angrily proposes that all certificates offered by the Secretary of Treasury should be "inscribed" with "1. The *bloody arm* of a soldier. 2. The *wooden leg* of a soldier. 3. A *soldier's heart* pierced with a bayonet. 4. The *broken heart* of a widow."[108] In this author's fantasy, the debt speculators would be forced to handle the bodies—arms, legs, hearts—of those who had been "grossly defrauded and injured." Written in 1792, after the ultimate passage of the anti-discrimination policy, the author's theatrical rhetoric admits defeat but does so by appealing to another moment from *Merchant of Venice*. This reverie about credit bonds dripping with the blood of American veterans imaginatively fashions speculators as Shylocks taking their pounds of flesh and shedding Christian blood. Unlike Portia, Hamilton's opponents may not have been able to gain relief for their "clients," but they could circulate tales that dramatized American fiscal policy as causing injury and violating justice.

The recurrent tendency to describe financial injury as literal violence and to demand readers respond with genuine and embodied sentiment reveals the fine linguistic tightrope the anti-Hamiltonians had to walk. On one hand, they insisted that "genuine" creditors were being deprived of the "true" and "real" value of their paper certificates. On the other hand, in order to present this truth, they necessarily resorted to metaphors and similes that could not help but reveal the shifting terrain of any symbolic currency. This explains, I think, why they so often turn to the language of sentiment and corporeal pain, an appeal designed to distinguish their position from their antagonists: not only are they expressing self-evident truths in plain-spoken language, but the authenticity of their position is validated when readers are made to feel the sorrowful losses of the original debt holders. Recognizing their unique rhetorical predicament, one anti-Hamiltonian writer explicitly invokes the ineffectual literary style of his position's arguments, characterizing the "awkward wit, that did no honor to the imagination" of those who try to express the "murmurs of the poor soldier." But the inadequacy becomes an advantage since what the anti-Hamiltonian writers lack in "wit" and "imagination," they make up with genuine and honest feeling. And so their words are ultimately successful, because they "race the heart" of their readers.[109] He thus argues that writers who oppose Hamilton trade in a sentimental currency that cannot be counterfeited.

This is why dramatic dialogues and monologues were an especially popular literary mode employed against public finance: they offered an ideal sentimental counterattack to Hamiltonian rhetorical flourishes. Consider, for example, "A Dialogue between a Soldier and a Tax-Gatherer," in which the Soldier plaintively cries, "I cannot pay my tax, my children have no victuals to eat, and if they had I have no fire to cook it.... Go, Sir, and tell Mr. _____ that he now enjoys the interest of a Certificate which once belonged to me... let that bargain satisfy him."[110] Against the recondite and mystifying prose of the financiers, these dramatic stylings gave literal voice to the "authentic" victims of Hamilton's plan. Webster, likewise, represents a dialogue between "soldiers" and a federal "Orator," in which the former refuses to countenance the government's fiscal arguments:

> We do not wish to enter into any conversation about *public faith* and *honor;* it seems to us, that this subject is not very proper to talk much of, at this time; for the *least said is soonest forgot;* but one thing we *know* and *feel,* that we could get *no more* than 2*s.* 6*d.* in the pound for our certificates; and our *necessities obliged* us to part with them for what we *could get.*[111]

Contrasting Hamilton's extended oratory and discussion about "public faith and honor" with the authority of what they "know and feel," Webster's tactic is to have the soldiers speak on behalf of debt discrimination in their "real" voices and on the basis of their genuine feeling and their apprehension of a self-evident truth. The dialogic form also emphasizes the miscommunication that Hamilton's opponents say is at the heart of finance. In many of these dialogues, the government spokesperson asserts that the amount the veterans received when they sold their certificates (even if it only consisted of three shillings for the pound) constitutes payment; the soldiers or widows express their conviction—their feeling—that such analysis is based on financial and linguistic trickery. In Webster's dialogue, for example, the soldier replies, "how [can] our sale of negotiable certificates…operate on our real earnings like an enchanter's wand, so as to annihilate them, or turn them into a mist."[112] We see a similar strategy in a letter protesting the public debt proposal, written in the voice of an old Irish soldier. Addressed to the "Printer" of the *Independent Gazetteer,* the letter is written in dialect, thereby reproducing the ostensibly genuine voice of the poor veteran who laments that his situation "is now in the hands of fine folks, who do not like to admit any body who has not new shoes" and that he has been "served such a dog's trick."[113] Whatever the real identity of these pseudonymous authors, the crucial point is that they construct their personas as antidote to what is said to be the fallacious arguments and fantastical currency offered by their opponents. Insisting on tales that reproduce the "authentic" voice of the fiscal victims of the Revolutionary War, or that compel "genuine" emotional affect, the critics of Hamiltonian finance contrast their narrative mode with the highly mediated systems of exchange implied by the new economy.

Advocates for Hamilton's system of public finance tried to counter with their own stylistic critique, essentially describing the opposition to a funded public debt—whether it was an absolute refusal of public credit, an advocacy for discrimination, or a rejection of state assumption—as nostalgia for a long-departed economic world. Responding specifically to Webster, for example, "Another Citizen of Philadelphia" insists that opposition to debt discrimination is not an attack on American patriots. Instead, he accuses those who write on behalf of discrimination of chronicling crude tales that cultivate sympathy only by fomenting rage at imaginary villains. Such stories, he explains, are constructed as "phantoms calculated to dazzle" weak-minded readers.[114] Another writer tries to discredit the proliferating stories about the "infamous speculators," explaining that, far from attempting to defraud farmers and soldiers, the traders performed a commendable service by taking on financial risk of purchasing financial instruments for which there was almost no market at the time. "Can these people…justly be called knaves and villains?"[115] Hamilton's advocates depict the farmers and veterans not as dupes of speculation, but as credulous readers who, unable to comprehend the principles of high finance, eagerly partake in the stories of speculative villainy that cast them as martyred victims. One author explicitly links the citizenry's economic illiteracy with their susceptibility to melodramatic plots. Opening with a brief stanza celebrating the soldier ("The patriot, whose unweared mind, / Toils for the good of human kind"), the essayist then describes the young nation as engaged in an infantile system of finance—one that is "imbecile, inefficient and confused, which marks the early stages of other nations." Hamilton's prejudicial opponents are anachronistically clinging to an unsophisticated system and unreasonably appealing to "the passion of their readers" in an effort to frighten them into a rejection high finance.[116] Another essayist describes the "bitter things" that are being written against "the chapter on Public Credit," and characterizing Hamilton's report as a textual remedy, it announces, "It is high time to turn over a new leaf, and see what can be inscribed on the fair pages of the future history of our country."[117]

Many of Hamilton's advocates published in the *Gazette of the United States*, the newspaper that served as the unofficial mouthpiece for Washington's administration, and even when not explicitly referencing public credit, the newspaper included essays advocating for Hamilton's plan. One author, for example, begins with an epigram that obliquely gestures towards the issues of finance that take up much of the rest of the newspaper's pages: "From annexing different ideas to words, men must always be at variance in their speculative reasonings."[118] What follows is an analysis of the vocabulary used to reference crucial theological tenets, and the essay concludes with a general assessment about linguistic practice and cultural advancement. Arguing that "much depends on the copiousness of a language," the author explains, "Languages, in their infant state, contain few words but names of sensible objects," before making the relatively commonplace observation that it is impossible to "convert rude nations" into "rational Christians" until they have a language that possesses "words for expressing abstract ideas."[119] These remarks on linguistic abstraction are an indirect retort to opponents of Federalist finance insofar as they suggest the spiritual and intellectual deficiency that accompanies linguistic simplicity. The intellectual speculation that is the hallmark of civilized Christians, the author posits, requires a "copious language" that transcends mere homology between word and thing. In similar terms, those writing against discrimination explain that the debt certificates do not represent a sum of money that is owed to a particular person, but instead stand for an abstract value whose meaning shifts according to who is willing and able to purchase at any given time. That this essay on language theory and theology speaks to finance is corroborated when the following article, written by one of Hamilton's advocates, argues for the necessity of increasingly abstract and federalized systems of taxation and public credit.

It also seems likely that this commentary on language and abstraction is a subtle rebuke to Madison who spearheaded the proposal for debt discrimination. After all, there was something deeply ironic in Madison's advocacy for stabilized representational value given his earlier commentary on language in Federalist No. 37. There Madison explicitly acknowledges the slipperiness of language, explaining that even when laws are written with the greatest possible care and deliberation, their meaning and application will necessarily be "obscure and equivocal" because laws require words. "No language," Madison posits, "is so copious as to supply words and phrases for every complex idea."[120] Madison is not suggesting that this makes law-making impossible: he is writing, after all, on behalf of the proposed Federal Constitution. But he is insisting that meaning happens not through intention and the writing of the law, but its practice, or what he calls "discussions and adjudications." Madison implies that this practical application becomes even more crucial when the legal concept is complex since there is a necessary correlation between the "complexity and novelty" of what is conveyed and the "inaccuracy" of the language used to describe it. Given Madison's assessment of the difficulty of stabilizing linguistic currency in Federalist No. 37, his demand for the firm value of the debt certificates—and a refusal to allow their value to be "adjudicated" through the market—must have struck his former colleagues as surprising.

The deficiency of the argument on behalf of discrimination, the Hamiltonians repeatedly protested, was the failure to understand the abstract value of public debt and the refusal to acknowledge that value was only relative to the market exchanges in which public credit served as currency. Debt discrimination was anathema not just because it would jeopardize international confidence in the instruments of credit, but because it fundamentally misconceived how these instruments operated in a system of global finance. The error of the veterans was that they fetishized the original loan of goods, specie, or services, and they imagined that the paper credit they received was a non-transferable representation for this loan. Had they retained ownership of the paper, Hamilton's advocates argued, then they could insist on this allegory. The Hamiltonians also explained how their opponents were likewise wrong in rejecting federal assumption of the debt, since it was predicated in a false conviction that the same government agency that took the debt also needed to offer repayment. In both cases, they engaged in a fallacy of literalism.

### Letter of the Law and the Bank of the United States

The dispute concerning literalism becomes even more imperative when the partisan feud shifts from public credit to Hamilton's subsequent proposal to establish a national bank. Here Hamilton's opponents accuse him not only of breaking financial contracts and violating the spirit of democratic law, but also for attacking the very letter of the United States Constitution. Hamilton provides his Report on a National Bank to the United States Congress in December, 1790, only eleven months after he had delivered the first on public credit. Hamilton conceived of all his financial proposals as an integrated endeavor, and the relationship between public debt repayment and the establishment of the national bank was especially interdependent since the newly circulating public debt certificates would constitute 75 percent of the bank's initial ten-million dollar capitalization. Similarly, Hamilton believed the bank's vitality would strengthen confidence in the public debt, thereby stabilizing the United States' reputation in the world's financial markets. And having learned something from his experience with the first Report, Hamilton attempted to anticipate objections to his bank proposal. He therefore spends pages arguing on behalf of the numerous possible benefits to come from incorporating the bank as well as disputing the anticipated arguments against it: that it will raise interest rates, eliminate other lending institutions, cultivate financial irresponsibility, and make gold and silver scarce.

As it turns out, Hamilton did not accurately predict the issue that would ultimately become the fulcrum of opposition to his proposed national bank: its constitutionality. This is why Bray Hammond suggests that the controversy surrounding the Bank of the United States should be conceived as a political dispute about the limits of federal authority rather than one about the specifics of economic policy.[121] But even as the terrain of the argument shifted, those arguing against the establishment of a national bank mounted their resistance by deploying many of the same rhetorical weapons with which they had waged their earlier wars against public credit: once again, they charged Hamilton with linguistic misrepresentation. They asserted that sanctioning the bank would manifest such a fundamental violation of the Constitution's meaning as to render any semiotic system unintelligible.

In what remains of this chapter I read some of the canonical documents of the debate surrounding the legislation that ultimately led to the establishment of the Bank of the United States in 1791, specifically Hamilton's Report on a National Bank, Madison's Congressional address opposing the Bank Bill, Jefferson's subsequent "Opinion on the Constitutionality of a National Bank," Attorney General Edmund Randolph's written response in opposition to the bill, and finally Hamilton's "Opinion on the Constitutionality of a National Bank" in which he responded directly to both Jefferson and Randolph. This constellation of texts provides the basic structure of a debate that, as Charles Beard stated at the beginning of the twentieth century, "first summoned to the political battle that high talent for analysis, deduction, reticulation, and speculative imagination which has characterized American constitutional conflicts from that day to this."[122] Two of Beard's terms, "reticulation" and "speculative imagination," are particularly salient since, as I will suggest, the encounter between the opposition parties was shaped by very different senses of the reticular structure of the American economy and by contrasting speculative projects. In using the term "speculative projects," I do not refer to the manifestly opposing opinions on financial speculation from the two partisan positions, but instead to an imagination of the future as a consequence of previous actions and events. As was the case in the debates surrounding public debt, the quarrel over the bank reveals two very different literary forms by which to describe the measurement of economic value and the analysis of economic consequences.

Hamilton's primary rationale for the bank is prospective: he wants to increase the future capital supply of the new nation. And so he tells a story to elucidate the interrelation between confidence, credit, and capital. He explains, for example, that one reason that banks can circulate capital beyond their metallic reserves is that while each loan is payable in gold and silver, "in a great number of cases, no actual payment is made" (577), and he illustrates his scenario by following debt from one hand to another:

> The Borrower frequently, by a check or order, transfers his credit to some other person, to whom he has a payment to make; who, in his turn, is as often content with a similar credit, because he is satisfied, that he can, whenever he pleases, either convert it into cash, or pass it to some other hand, as an equivalent for it. And in this manner the credit keeps circulating, performing in every stage the office of money, till it is extinguished by a discount with some person, who has a payment to make to the Bank, to an equal or greater amount. Thus large sums are lent and paid, frequently through a variety of hands, without the intervention of a single piece of coin.   (577)

In Hamilton's narrative, credit is the protagonist: people are the vehicles through which money moves, and human confidence in its representative function is what allows its circulation to continue. Although his story provides an artificial conclusion or "extinguish[ment]" when it narrates the loan's return back to the bank, his tale also implies the potential for the ceaseless movement of capital. He later marvels at the reticular structure of credit and "the almost infinite vicissitudes and competitions of mercantile enterprise" (578). As in his first Report, he tries to give expression to a complex economic system that can only be understood as consisting of the beliefs and actions of people in the aggregate. To do so he deploys the metaphor of waterways. "The Bank," he explains "furnishes an extraordinary supply for borrowers," and its "copious stream" will take a "natural course" in which, as the "circulation of the Bank is extended, there is an augmentation of the aggregate mass of money answering the aggregate mass of demand" (583). In Hamilton's financial vista, the plains are always aqueous but never flooded because its boundaries adjust themselves to capital volume.

Yet even as Hamilton's narrative emphasizes a natural economic current in which individual creditors and debtors serve as valves for a larger system of capital intake and outtake, his proposal nevertheless asserts the primacy of individual economic agents. These individual debtors and creditors, he argues, cannot see themselves as integrated into this network, but make judgments on the basis of their immediate private needs. Assuming that oft-cited line from Adam Smith—"It is not from the benevolence of the butcher, the brewer, or the baker that we expect our dinner, but from their regard to their own interest"—Hamilton asserts self-interest as the necessary foundation for a national bank.[123] Accordingly, the bank must be "under a *private* not a *public* Direction, under the guidance of *individual interest,* not of *public policy*" (601). A public bank would necessarily fail, according to Hamilton, because it would be "too much influenced by *public necessity*" (601), which necessity would be a "canker, that would continually corrode the vitals of the credit of the Bank" (601). A privately held bank, by contrast, would elicit the careful management of owners whose personal fortunes would be at stake. And so Hamilton gives oblique expression to one fundamental paradox of economic science, which is that even as it is dedicated to studying social interaction, it theorizes on the basis of individual human choices. Because Hamilton has no confidence that individuals can make sound decisions in the face of public exigencies, he makes the national bank a private corporation.

The private corporatism of the national bank was certainly one reason Hamilton's proposal was met with such hostility, and Jefferson begins his attack on the proposal, "Opinion on the Constitutionality of a National Bank," with a litany of charges against corporations more generally, stating their fundamental violation of laws of mortmain, alienage, descent, distribution, forfeiture, and escheat. Although Jefferson begins with this broad range of accusations, he ultimately follows Madison's initial strategy of resistance, which was to claim there was no constitutional authority by which the federal government could incorporate a national bank. Madison first makes this maneuver in a last-ditch effort to stop passage of the Bank Bill.[124] On February 2, 1791, as the bill moved closer to a vote, Madison addressed Congress with his objections. He began the speech by rehearsing the familiar Country Party associations between banking and corruption, the very same arguments that Hamilton had anticipated in his Report: banking's tendency to foment corruption, avarice, and irresponsible speculation. But pivoting his rhetoric substantially, Madison declares all these issues to be irrelevant since everything depended on the more basic issue of whether "the power of establishing an *incorporated bank* [was] among the powers vested by the constitution in the legislature of the United States." The simple answer to this question, Madison asserted, was no: "it was not possible to discover in [the Constitution] the power to incorporate a Bank."[125] His speech begins to circulate in American newspapers within the same month, establishing the terms by which generations of politicians would assail Federal finance.[126]

The primary weapon in Madison's salvo was a detailed textual exegesis of Article I, Section 8 of the United States Constitution. He proposes that the only possible justification for the bank would be located in three clauses from this section, and then argued that the bank's establishment was not textually warranted by any "fair construction" of these clauses. Madison's logic went even further to maintain that there was no legal provision for the bank's incorporation, as he also uses the proposed bank as a litmus test by which to construct a constitutional hermeneutics. For Madison, the problem was not simply an economic one in which the national bank could cause irreparable harm to state banks by interfering with their business, but that establishing the bank would authorize an interpretation of the Constitution that would fundamentally contradict the basis of government. This is why at the head of his speech, Madison lays out "preliminaries to a right interpretation." In the first of these preliminaries, he stipulates that "an interpretation that destroys the very characteristic of the government cannot be just." He suggests, in other words, that if the consequences of an interpretation betrays what is self-evidently true, then this reading must be erroneous. Here engaged in his own speculative imagination, Madison emphasizes "consequences": "Where a meaning is clear, the consequences, whatever they may be, are to be admitted—where doubtful, it is fairly triable by its consequences."[127] The consequences in this case, Madison explains, "would give to Congress an unlimited power," a power that fundamentally "destroyed" the framers' intention to establish government "as composed of limited and enumerated powers."[128] In setting his opposition to the bank in these terms, Madison continues the tendency of anti-Hamiltonian critique, which is to argue economic policy within a framework of literalistic interpretation.

Conventionally we understand this particular dispute between Hamilton and Madison as hinging on the distinction between loose and strict constructions of the Constitution, but we might also consider the respective narrative theories that inhere within these interpretive paradigms. Madison's strict constructionism offers something like the inverse of Hamilton's speculative mode. Madison does look ahead to future effects and consequences, but instead of reading them as contingent products of what Hamilton described as "infinite vicissitudes," he judges them in relationship to original intention. Whereas Hamilton sees the Constitution as establishing an inviolable contract that is also embedded in longer narrative strands over which even the most immediate participants cannot have full control, Madison sees the founding document of the United States precisely as he saw original instruments of public debt: as an intentional transaction unstitched from the manifold events that precipitated it and the infinite ones that might follow. In his speech, Madison briefly entertains something like a Hamiltonian narrative, even invoking some of his opponent's characteristic phrases, when he muses: "If implications, thus remote and thus multiplied, can be linked together, a chain may be formed that will reach every object of legislation, every object within the whole compass of political economy."[129] Here Madison registers the consequences of a loose Constitutional interpretation as the production of a reticulated web of remote causes. And his response to this labyrinthine horror is to return to a fundamental rule of interpretation: "the latitude of interpretation required by the bill is condemned by the rule furnished by the constitution itself."[130] In other words, Madison refuses to consider the remote and linked chain of implications by returning to the fundamental truth on which he asserts the Constitution must be read: as a document of limited powers. He thus inveighs against the bank by demanding a reading of the Constitution as a profoundly nonspeculative fiction.

Once again, as Madison turns his eye to economic policy, he substantially revises the literary theory he presented in his earlier writing on behalf of the Constitution. As I suggested, his arguments in Federalist No. 37 were predicated on the conviction that meaning could not be secured by intention. But only a few years later, he organizes opposition to Hamilton's proposed bank by insisting that the language of the Constitution could only be read in relationship to authorial design, which he declares was manifestly and self-evidently to limit federal authority. It is a particularly striking revision since the fundamental purpose of Madison's earlier meditation on linguistic incertitude was to elucidate the difficult political task of measuring the "due proportions" of power and liberty, of state and federal authority, and of legislative, executive, and judicial jurisdiction. So obscure are these matters, Madison inveighs, that they have "puzzle[d] the greatest adepts in political science."[131] Only four years later, in rallying opposition to Hamiltonian finance, Madison clears away what he had earlier seen as irreducible linguistic and political obscurity.

Despite Madison's objections and ingenious Constitutional critique, the bill passed easily, at which point the only viable option was to try to convince President Washington to veto the legislation. Although Washington was predisposed to accept his Treasury Secretary's grand plan for resuscitating the American economy, he was also somewhat receptive to the possibility of a veto in no small measure because he worried that a national bank located in Philadelphia could pose a threat to the planned capital on the Potomac River. As part of this concerted strategy to secure the veto, Madison worked in tandem with Jefferson, who provided Washington his own "Opinion on the Constitutionality of a National Bank," largely based on Madison's Congressional speech. We are more familiar with Jefferson's "Opinion" only because, beginning in the 1830s when it was published, Jefferson's text came to epitomize a strict interpretation of limited Congressional authority.[132]

Like Madison, Jefferson emphasizes a hermeneutics that stresses textual literalism, and only indulges in speculation in order to prove the illegitimacy of establishing a bank. He asserts that *were* he to interpret the Constitution as authorizing the bank, this reading would nullify the meaning of the rest of the document. Laying the ground for a longstanding alignment between forces hostile to finance and those in support of state sovereignty, Jefferson identifies the Tenth Amendment—"all powers not delegated to the United States, by the Constitution, nor prohibited by it to the States, are reserved to the States or to the people"—as the "foundation" of the Constitution.

Again, as with Madison, Jefferson believes the erection of a national bank doesn't merely violate state rights' but also fundamentally attacks linguistic sense: "To take a single step beyond the boundaries thus specially drawn around the powers of Congress [by the Tenth Amendment], is to take possession of a boundless field of power, no longer susceptible of any definition."[133] One unusual feature of Jefferson's argument is that even as he is warning against vagrant readings of the Constitution and thereby emphasizing its narrow and cohesive structure, he also identifies the text's essential basis as located in an annex, an amendment that at the time that Jefferson wrote his "Opinion" had not yet been approved (and would not be for almost a year). Yet even as Jefferson locates the limitations of federal authority in what is, as of January 1791, a supplemental document, his opposition to the bank is premised on the assertion that the Constitution offers no expressed or specified approval of such an institution.

Figuring Congressional power as a voluptuous female body, Jefferson describes the Constitution's authors as crafting the text "to lace them up straitly within the enumerated powers."[134] Jefferson likewise employs a metaphor of female sexuality in his discussion of the Necessary and Proper clause. While Jefferson admits that the bank might provide a "convenient" mechanism by which to help the government collect taxes (one of the enumerated powers), he also stresses the denotative difference between *convenience* and *necessity*: "Nothing but a necessity invincible by any other means, can justify such a prostitution of laws, which constitute the pillars of our whole system of jurisprudence."[135] To interpret Article I, Section 8 as authorizing the incorporation of the bank as "necessary and proper for carrying into Execution the foregoing Powers," according to Jefferson, is to let Congress tumble out of her stays and prostitute the "whole system of jurisprudence." We might notice that Jefferson's metaphors invoke precisely the same sexualized rhetoric as that employed against Hamilton's public credit proposal, a rhetoric that was itself imported from arguments made against the Bank of England a century earlier.

Also significant is Jefferson's metaphoric stress on constriction and narrowness, which leads us to ask why the argument on behalf of Constitutional literalism lends itself so readily to figures of tight fastenings. The word "constrict," from which we derive the term frequently used to describe this approach to Constitutional interpretation as "strict," comes from the Latin word *stringere* or "to draw tight." To read the Constitution strictly is therefore to refuse any slack between word and interpretation. By contrast, the bank's proponents argue for a "loose" construction, from Middle English *loos* or "free from bonds." The other term frequently used to describe this "loose" interpretation of the Constitution is "implied," a word that both Madison and Edmund Randolph use extensively in their assessments of the bank's constitutionality. Madison, for example, describes the dangers of implication in a passage cited earlier, "If implications, thus remote and thus multiplied, can be linked together, a chain may be formed that will reach every object of legislation, every object within the whole compass of political economy." As I suggested before, Madison here briefly entertains a Hamiltonian narrative that conceives of Constitutional language as a reticulated sequence of "remote" and "multiplied" causal strings. The word "implicate" emphasizes this conception of causality as a netlike structure, since the original meaning of the word was to be entwined, entangled, or knitted together. But Madison recoils at the consequences of such an interpretation of the Constitution that would allow readers to stitch loose connections between words and future exigencies: such a reading would allow "the whole compass of political economy" to be subject to Congressional power. In his advisory letter to Washington, Randolph similarly describes the dangers of implication: "To be implied in the nature of the federal government would beget a doctrine so indefinite, as to grasp every power."[136]

In this way we see that Jefferson, Madison, and Randolph not only posit Hamilton's proposed bank as outside the circumference of Congressional authority, but they also articulate a literary theory that repudiates the very plot structure of modern economics that animated Hamilton's financial proposals. The bank debates thus bring to the surface the fundamentally different assumptions the two sides make about the intersection between economics and narrative. In insisting that words are limited to narrow definitions and to their user's original intentions, the Jeffersonians posit a narrative system that refuses ambiguity and conjecture. By contrast, the ambiguity of the future is precisely what motivates Hamilton to propose a national bank with a large capitalization: he imagined that both its size and its centralization would make it better capable of handling the "exigencies" he anticipated would befall the new nation. For Hamilton, the bank would be an institution adaptable to an uncertain future, and it was precisely this unpredictability that required a more generous interpretation of Congressional authority.

Hamilton provides his response to Madison, Jefferson, and Randolph in his "Opinion on the Constitutionality of a National Bank," a document he wrote at the behest of Washington, who sought out Hamilton's counsel before deciding whether to sign or veto the bill. Washington writes Hamilton, "I give you an opportunity of examining & answering the objects contained in the enclosed papers."[137] The "enclosed papers" included both Jefferson's and Randolph's opinions, and in his long rejoinder Hamilton attempts a methodical critique of both texts. We get a clear sense of his scrupulous approach in his notes he produced in preparation, which are organized as if the constitutional challenge was a bookkeeping problem: he records Randolph's arguments on the left-hand side of his page and his own rejoinders in the right-hand column. In this way, he strives to reveal the deficiency—the literal deficit—in his opponents' arguments. But while Hamilton employs the formal structure of arithmetic to engage the analysis, his evaluation is steeped in literary criticism. Indeed, the argument concerning the constitutionality of the bank strongly resembles the first feud over the public debt in its emphasis on issues of style and signification. Once again Hamilton's opponents accuse him of a loose argumentative practice designed to obfuscate and misrepresent his venal ambitions, and they correspondingly posit their own textual production and exegesis as legally and literarily scrupulous and transparent. Hamilton conversely suggests that their attempts at legal and literary exactitude—their narrowing of both the compass of federal authority and of lexical definition—are based on an erroneous understanding of finance. For Hamilton, their misreading yields both poor economic policy and a fundamental distortion of the Constitution.

Much of Hamilton's "Opinion" is dedicated to an evaluation of Madison's, Jefferson's, and Randolph's use of the word *necessary*, the definition of which becomes paramount not only to Hamilton's defense of the bank but also his conception of Federal sovereignty. He writes, "It is essential to the being of the National government, that so erroneous a conception of the meaning of the word *necessary*, should be exploded" (618). And he proceeds to ignite this blast by rebuking their usage of the word according to three very different criteria. First, he simply says that Jefferson and Randolph are not using the word according to any conventional definition. "To understand the word as the Secretary of State does," Hamilton opines, "would be to depart from its obvious & popular sense. . . . It would be to give it the same force as if the word *absolutely* or *indispensibly* had been prefixed to it" (618). In so arguing, he grants literality as the standard by which to evaluate the Constitution, but also asserts that Jefferson does not abide by his own principles of evaluation.

His second critique begins with a similar assessment, which is that Jefferson's analysis rests on a fundamentally "restrictive interpretation of the word [necessity]" (617). But here the significance of the misreading is more consequential, as Hamilton asserts that were we to accept Jefferson's reading of the word, then the only warrant for the constitutional exercise of federal power would be circumstances both "*casual & temporary*" (617). For Hamilton, the criteria by which Jefferson distinguishes necessity from convenience entirely depends on highly situational and contingent contexts. Using Jefferson's own example to clarify his point, Hamilton explains that the only reason that a national bank is not "necessary" is because state banks "*happen to exist to day*," but these state banks "may disappear to morrow" (617). As such, he claims that Jefferson's argument about the bank's unconstitutionality entirely depends on happenstance: were state banks to disappear, then the national bank would prove necessary and therefore constitutional. Jefferson's reading of the word "necessary," therefore, constitutes a "*radical* source of error," because "the *expediency* of exercising a particular power, at a particular time, must indeed depend on *circumstances*; but the constitutional right of exercising it must be uniform & invariable—the same to day, as to morrow" (617). Hamilton thus significantly turns the tables on his opponents, maintaining that while they think they are crafting their arguments according to narrow and invariable linguistic rules, their interpretive theory actually subjects the Constitution to casual and temporary considerations.

His third argument offers an entirely different tactic, which is to reject the very premise of Madison's and Jefferson's literalist hermeneutics and instead to emphasize the "expediency" of the exercise of power. Hamilton thus announces, "an adherence to the letter of [Constitutional] powers would at once arrest the motions of the government" (621). Hamilton plainly articulates his doctrine of implied powers: were governance restricted only to powers explicitly enumerated by the Constitution, he posits, the wheels of government would come to a grinding halt. Conceiving of the language of the

Constitution much the same way he conceived of the monetary language of public credit, Hamilton's interpretive theory emphasizes suppositious consequences and not original intentions. "Nothing is more common," he explains, "than for laws to *express* and *effect*, more or less than was intended" (625). Attempting to shift the dispute away from questions of authorial intention, Hamilton acknowledges that there is a distinction between "implied" and "express" powers, but also offers a third category he calls "resulting" powers. To explain, he conjures a speculative example. "It will not be doubted," he insists, "that if the United States should make a conquest of any of the territories of its neighbours, they would possess sovereign jurisdiction over the conquered territory. This would rather be a result from the whole mass of the powers of the government & from the nature of political society, than a consequence of either of the powers specially enumerated" (615–16). Hamilton here imagines a future territorial conquest so as to prove the necessary limitations of enumerated powers. It is self-evident, he insists, that national sovereignty would extend over this new territory, and yet he also observes that there would be no express legitimization for this authority in the Constitution, the language of which cannot imagine the shape or character of this only conjectural conquest. The scenario, for Hamilton, reveals the fallacy of the Madisonian interpretive paradigm, which presumes temporal stasis—that the future nation will perpetually take precisely the same shape it does in 1791. By choosing the word "result" instead of "imply," Hamilton posits change as inevitable: the socio-economic conditions of the nation will necessarily mutate and so the literary analysis of the constitution must allow for unforeseeable results and consequences.

This attention to future consequences is central to Hamilton's doctrine of implied powers. Indeed Hamilton articulates this concern in one of his earliest expressions of the doctrine when, in Federalist No. 23, he remarks, "The circumstances that endanger the safety of nations are infinite and for this reason no constitutional shackles can wisely be imposed on the power to which the care of it is committed."[138] We might note that in this early articulation of Federal power, Hamilton depicts what Jefferson and Madison had envisioned as "stays" and "fastenings" as "shackles," thereby transforming the representation of the Constitution as a well-supported female body into a slavish one that is incapable of protecting a vulnerable nation. Hamilton wants his Constitution unfettered so that it can respond to currently unimaginable scenarios and events (like, for example, new territorial conquests). Hamilton continues to put stress on infinite possibility in his explanation for the necessity of the bank stating, "The means by which national exigencies are to be provided for, national inconveniences obviated, national prosperity promoted, are of such infinite variety, extent and complexity, that there must, of necessity, be great latitude of discretion in the selection & application of those means" (620). In both cases, Hamilton tacitly accuses his opponents of imaginative deficiency in refusing to envision the countless possible plotlines by which the United States might rise or fall.

In his initial ledger written in response to Randolph's opinion on the bank, Hamilton had registered precisely this same critique. In the left column, Hamilton records Randolph's enumeration of powers that relate to the laying and collection of taxes, which includes the need "to ascertain the subject of taxation," "to declare Quantum," "to *prescribe mode of Collection*," and "to ordain the manner of accounting." In his right-hand column Hamilton remarks, "This an infinite chapter" and then he himself enumerates some of the specific items that he thinks fall under this infinitude: "creation of districts & ports," "of officers," "compensation," "penalties," "what places to be paid at," "oaths," "Mode of recovery," etc. Hamilton clearly does not mean for his own tally to be exhaustive, but instead to capture the remarkable insufficiency of Randolph's abbreviated accounting. In his letter to Washington, Hamilton concentrates on this inadequacy, asserting that the doctrine of express powers "must depend on the accuracy of the enumeration." Hamilton continues, "If it can be shewn that the enumeration is *defective*, the inference is destroyed. To do this will be attended with no difficulty" (628). Much of his task in the "Opinion on the Constitutionality of a National Bank," is therefore to express the omissions and ellipsis of his opponents, and in so doing, to reveal the complexities entailed in the tasks relevant to the national bank. In narrating what Hamilton describes as this "immense chapter" (628) he also exposes what he sees as the fallacy of his opponent's interpretive methodology.

## Encyclopedic Order

The contentious debates about both the public debt and the national bank were clearly animated as much by divergent understandings of language as they were by disagreements over economic policy. Given the significance all the participants place on textual interpretation, we might profitably schematize the two partisan positions according to a distinction that Umberto Eco uses to explain two approaches to semantic representation: the *dictionary* and the *encyclopedia*.[139] According to Eco, lexicography is a project of delimited identity: "items [are] explained by a concise definition," and the dictionary thus "is expected to take into account only those properties necessary and sufficient to distinguish that particular concept from others."[140] The crux of the dictionary is that it disallows transversal explanation: the definition of a word should not require explanation through other words but should be sufficient to itself. Eco illustrates the point with the example of the word "dog," which can be defined through a familiar taxonomy: it is an animal, a mammal, a domesticated canine. This sufficient definition does not, however, articulate many other features common to dogs (that they bark, that they are associated with faithfulness, that they are also a source of fear). The dictionary model also cannot give expression to metonymy: there would be nothing to explain the phrase "dog tired" (which depends on an understanding of exhaustion that always follows canine energetic bursts), or to understand the familiar connection made between dogs and postal workers (which is paradoxically based on antipathy), or the phrase "to hound," (which also depends on a knowledge of the indefatigable persistence associated with dogs). All such features, and there would of course be infinite others, would constitute "matter for the encyclopedia," to a "potentially orderless and limitless galaxy of elements of knowledge of the world."[141] The encyclopedia approaches the linguistic world it represents not as a collection of discrete words, but by assuming that "that every item of a language must be interpreted by every other possible linguistic item, which…can be associated with it. Every sign can be interpreted by another sign that functions as its intepretants."[142]

The distinction Eco draws between the dictionary and encyclopedia provides us with a tidy analogy for the dispute surrounding both economic policy and constitutional interpretation in the 1790s. Insofar as a dictionary establishes meaning by stitching a "necessary and sufficient" attachment between sign and signified, it mirrors the hermeneutic strategies of Madison and Jefferson who approached the Constitution's enumeration of powers according to this selfsame emphasis on both concision and identity. It is not only that Jefferson, Madison, and Randolph assessed the proposed national bank as trespassing beyond the "necessary and proper" clause of the Constitution, but their strict constructionist hermeneutic also presumes a semiotic theory in which every word of the Constitution is necessary and sufficient: there can be no implicative reading. They approached economic transactions in precisely the same fashion: as acts of representational exchange that should be understood in isolation and as a closed system. Any single exchange—a farmer trades one-hundred bushels of wheat to a buyer for a fifty-eight dollar credit note, for example—is like the word "dog": its meaning is bounded by this particular transaction the successful completion of which establishes the identity between sign (fifty-eight dollars of value) and signifier (the one-hundred bushels of wheat). What this reading fails to register, however, are the fluctuating prices of wheat, of currency rates, of the reliability of the creditor's note—and each of these variables are themselves influenced by myriad factors, including supply, demand, labor costs, shipping costs, and rent. Following Eco, we might say that all these are "matter for the encyclopedia."

Such an encyclopedic approach to both language and economic exchange is characteristic of both Hamilton's Constitutional reading and his economic policy. His dedication to a loose interpretation of the Constitution, for example, assumes that both the law and the words that write it must be capable of adapting to fluctuating values. And he indicts the analyses offered by Jefferson, Madison, and Randolph for their imaginative and linguistic poverty: they fail to comprehend the enormity of the many tangential and contingent causes and effects that surround the business of governance. Hamilton also reads economic relations as structured by exactly this same polydimensional encyclopedic model. Even as he holds singular points of exchange—the financial contract—as sacrosanct, he fashions his policy by speculating on the myriad events previous to and consequential from these individual contracts. And notably, as we discovered earlier in this chapter, Hamilton came to this conceptual schema through his own reading and study of Postlethwayt's *Universal Dictionary of Trade and Commerce*. Although Postlethwayt uses the word "dictionary" in his title, the text's prefatory notes and its recommendations for cross-references epitomize the associative and rhizomatic structure that Eco designates as encyclopedic.

Postlethwayt's text was one of the many encyclopedias of the eighteenth century, the most important of which was the grand enterprise of Denis Diderot's *Encyclopédie*, which had, as Jean le Rond d'Alembert explained in his "Preliminary Discourse," possessed two ambitions: to "contain the general principles that form the basis of each science and each art, liberal or mechanical" and to "set forth as well as possible the order and connection of the parts of human knowledge."[143] Jefferson was also profoundly influenced by the *Encyclopédie*, famously organizing his own library around the taxonomy it established: a tripartite division of knowledge into Memory/History, Reason/Philosophy, and Imagination/Poetry. In so doing, Jefferson aligns himself with an encyclopedic imperative towards an orderly mapping of general principles—what d'Alembert describes as the "tree which will gather the various branches of knowledge together under a single point of view to indicate their origin and their relationships to one another."[144] Yet D'Alembert does not solely rely on the metaphor of a tree to describe the *Encyclopedie*, choosing also to characterize it as "vast labyrinth" that does not easily facilitate this singular point of view. In his introductory notes to the *Encyclopédie*, he explains that the "Systematic Chart" (the system by which Jefferson organized his library) is a "world map" through which the viewer can "glimpse the secrets that relate [one system of knowledge] to another"; by contrast, the many individual articles of the *Encyclopedie* provide "highly detailed maps" of local information that can only be known to "inhabitants or to travelers"—to those, in other words, who are lost in the labyrinth.[145]

The distinction that d'Alembert draws here between a bird's-eye and a localized map helps reveal the fundamental difference between the two conceptual systems by which Hamilton and Jefferson imagined their economic world. For the Jeffersonians, as I will consider at length in the following chapter, economic analysis was a kind of poetry: it offered abstract and timeless theorems that transcended the contingencies of history. And from this vantage, the vast constellation of economic participants and transactions could be comprehended in one glimpse and recorded as a simple tally. Hamilton's approach, as we have seen, was conversely to construct policy by assuming an infinite number of possible storylines. Forever lost in the weeds of individual economic decisions, Hamilton's early writing about finance explains that any singular perspective will be unable to represent the immense and heterogeneous scale of economic affairs. To use Eco's terms, then, Hamilton does not map a tree, but rather describes a labyrinth. He conceptualizes economic science as implicative and speculative fictions.

Hamilton's decision to describe and explain the haphazard causality of an emergent capitalist economy is motivated by his dedication to mimesis: he doesn't want to explicate capital movement by simplifying it through abstraction, but by replicating its complexity. He explains, for example, that one fundamental flaw of economic science is that although its "abstract calculations...[are] geometrically true," they generate conclusions that "are false as they relate to the concerns of beings governed more by passion and prejudice than by an enlightened sense of their interests."[146] Hamilton early on recognized a fundamental paradox of economic theory, which was that the objects of its study didn't necessarily follow the fundamental law that economic individuals were supposed to adopt: self-interest.[147] Almost 200 years before the advent of the subfield of behavioral economics, Hamilton similarly recognized that any attempt to explain economic systems had to recognize that individuals made decisions on the basis of passion and prejudice as much as rational self-interest. His reports attempted to bring this recognition of human realism into public policy.[148]

{ 2 }

# Jefferson and the Simple Story
# of Pastoral Economies

In Thomas Jefferson's "Thoughts on English Prosody" (1768), he includes sixty-one citations from English-language verse, many of which include what we now consider to be the standard fare of the eighteenth-century poetic diet: Milton, Pope, Addison, and Gray. But the poet Jefferson cites most (indeed, his verse constitutes almost 25 percent of the citations) is the now infrequently read William Shenstone.[1] Jefferson read Shenstone from the two-volume edition of his work he purchased in 1765, and no doubt he was drawn to the poet because of Shenstone's reputation for landscape gardening and his famous home and gardens, Leasowes.[2] Shenstone had dedicated his life to the development of his gardens that by mid-century were renowned, serving as an inspiration for Jefferson's Monticello. Thomas Whately praises them in *Observations on Modern Gardening* (1770), a book Jefferson took with him when he travelled to Europe in 1786, a trip which included a visit, with John Adams, to Leasowes. Jefferson recalls, "I always walked over the gardens with [Whately's] book in my hand, examined with attention the particular spots he described, found them so justly characterized by him as to be easily recognized, and saw, with wonder, that his fine imagination had never been able to seduce him from the truth."[3]

In *Observations on Modern Gardening*, Jefferson would have read an admiring description of the gardens that Whately said exemplified a symbiosis between the poet and his environment, presenting a "perfect picture of [Shenstone's] mind, simple, elegant, and amiable."[4] Whately further declares that Leasowes so embodies "the ideas of pastoral poetry," that it is impossible to determine "whether the spot inspired his verse; or whether, in the scenes which he formed, he only realized the pastoral images which abound in his songs."[5]

*Speculative Fictions: Explaining the Economy in the Early United States.* Elizabeth Hewitt, Oxford University Press (2020).
© Elizabeth Hewitt.
DOI: 10.1093/oso/9780198859130.001.0001

And yet when Jefferson visited the site, he expresses disappointment: "This is not even an ornamented farm—it is only a grazing farm with a path around it, here and there a seat of board, rarely anything better" (625). Despite, then, his insistence that Whately was never in error in his observations and judgments, and that his "fine imagination" always protected him from any seduction away from the truth, Jefferson records a very different assessment of Shenstone's gardens: not of pastoral simplicity but rural decrepitude.

Jefferson blames the property's decline on Shenstone's failed fortune, speculating that "Shenstone had but three hundred pounds a year and ruined himself by what he did to this farm. It is said he died of the heart-aches which his debts occasioned him."[6] Given Jefferson's own fear of debt, he was no doubt particularly distraught by the declining state of the grounds occasioned by financial insolvency. Jefferson likely knew the stories of Shenstone's financial predicament from Samuel Johnson's *The Lives of the Poets*, which recommended Leasowes as "a place to be visited by travellers, and copied by designers," but also firmly established Shenstone's reputation as an improvident property owner. While admiring his obsessive care for the estate, Johnson also notes that Shenstone's "delight in rural pleasures" was oriented "more to the improvement of its beauty than the increase of its produce." Johnson further suggests that Shenstone's death was "hastened by his anxieties" over the financial burden occasioned by his obsessive interest in the gardens that bore no profit.[7] Yet even as he takes Shenstone to task for his lack of attention to economy, Johnson also effectively establishes the poet as the quintessence of an eighteenth-century version of the pastoral that depended on a radical distinction between profit and poetry. This is the species of pastoralism that, as Raymond Williams once wrote, represents only "an enamelled world."[8] Leasowes is beautiful because, like pastoral poetry, its function is an aesthetic of simplicity and not a productive economy. John Adams expressed a somewhat similar judgment after his visit, saying: "Shenstone's Leasowes is the simplest and plainest, but the most rural of all. I saw no spot so small that exhibited such a variety of beauty."[9] For Jefferson, however, the plainness of the garden—that it is was "unornamented" and only a "grazing farm"— marred its beauty because its plainness also reminded him of scarcity, of the fact that funds are required to make gardens grow, and that these funds only come when gardens yield produce that can be transformed into capital.

Johnson praises the inefficient pastoral beauty of Shenstone's gardens, but dismisses Shenstone's poetry for much the same reasons that Jefferson disliked the landscape: for bringing the realities of an agricultural economy to the surface. Johnson particularly singles out Shenstone's *Pastoral Ballad* (1755), about which he says, "an intelligent reader, acquainted with the scenes of real life, sickens at the mention of the *crook*, the *pipe*, the *sheep*, and the *kids*, which it is not necessary to bring forward to notice, for the poet's art is selection, and he ought to shew the beauties without the grossness of the country life."[10] Johnson condemns Shenstone both for revealing "the grossness of the country life" and for misrepresenting this "real life" as just so many pastoral objects: crooks, pipes, sheep, and kids.[11] Other eighteenth-century readers were similarly unkind in their judgment: Horace Walpole, for example, referred to Shenstone as "that water-gruel bard," pointedly remarking on the inefficiency of Shenstone's poetic work: "he was labouring all his life to write a perfect song, and . . . never once succeeded."[12]

For Jefferson, however, Shenstone's poetry was valuable precisely because it appeared to occasion no labor from the poet and cause none for his readers. The uncomplicated mediocrity of Shenstone's verse is the source of its beauty and pleasure. In "Thoughts on English Prosody," for example, Jefferson observes that the variances of English accentual verse make it such that, for many poems, "No two persons will accent the same passage alike." By way of example, he cites two passages from Shakespeare's *Julius Caesar* and one from *The Tempest*, and he muses, "each word teems with latent meaning" and that "no man but Garrick ever drew their full tone out of them" (612). Shakespeare's lines thus present a motherlode of meaning that only the most skilled of readers can secure. Jefferson uses Shenstone to illustrate the opposite case: an example "wherein little differences in the enunciation will not change the meaning sensibly" and it is "easily enough read" (612). Like even rows in a garden plot, Shenstone's verse offers an easy and simple metrical regularity. And it is perhaps for this reason that one biographer refers to him as one of Jefferson's "favorite poets."[13]

There might be some humor in Jefferson's celebration of a now minor poet and his pastoral renderings of lovelorn boys wandering into the "verdure" of the trees, save for the fact that Jefferson's poetic tastes are an especially tender subject for contemporary literary scholars given his infamous dismissal of Phillis Wheatley's verse as "below the dignity of criticism" (267).[14] Jefferson's contemptuous remarks are, of course, offered in *Notes on the State of Virginia*, the quintessential expression of American pastoralism. As Leo Marx writes, "Nowhere in our literature is there a more appealing, vivid, or thorough statement of the case of the pastoral ideal than in *Notes on Virginia*."[15] Wheatley also wrote pastoral poetry, a fact that Jefferson must have known since he opted to classify her volume, *Poems on Various Subjects Religious and Moral* (1773), in the sub-section of his library titled, "Pastorals, Odes, Elegies," along with his copies of Shenstone's volumes.[16]

Like Jefferson, Wheatley was herself familiar with Shenstone and owned a copy of his work.[17] She almost certainly would have been familiar with Shenstone's "An Elegy on the Miserable State of an African Slave," which was included in the publication of Granville Sharp's *An Essay on Slavery* (1773).[18] Shenstone's "Elegy" offers a distinctly anti-pastoral portrait of the Atlantic slave trade: the poem's imagined speaker is an African man torn from "Lybian shores" who describes a pestilence brought by European traders, rhetorically asking, "Shall foreign plagues infest this teeming land.../ Here the dire locusts horrid swarms prevail; / Here the blue asps with livid poison swell?"[19] And the poem's speaker reproaches the pastoral pretensions of white Europe, establishing a direct causal relationship between America's "fertile plains" and the destruction of Africa and its people: "Rich by our toils, and by our sorrows gay, / They ply our labours, and enhance our pains." Published with Sharp's work, and also republished in American miscellanies alongside William Cowper's poetry, the poem is manifestly harnessed to anti-slavery politics.

But the poem's original context significantly obscures this politics. First published as "Elegy XX," the poem is part of a larger set of "Elegies, Written on Many different Occasions," and the sentiment of these poems is more predictably pastoral. The first of the elegies begins, "For rural virtues, and for native skies, / I bade Augusta's venal sons farewell," establishing a conventional calculus of rural virtue as antidote to the corruptions of the court.[20] Moreover, the original "Elegy XX" begins with a narrative explanation that the speaker only uses the term slavery metaphorically to describe his own amorous devotion: "He compares his humble fortune with the distress of others; and his subjection to DELIA, with the miserable servitude of an African slave." When in the third stanza, the speaker exults, "Slave tho' I be, to Delia's eyes a slave," it is only a figurative slavery. But in the very next stanza, the poem shifts its gaze to the "poor native [on] Lybian shores," and the speaker even condemns the "vacant bards" for making "mockery of grief" by asserting a comparison between the lovelorn shepherd and the captured African. If, however, the speaker chides both himself and poetry for the false comparison between a metaphoric and a literal enslavement, then the poet nonetheless uses the "muse" to capture and translate the slave's "tender plea" into an elegiac song.

Wheatley takes up the very same topics in her own pastoral elegy, "On Imagination." But unlike Shenstone's speaker, who admits he can only imagine the grief of slaves and their exile from fertile gardens, Wheatley's poem depicts imagination as a powerful tool of mastery. Wheatley's speaker metaphorically "fetters" herself to an imagination that can actually revitalize a ruined landscape. Attaching herself to a "Fancy" that breaks the "iron bands" of "frozen deeps" and "bid[s] their waters murmur o'er the sands," Wheatley's speaker gives her readers a treasure trove of pastoral delights:

> Fair *Flora* may resume her fragrant reign,
> And with her flow'ry riches deck the plain;
> *Sylvanus* may diffuse his honours round,
> And all the forest may with leaves be crown'd:
> Show'rs may descend, and dews their gems disclose,
> And nectar sparkle on the blooming rose.[21]

Yet Wheatley's poem does not remain long in this fertile imaginary land, and in the concluding stanza, the speaker, "reluctant leave[s] the pleasing views, / Which *Fancy* dresses to delight the *Muse*." While Shenstone's poem concludes by allowing the imagined speaker, the kidnapped slave, to fancy himself in heaven, "Where tufted flowrets paint the verdant plain," Wheatley's speaker returns to the desolate world of winter and the "northern tempests [that] damp the rising fire." Her poem thus offers something like the inverse of Shenstone's. He lambastes imaginative projection but then indulges it, concluding with the imaginative consolation of the Christian pastoral. Wheatley allows the indulgence of fancy, but then returns to the cold climate of Boston and enslavement, thereby signaling the very real limitations of the imaginative power she is harnessing.[22]

We see something similar in Wheatley's "An Hymn to Morning," which likewise calls on the power of poetry (the "honour'd nine") to

"Assist my labours." And the appeal yields the "shady groves" and "verdant gloom" that shades the "poet from the burning day."[23] But the cooling shade engendered by the pastoral tradition, which can convert the shepherd's labor into otium, is not sustained in this poem. The sun climbs higher into the sky, and the speaker acknowledges that "his fervid beams too strong," she must "conclude[e] th' abortive song." Here Wheatley mobilizes the vocabulary of the pastoral, but the poem instead harnesses the energy of the georgic in so far as it emphasizes the labor and toil required to make both gardens and poems grow.[24] Indeed, this ceaseless labor is emphasized by the poem's partner, "An Hymn to Night." The poem predictably praises the night for providing the "placid slumbers" that will "sooth each weary mind," but this solace is no sooner described than the speaker remembers that evening and morning are inextricably bound: "At morn to wake more heav'nly, more refin'd; / So shall the labours of the day begin."[25] Wheatley's aestheticized dawn and dusk thus cannot be separated from the perpetual repetitions of daily toil.

We should keep Wheatley's analysis of the deficiencies of the pastoral imagination in mind when we reread Jefferson's critique of her verse.[26] Scholars have largely read Jefferson's commentary as a strategy by which he can rationalize racism: simply put, a derogation of her poetry as imitative is a necessary move in a justification for chattel slavery that depends on excluding black persons from the vaunted rights and happiness of man. But we might also note that a denigration of her poetry is equally crucial to Jefferson's devotion to the pastoral as both poetic mode and political ideology, a devotion that finds its apotheosis in Jefferson's exultation from *Notes* that "Those who labour in the earth are the chosen people of God, if ever he had a chosen people, whose breasts he has made his peculiar deposit for substantial and genuine virtue" (290). Wheatley's own pastoral writing presents a challenge, then, for two reasons. First, her status as African slave is a reminder that, in the United States, many of those who labored the earth were "chosen" to be human chattel. Second, and this accounts for why Jefferson adamantly stresses Wheatley's incapacity at "imagination," because her verse deliberately contradicts one fundamental premise of pastoralism, which is that poetry can unfetter agricultural practices from their real material conditions. Even as she writes odes to imagination that successfully deploy pastoral imagery, her work acknowledges that poetry cannot transport the slave laboring under the hot sun to shade. Nor, her verse implies, can a poetic imagination sustain the pastoral ideal of small-scale subsistence farming in a landscape increasingly devoted to agrarian capitalism.

Except, of course, this ideological reconstruction is precisely what the pastoral does, and Jefferson and his party were remarkably effective in sustaining a particular ethos of agrarian life even as the forms of that life radically shifted. As William Dowling argues, Jefferson and his party spun such a compelling story about American democracy that he all but "neutraliz[e] any competing vision of the American republic."[27] And the key to their political and poetical ascension, Dowling continues, was their monopolization of the language of agrarian virtue: the Jeffersonians had the "power to convince Americans that they actually inhabit[ed] the fantasy of natural innocence contained in works like Crèvecoeur's *Letters from an American Farmer.*"[28] This is not to say that Jefferson actually conceived of agricultural production as divorced from capital markets: he always assumed that the sales of American produce on the global stage would be the key to national wealth. The same chapter that rhapsodizes about "those who labour the earth" also proposes that cotton, wool, flax, and hemp be exported. As we will see, American "pastoralism" is also entirely coterminous with laissez-faire capitalism because in the Jeffersonian version of the free market, there is no entropy: the system cannot wind down. In this chapter, I argue that the real attraction of the pastoral for Jefferson and his party is located less in its rural setting than on the presumption that wealth is easy to maintain—that the shepherd's song and the sheep are self-sustaining. If the deteriorating state of Leasowes offered a visual rebuttal to this assumption, then Shenstone's poetry, with its effortlessly readable lines, sustained it. The pastoral offered a simple explanation of a complex system, and it is this simplicity that has shaped the discursive history of American political economy.

## American Pastoral

Stuart Curran observes, "Nothing better exemplifies the intractability of generic definition than pastoral."[29] Paul Alpers argues something similar when he chides a critical tendency to use the term pastoral with "ungoverned inclusiveness."[30] Both critics identify the definitional capaciousness of the term, and Curran specifically compares the

genre to a dysfunctional monetary "currency" that must constantly
"adjust [itself] to the local economy."[31] His metaphor also suggests
that we loosely trade in the pastoral, failing to register that the genre's
value necessarily depends on the economic world from which it is
deployed. Other scholars of the pastoral make similar claims, albeit
with different critical agendas. Annabel Patterson, for example, eschews
any attempt to define the pastoral, but does stress that the pastoral's
meaning for its readers is deeply situated in historical moments.[32]
Lawrence Buell makes the same argument about the American pastoral more specifically when he states, "American pastoral representation cannot be linked to a single ideological position."[33] Yet in this
regard, there is nothing unique about the pastoral: other literary
genres mutate and evolve over time, and other literary genres thwart
any single ideological argument. What does mark the pastoral as
exceptional, however, is that the appeal to both timelessness and
universality is crucial to its formula, if not its practice. And thus, the
pastoral becomes, as many of its critics have remarked, imbued with
a deeply paradoxical structure. If the "high noon of pastoral pleas-
ance," as Curran proposes, is located in the "momentary delight into
an untrammeled mode of existence withdrawn from temporal concerns, temporal costs," then it is also the case that this Arcadian
dream is an impossible one.[34] And from Virgil on, the pastoral and
georgic modes have always offered double-voiced expressions of
temporal retreat: one song spun the fantasy of agrarian leisure and
labor, while the other acknowledged that the material conditions of
this life of plenty were already threatened by geo-political realities.[35]

This paradoxical structure, so fundamental to the genre, necessarily mutated in the American context since unlike the classical pastoral, in which the idyll was located in an unrecoverable past, or the
Christian pastoral, in which it is imagined as a possible millennialist
future, the particular mythos of North America was the presence—
both temporal and spatial—of the lost Golden Age.[36] From the very
beginning of English colonization of North America, its soil was
promoted as providing the temporal transport essential to the pastoral.[37] Its fertile ground would produce new and abundant commodities that could substitute for old world goods and sustain an ever
growing population. Its vast real estate would absorb the superfluous
population of the old world. This is the calculation that James
Madison makes in his 1791 *National Gazette* essay, "Population and
Emigration," to predict the substantial economic rewards for both

the United States and Europe because American soil could sustain a larger global population with foodstuffs and raw materials.[38] His text, working from political arithmetic and economic statistics, does not seem the stuff of pastoral, but the basis of his argument is saturated by the genre's idyllic assumptions. Limitless territorial expansion for the nation's white citizens will keep the country perpetually in that historical and economic sweet spot located between savage wilderness and corrupt civilization.

We can see this same logic play out in a more familiarly pastoral setting in Mercy Otis Warren's lyric, "Simplicity" (1790). The poem rewinds us to the past as we travel back to a classical age allegorized by a "virgin" goddess who rises from the sea and beholds her "happy race, / Who ne'er contested titles, gold, or place...[before] commerce's whiten'd sails were wafted wide."[39] But we also travel to a Scriptural past, "that ideal golden age...in dark oblivion lost, / The sons of Adam know it to their cost." Warren's focus on narrative time is also sounded by the distinctly stadialist history she offers: the poem rehearses the fall of Rome, in which "High-wrought refinement— usher'd in replete, / With all the ills that sink a virtuous state"; the fall of Carthage, of which she states that "Commerce! The source of every narrow vice" was single-handedly responsible for "blott[ing] out Carthaginian fame"; and the fall of the Hanoverians in which "George's folly stains his grandsire's crown [because] fancy craves what nature never taught." The poem calmly narrates stories about these fallen empires: "While time rolls on, and mighty kingdoms fail." Yet there is also something profoundly vertiginous in Warren's chronometry, which fashions the temporal sequences of fallen kingdoms into a simultaneous and allegorical "vortex of European crimes" that confirms a transhistorical truth about the dangers of commercial wealth. In opposition to this whirlwind of history, however, the poem gazes toward "Columbia free" as a geographic reprieve that also can return us to where the poem begins, "Deep in the Bosom of old Time."

Warren's appeal to a literalized new Golden Age on North American territory is a consistent theme in American poetry of the early Republic. For example, of the forty-five poems that are included in the section, "From American Poets," of Mathew Carey's *The Beauties of Poetry* (1791), the first poetry anthology published in the United States, almost 40 percent of them invoke this basic pastoral theme of an idyllic agrarian landscape. The first American poem in the anthology is Timothy Dwight's "Columbia," which apostrophizes "Columbia" as the "noblest" reign because "Most fruitful thy soil," and, like Warren's poem, explicitly contrasts this agricultural plentitude against European desolation: "To conquest, and slaughter, let Europe aspire; / Whelm nations in blood, and wrap cities in fire."[40] Like Warren, Dwight forecasts a happy American simplicity primarily through historical juxtaposition against Europe's failures.

Other pastoral poems in the anthology provide even less equivocal celebrations of American agrarianism. *Beauties of Poetry* includes several contributions from Dwight's fellow Connecticut Wit, David Humphreys, who gives full-throated expressions to agrarian idealism. In "Future state of the western territory," for example, Humphreys extends the geographic range of the American idyll as he rhapsodically celebrates the "vernal glories in perpetual bloom," "fragrant groves," and "rural ease" that will soon sprout up along the "fair Ohio." As the title makes clear, the poem offers an early expression of Manifest Destiny in its imagination of a soon-to-be realized Arcadia alongside the banks of the Ohio River in the recently acquired U.S. territory. The poem catalogues the bounty that will emerge from this new promised land with no mention of a threat:

> But golden years, anew, begin their reigns,
> And cloudless sun-shine gild salubrious plains.
> Herbs, fruits, and flow'rs shall clothe th' uncultur'd field
> Nectareous juice, the vine and orchard yield,
> Rich dulcet creams, the copious goblets fill,
> Delicious honey from the trees distill.[41]

And even when it acknowledges the hazards most likely to wreck this delectable paradise, it quickly dispatches them. In this always already cultivated wilderness, the poem explains, the indigenous people have disappeared: "Nor shall the savages of murd'rous soul...On the pale victim point the reeking blade; or cause the hamlet, lull'd in deep repose, / No more to wake." The new American shepherds can sleep easy because the Indian has already been "rous'd" from his "lurking place." And just as the poem rescues its Ohioan Arcadia from the "savagery" that comes before, it will protect against the "civilization" that comes after. Thus, the poem speculates a future in which "cities rise, and spiry towns increase, / With gilded domes," a world of such wealth that "rich Commerce [will] court the fav'ring gales, / And wond'ring wilds admire the passing sails." The poem navigates its own vision as supply chain following the produce alongside the Ohio River to the cargo being delivered up and down the "stormy Huron," to the "wild Ontario," and finally into the port of Mississippi. The poem, however, reassures its readers that there will be no danger from this commercial traffic: it will not threaten the idyll because the "unbounded deserts" of the United States will allow its citizens to escape the clock of a stadialist future, instead providing the "last retreat of man."

These three poems bring into relief what it is about the pastoral that seems to haunt its critics: that it is a literary mode primarily "motivated by naïve idyllicism."[42] Alpers asserts that this assumption was one of the "irritants" that led him to undertake his project. Pastoral writing, he insists, is "far more aware of itself and its conditions than it has usually been thought to be, or even capable of being."[43] This insistence on pastoralism's self-consciousness about its manufactured simplicity is a consistent theme across its critics. Alpers, Williams, Marx, Patterson, and Buell address a diverse set of literary periods and canons, but they have consensus in claiming that the innocent charm of the pastoral is always hitched to a more complicated and canny aesthetic and/or ideological project.[44]

What, then, are critics to do with an American pastoral like Humphreys's or Warren's in which there seems to be nothing *but* simplicity—in which there is no attempt, as Lawrence Buell puts it, to register the "gap between pastoral as ideological construct and pastoral as social program," in which there is no ironic separation between what the poem says and what it means?[45] Humphreys envisions a new golden age in which there is no contradiction between *homo economicus* and *otium*, between utopia and practice. Warren fantasizes Columbia as both a historical and geographic reprieve from the storms of history. Insofar as this poetry seems to offer a straightforward embrace of a retrograde economic fantasy, the answer to the question is that critics simply ignore it. And yet even as we have paid scant attention to early American pastoral verse, critics have emphasized the centrality of pastoralism as a key concept of American literary culture. And so we have the strange situation in which poems by some of the first American-born poets publishing in the United States are absent from the critical canon even as they epitomize a set of remarkably familiar ideological projects.[46] And instead of examining this poetry as the source of American pastoral ideology, critics turn to Thomas Jefferson's *Notes on the State of Virginia*—a prose work that pushes at the generic edges of the pastoral in that it engages topics far outside the scope of the agrarian landscape and husbandry.

In his landmark study of antebellum American agrarianism, Allan Kulikoff rejects the association between Jefferson and pastoralism: "Jeffersonians rarely adopted images from pastoral tradition."[47] Kulikoff argues that Federalist authors were actually more likely to utilize pastoralism in the service of their political arguments. As corroboration of his position he points to the poetry of Timothy Dwight and David Humphreys, and a novel by fellow Connecticut Federalist, Enoch Hitchcock's *The Farmer's Friend* (1793). Kulikoff's work is a useful corrective to the conventional association between Jefferson and pastoralism, in which Jefferson's vision of America was a "Vergilian paradise magnified a thousand times."[48] It likewise challenges Dowling's claim that the Jeffersonians had an exclusive monopoly on the rhetoric of agrarian idealism. Yet Kulikoff also clearly overstates the Federalist cornering of the pastoral market, since Mercy Otis Warren and Philip Freneau, to just name two examples, were both Jeffersonians who wrote pastoral verse. Moreover, even the case of *The Farmer's Friend* complicates a simple partisan argument since, while the novel offers a panegyric to American farmers (to whom the work is dedicated), it also explicitly cites passages from Jefferson's *Notes on Virginia* as the source material for the mythos of the American pastoral.[49]

Kulikoff's reluctance to read Jefferson's *Notes* as canonical text of the American pastoral is motivated by a longstanding historical debate concerning Jeffersonian political economy. On one side were historians associated with the "republican synthesis" who saw the rhetorical strains of Democratic-Republicanism as tied to an enduring intellectual tradition of civic humanism that made its way to the American politics through British Country Party ideology. The critique of Hamiltonian finance, they argued, was deeply inflected by an Augustan rhetoric that moralized against luxurious excess and speculative valuation. J.G.A. Pocock can thus describe the philippics levelled against Hamilton as work "in which the ghosts of Swift and Bolingbroke stalk on every page."[50] And certainly the consistency with which Hamilton's detractors labeled him an American Walpole corroborates this assessment about the potency of Country Party ideology for Jeffersonian critique.

On the other side, however, were historians who argued that Jefferson could not be neatly assimilated to this Country Party tradition.[51] They asserted that the third President had been misrepresented as an economic conservative doomed, as Joyce Appleby put it, to play the part of a "heroic loser in the battle against modernity."[52] Such scholars maintained that what appeared to be Jefferson's pastoral emphasis on husbandry and individual landownership was actually an economic plan that depended on the large-scale export of staple crops to a European market. In his study of what he designates as the American "georgic," Timothy Sweet makes a very similar claim, explaining that Jefferson's agrarian vision was fundamentally oriented toward the capital market.[53] In their arguments on behalf of this liberal Jefferson, scholars explicitly distinguish Jeffersonian economic policy from poetics. As one historian highlights the distinction: do we see Jefferson as a disciple of the free market and a "herald [of] modern capitalism" or does he "look backwards to an idealized Arcadia of philosophical farmers"?[54] Kulikoff frames the argument in similar terms when he holds a literary scholar as responsible for establishing the association of Jefferson and pastoralism, accusing Leo Marx's *Machine in the Garden* for "exaggerate[ing] the pastoral imagery in Jefferson's thought."[55]

But Marx was similarly reluctant to link Jefferson to any naïve pastoral tradition, and his classic study of the agrarian mythos argues that there were two versions of American pastoralism. One believed that in the new United States, "it still was not too late...to establish a home for rural virtue."[56] Marx identifies J. Hector St. John de Crèvecoeur's *Letters of an American Farmer* (1783) and the anonymous pamphlet, *The Golden Age* (1785) as epitomizing this "simpleminded" pastoral, although we can easily imagine him applying the label to the works of Warren, Dwight, Humphreys, and Hitchcock.[57] The other version, designated as "complex" pastoralism, sagaciously recognized that this agrarian fantasy was only ever an imaginative projection.[58] Jefferson's *Notes,* according to Marx, is the quintessence of the complex pastoral. Unlike its simple brethren, Jefferson's *Notes* does not want to "mask the real problems of an industrial civilization," but instead to give expression to the "counterforces" threatening to disrupt the idyll.[59] Yet Marx also posits Jefferson's invocation of moral virtue as deliberately eschewing any economic calculus: Jefferson does not care that "an agricultural economy may be economically disadvantageous," because "he rejects productivity and...material living standards, as tests of a good society."[60] Marx therefore defines Jeffersonian pastoralism through its opposition to economic concerns, but also simultaneously declares this poetry to be perspicaciously aware of an emergent commercial capitalism.[61] It would seem therefore that Marx and Kulikoff have a similar motivation: to distance Jefferson from a pastoral poetics that expresses idyllic escapism without critique.

Yet this vindication of Jefferson stands in stark opposition to the very terms that the Jeffersonians used in their battle against Hamiltonian finance. As we saw in the last chapter, the most frequent accusation made against Federalist finance was that its proponents wrote with a deliberately complex style designed to obfuscate and confuse its readers. And they conversely appealed to the simplicity of both their own literary style and political assumptions. They argued, for example, that public debt was abhorrent because it signaled slavish dependence to a creditor that necessarily undermined the personal autonomy said to be the centerpiece of democracy. They argued that a national bank was a talisman of political corruption because it consolidated power under one corporate body. And, as we will see in more detail in this chapter, they saw Hamilton's proposal to support American manufacturing as a direct repudiation of democratic principles because it discouraged landownership, which was said to be the only firm ground on which political liberties could be cultivated. In each case, we read an argument on behalf of *integrity*: debt attaches individuals to the pleasures and demands of other bodies; banks link individuals into monstrous corporate bodies; and manufacturing turns individuals into body parts (hands) that cannot own their own labor or land. We typically theorize this stress on personal integrity, or the indissolubility of the subject, as being the crux of political liberalism. And it was certainly in these terms that Hamilton's opponents judged his economic proposals as a betrayal of American liberty and a repudiation of the promise of individual political and economic sovereignty. But this political critique is also inextricable from the critique of literary style—that the Reports were purposefully abstruse. In other words, the demand for a simple explanation of American finance was also a demand for stories with simple and integral economic actors. We don't typically use the language of simplicity to talk about political theory, but we could. Individual sovereignty presupposes a self that cannot be divided—which is to say, it is uncompounded. The sovereign self is quite literally a simple self: *simplus* or onefold. The importance of the concept of simplicity to Hamilton's critics is not only, then, that his complex plots confused "simple" readers, but that his proposals enmeshed "simple" individuals into serpentine economic systems from which they could not extricate themselves. The Jeffersonian strategy thereby was to tell stories about the American economy that could disentangle individuals and individual households from the manifold economic systems on which they were necessarily dependent.

The "simplicity" of the pastoral thus becomes useful in the American context not because of its association with agrarianism, and not because it fantasizes an idyllic past as a plausible future, but because it provides a remarkably compelling way to tell stories about complex economic relations. This is why the language of agrarian virtue has had such durability in American literary and political history even though the material conditions of the nation did not support this vision. As Buell puts it, these fabulations were "defeated even before being expressed in mature form by Jefferson."[62] Pocock makes the point even more extravagantly: "From Jefferson to Frederick Jackson Turner and beyond, it was a commonplace that sooner or later the frontier would be closed, the land filled, and the corruptions of history—urbanisation, finance capital, 'the cross of gold,' 'the military-industrial complex'—would overtake America."[63] The reason Jeffersonian fables about the productive power of American husbandry and the natural efficiency of laissez-faire economic policy have remained so firmly entrenched, even in the twenty-first century, I want to argue, lies in the explanatory methodology of the American pastoral tradition.

## Poetics of the Representative Anecdote

The perpetual charm of American pastoralism is that it narrates the complexities of modern economic life as the tale of an unimpeded, wholly integral individual. Its aesthetic is so seductive not because it convinced its readers that the bucolic fantasy of the independent freeholder was viable, but because it could explain the wide-ranging economic systems in which people organized their lives as if they were simple—and singular—household economies. In some ways, then, I am echoing William Empson's famous definition of the pastoral as the literary form whose fundamental purpose is to put "the complex into the simple."[64] For Empson, the substitution or displacement was primarily a reference to objects, characters, or themes: the pastoral allowed "simple people" (like shepherds) the ability to speak "in learned and fashionable language."[65] The pastoral project of the early United States works somewhat differently: it takes the learned and difficult concepts of the emerging discipline of economics and it makes them simple.

One method of this simplification is through figures of substitution and displacement: allegory, metaphor, metonymy. To see this in action, we might also look more closely at the infamous Query Nineteen from Jefferson's *Notes*. Marx reads this moment as emphasizing what he characterizes as a schism between the "spare language of political economists" and the "highly figurative, mythopoeic language" that describes farm laborers as the "chosen people of God."[66] Jefferson's language certainly turns metaphoric when he represents American farmers as Israelites and as the motherlode for American virtue, announcing that God has made them a "peculiar deposit for substantial and genuine virtue" (290). But we should not understand Jefferson's metaphoric turn in this long paragraph as shifting away from the language of political economy since his metaphor-making is absolutely crucial to his political arithmetic—an arithmetic that depends on simplification. Because the paragraph is colored with the panegyric to "those who labour in the earth," and because Jefferson embraces the republican argument that "Dependance begets subservience and venality, suffocates the germ of virtue," the passage has frequently been interpreted as an endorsement of economic self-sufficiency. But Jefferson is notably making the opposite claim: his manifest proposal is that American agricultural goods (this short chapter is largely focused on textile crops—cotton, wool, flax, and hemp) should be exported to Europe and imported back as manufactured products. Even as Jefferson is casting industrial manufacturing out of his garden, he is describing a garden that is fully integrated into a global commercial marketplace.

Why, then, is this famous passage taken as the epitome of the American idyll and not an archetypal statement of the United States' imbrication in international trade? One explanation is that it is a function of Jefferson's calculations:

It is better to carry provisions and materials to workmen there, than bring them to the provisions and materials, and with them their

> manners and principles. The loss by the transportation of commodi-
> ties across the Atlantic will be made up in happiness and permanence
> of government.   (291)

Here Jefferson compares the relative productivity of a national economy exclusively dedicated to exporting raw goods against one that
developed a domestic manufacturing base. Although he acknowledges the fiscal "loss[es]" that will come from the expense of importing manufactured goods, he also insists that these will be offset by
political gains ("happiness and permanence of government"). The
rhetorical finesse here is to associate export trade with the "happiness" and virtue that he has already tied explicitly to economic self-
sufficiency. Americans should disavow manufacturing, he writes,
because "dependence…suffocates the germ of virtue" (290–91).
Quite remarkably, Jefferson's recommendation for a voluminous
export and import trade are drawn as a portrait of economic autarky,
and the pastoral poetry of the chapter is found in his highly abbreviated description of the global market. What he celebrates as the
simple sufficiency of the independent Virginia farmer would involve,
for example, moving Virginia flax to a Philadelphia merchant, to a
Boston exporter, to a London importer, to a Manchester mill owner,
to a London exporter, to a New Yorker importer, to a Virginia merchant, and back to our farmer in the form of a linen shirt.

Jefferson offers another strategy of simplification in the next metaphor he deploys in his impassioned castigation of urban life:

> The mobs of great cities add just so much to the support of pure
> government, as sores do to the strength of the human body. It is the
> manners and spirit of a people which preserve a republic in vigour.
> A degeneracy in these is a canker which soon eats to the heart of its
> laws and constitution.   (291)

Jefferson uses the orthodox metaphor of the social body as an individual human body in order to describe the influx of a population of
wage earners as "sores" and "canker[s]" that will destroy the American
state. The rhetoric of foreign contagion follows directly from the earlier
statement that inveighs against importing the "manners and principles"
of immigrant workers. Jefferson thus establishes the metaphoric
body of the United States as singular, as an integer, which must resist
"degeneration," a word that literally means to lose the qualities proper

to itself. Here too, then, even as Jefferson is making an argument on behalf of an import trade, the simplicity of his metaphoric substitution—the nation as a singular healthy body—allows for the conventional interpretation of this passage as the epitome of American pastoralism. What is pastoral about this moment, therefore, is not the bucolic landscape on which the American farmer labors (which notably Jefferson does not describe at all), but rather the construction of the American farmer as a "representative anecdote" by which to describe the whole of the American economy.

"Representative anecdote" is the phrase Alpers uses to describe the essential generic project of the pastoral, which is to offer "a brief and compendious rendering of a certain situation or type of life."[67] For Alpers, the life of the herdsman, and not the agrarian landscape on which he roams, is the representative anecdote that characterizes the pastoral. I argue that we should broaden Alpers's definition and consider the essence of the pastoral to be the very notion of the representative anecdote. Jefferson's work epitomizes pastoralism because he explains the intricate realities of global capitalism through a "brief and compendious rendering": a simple anecdote of a virtuous laborer.

Jefferson deploys the very same anecdotal method in his 1789 letter to James Madison, in which he famously outlines his belief that "the earth belongs in usufruct to the living" and rhetorically asks, "Whether one generation of men has a right to bind another" (959). The letter is a canonical one in Jefferson's enormous epistolary corpus because it provides a quintessential statement against legislative conservativism. Jefferson establishes a mandate for perpetual social deliberation, a political model in which the legal decisions of one generation would never impinge on their descendants. This is the letter said to reveal Jefferson as radical in that he manifestly rejects any system of government founded on custom and to which each new generation is bound to give consent. However, as Herbert Sloan argues, Jefferson's letter is more deeply concerned with economic than with legislative inheritance. It must be read, Sloan states, "first and foremost [as] a confession of what debt meant to Thomas Jefferson."[68]

For Jefferson, a debt that contracted descendants to financial obligations to which they had not consented violated the liberties of that future generation. This is why, Sloan continues, "Debt was a horror, a nightmare; [Jefferson's] debts stood between him and the realization of his hopes—just as the public debt stood between America and the hopes he cherished for it."[69] And Jefferson makes this argument against intergenerational debt by appealing to the integrity of an individual's body: "The portion occupied by an individual ceases to be his when himself ceases to be, and reverts to the society." Property, in his formulation, can only be owned by a person who possesses being: when this person "ceases to be," which is to say, when the property that was their body dies, their property necessarily "reverts to the society." Jefferson extends his analysis to reference a broader social body: "what is true of every member of the society individually, is true of them all collectively, since the rights of the whole can be no more than the sum of the rights of the individuals" (959–60). Jefferson's illustration assumes a social body comprising individual parts, each of which is a synecdoche for that whole body. This amalgamated social body cannot, according to Jefferson, compel future bodies to assent to its own political and economic contracts. But this argument raises a fundamental problem, which is how to calculate the borders of a social body that, unlike an individual, has no clearly defined moment of birth or death.

David Hume—about whom Jefferson is clearly thinking— registered precisely the same complication in his own meditations on generational inheritances in "Of the Original Contract" (1752). Hume writes:

> Did one generation go off the stage at once and another succeed, as is the case with silkworms and butterflies, the new race, if they had sense enough to choose their government, which surely is never the case with men, might voluntarily and by general consent establish their own form of civil polity without any regard to the laws or precedents which prevailed among their ancestors. But as human society is in perpetual flux, one man every hour going out of the world, another coming into it, it is necessary in order to preserve stability in government that the new brood should conform themselves to the established constitution and nearly follow the path which their fathers, treading in the footsteps of theirs, had marked out to them.[70]

While Hume asserts the impossibility of an integrated generational body, Jefferson entertains the notion. Ironically relying on the very same actuarial statistics that Hamilton used to calculate tontine repayment schedules in his Report on Public Credit, Jefferson writes:

> Let us suppose a whole generation of men to be born on the same day, to attain mature age on the same day, and to die on the same day, leaving

a succeeding generation in the moment of attaining their mature age all together. Let the ripe age be conceived of 21. years, and their period of life 34. years more, that being the average term given by bills of mortality to persons who have already attained 21. years of age. Each successive generation would, in this way, come and go off the stage at a fixed moment, as individuals do now. Then I say the earth belongs to each of these generations during it's [sic] course, fully, and in their own right. The 2d. generation receives it clear of the debts and in-cumbrances of the 1st., 3d. of the 2d. and so on. For if the 1st. could charge it with a debt, then the earth would belong to the dead, and not the living generation.    (960)

Here Jefferson assumes the basic premise of statistical analysis: that an arithmetic mean can substitute for diverse data. His formulation reveals the essentially metaphoric function of all statistics. Jefferson's speculative allegory—"let us suppose"—provides him with a repre-sentative anecdote that allows him to fashion a single corpus for a multitude of men. In this simple substitutive method lies the allure of Jeffersonian economics.

## American Physiocracy

The logic of the representative anecdote is also crucial to the political economic science most directly associated with agrarianism, French physiocracy. Many of Hamilton's most vocal critics regularly deployed the language and arguments of the physiocrats. Indeed, although we have tended to understand the Jeffersonian critique of Hamiltonian finance as deeply inflected by Augustan republican rhetoric, in many ways, this French economic school had greater resonance for the Democratic-Republican Party.[71] Physiocracy (a neologism meaning "the governance of nature") is the name given to the eighteenth-century school of philosophers and scientists who developed what is thought to be the first systematic attempt to ana-lyze the concept of value in political economy. Their crucial tenet, and the one by which physiocracy is best known to modern readers, was that natural resources and produce constituted the sole source of national wealth. The only way to increase the wealth of the nation, they argued, was to increase the efficiency and productivity of the labor that translated nature into commodities. And the only legiti-mate taxation was to be taken from the profit (the net revenue) that came from the produce of cultivated land.

Because the physiocrats located all value in the soil—declaring all manufacturing labor to be "sterile" or unproductive—they have been caricatured as economic traditionalists. This is the reason that there has been a tendency to assume a basic similarity between the literary modes of pastoralism and the political economic theory of physiocracy, and to see in both an idyllic strain. But the French économistes were not harkening back to any past social order: they were attempting to establish a new scientific method by which to understand the production of value. The claim that real wealth could only be located in produce from the earth was motivated by a practical recognition of France's large and fertile landmass—one that also characterized the United States—and a desire to understand why, despite this potential wealth, France economically lagged behind Great Britain.

Moreover, and even more crucially for my argument, the originality of physiocratic thought was not located in their assignation of soil as the source of value, but rather in their methodology. As Paul Cheney explains, "they were able to establish scientifically what had hitherto been a matter of conjecture."[72] The core of their scientific authority was located in their resistance to theoretical speculation: they maintained that economics was not a predictive science but should be formulated from an apprehension of permanent and natural laws. They stipulated that the basic principles of economic systems, like Newton's laws of physical matter, were timeless and universal. And so, as Cheney explains, the physiocrats defined their method in opposition to history. This assessment was made plainly by the leading figure at the center of the movement, François Quesnay, a physician to Louis XV. Quesnay asserted that the physiocrats were not "to seek lessons in the history of nations," precisely because such history offered nothing "but an abyss of disorders."[73] Quesnay's protégé, Pierre Du Pont de Nemours, with whom Jefferson maintained a long-standing correspondence, offered a similar indictment of historical methodology, asserting that history necessarily failed to offer any clear standard on which to base economic decisions and policies. For Du Pont, physiocracy offered a way to make sense of the "infinity of variable circumstances" that were otherwise "difficult to disentangle and to evaluate."[74] As Ronald L. Meek explains, the paramount achievement of the physiocrats was their recognition that "We are unfree ... so long as we do not understand the necessities by which we are bound in our society; and we can understand these necessities, in a society as complex as ours, only if we use the methods of simplification, selection, and generalization in our analysis of it."[75]

In response to the tangled chaos and contingency of modernity, the physiocrats declared their practice to be located, first, in the collection of meticulous data, and second, and most crucially, in the axioms and laws that could transform these myriad statistical details into the "true and simple principles" of political economy.[76] It is for this reason that Joseph Schumpeter identifies physiocracy as critical to the development of modern economic science and declares Quesnay to be a prototype for the econometrics that would dominate the discipline in the twentieth century.[77] We should observe the basic similarity between this imperative to escape the disordered abyss of history and the imperative of Mercy Otis Warren to conceive of the American landscape as a refuge from the "vortex of history." In both pastoralism and physiocracy, we locate an imperative to transcend the details of time and place for the "simple principles" of mathematics and representative anecdotes.

In physiocratic science, the manifesto for "simple principles" and mathematical laws was neatly embodied in the icon of the movement, the *Tableau économique* (see Figure 2.1), first produced by Quesnay in 1758.[78] Quesnay's table provided a visual illustration of the central physiocratic premises: that market exchanges followed universal laws transcending the vicissitudes of history and human behavior; that the best way to discover these laws was to substitute the countless variables involved in real economic exchange with simplified abstractions; and, finally, that the model of these abstractions should be represented as theoretic ideal.[79] Quesnay translated all of this into his famous *Tableau économique*, which the other "founding father" of physiocracy, the Marquis de Mirabeau, publishes first in his *L'Ami des hommes* (1760) and then in *Philosophie rurale* (1763). An English translation, titled *The Œconomical Table,* soon followed in London in 1766, and it included several versions of the table, as well as Mirabeau's and Quesnay's explanations of the by-then famous illustration.[80]

The significance of the chart to eighteenth-century political economic thought cannot be underestimated. Mirabeau claimed that the *Tableau* was, along with "writing" and "money," one of the "three great inventions which have given stability to political societies," going so far as to assert that the table "completes them both [writing and money] by perfecting their object."[81] We might be skeptical about the hyperbole of Mirabeau's assessment save for the fact that Adam Smith cites it ten years later in his *Wealth of Nations.*[82] Smith was familiar with

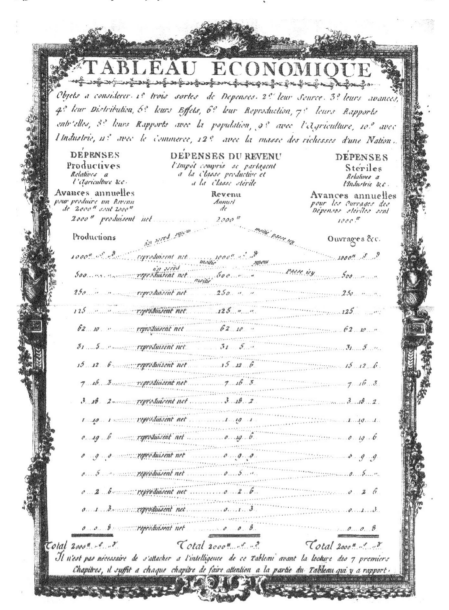

2.1 *Tableau Economique from* Élemens de la Philosophie Rurale, *1767*

Quesnay's work, having met him in Paris in 1765 at the urging of
David Hume. And although *Wealth of Nations* disputes the physiocratic emphasis on the primacy of agricultural production, Smith's
deep appreciation for the earlier work of the économistes is indicated by the fact that he had planned to inscribe the book to Quesnay
before the death of the latter in 1774.[83]

Quesnay's table is crucial to physiocracy in two fundamental ways. First, it visually documents the major assumptions of the economic school. Dividing the nation's economy into three fundamental classes—landowners, agricultural laborers, and manufacturing laborers—the chart describes the movement of expenses and produce between these classes to show that wealth (production that is not consumed) is exclusively generated from agricultural labor: all other labor is "sterile" or unproductive. Thus, the chart shows that the original revenue of 600 livres is distributed to those who work on the land (the left side of the chart) and those who work in industry (the right side of the chart), but only agricultural workers produce or return value (300 livres). For Smith, the table represents his own theoretical ideal, a "state of the most perfect liberty, and therefore of the highest prosperity" in the unimpeded distribution of wealth throughout a nation.[84] Indeed, Quesnay designed the table to allow its readers to trace the movement of capital through its myriad exchanges and expenditures and realize that, if unencumbered by artificial obstacles in the way of taxes or tariffs, there will always be surplus. The table thus visually documented the rationale for physiocratic commitment to free trade. Quesnay came to his laissez-faire theories by way of his practice as a Versailles physician: he conceived that any blockage to the circulation of capital would be as disruptive to economic health as obstacles to the free passage of bodily fluids would be to a human body. In his letter to Mirabeau that accompanied the original version of the *Tableau*, Quesnay says that "recourse to medical knowledge" is essential to his diagnosis of the economic ills plaguing the French state.[85] Adam Smith confirms the importance of his anatomical training, referring to Quesnay as a "speculative physician" whose economic theory asserted that "only by a certain precise regimen of diet and exercise"—by an "exact regimen of perfect liberty and perfect justice"—could the state thrive.[86]

Secondly, the table visualizes the physiocratic method in that it simplifies and regularizes what might, according to the long perspective of history, be incomprehensibly complicated. In the same letter to Mirabeau, Quesnay remarks that one critical advantage of the visual chart is to allow readers "a way of meditating on the present and on the future."[87] The table thus translates the heterogeneous and messy exchanges between farmers, landowners, and manufacturers into one static image and this "tremendous simplification," as Schumpeter puts it, is key to physiocracy.[88] Recognizing that any modern

economic system comprises millions of exchanges and transactions—
the "infinity of variable circumstances"—Quesnay proposes that the
best way to represent this complexity is through a radical simplification of the vast system into the paradigmatic shape of the zigzag. In
a letter to Mirabeau he writes, "the zigzag, if properly understood,
cuts out a whole number of details, and brings before your eyes certain closely interwoven ideas which the intellect alone would have a
great deal of difficulty in grasping, unravelling, and reconciling by
the use of the method of discourse."[89] His strategy is to capture the
enormity of economic exchange by substituting the comprehensive
image of the chart for the narration of the individual transactions
happening in real time. Quesnay insists that the mind is incapable of
"grasping, unravelling, and reconciling" the movement of capital
with an economic system in narrative form. This analysis explains
Mirabeau's claim that the *Tableau* fulfilled the inventions of writing
and money, since, according to Quesnay, writing or "discourse"
cannot sufficiently explain monetary systems. His table, by contrast,
allows the reader to picture the "interconnections" that constitute
the economy in a "single survey...so that we can contemplate them
at our ease without losing anything from sight and without the mind
having to worry about putting them in order."[90] Quesnay's zigzag
alleviates the need to put events "in order," because it renders cycles
of production, consumption, and exchange as synchronic: we can
visualize them at one glance.[91] The *Tableau* fulfills the ahistorical
imperative of physiocratic method as it compresses the vicissitudes
of time into one paradigmatic year and three paradigmatic, even
allegorical, "characters": the landowner, the agricultural laborer, and
the manufacturing laborer.

Karl Marx's admiration for the physiocrats was precisely a consequence of this comprehensibility: their analysis offered a simplified
abstraction of the otherwise obscure details of economic exchange.
Marx discusses the physiocrats at length in the second chapter of
*Theories of Surplus Value* (1861–63), where he begins with the assertion,
"The analysis of *capital*, within the bourgeois horizon, is essentially
the work of the Physiocrats."[92] The physiocrats, he continues, were
the "true fathers of modern political economy" because they were
able to explain with remarkable clarity what later classical economists obscured: surplus value.[93] Given the evident differences
between Marx's historical materialism and the physiocratic method's
exile of economic exchanges from both history and social relations,

Marx's appreciation may seem strange, but for Marx, it was precisely this distortion that illuminated "the whole production process of capital."[94] Even as the physiocrats epitomize what Marx judges as the fundamental flaw of classical economy, which is to read historically contingent forms of bourgeois economy "as fixed immutable, eternal categories," this failure allowed the physiocrats to identify surplus value so plainly.[95] Physiocratic analysis was revelatory, according to Marx, because it made agriculture—the production of food that literally sustained and reproduced the agricultural worker and was returned back to the landholder in the form of rent—the *representative anecdote* to explain the complex realities of capital.[96] Because the agricultural worker sustains himself with his production, unlike the mechanical worker for whom the "process is mediated through purchase and sale," and because the agricultural laborer returns some of his agricultural surplus in the form of rent, a "third element...not found in industry," the fact of surplus becomes perceptible.[97]

This surplus is visualized in Quesnay's *Tableau*, which reveals the disparity between what it costs to sustain the agricultural worker and what he returns back to the landowner, by isolating and highlighting the 600 livres in the first top left-hand *zig*. In explaining the zigzag to Mirabeau, Quesnay states that the *Tableau* will allow him to see that the labor of the husbandman (unlike the manufacturer) "produces more than their expenses."[98] Marx also praises the abbreviated clarity of Quesnay's chart when he exclaims that in "no more than five lines which link together six points of departure or return," Quesnay is able to show "the origin of revenue, the exchange between capital and revenue, the relation between reproductive consumption and final consumption,...and finally to present the circulation between the two great divisions of productive labour..as phases of this reproductive process." Marx thus celebrates the *Tableau* as "an extremely brilliant conception, incontestably the most brilliant for which political economy has up to then been responsible."[99]

Marx's interest in the physiocrats also brings to the fore what has often been obscured by the agrarian focus of the French économistes, which is that even as their economic theory was oriented towards "rural life," their focus was on capitalist economies. Although their exclusive emphasis on agriculture gives their analysis a "feudal semblance," the crux of their argument is to present "the landowner as the true capitalist."[100] According to Marx, physiocracy examines feudalism "from the viewpoint of bourgeois production," but through this selfsame analysis, "bourgeois society is given a feudal sem-blance."[101] Marx's argument here goes some way, I think, in making sense of the American pastoralism of Thomas Jefferson. The finesse of physiocratic analysis was that it described a relationship of appro-priation, in which an owner received the surplus labor power. Yet it represented this appropriation as natural and self-evident—as "a gift of nature, through whose co-operation a definite quantity of organic matter—plant seeds, a number of animals—enables labour to trans-form more inorganic matter into organic."[102] This "feudal sem-blance," Marx continues "was bound to win a number of feudal lords as enthusiastic propogandists of a system which, in its essence, pro-claimed the rise of the bourgeois system of production on the ruins of the feudal."[103] It is unlikely that Marx was counting Jefferson as one of these feudal lords, but his commentary explains why physioc-racy would have appealed to a particular version of Jeffersonian agrarianism that depended an obfuscation of the deep contradic-tions between a pre-capitalist fantasy of virtuous landowners amidst a bountiful nature and a commitment to a laissez-faire economic policy as the mechanism to amplify national wealth.

Marx's analysis also allows us to see the compelling power of phys-iocracy's explanatory simplification for two of the most prolix American writers arguing on behalf of a Jeffersonian economic policy in the 1790s: George Logan and John Taylor. Like their ideo-logical helmsman, both men were landholders. Taylor was the owner of a large Virginia slave plantation, while Logan was a Quaker farmer outside of Philadelphia. Both men served in the United States Senate. Both men were agronomists and published practical treatises on husbandry. And both began their writing careers in the early 1790s writing essays and pamphlets that systematically attacked Hamilton's fiscal proposals while also articulating the central physiocratic credo that agricultural produce was the only true source of national wealth and legitimate source of taxation. Throughout their careers, both men would write frequently and vociferously on behalf of the moral and civic virtues to be gained by an agrarian economic base.

Because of their manifest agrarian predilections, most of the fairly limited scholarship on both authors links them to an American pas-toral tradition that is said to span both mythopoeic ideal and social policy. So, for example, Chester Eisinger says of Logan that his writing "constituted the *summa* of agrarian thought"; and Robert Shalhope, whose biography of Taylor is subtitled "Pastoral Republicanism," argues that Taylor's work exemplifies "a pastoral ideal that could not be contained by literary design."[104] Their crafting of a particular story of American economic liberalism draws its ink, as it also did for Jefferson, from the wells of pastoral poetry and physiocratic political economy. But because cultivated land is the necessary ingredient of both traditions, we have been inclined to focus our exclusive attention on agrarianism. I propose we concentrate instead on their use of simplified explanation. Logan and Taylor propose that their exegeses of economic systems can transcend the messy contingencies of history and social exchange: they transmute a world of mediated and dependent relations into an autarkic idyll.

## George Logan's Simple Truths

Although we consider Jefferson as the spokesperson on behalf of American agrarianism, George Logan in fact gave public expression to this dominant strain in American political rhetoric. Thus, even as he is probably best known to students of American history as the namesake of the Logan Act of 1799, which forbids individual citizens from negotiating with foreign governments, Logan was more importantly one of the most prolific writers in the service of Jeffersonian resistance to Federalist finance policy. A Philadelphia Quaker, landowner, and politician, Logan's language substantially shaped the terms by which the Democratic-Republic Party offered its critique of Hamilton's proposals. According to one historian of the period, when Jefferson returned from Paris in late 1789, he "entrusted the attacks on the Federalists' economic project to George Logan."[105] Fulfilling Jefferson's faith, Logan provided counterattacks to each of Hamilton's Reports.

In its general contours, Logan's indictments of public debt, excise taxes, the establishment of a national bank, and protectionist economic policies were made in familiar terms: as repudiations of the young nation's democratic political ideals. But more than any other writer of the time, he articulated his objections with an emphasis on political economy, and his arguments were fundamentally shaped by his own affinity for the French physiocratic tradition. In her study of physiocratic influence on American economic thought, Manuela Albertone identifies Logan as "an authentic American Physiocrat."[106] Her use of the word "authentic" intends to convey something more than Logan's fondness for agriculture, and she explains that the terms by which Logan repudiated Hamilton were explicitly framed with the language of French political economic theory to which he had been introduced while living in France. As she puts it, "Physiocracy was a weapon to wield against Hamilton and the Federalists."[107]

Logan began his public opposition to Hamilton immediately after the first Report on Public Credit was published in January of 1790, and it originates in the pages of Eleazer Oswald's *Independent Gazetteer and Agricultural Repository*. His newspaper had been published daily since 1782, but in January of 1790, Oswald announces a change to a weekly format because he means to direct his paper "exclusively to the wishes and circumstances of the Farmers in general."[108] He also advertises that several men, including Logan, had formed a society "similar to that of the Œconomical Society in France," and that these men would contribute articles for the newspaper. Logan's "Address to the Yeomanry of Pennsylvania, by a Farmer" appears in the first issue of the newly established weekly newspaper, the very same month that Hamilton's Report on Public Credit is delivered. They continue for several weeks, and are subsequently collected into a volume that is published a year later also by Oswald as *Letters Addressed to the Yeomanry of the United States: Shewing the Necessity of Confining the Public Revenue to a Fixed Proportion of the Net Produce of the Land; and the Bad Policy and Injustice of Every Species of Indirect Taxation and Commercial Regulation.*[109]

This long title makes Logan's physiocratic predilections explicit as it articulates two key tenets of physiocratic fiscal policy: that the only legitimate tax was based on the net profit of the land and that commercial regulation was anathema to healthy economic production. Given the clear policy claims marked in the pamphlet's title, we might imagine that Logan will delve into the details of taxation. For the most part, however, Logan avoids the minutiae of economic statistics, stating instead that his work is premised solely on the "universal and immutable laws of nature." He begins, for example, with an appeal to the "simple truth" that the only justification for civil society is when "pastoral life" becomes sufficiently large that a "firm, established government becomes equally necessary to support each individual citizen in the right of soil, and the advantages and profits arising from his labor" (5). Or, as he later puts it, although nature is "naturally fruitful," it is insufficiently fruitful "for the support of civil society without cultivation" (15). Logan thus begins by establishing a mutual reciprocity between agriculture and civil governance, between nature and cultivation. The only justification for government is the obligation to make agriculture more productive and efficient, and the only criteria by which to evaluate the effectiveness of social law is to assess how it contributes to the productivity of the soil and its laborers.

Because so much turns on the premise of the productivity of agriculture, and because the letters are explicitly addressed to the "Yeomanry of Pennsylvania," we might also expect that they would emphasize husbandry. Logan was, after all, renowned for his knowledge of agronomy: Jefferson identified him as "the best farmer in Pennsylvania, both in theory and practice," and Logan's study of crop rotation was one of the first systematic experiments in United States agriculture.[110] The primary reason that Oswald highlighted Logan's contributions in the new manifestation of his *Independent Gazetteer* was his fame as a farmer and owner of Stenton, a "model estate" that served as a laboratory for numerous agricultural experiments.[111] But just as Logan's letters do not emphasize the details of tax policy, neither do they provide instructions for improving the soil. Their sustained focus is instead to describe the ways Federalist finance harms the economic health of the new nation. Logan writes not as an agronomist, but as a political economist; or rather, he collapses the difference between the two, suggesting that the political health of the state can be determined by the quality of its soil and that the quality of its soil can be determined by the political health of the state.

Following a key tenet of physiocracy, Logan argues that cultivating a "perfect free commerce" (18) is the key to establishing this political health, and he directs much of the polemic in the pamphlet against government intervention. The nation and its soil can only be productive when there is unimpeded movement of capital through its body. Like Quesnay, Logan had been trained as a physician, and his adaptation of Quesnay's theories indicate that he too took seriously the correspondence between the national body and the human body, especially emphasizing the analogy between the circulation of capital and the circulation of blood. As Logan puts it, tariffs and excise taxes "clog and impede every exertion of [the nation's] citizens" (23). In this formulation, not only will governmental regulation impede the free flow of capital through the nation, but it will also impede the efficiency and energy of individual workers. Logan's analysis thus depends on a metonymic connection between a healthy and fertile soil, a healthy and prosperous nation, and a healthy and vigorous citizen-farmer. The well-being of each, he argues, disallows governmental fiscal interference, which is depicted as both a toxin and an obstruction.

Logan's pamphlet also draws inspiration directly from physiocracy in articulating a fundamental distinction between "productive" and "unproductive labor" and classifying agriculture as the only form of productive labor because it "does not merely pay the expence of subsistence, but also furnishes a surplus" (15–16). Like Quesnay, Logan identifies this "surplus" as the capital that emerges at the end of the paradigmatic year to reinitiate, or reproduce, the circulation of value on which national wealth depends. There is, however, a crucial difference between his analysis and Quesnay's: Logan emphasizes this surplus as emerging from an individual household economy. "The cultivation of the land," Logan writes, "does not merely pay the expence of subsistence, but also furnishes a surplus more or less considerable, according to the ability or independent situation of the Farmer" (15–16). Logan thus translates Quesnay's analysis of national economies and social class into a story about "*the* Farmer, *his* family, and stock" (15). This appeal to the "independent situation of the Farmer" changes the analysis of Quesnay's table in significant ways. First, Logan reverses the allegorical logic of Quesnay's original model. While Quesnay simplifies the exchanges of numerous landowners, agrarian laborers, and manufacturers into the static schema of his *Tableau*, Logan literalizes the model as a mimetic representation of the incorporation of an individual landowner into a national economy. Quesnay's table depended on a metaphoric substitution of a vast citizenry and their individual economic transactions into allegorical social classes. The *Tableau* visualized the efficient movement of capital in order to explain how certain kinds of governmental policy—price fixing, tariffs, trade restrictions, indirect taxes—caused blockages that necessarily decreased national wealth. Logan is making similar arguments about national wealth, and this is why he proposes that it is "the interest of the government, and of every class of citizens" that the "surplus" be as large as possible (15–16). But in emphasizing the "surplus" as the product of individually owned farms, Logan transforms the physiocratic model of national economic equilibrium into a descriptive illustration of a single individual's economic choices. Logan thus further simplifies the "tremendous simplification" that Schumpeter identifies as the essence of physio-cratic methodology.

Second, unlike Quesnay who manifestly states that his agrarian economy depends on large-scale farms "fully cultivated by the best possible methods," which are themselves made possible through enormous capital investments, Logan is circumspect in explaining what agrarian practice in the United States should look like.[112] He sounds a clarion call on behalf of agriculture in the most basic of terms: because only nature provides an unmediated source of human subsistence, it is "in the interest of all, that Agriculture should be the most productive possible, [and] it is the duty of all to encourage and promote it" (16). And he adheres to Quesnay's assumptions when he acknowledges that the key to productivity is capital investment: "This must be accomplished by devoting large sums of money to those previous expences necessary to making the land fertile" (16). In later work, Logan specifically remarks on the inefficiency of small-scale farming: "it is asserted, that our farms in America are too large; I would rather say that the *purses* of the yeomanry are too weak, to carry on agriculture to their own profit, or to the advantage of the country."[113] For Quesnay, the source of this capital is clear: it emerges from the net surplus returned back to the landlords at the end of a year. But Logan is less patent in his own explanation of the source of these "large sums of money" that will make the soil productive enough to secure the "happiness" of the citizenry.

Logan is less clear because he does not distinguish between house-hold and national economies. The significance of this elision is apparent when Logan illustrates the formula from which the net sur-plus derives. Taking his terms directly from physiocracy, he explains the difference between "primitive" and "annual expences." The former consists of "instruments of husbandry, horses, oxen, and other animals necessary on a well regulated farm"; the latter "consists in the support of the Farmer, his family, and stock, from one harvest to the other" (16–17). For the physiocrats, the "net produce" is what returns back to the landlord after both primitive and annual expenses are met in the form of rent and produce. Logan's analysis by contrast describes the expenses of an individual freehold: the farmer, who both owns and labors the land, must deduct his own expenses (mort-gage, animals, seed, food, clothing, tools, hired labor, etc.) from his gross product, and he is thus left free to capture the surplus as profit that can be returned back into the next harvest. As such, even as Logan is telling a story about the self-sufficient American farmer that echoes the earlier mythos crafted by Jefferson, his analysis depends on the economic suppositions of large-scale agricultural capitalism. In this way, we can see how the appropriation of labor as profit that Marx thought Quesnay's *Tableau* made so apparent is remystified by Logan's pastoral tale.

As a Quaker, Logan neither owned slaves nor supported the institution, but his explanation of American agriculture both references and disguises the fact that slave labor constituted a considerable portion of both primitive and annual expenditure. In the case of "well regulated farm" worked by enslaved people, for example, primitive expenses would include the purchase of human labor as chattel, and perhaps this is what Logan is sanitizing in his reference to "other animals necessary." Similarly, annual expenses would include the costs of feeding, clothing, and housing slave laborers and, therefore, likely what Logan has in mind in his use of the term "stock." But Logan does not reference the actual fact of slave labor, instead appealing to the revolutionary rhetoric of slavishness to describe the tyranny of taxation: if his readers accept Federal taxation, he intones, "you may be regarded as slaves to support the pageantry of government, but cannot be esteemed freemen, acquiring property for yourself" (19). Here too Logan draws an idyllic model of the self-sustaining farmer, freely "acquiring property" for himself, even as his economic analysis depends on the suppositions of large-scale and capital intensive farms, which in the United States of the 1790s included land that was labored by slaves, hired hands, and tenant farmers. Logan can obscure the fact that farm labor was performed by these kinds of laborers because of another crucial revision he makes to Quesnay. The *Tableau* makes a clear distinction between the landholders and agricultural laborers, ultimately placing the surplus back in the hands of the landowners who start the annual process anew by dispensing their capital to labor. Logan, by contrast, eliminates the difference between those who own the land and those who labor on it, effectively collapsing the two columns of the table, since his "farmer" is both proprietor and laborer. In so doing, he erases the complications that wage laborers and chattel slaves present to his vision of agrarian capitalism. As we will see, both Hamilton and Adam Smith will highlight the significance of this conflation.

Logan's emphasis on the individual farmer also revises the physiocratic model in that it allows him to argue that the national wealth will mirror the economic condition of its best farmers: the more capital that any individual possesses, "the better will be the cultivation, and the greater will be the profit to the farmer, and to the state" (17). For Logan, the aggregate surplus of all the individual American farms and plantations constitute "the great mass of wealth of the community," which will be "distributed among the citizens according to their industry and merit" (17). Logan reads Quesnay's table, in other words, as an input-output table—as if it were an account book of both national and personal revenue.[114] But this is not what Quesnay intended. As we have seen, for Quesnay, the *Tableau* demonstrated the ideal conditions in which a prosperous agricultural economy, unimpeded by indirect taxes, is able to fully fund original advances: it represents a perfect equilibrium, or "state of bliss," in which capital holders are never at a deficit.[115]

Logan by contrast is describing a strategy for economic growth— in which the surplus can be "more or less" depending on the relative productivity of the individual laborer. Logan's analysis is remarkably similar to what we now call supply-side economics. He proposes a reduction of governmental regulation and taxation in order to increase the incentive and revenue of individual producers. And therefore, even as he insists that the riches of the soil will descend to the whole of the population, he also explains that the distribution of wealth will be made according to the "industry and merit" of individuals (17). And so, Logan's analysis of national wealth atomizes into a story of the enterprising individual whose work allows him to reap more private rewards. Logan's revisions help bring to light what clearly was so compelling for him about physiocratic analysis, which is its ability to translate and distill the heterogeneous and exogenous forces affecting the financial, labor, and monetary markets of the American economy at the end of the eighteenth century into a tidy tale of a hardworking freeholder. Logan can thus write, "To proportion your expences to your income, is a maxim as necessary to be attended to by government, as by individuals" (37). We can see the significance of Logan's move by employing the vocabulary of contemporary economic science: Logan draws on the macroeconomic relations the physiocrats theorized between wealth production and the dictums of free trade, but he reshapes these large forces into a microeconomic analysis of one individual's economic choices.

Logan thus spins a yarn about the yeomen farmer laboring to provide food stuffs that obscures the crucial fact that the value of these food stuffs depends on a price that fluctuates with the whims of a global marketplace. After all, Logan admits that the "net produce" depends not only on the quantity of produce, but its "value," which is the price at which the food commodities will be exchanged on the market. It is in the "interest of every class of citizens, and of the government itself, that the produce of the land ... should bear the greatest possible price, by means of a perfect free commerce" (18). Logan assumes that "perfect free commerce" will yield the natural price: the price at which any given commodity should trade in the absence of the distortions of governmental intervention (e.g. indirect taxes, excises, or tariffs). But while Quesnay's *Tableau* assumes this natural price as the basis for economic equilibrium, Logan quite differently suggests that this "greatest possible price" will be captured by both the nation as a whole and by the individual consumers and producers that constitute it. Thus Logan appeals to an explanatory system that describes how high agricultural prices paid by foreign consumers can reap wealth for the nation's landowners, but he uses the formulation to describe a utopian economy that rejects "an extensive commerce" and in which "every class of citizen" gains the monetary upper-hand against his or her trading partner (33).

This impossible schema depends on Logan's metaphoric substitution of the body of the nation with the body of the farmer/landlord— as we see when Logan claims: "perfect free trade will always ensure to the Farmer the highest price for his produce, by bringing purchasers of every denomination to his very doors" (42). His use of the singular, "the Farmer," suggests both an allegory and a literal description. But the real marketplace, comprising as it does a tangle of actors, desires, and motivations, reveals the limitation of the allegory. The farmer who commands the highest price might be undersold by the farmer who can sell more goods because he reduces costs. The farmer who commands the highest price will be taking his monies from purchasers at other ends of the supply chain—from the very people who are laboring the soil or producing the tools necessary to bring the commodity to market. Logan's allegorical "Farmer" allows him to rewrite these messy and unequal exchanges as "an amicable exchange of property" (43). In his simplification of the competing economic interests that bring together buyers and sellers into his own representative anecdote of the well-rewarded farmer, Logan establishes a powerful paradigm in popular economic writing, which is that state economies are only larger versions of household economies. This assumption has retained its power some 200 years later as politicians still reference the American national debt as an example of fiscal mismanagement equivalent to personal profligacy.[116]

Logan likewise proposes the autarkic farm as a paradigm for the broader American economy in an essay published in Philip Freneau's *National Gazette* directed exclusively to Virginia farmers. Here Logan suggests that the freeholder might be able to employ his "poor neighbors" in the production of manufactured goods, alleviating the need for the landowner to make purchases from merchants or foreign nations. He suggests that poor neighbors could manufacture the farmer's wool, flax, or cotton into textile and "receive the produce of the farm in pay for their services." In this way "a simple exchange of property takes place between the manufacturer and farmer, greatly to the advantage of both."[117] In this case, Logan's "simple exchange" even eliminates the need for money. Yet we begin to recognize the fallacy of his accounting when Logan descends into the details of his example. He writes,

> I have now a coat in use made from the wool of my farm which stand me in but five shillings per yard. English cloth of the same quality cannot be purchased out of the stores for less than seven shillings. I am convinced from experience that a steady attention to domestic manufactures makes at least a saving of fifty per cent to the American farmer, particularly where his family is numerous.[118]

We might observe, first, that in order to prove the economic advantage of his non-monetary proposal, Logan resorts to currency. Only by appealing to the common denominator of the shilling can Logan compare costs and assert that there is a savings for the American farmer engaged in "domestic manufacturing." Logan's example of simple barter thus provides for us a lovely instance of what Marx describes as commodity fetishism: the two coats encounter each other as a social relation between objects. Whether the fabric is spun by the English factory laborer or the poor neighbor, whether they are paid in shillings or wheat, the cloth they spin and weave only has value when it comes to the landowner at a price per yard. Logan's account of this "simple exchange" also makes it hard to reckon how the poor neighbor will gain his own advantage in this transaction, since the key to the price reduction for the farmer seems largely to depend on reduced labor costs. And we might also note that Logan's arithmetic is itself simplified, since he rounds up the actual difference in costs (40 percent) to announce a 50 percent savings. In short, there is nothing simple about this economic exchange save for how Logan chooses to tell it.

Logan emphasizes the utility of his explanatory method and claims that the Hamiltonian narrative debilitates the economic health of individual households and the nation. He writes, "The immutable principles of political economy cannot be diverted or frustrated by the false opinions of speculative men" (25). "Speculative men" is a reference to those advocating on behalf of speculation through the establishment of public credit, a national bank, and corporations, as well as those individuals purchasing these stock shares and public debt certificates, all of which are judged by Logan to obstruct the free flow of capital. But his formulation also opposes the "immutable principles" of physiocracy to an interpretive methodology that itself diverts and frustrates this self-evident truth with its own corrupt speculations. According to Logan, then, the problem with "speculation" is not merely that it is the system used by "crafty financiers" (25), but that it enables an explanatory method that obscures what Logan maintains is the self-evident and naturalized translation of value from soil to commodity, to money, and back to soil. He routinely charges his adversaries of willfully misrepresenting and complicating what he maintains is the "natural" simplicity of capital movement. Throughout his work, Logan will accuse those advocating for national finance of making economic science more difficult than it needs to be solely for the purpose of intimidating the citizenry. They make economics, he writes, "a mysterious and impenetrable science" so that "no one knows what sums of money are actually raised—no one becomes acquainted with the manner of expenditure."[119]

In this way, Hamiltonian explanation causes the same harm to the body politic as that caused by merchants and bankers: it depletes the intellectual and economic energies of the nation and individuals. "[S]tatesmen and lawyers," he charges, strive to "render the science of politics impenetrable to the people," and they have introduced "a labyrinth of errors, inverting the order of nature" (7). Logan frequently characterizes Hamilton's writing as "inveloped in darkness and mystery," insisting that this opacity is intended to deliberately confuse his readers, to cultivate their "indolence" and credulity so they passively come to accept his opinions as truth (5). Logan often comments on the unnecessary length of Hamilton's reports, specifically charging him of using tedium as a strategy of obfuscation. To read Hamilton, Logan lambastes, is to fall under either "mental fatigue, or implicit faith" (22) that necessarily quells both skepticism and resistance: his "long reports on finance, by fatiguing the memory confound the judgment, and force his readers into such a labyrinth of error, that the clue of decision has no length enough to reach the extensive mazes of a wandering imagination" (5). Because Logan repeatedly metaphorizes Hamilton's economic explanations as labyrinths, as linguistic puzzles designed to disorient readers, we might conceive of his own textual project as a sort of Ariadne's thread, a clue by which his readers could move through the heterogeneous topics raised by Hamilton's Reports.[120]

This is not, however, Logan's gambit, and he instead offers his own short pamphlets and letters according to an entirely different narrative template. There is no need to unwind the long narrative threads that tie individuals together. There is no need to disentangle the various economic dependencies that link farmers to laborers, buyers to sellers, bankers and merchants, debtors to creditors. There is no need to provide long reports forcing readers into tedious economic details. Challenging his audience—"How long will you suffer yourself to be duped by [Hamilton's] low cunning and artifice"—Logan exhorts his readers to study physiocracy through his writing. His work will emphasize the single truth of political economy: that the sole purpose of governance is to protect natural rights, the essence of which is the protection of individual property. This appeal, he says, requires no laborious explanation precisely because its truth is self-evident or natural. His analysis thus does not constitute a clue to unravel what Hamilton tangles, but a bulwark to defend against the maze itself. His plain-spoken letters provide instruction in a "science of political economy" established by "a few enlightened men in France," to "enlighten the minds of free citizens by substantial and immutable truths" (7–8). The doctrine of the "heaven-born French philanthropy," he opines, will tear asunder the "veil of hypocrisy" (23) that Hamilton weaves.

This assumption underlies all his work: if he can teach his readers the "just principles of political economy," then they will be able to defend themselves against the devious plots of the moneyed social elite trying to obscure and confuse the "immutable truths" of wealth and value. The key is the recognition that the "science of political economy in no instance is subject to uncertainty, but a pleasing uniformity is discoverable in every part of it" (7). Although the term, "pleasing uniformity" might seem an allusion to Crèvecoeur's description of an American agricultural economy in which a "pleasing uniformity of decent competence appears throughout our habitations," Logan notably is not describing a standardization of income in which every farmer will earn roughly the same amount of profit relative to his acreage.[121] After all, Logan argued that the rewards for the farmer would follow his individual rate of productive efficiency. Logan instead uses the term "pleasing uniformity" to characterize the system of economic analysis he employs. The pleasure emerges not from the happy medium between poverty and luxurious excess, but from the scientific scheme by which he calculates happiness. The pleasure is specifically located in the fact that the science is not speculative: it is in "no instance subject to uncertainty." Logan thus represents his own economic analysis as fundamentally opposed to Hamilton's not merely because of its familiar salvos against speculation and leverage, but because it offers an explanation of capital movement that can escape the contingencies of history.

## John Taylor of Caroline's Simple Vocabulary

This narrative and methodological premise was also central to the other prominent writer enlisted to oppose Hamiltonian finance, John Taylor of Caroline, so-called because he was one of the major landholders of Caroline County, Virginia. Like Logan, he published extensively about agricultural practice and vehemently denounced public finance, tax policies, and the Bank of the United States. Unlike Logan, he was a slaveholder and owned three large plantations in Caroline County, whose primary workforce was black slaves. By 1810, he owned 145 people who worked 2245 acres and was the largest slaveholder in his county.[122] Because his wealth derived from real estate, and because he was one of the major spokespersons against national banking and public finance, historians have long focused on Taylor's agrarianism, often employing the language of both pastoralism and physiocracy to describe his work.[123] Like Logan, Taylor's economic theory was formed through his reading of the physiocrats, and he followed their basic dogma in advocating for agricultural production as the foundation for personal and national wealth and in protesting governmental financial intervention.

Taylor begins his philippic against Hamilton in the pages of the *National Gazette* under the penname of "Franklin" in 1793.[124] In this handful of essays, Taylor accuses Hamilton of willful obfuscation in both his literary style and his fiscal accounting: "Democracy delights in public knowledge—Simplicity ought to be the garb of her fiscal arrangements," and "It is the character of truth to be simple and consistent."[125] The pseudonymous Franklin thus appeals to "simplicity" as a paradigm for good governance, fiscal accounting, and literary practice. Effacing any meaningful distinction between storytelling and bookkeeping, Taylor begs his readers to aid him in "unravelling the whole plot" and join him in demanding access to the books of the Treasury Department and the Bank of the United States.[126] The controversy that motivated these pages began when a Virginia congressman publicly accused Hamilton of misusing Dutch credit to repay a loan due to the Bank of the United States in the initial establishment and charter of the Bank. Because the Federal government did not have sufficient funds to purchase the requisite two million of the ten million shares that constituted the Bank's original capitalization, the Treasury Department drew the two million from commissioners selling government securities in the Amsterdam market. But in order to avoid shipping two million dollars across the Atlantic to purchase the stock, and then having to remit the currency back across the ocean to repay the loan, Hamilton conceived an ingenious solution: the Bank bought the government securities in Amsterdam, and credited the monies to the United States Treasury who used this credit to purchase the two million dollars of Bank of United States stock. As Bray Hammond explains, "Technically this consummated the purchase of the stock with funds borrowed in Europe."[127] But Hamilton's opponents, including Taylor, saw it much differently, as a "system of œconomy and finance" designed to cultivate "mysteries and obliquities" that would engross financiers and governmental agents at the expense of the people.[128]

For his own part, Hamilton responded to the accusations with only barely concealed rage. Hammond characterizes the reply as "detailed, sarcastic, and calculated to overwhelm his inquisitors with particulars if not with light."[129] Needless to say, the barrage of details Hamilton produced in response did nothing to assuage his accusers, since it merely confirmed their conviction that the complexity of the particulars was part and parcel of a strategy of obfuscation and malfeasance. Taylor, in fact, describes Hamilton's "indecent" response as "seventeen pages of sophistry."[130] This conflation of fiscal intricacy, explanatory complexity, and fraud characterizes the incendiary rhetoric between political antagonists during the 1790s. Taylor, like others in his party, accused Hamilton of various forms of illegalities: that he embezzled money to pay for political favors, or that he misrepresented funds in an effort to deceive Congress and avoid repayment of debts to France. But evidence of the crimes was always located in the bookkeeping they could not explain. Taylor thus demands that Hamilton provide a simple and "plain statement of public funds," asserting that numbers cannot lie: "Of what do these funds consist? Of dollars and cents. How can dollars and cents be comprehensible exhibited? By figures." Taylor asks his readers: "Are not contradictions, and unintended transmutations of fiscal entries, indicative of a design to deceive and mislead?"[131] Proof of criminality is therefore located not in action but in the *representation* of action, in the Treasury Department's obscure financial records and prolix narration of the movement of funds between institutions and nations. But, as was the case with Logan, despite Taylor's admonishment to help "unravel[] the plot," his own strategy is not to untangle but to cut the Gordian knot.

Taylor continues this line of attack with the publication of *An Enquiry into the Principles and Tendency of Certain Public Measures* (1794). Taylor writes James Madison about the project in the spring of 1793, observing that the activities of the previous Congressional session had "trodden on each others heels, in too rapid succession for much reflection," but that now the events had begun "to exhibit an unity of design," he had begun to compose the essays that would ultimately constitute *An Enquiry*. He asks Madison's opinion on the essays and his advice on where best to publish them, expressing a disinclination for newspaper publication because they are "mere ephemere" and also have limited "sphere of [] circulation."[132] Madison approved of Taylor's work, so much so that he forwarded the essays to Thomas Jefferson in August 1793, commending Taylor's writing for its "many strokes of imagination, and a continued vein of pleasantry & keen satire, that will sting deeply."[133] It was probably either Jefferson or Madison who subsequently delivered the manuscript to Freneau who anonymously published two of them the following month.[134] The publication caused Taylor some consternation, and he writes Madison to thank him for his approbation, but also to complain that the newspaper publication was "both unwise and indelicate," further explaining that the "mutilated anticipations, will weaken its effect" and "the performance will exhibit the ludicrous aspect, of a compilation from his news papers."[135]

Taylor's anger at the publication in the *National Gazette* is curious. Although he had expressed concern about the limited range of newspaper publication, Taylor knew that newspaper essays were frequently reprinted and therefore could cover considerable geographic ground. His own Franklin essays had been republished in Philadelphia's *Dunlap's Daily Advertiser* and in the *New-York Daily Gazette*. But we can get a better sense of his objections to newspaper publication by considering the terms through which he makes his complaint to Madison: the newspaper "mutilated" his work and presented it in a "ludicrous aspect." The term "mutilate" indicates Taylor's conviction that the fifteen chapters of the ninety-page pamphlet constituted a cohesive whole and that newspaper publication violated the work's integrity. The "wholeness" of the work would be harmed in part because of the delay in periodical publication: rather than consuming the essays in one setting, his readers would read it piecemeal and with temporal interruptions. But more critically, the mortal wound would come from the newspaper's erosion of the clear borders of the text. Unlike the essays in the pamphlet, which are clearly enclosed by the covers and that we are encouraged to read from start to finish, the newspaper essay is surrounded by other texts: its meaning and sense is ineluctably shaped by its proximity to the other essays within the four pages.

To read an essay in a newspaper, even one as partisan as Freneau's *National Gazette*, is to see an object as one component in a larger system of texts. The first of Taylor's essays published by Freneau, for example, concludes with a strong embrace of laissez-faire trade: "when a general friendship prevails between the people of different nations, courts and kings will instantly be annihilated, or rather their fall will be a natural consequence of a friendly coalition among mankind, founded upon the basis of free and universal commerce."[136] But Taylor's assessment is necessarily tempered by the substance of the two surrounding essays, both of which describe the geopolitical conflict of the French Revolutionary Wars, including the recent Siege of Toulon, in which British and Spanish forces had attempted to capture France's primary naval arsenal. Taylor's preference for an autonomous text also takes on considerable significance when we consider how much his critique of Hamiltonian finance puts its stress on the term "system." For Taylor, Hamilton has constructed a devious and perplexing system of financial instruments and institutions (public credit shares, bank stock, excise taxes), in which the multitude is unknowingly entwined and on which the influence of the Federalist Party rests. The word "system," which permeates Taylor's writing, is not incidental to the critique, since it emphasizes a vision of the economy comprising multiple and interconnected parts, each of which depends and affects the others. Any newspaper—even Freneau's— would constitute the very kind of system he seeks to critique.

For Taylor, the economy is a system that can be explained by "natural" and simple truths: his work will rely on "plain and unerring arithmetic."[137] His task is to "repel the deceitful efforts" by which the American people have been "deluded," and to provide reckonings and statements that are "self evidently true," thereby allowing knowledge to "flash in upon our minds" (6). As we have seen, this appeal to a plain style is characteristic of Hamilton's critics, but what makes Taylor unusual is that even as he hitches his rhetorical wagon to a "plain and unerring arithmetic," his writing engages a baroque figurative language. The first chapter of the pamphlet begins, for example, with an "allegory" of the United States as a spoiled child, which then shifts, through a simile, to an "ill weed" (2). This agricultural metaphor continues as he declares his own writing as laborious husbandry, a bulwark against a political "laziness" that will otherwise leave the nation "in the possession of tares and thistles" (3). This agricultural metaphor would seem to be an ideal one to establish a contrast between Taylor's orderly pasture and the weed-ridden field of Hamiltonian finance. But in the following pages Taylor tries out a range of other figures, variously describing banks, public debt, and taxes as a "devouring monster" (9), a "Pandora's box" (9), "an established church" exerting tyrannical thrall over a nation (15), a "political papacy" selling "paper indulgencies" (20), a "whore…rule[d by] her own insatiable appetite, and not the ability of her paramour" (30–31), a "conjurer's wand" (39), a "doctrine of transubstantiation" (39), a "wound" that is made to "bleed afresh" (42), a "flying squadron, whose object it is to divide the great mass of the people" (88), and, in the final paragraph of the pamphlet, as the idol from Nebuchadnezzar's dream that is smashed into dust (92).

I pause over Taylor's figurative excess for two reasons. First, it would seem to belie Taylor's stated dedication to a plain and simple literary style. Second, it flies in the face of the standard republican critique of finance as the misrepresentation of real, or inherent, value. Taylor clearly appeals to this Augustan tradition in his suggestions that bankers and speculators shore up their wealth through "hireoglyphicks upon paper" (16) or that they "traffic in ideas, not in substances" (9). Yet his own comparisons of Hamiltonian finance to thieves, monsters, tyrants, and sexually voracious women would seem to indicate that illusory signification is not where the primary dangers lie. After all, if the gap between monetary signs and value were Taylor's major concern, then why would he trade in that self-same currency by using metaphors that so clearly expose the distances between tenor and vehicle? The danger of a bank share is not that it is paper, nor is it that it only represents a percentage of an unstable and fluctuating whole. The peril, I suggest, is one of causality and not signification. Taylor is perfectly sanguine with the premise of fictitious money: instead, what is so infuriating about Hamilton's "system" is that it is composed of incalculable component events, actions, institutions, and actors. It is a "machine of such wonderful cunning contrivances," Taylor writes, it is almost impossible "to comprehend its mechanism" (11). Taylor's imperative is to refashion Hamilton's causal "tricks" into a "simple vocabulary" (9) and to refashion Hamilton's "perplexity" into a "simplicity" (47), so that its machinations might be exposed. As was the case for Logan, Taylor's indebtedness to physiocracy is located not only in his espousal of their key tenets, but also in their demand for explanatory simplicity.

Taylor begins this project in earnest with a metaphoric description of the Bank of the United States as "the master key of that system, which governs the administration. It could unlock a depository of secrets" (7). According to Taylor's analogy, the Bank is the key to the Federalist financial system and its deception. Eschewing a metaphor of the labyrinth, in which we would need to unravel a narrative and a clue, he presents us with an image of easy access to truth. Taylor admits "although it might redound to our amusement to trace this operation [by which a bank profits], it would contribute but little to our edification. The conclusion will be better evinced by a few strong lines, than by an assemblage of the most diversified colourings" (9–10). And so Taylor presents his own sentences as the metaphoric code that will unlock the business of banking: his pamphlet will reveal the mysteries instantaneously, as a "flash upon our minds" (6). Banking, he explains, "is simply a reiterated exchange of obligations for the payment of money. A. gives his *bond* to B. and receives B's *bond* in exchange" (8). In this exchange, "A. pays B. an interest, whereas B. pays none." When Taylor specifies that "A" is the "community" and "B" is the bank, it seems that the "exchange of obligations" he describes is one in which an individual takes a loan from a bank: A's bond is the promise to repay the debt with interest and B's bond consists of the notes that function as credit. Yet as Taylor continues to elucidate this "simple" transaction, he revises the account. He recasts what had been an interaction between two individuals as an exchange between "two classes": the "stockholders...of the bank" constitute one class and "all those who deal with the bank" form another (8). Taylor's new schema divides the economic world into debtors and creditors, thereby effacing the fact that many people occupied both roles. Taylor himself, like all plantation owners, would have taken on substantial debt to secure sufficient capital to pay for the necessary expenses to get him to the next annual harvest; but he also extended credit to those who purchased his produce and who leased his land, equipment, or enslaved laborers. His rendering, however, demands that each economic agent only occupy one position.

Taylor also adjusts his tale in that he no longer depicts banking as an "exchange of obligations for the payment of money," but rather like a "barter of two commodities," in which those who "deal with the bank...deposit their bonds or notes carrying an interest, and receive in exchange the bonds or notes of the stockholders [of the bank], carrying no interest" (7–8). The intention here is to depict a bank's interest charges as the illegitimate basis of their profit. But instead of appealing to the more conventional derogation of interest as usurious, Taylor renders bonds and notes as a commodity and, even more unusually, he depicts the exchange of these monetary instruments as "barter," an economic transaction that is defined by its nonmonetary quality. This strange, even oxymoronic, characterization of banking as barter is motivated not by a conviction that money has a use value, but by Taylor's desire to sidestep the details of usury statutes. Taylor can simply assert that interest is illegitimate because it distorts what would otherwise be an equal exchange of commodities: $x + \text{interest} > x$. Taylor's formula means he does not need to explain why the one-point difference between the 5 percent rate, authorized by Virginia statute, and the 6 percent discount rate charged by the Bank of the United States constituted an injurious fraud.[138] Illegitimacy, according to Taylor's logic, does not stem from any of the financial particulars: not on the terms of the rate and not on whether interest was calculated according to simple or compound formulas.[139] The fraudulence of the Bank, for Taylor, is more fundamentally determined by the fact that their profit is certain: they gain without risk.[140] We see how important this lack of hazard or risk is to Taylor's argument when he further adjusts his metaphor. Now banking is not inequitable barter, but a "species of hazard, called the A. B. C. table, except that the latter proposes to the adventurers some chance to win; the bank can never lose" (8).

This rendering of the Bank as a rigged game is not however sufficient to provide Taylor the key with which to "unlock the depository of [Hamiltonian] secrets," because his metaphor fails to identify the victim. Although Taylor's explanations stress a dyadic structure in which there are manifest winners and losers, he also declares that "it is not so easy to discern upon whom this loss falls" (9). The real power of Hamiltonian finance, he suggests, is not that they cheat and always win, but that they obfuscate the identity of their dupes. The loss does not fall, Taylor explains, on the "immediate gamblers" who only serve as the "brokers between the bank and those who really suffer by the institution" (10). Those who "really suffer" consist of "the original sellers of whatever labour produces, and the consumers of the wares the brokers deal in" (10). We see then a triangulated structure in which the monolithic Bank of the United States manipulates its brokers into perpetrating a wholesale fraud against the rest of the nation: "the whole agricultural, mechanical, professional and mercantile interests of the community" (10). It is upon the labor of these "aggregate" interests that the "devouring monster" of the Bank of the United States gorges. The advantage of the portrait of the Bank as a monster or as a swindler is that it clearly designates his story's antagonist, but the drawback is that these metaphors fail to explain how the Bank can continually perpetrate its violence without its victims recognizing the injuries. To explain this "cunning," Taylor further adjusts his metaphor, depicting Federalist finance as an "ever running fountain of wealth" linked to "numberless devious streams" that surreptitiously draw wealth away from the nation's citizens (10).

In many ways, this representation of the national economy as system of waterways through which currents of labor flow, and from which wealth is slowly siphoning into the coffers of the bank, captures the diffuse economic relations that are, indeed, fundamental to the financial system that Taylor means to critique. Indeed, the metaphor of capital circulation as blood through a body, or water through a nation, was frequently employed both by the physiocrats and Adam Smith. Yet Taylor refuses to diagram these intricate tributaries for his readers, insisting that there is no need to "perplex[] ourselves, to trace out the various modes, by which the first dealers with the bank are reimbursed from the wealth of the aggregate" (10). Or, as he puts it in another pamphlet published only a year later, "Shall I go into a tedious and intricating enquiry concerning the causes of danger or shall I endeavor to save it."[141] Like Logan, Taylor devotes himself to identifying what he declares as the devious perplexities of Hamiltonian finance, but he will not entangle his own prose in explicating them. Taylor adamantly refuses to unwind the Hamiltonian plot that so captivates him, because were he to retrace the plot, he would countenance a vision of economic interdependence that is itself anathema. As such, he represents the labyrinthine Hamiltonian plot not as a mimetic portrait of the emerging American economy, but as its distortion.

His own literary project, by contrast, will identify clear causal chains and easily identifiable protagonists and antagonists. His response to the "indelible hieroglyphic of the principles and designs of administration," which are "probably impossible to unravel" (41) is to script a melodrama that identifies one individual, Alexander Hamilton, as the original source of all harm. "The person who framed the system," Taylor writes, "was certainly capable of contemplating, and of guiding its effects." This sentence declares Hamilton to be not only the sole author of a financial "system," but also in total command of the consequences of his actions. His "contemplated intention," Taylor continues, was to "erect[] an enormous aristocracy or monied interest" (41). Taylor thus paints a portrait of Hamilton as diabolically "transplant[ing] the constitution from democratic ground, in which it might flourish, to aristocratic soil, in which it must perish" (42). And repurposing his waterworks metaphor, Taylor describes Hamilton as the chief engineer of a plan to strangle state sovereignty: "Without pulsation, without elasticity they will dwindle gradually into a tale that has been told, they will crumble and dissipate, like a corporation of beavers, whose waters have been drained away" (43). Taylor is making two somewhat different arguments in these accusations. First, he depicts Hamilton as what Adam Smith called the "man of system"—the individual legislator who believes that he can both fathom and control the complexities of the market and, in so doing, interfere with the natural flow of capital. Second, he pits himself against Hamilton in an authorial competition. Accusing Hamilton of writing a plot designed to both obscure and obstruct the movement of wealth through the nation, Taylor tells a simple tale about how one man tried to seduce a nation into abandoning its democratic principles.

## Manufacturing the Simple System

The many texts inveighing against Hamilton's proposals expressed horror at a world in which individuals were dwarfed by immense economic systems that attached individuals to countless other people in temporally and spatially unfathomable sequences of exchanges. The response was not, however, to explicate and trace the global supply chains and fiscal dependence in which the citizenry was implicated, but to craft narratives that imaginatively restored economic independence to this new commercial landscape. Because so many of these authors have set their stories in pastoral settings, we have tended to assume that agrarianism is the critical detail: following Country Party rhetoric, they posited farming as a virtuous last ditch defense against the emerging specter of financial capital. But the importance of the pastoral mood in which so many of these critics operate is just as crucially located in its methodology, in the appeal to the representative anecdote. The essential element of their narrative is plot and not setting: they atomize large-scale economic relations into a story of an individual body that can be disentangled from the contingencies of the global market. We can best see this emphasis on formal structure when we turn to Logan's response to Hamilton's Report on Manufactures (1791) wherein Logan departs from the essential tenet of physiocratic economic theory and does not distinguish between agricultural and manufacturing labor.

Although Logan originally cultivates his argument in the rich rhetorical soil of antagonism between farmer and merchant, between landowner and banker, as his career continues, his critique of Federalist policy expands beyond an exclusive identification with the "yeomanry" and "farmers" to whom his original pamphlets are directed. In 1793, for example, he publishes a broadside that reproduces the physiocratic argument against indirect taxation. But this pamphlet is addressed to "The Citizens of the United States," and he asserts that excise taxes will draw wealth away from both agricultural and non-agricultural workers, both of which constitute the "laborious part of the community."[142] Logan thus makes a substantial break with physiocracy, aligning himself with Adam Smith in establishing non-agricultural workers as capable of producing national wealth. We see evidence of this shift as early as 1792, when Logan explicitly responds to Hamilton's Report on Manufactures. He adopts his conventional alias, publishing as "A Farmer" when he first prints the response in the *Independent Gazetteer*, and then again when it is republished as *Five Letters Addressed to the Yeomanry of the United States, Containing Some Observations on the Dangerous Scheme of Governor Duer and Mr. Hamilton to Establish National Manufactories* (1792). But although he writes as a "Farmer," and he addresses his letters to a "Yeomanry," the latter term has become much more capacious, comprising "the farmer, the mechanic, the manufacturer, and useful laborer."[143] For Logan, the danger of Hamilton's proposal is not the endorsement of manufacturing or even corporatism per se, but Hamilton's explanation of the component parts of the national economic system. Once again, he accuses Hamilton of designing a financial system as a "curious and complicated machine," and Logan proposes his own work as a disclosure of the "secret of modern science of finance" that will lay bare the mechanics of appropriation.[144]

The general assumption about Hamilton's Report on Manufactures, released on December 5, 1791, is that it was his least influential in that, unlike the Report on Public Credit and the Report on a National Bank, it did not result in any lasting federal policy. Yet it is also understood to be the most prescient insofar as it anticipated a national economy that for the next century and a half largely depended on an expanding manufacturing base. The Report is also significant because Hamilton uses it to articulate the large contours of his own economic philosophy, and the first several pages comprise Hamilton's paraphrase of the prevailing consensus on the dangers and impracticalities of encouraging manufacturing in the United States. Most scholars identify Adam Smith as Hamilton's primary interlocutor, yet the political economic adversary that Hamilton combats in the opening pages is more obviously physiocracy: so much so that one historian describes the Report as a "point-by-point

rebuttal of the Physiocratic positions."[145] Hamilton's rhetorical strategy is to imitate the arguments of the physiocrats, pretending citation by placing them within quotation marks even though he is
drafting the sentences:

> "In every country (say those who entertain them) Agriculture is the
> most beneficial and *productive* object of human industry. This position,
> generally, if not universally true, applies with peculiar emphasis to
> the United States, on account of their immense tracts of fertile terri-
> tory, uninhabited and unimproved. Nothing can afford so advanta-
> geous an employment for capital and labour, as the conversion of
> this extensive wilderness into cultivated farms. Nothing equally with
> this, can contribute to the population, strength and real riches of the
> country."[146]

Hamilton here parrots the expressions of Quesnay, Mirabeau, and
Du Pont, but also summarizes physiocratic thought using the language that most of his American readers would have associated with
Jefferson, Logan, and Taylor. Hamilton next rearticulates the laissez-
faire argument that defines physiocracy: "To endeavor by the extraordinary patronage of Government, to accelerate the growth of
manufactures, is in fact, to endeavor, by force and art, to transfer the
natural current of industry, from a more, to a less beneficial channel"
(648). Here Hamilton explicitly deploys the metaphor of circulation
that is so crucial for both Quesnay and Smith, rightly anticipating
that one objection to his plan might be the claim that it would have
the consequence of shunting or blocking the natural movement of
capital.[147] And finally Hamilton rehearses the argument that French
économiste theory is particularly suitable for the United States
because, like France, the new country possesses a large land mass. In
the broad strokes of only three paragraphs, Hamilton captures the
physiocratic objection to his proposal to advance American manufacturing.

Hamilton concludes this paraphrase of his imagined detractors by
acknowledging that they are based on "respectable pretensions." But
he pivots by claiming that even as such arguments are largely true, it
is also the case that "general theories [also] admit of numerous
exceptions." He objects to physiocratic analysis, therefore, less on the
basis of specific claims made about the relative profitability of agriculture versus manufacturing, or the relative advantages of agriculture

when land is not scarce, or, conversely, the dearness of labor when the population is small. He bases his objection instead on a more generalized indictment of the methodological pretensions of physiocracy, which is that it argues for a "general theory" presuming timeless laws that refuse to admit of any exceptions. Hamilton further challenges the fundamental dogma of physiocracy by claiming that their general theories about the exclusive productivity of agricultural labor have "not been verified by any accurate detail of facts and calculations" (236). For Hamilton the flaw of economic science is not that it mystifies its subject, but that it tries to formulate universal laws with insufficient empirical evidence.

Having gained some experience from the opposition to his earlier Reports, Hamilton charges his opponents with verbal subterfuge. He indicts physiocratic analysis for its own deceptions, declaring the physiocratic presumption that when "nature co-operates with man...the effect of their joint labour must be greater than that of the labour of man alone" to be a doctrine that is "both quaint and superficial" (652). The only difference, Hamilton explains, between the rent secured as the "nett surplus" from the soil and the "ordinary profit" that returns to the factory owner is semantic: it "appears rather *verbal* than *substantial*" (653). Hamilton continues this lexical argument when he suggests that physiocratic vocabulary also conflates two kinds of agricultural profit—the "*ordinary profit* of the Stock of the farmer and *rent* to the landlord"—under one term, "rent." Conversely, in the case of manufacturing, the "ordinary profit" of the labor and the repayment on the capital advanced by the owner all fall under one name: "profit." This "formal or verbal distribution," Hamilton concludes, "constitutes the whole difference in the two cases" (653). Hamilton's analysis draws here heavily from Smith's own consideration of the nomenclature used to describe different kinds of monetary gain—wages, profit, rent—from his chapter from *Wealth of Nations*, "The Component Parts of the Price of Commodities." Smith remarks that while these gains are easy enough to distinguish when they belong to different persons: "when they belong to the same they are sometimes confounded...at least in common language."[148] Smith thus highlights the fact that economic analysis is substantially shaped by discourse.

Hamilton's implicit reference to Smith's discussion of economic nomenclature also suggests that he is engaged in an oblique discussion about the role of slavery in American agriculture. In the passage from *Wealth of Nations* to which Hamilton alludes, Smith explains the slipperiness of economic vocabulary by way of a particular example. Smith remarks on the situations of "North American and West Indian planters" who, because they are both farmers and landlords, "should gain both the rent of the landlord and the profit of the farmer." But the plantation owner is apt, Smith explains, "to denominate his whole gain, profit, and thus confounds rent with profit."[149] Smith's concern here is primarily one of vocabulary—the fact that profit and rent get conflated in the Americas. As we have seen, Logan makes a similar collapse in his assumption that farmer and landlord are one person. But Smith's use of the term "planter," and his reference to North America *and* West India, make it clear that he is also describing a specific kind of agrarian labor economy: a "planter" owns a "plantation," which means that his slave laborers pay no rent and receive no wages. This is why, Smith adds, "we seldom hear of the rent of a plantation, but frequently of its profit."[150] The conflation between rent and profit, Hamilton implies, effectively obscures the appropriation of labor (of slaves, of tenant farmers) from which the ostensible virtue of agrarian wealth flows. Hamilton is also signaling to his readers that agriculture—at least as it is practiced in the Americas at the end of the eighteenth century—was as much a capital enterprise as was manufacturing. Landowners advanced large amounts of capital, which took the form of money, stock and land, and they took their interest in the form of both rent and profit.[151] Hamilton thus is not only arguing for the productivity of both agricultural and manufacturing labor, but he is also trying to explain the capitalized structure of any agricultural enterprise.

Logan's direct response to Hamilton's Report on Manufactures concedes the former point but rejects the latter. Just as his earlier analysis of an agricultural economy did not distinguish between landowner and worker so as to conveniently elide *who* was appropriating the value of the labor, so too does Logan here ignore the substantial differences that would exist between a manufacturer who sells the goods he produces and a manufacturer who sells the labor with which he produces these goods. Such distinctions are irrelevant to Logan because his goal is not to reveal the circuits of capital movement through the American economy but to identify Hamilton's proposal as a violation of free labor. Taking his cues from the physiocrats and from Smith, Logan identifies the danger of Hamiltonian finance as that which blocks, shunts, misdirects, or leeches capital from a freely circulating system. He explicitly invokes Smith to validate his argument on behalf of free trade, citing a passage from *Wealth of Nations* often taken to be the summa of economic liberalism: "to prohibit a great people…from making all that they can of every part of their own produce…is a manifest violation of the most sacred rights of mankind."[152] The citation was a popular one among American audiences, because its immediate context involved a discussion of British restriction on the economic liberties of her North American colonies. Regulation, Smith explains, "effectually prevents the establishment of any manufacture of such commodities for distant sale," and thus "confines the industry of her colonists in this way to such coarse and household manufactures as a private family commonly makes for its own use."[153] Smith assumes a correlation between the economic health of a family and a state, and he points to the primitive ("coarse") economic condition of a single household as evidence of the stunted development of the whole colony. In describing the necessarily deleterious consequences that come from state intervention, Smith subtly draws a distinction between justice and wealth. British policy, he says is "unjust," but it has "not hitherto been very hurtful" because the high cost of labor in the colonies means that they still find it economically advantageous to import manufactured goods. For Logan, however, this distinction does not pertain, and his own pamphlet's manifesto on behalf of free trade is made irrespective of the material consequences of any given economic policy. Indeed, what Smith identifies as the symptom of economic inefficiency—a private family forced to manufacture their own household goods—is precisely what Logan elsewhere identifies as a virtue insofar as it exemplifies economic autonomy.

The essential condition for economic liberty, according to Logan, is the possession of an undivided body. This explains why Logan's response to Hamilton's Report on Manufactures is to assemble American laborers into a unified class or corpus, and to accuse Hamilton of a policy of socio-economic fracture. He poses his own model of an integrated American laboring class against what he describes as Hamilton's vision of divisive corporatism and private interests. By grafting farmers, mechanics, manufacturers and all "useful laborers" (8) into one integrated economic body, he can also craft a story of economic liberty that makes government the only real excrescence. Logan thus assembles his chorus of workers as univocal in their call for laissez-faire capitalism. When asked the

best way to encourage commerce and wealth, Logan states, all
Americans "engaged in agriculture, in manufactures, in mechanics,
and even in the Cod fishery" have the same answer: "*Let us alone*"
(19). His formulation of laissez-faire as *laissez-nous faire* should draw
our attention to the boundaries that shape the corpus of the "us" that
is ostensibly free from interference. He makes it clear in this pamphlet that he imagines the "us" to include a heterogeneous array of
American workers across many different industries. And so, in this
early challenge to American corporatism, Logan appeals both to the
language of labor rights and to laissez-faire capitalism: his work thus
presents us with an early example of the coincidence between economic liberalism and American populism. Unlike Smith, for example, who explains the unequal distribution of profits and wages
across socio-economic class by pointing to the need for greater
remuneration on behalf of those who take greater financial risks,
Logan simply effaces the distinction between different kinds of
financial rewards. The "us" can be united because, in Logan's formulation, there is no essential difference between wages, profits, and
rent: they are just different words for the ways that individuals take
property in labor. Through this lexical simplification, Logan can
represent the self-interests of the cod fisherman, tobacco picker,
hat maker, weaver, importer, or plantation owner functioning as
part of one fully integrated system: the motley assembly of economic transactions becomes homogeneous capital coursing through
the body politic.

Simplification is therefore the essential methodology of Logan's
project. And again, we should recognize that even as Logan repeatedly accuses his political enemies of willfully overcomplicating discussions of economic relations, he does not himself offer more
transparent explanations of these relations. He might, for example,
have delved into the details of tariffs, one of the specific policy proposals that he found so abhorrent. He could have tried to explain the
manifold consequences that might follow from a tariff imposed on
British textiles: that the cost would be felt first by importers, who
would likely pass it on to consumers further down the supply chain.
He could have tried to explain that in response to the higher cost,
consumers would be encouraged to patronize domestically produced fabric, but that as they adjusted their own economies to these
higher prices, they would likely make purchasing choices that would
affect other sectors of the economy. Or we might imagine that Logan

would want to dispute Hamilton's supposition that a rise in domestic manufacturing would increase the prices of American raw materials, thereby raising the profits for American growers.

Logan does not opt to explain or elucidate any of these long sequences of economic dependencies, instead asserting the fundamental equivalence of every link in the chain. Rather than provide his readers with a narrative account of the relationship between tax policy, manufacturing costs, labor costs, and national revenue, he illustrates the economy as a sequence of unvaried components: "A chain does not derive its strength and utility from being composed of a few heavy links, and the remainder weak and ill conditioned, but from every link being as much as possible of equal power" (21). Let us set aside the irony of Logan's choice of a chain to metaphorize the power of free trade, focusing instead on the fact that the metaphor depends on the presumption that all constituent links of the economy constitute an integrated system. Equally crucial is that the interconnected loops in Logan's figural chain eschew any causality: one link does not affect another, but are simply conjoined into one amalgamated body. Logan thus selects a metaphor that recognizes that economic exchange involves the configuration of manifold parts, but the figure also demands a fundamental equivalence between the individual links and the chain as a whole. Logan's metaphor is thus characteristic of the broader project of Jeffersonian opposition, which is to represent each individual as metonymic for the operations of an entire economic system.

Logan derives this substitutive method from Quesnay's *Tableau*, which similarly compresses three links into the synthetic zigzag. Logan also takes his design from Jefferson—and more specifically from Jefferson's 1789 letter to Madison, which Logan reprints verbatim (without any reference to Jefferson) in one of his oppositional pamphlets.[154] In that letter, as we saw, Jefferson not only inveighs against public debt, but he also indulges a fantasy of generational incorporation, imagining a "whole generation of men to be born on the same day, to attain mature age on the same day, and to die on the same die." Jefferson's metaphor, however, obscures the crucial issue of how to ascertain the boundaries of a system that extends beyond an individual person. What, for example, are the grounds by which Logan judges the Society for Establishing Useful Manufactures as obstruction or alien appendage? Why is public credit, which we could understand as capital flowing through the nation's veins,

instead represented as vampirically draining wealth? Why is the
Bank of the United States, which we could understand as a heart,
pumping capital into a national economy, depicted as a malignant
growth sapping the nation's energies? Why are excise laws, which
fund the national government, represented as parasitic legislation
that slowly siphons productive labor from the body politic? The
laissez-faire explanation is that capital must circulate through the
body like blood, but this analogy begs a more basic question of
how to locate the borders of the "natural" body through which this
capital flows.

Faced with the need to map the geographical and temporal edges
of an economic world that stretches at the limits of any one person's
understanding, Logan posits his desire to consider "the whole
Universe as one system, composed of infinite other lesser systems,
and these again of others."[155] From this assertion, he forges a series
of analogies: just as the Earth is only a "lesser system" within the
immensity of the universe, so too is an individual person a lesser
system in social body "made up of individuals," and so too are different parts of each individual ("eye, hand, &c.") lesser systems in the
large human body that is itself a "system of vessels, glands, and liq-
uids," which themselves comprise microscopic systems, the "smallest
particles of matter" (5). Logan's response to the inability of the human
mind and eye to apprehend the scope of the incredibly small and
distant scale of the universe is to theorize radical integration into
"one universal whole system" (4). He argues for the fundamental
congruity between the "smallest particles of matter" and "those
luminous Bodies observable in the Heavens" (4). He is also arguing
for the necessary congruence between the lesser systems of agriculture, mechanics, and manufacturing: each sector is inextricable from
the "one universal whole system." In the face of the infinite scale of
economic causality, then, Logan's analysis seems to rest on the notion
that any "lesser system" will serve as a model or paradigm for the
immense system in which it is located.

Yet Logan's own observations about economic praxis fail to corroborate his theory, and he acknowledges considerable dissension
between the classes. Manufacturers, for example, want their "Fellow-
Citizens [to] give a preference to the produce of their industry, over
Foreign Manufacturers," but merchants resist domestic manufacturing
because their profit lies in traffic and thus they seek to "support[] the
prosperity of the Foreign Manufacturer" (8). Although agricultural

laborers might be isolated from this particular dispute because they "are so advantageously situated, that they can manufacture, immediately from their own Farms, all the Woollen and Linen Cloth necessary in their families," Logan acknowledges that their "peculiar interest" would be to support domestic manufacturing since it would provide a "certain and steady market at their own doors, for the surplus produce of their industry" (9). Logan's integrated vision will therefore require the exile of the merchant, as this class becomes an impediment to the mutualism between farmer and manufacturer. But just as soon as Logan casts the merchant from the garden, another problem looms when he realizes that American manufacturing labor cannot be purchased as cheaply as it is in Europe and India. Admonishing American consumers against purchasing cheaper foreign goods, Logan tells his readers that their bargains are made at the expense of global labor, whose bodies bear the injuries of "horrid outrages" (11). He further suggests that American manufacturing ought not try to compete with these foreign factories: instead of attempting to buy American labor at this price, "every manufacturer should have such an equivalent for his labour as to enable him to live with comfort; to educate his children and to preserve something for the support of his family in case of unavoidable accident" (9).

Logan is thus both arguing for the natural efficiencies of an unregulated labor market while also making the case for a minimum wage that will not only reproduce the worker's labor but also provide the worker with "comfort," education, and life insurance. But rather than spelling out the necessary conflict between high profits and high wages—that is, between two classes of American capitalism—Logan scapegoats foreign manufacturing, arguing that reliance on foreign goods constitutes the sole impediment to a naturally efficient market:

> It has made the Farmer tributary to the Storekeeper; the Storekeeper, to the Merchant, of Philadelphia; the Merchant of Philadelphia, to the Merchant of Great Britain. The Credit thus given, can, at any time, be withdrawn; the Debts thus contracted, can, at any time, be demanded; and the Peace and Comfort of a numerous Body of American Citizens are now, and have long been, at the Mercy of British Merchants, and of the British Court.[156]

If at first glance his use of the word "tributary" to designate this supply chain suggests the metaphor of waterways and the smooth passage of capital, then this is not the force of the phrase, which instead stresses the other denotation of the word, a person who must pay tribute to another. As such, he does not depict the global supply chain as "one universal whole system" but as a shackle that threatens to drag down the American farmer. Thus, Logan advocates for cutting the links of dependence, telling his readers that American agricultural and manufacturing production should constitute its own integrated economic circuit, insulated and indemnified against foreign influence. In so doing, Logan advocates for both a free market economy and economic nationalism.

He can make both claims because the plot of the story he tells remains the same regardless of whether he is proposing agriculture or manufacturing as the source of American wealth, and regardless of whether he is fomenting against market interference or espousing protectionism. In each case, his protagonist—be it a farmer, manufacturer, or nation—comprises its own autonomous system, its own "natural market" that runs at optimum efficiency and profitability. This Jeffersonian strategy of simple explanation is where the real force of the American pastoral lies. And it is an explanatory story that still shapes our lives, as it is adopted by people across the political spectrum. Indeed, in his classic history of American banking, Hammond observes the remarkable shift in political economic alliances that occurs in the twentieth century:

> [I]t has become the economic posterity of Alexander Hamilton that complains of centralized authority and...resists what it considers an unconstitutional interference with human rights—that is, property rights and business. And it is the professed posterity of Thomas Jefferson—now more industrial than agrarian—which fears the evil of a weak governmental authority and...has out-Hamiltoned Hamilton in elaborating the federal government's apparatus for the guidance of economic behavior. There persist to-day, accordingly, two political groups with economic differences that are reminiscent of those that divided Americans in 1791, but the two, like Hamlet and Laertes, have switched weapons.[157]

This shift in weaponry has only increased in the twenty-first century where the Republican Party rails against governmental regulation while also advocating for protectionist policies that support a vision of economic nationalism. Contemporary politics still relies on the allure of the narrative crafted in the 1790s. In their objections to

Hamiltonian finance, the Jeffersonians did not attempt to teach the populace about their precarious position in the immense system of global capital but rather manufactured a story that cultivated a fantasy of economy autonomy. Over 200 years later, even as financial institutions and derivatives have become increasingly byzantine, spilling across the borders of nations and corporations, we steadfastly rehearse that same story: one that demonizes the language of finance while simultaneously allowing us to celebrate its business.

# Stories without Plots

The first two decades of American economic development were shaped not just by material transformations of westward expansion, technological inventions, and capital growth, but by the stories used to explain this development to the nation's laborers, consumers, buyers, and sellers. As we have seen in the preceding chapters, there were two distinct narrative strategies to describe the emerging economy. The first can be seen in Hamilton's Reports, designed not only to make and justify economic policy, but also to provide a mimetic narrative representation of the United States' integration into the global economy. The second is found in the opposition to Hamilton, and here the ambition was not mimetic but synthetic. These explanations did not strive to represent the complex sequences of human economic activity, but instead to distill the compound actions of desire, labor, and consumption into a static model.

In the last chapter, I identified this Jeffersonian narrative, with its emphasis on temporal condensation and simplification, in relationship to the literary tradition of the pastoral. But insofar as the central motif of this writing was a self-interested individual who rationally negotiated and profited with other equally self-interested individuals, then another literary tradition is probably the more obvious source. It is, after all, the economic bildungsroman that we most closely associate with narratives of capital accumulation, and literary historians have long understood the novel as the genre best suited to describe capital economies.[1] Karl Marx, for example, identifies Daniel Defoe's seminal novel of capital acquisition, *Robinson Crusoe*, as a key text in the arsenal of classical political economists. He begins *Grundrisse* by deriding Adam Smith's and David Ricardo's investments in the "individual and isolated hunter and fisherman" as still more evidence of the "unimaginative conceits of the eighteenth-century Robinsonades."[2] Their delight in Crusoe's ascendance from wreck to

*Speculative Fictions: Explaining the Economy in the Early United States.* Elizabeth Hewitt, Oxford University Press (2020).
© Elizabeth Hewitt.
DOI: 10.1093/oso/9780198859130.001.0001

riches as a story of economic independence is, according to Marx, a symptom of their refusal to see that the production of any individual is necessarily situated within the "most developed social relations."[3] This is why Marx also summons Crusoe in the first volume of *Capital*: "Since political economists love Robinson-Crusoe stories, let us first look at Robinson on his island."[4] Marx values the story of Crusoe on the island for much the same reason he valued Quesnay's *Tableau*: just as the simplicity of the *Tableau* allowed him to visualize the landowner's engrossment of the farm laborer's surplus value, the singleness of Robinson—the fact that he is only one man—provides a clear illustration of how commodities congeal the value of labor. As Marx puts it, "In spite of the variety of his work, he knows that his labour, whatever its form, is but the activity of one and the same Robinson, and consequently, that it consists of nothing but different modes of human labor."[5] The novel's plot is thus the occasion by which social exchange can be made transparent: "All the relations between Robinson and the objects that form this wealth of his own creation, are here so simple and clear as to be intelligible without exertion."[6]

Marx's literary criticism reveals a crucial feature of classical economic theory and the novel form, which is that both have historically constructed their plots as totalizing systems organized around individual protagonists.[7] This is why, in musing over the limitations of Defoe's paradigmatic novel of *homo economicus*, David Harvey asks why economists do not rather turn to Defoe's *Moll Flanders*, which he remarks is less a story of individual economic agency than of a commodity moving across the globe.[8] But even as a commodity, Moll is the object around which the social world is oriented and the novel's plot subsequently is required to delimit its stories of modern capital. In this way, *Moll Flanders* resembles the contemporary genre of the commodity history, which Bruce Robbins has persuasively described as another form of economic bildungsroman: "each commodity takes its turn as the star of capitalism's story...a self-sufficient protagonist."[9] Robbins is making an ideological critique: that these narratives displace the agency of exploitation from capitalists to commodities. But his observation also raises a formal problem: faced with an economic world that is too vast to diagram, in which there is no possible way to imagine the contingent causes and consequences from any single transaction, no matter how small, is it any wonder that authors build their stories around the armature of the bourgeois individual or the bourgeois object?

In concurring with Georg Lukács's assessment of the compensatory power of the novel—"The novel is an epic in an age in which the extensive totality of life is no longer directly given, in which the immanence of meaning in life has become a problem, yet which still thinks in terms of totality"—I do not intend a critique of the genre's politics, but to ask a basic question about literary history.[10] Were there other literary forms available to model an economic world in which no single individual, nation, institution, or commodity possessed motive force? Was there an imaginative form that could better articulate the long supply chains that brought people across the globe into perilous dependence? Was there a literary form that would express the fundamental contradiction between aesthetic unity and economic contingency and that would communicate the truncated and fragile structure on which individual actions were strung? Was there a way to tell stories about human life in a world characterized by the anonymous exchanges of commercial capitalism that didn't strive to recover the immanence of meaning, but instead would transmit experience?[11]

This chapter argues that the periodical essay was one literary form that set out to accomplish these representational ambitions, modeling its own speculative plots on the reticular structure of the modern economy. Given the codified generic conventions of the periodical essay, it may seem counterintuitive to suggest it as a form well adapted to capture the limitless vicissitudes of economic exchange. But I argue that the key feature of the genre lies less in the fairly predictable set of topics it addresses, than on the narrative infrastructure through which the periodical essayist displays his various essayistic goods. In what follows I consider periodical essays by Philip Freneau, Judith Sargent Murray, and Charles Brockden Brown, suggesting that when we attend specifically to their plotting of social relations, we can recover an alternative attempt to explain emergent economic systems to the nation's readers. Although their political positions did not align, their periodical essays follow the imperative of Hamilton's Reports in attempting to reproduce mimetically the intricate structure of modern financial and capital markets.

## Stores and Magazines

I am describing the periodical essay as a particular genre of writing that we can classify together because of its adherence to formal rules and its tendency to engage regular themes and tropes. But as the name makes clear, it is also a genre that is inextricably connected to the media in which the essays were published and circulated. This media, the periodical or magazine, was defined by its capacity to hold sundry texts. Eighteenth-century magazines and newspapers give expression to a literary landscape that had not yet been neatly sorted into modern disciplinary categories. As we saw in the previous chapter, it was precisely the motley arrangement of the newspaper and magazine that led John Taylor to wish to avoid publication in their pages. One of the earliest scholars of the periodical, Frank Luther Mott, identified this "eclecticism" as the most remarkable feature of the early American magazine.[12] The magazines Mott selects as the most significant of the post-Revolutionary period emphatically emphasize their generic range: *The Columbian Magazine; or Monthly Miscellany* advertises itself as "Containing a View of the History & Manners & Literature & Characters"; *The American Museum* declares itself to contain "essays on agriculture, commerce, manufactures, politics, morals and manners"; and *The Massachusetts Magazine* announces that its pages would contain "poetry, music, biography, history, physics, geography, morality, criticism, philosophy, mathematics, agriculture, adventure, chemistry, novels, tales, romances, translates, news, marriages and deaths, meteorological observations, &c., &c."[13] As with the encyclopedias of the eighteenth century, the pages of the magazine bear witness to an imperative towards categorical capaciousness.

It is within the hodgepodge of these eighteenth-century American magazines that we find the periodical essay: almost any single issue will consist of at least one of these periodical essays. All are written under the persona of an anonymous author about a wide variety of topics, and all are modeled explicitly on Joseph Addison and Richard Steele's *Tatler* (1709) and *Spectator* (1711–12). Sometimes the titles consist of just one or two essays before the series expires; others extend into the dozens and are published over several years. Probably the best known (and earliest) of such series is Benjamin Franklin's "Silence Dogood," published in his brother's *New-England Courant* (1722), but the form dominated the periodical press in colonial and early national North America throughout the century. "The Meddlers Club," "The Monitor," "The Hermit," "The Prattler," and "The Correspondent" constitute just a handful of the many titles published throughout the North American colonies before the

Revolutionary War. And the trend expanded after Independence: the major magazines of the early national period, the *Columbian Magazine*, the *American Museum*, the *Massachusetts Magazine*, and *The Port Folio* all regularly included series from essayists written in the Addisonian style. Like the magazine itself, these essays extolled variety as the best way to represent the cacophony of urban and commercial life, as well as to appeal to the greatest number of readers.

This formal commitment to expressing the details and minutiae of modernity made the periodical essay a privileged vehicle for discussions of "the commerce of everyday life."[14] And the historical coincidence of the emergence of periodical essay, novel, and magazine has linked all three in a critical tradition emphasizing the nexus between literary forms and economic systems. Richard Squibbs describes the "common impulse . . . to lump the genre [of the periodical essay] in with the magazines that emerged in its wake, often presenting it as one more piston in the engine of early modern commercial culture."[15] I heed Squibbs's cautionary advice that we not succumb to the temptation to collapse media (magazine), genre (periodical essay), and social form (commercial capitalism), but their intersecting history does allow us to consider the question that motivates this chapter: how did the periodical essay attempt to narrate the movement of goods and money?

The periodical essay, I argue, provides a narrative structure that tries to express the complexity of economic systems. I intend the term "complex" to oppose the key term from chapter two, "simple." Instead of explaining and describing an economic system by pruning the parts down to one, the periodical essay tries to express the many, or compound, parts that define it. I also choose the term so as to invoke the resonances of "complexity" as it is exercised in contemporary economic and social theory. Used variously across a range of disciplines, the expression can reference the heterogeneous and contingent noumenona of social and natural environments, and it can describe the phenomenal experience of disarray in the face of such experiential plenitude. My interest is primarily on the latter as I want to suggest that the periodical essay offered a different formal strategy to explain the tangle of economic relations that so frequently served as its subject. The periodical essay was exceptional in that it called attention to the numerous relations of interdependence that constituted any singular moment of economic exchange, thereby tacitly acknowledging that any single plot line was unable to reproduce the entirety of a social system. The representation strategy of the Addisonian essay is thus to reproduce the complexity of the reality it sets out to describe.[16]

In Addison's *Spectator 367* (1712), for example, readers are asked to consider the many economic agents that are implicated in the manufacturing of the periodical, and the essay traces the generation and distribution of the commodity Mr. Spectator is producing, marveling at the many systems required to move the magazine through the market. He does so by providing a detailed survey of the many people and industries employed in bringing his work into the arms of his readers: "[O]ur paper-manufacture," he explains, "employ our artisans in printing"; manufacturing the paper on which the work is printed "affords work for several hands," which includes the "poor retailers," the "merchant," and a "fresh set of hands" who work in the paper-mill; these manufactories allow landowners to "raise their rents"; and finally many "get their daily sustenance by spreading," or delivering, the magazine. As he summarizes, "when I trace in my mind a bundle of rags to a quire of Spectators, I find so many hands employed in every step they take through the whole progress, that while I am writing a Spectator, I fancy myself providing bread for a multitude."[17] There is undoubtedly something facetious in this self-congratulatory exultation, but we should also acknowledge that what he describes is accurate: the production of a single commodity necessarily involves countless other people, and the essay gives expression to these far-flung economic results. Moreover even as the Spectator exults in his power to "provid[e] bread for a multitude," he also subtly indicates the less positive consequences that come from the manufacturing of his product. He notes, for example, that the increased demand for paper leads to the construction of more paper mills and that because of these mills, landowners can "considerably raise their Rents." The essay posits this as an economic advantage because it increases revenue for landowners and because, as he puts it, "the whole Nation is in a great measure supply'd with a Manufacture, for which formerly she was obliged to her Neighbours."[18] Yet there are inevitable costs to this gain. Those who rent are forced to pay more, and thus the advantage the mill worker received from his employment is attenuated by the fact that his wage is effectively diminished by increasing living costs. Likewise, higher rent prices will necessarily increase the prices of food and textiles, and these costs will ultimately be borne by consumers further down the supply chain. Here, then, even as the periodical essay celebrates the large commercial enterprise circling around its own production, its description cannot help but register the possible consequences that descend from what it originally registers as an unalloyed good.

And so, even as we tend to consider the periodical essay as a genre that propagates homilies and polite sensibility, it also relentlessly reminds its readers that our individual vision of the world is inevitably limited and incomplete. Indeed, one reason the series often take their titles from leisure activities—Idles, Rambles, Rhapsodies, and Trifles—is to insist on the distinction between these casual reveries and a systemic method. Therein lies a notable distinction between the categorical projects of the periodical essay and the encyclopedia: where the encyclopedist demands comprehensiveness, the periodical essayist is satisfied with parts. One such self-titled "Essayist" suggests precisely this goal in his defense of the form: "Those few, but precious moments of leisure, which occur even in the busiest scenes of life, may be very conveniently and profitably employed in reading a book, that consists of small and unconnected parts."[19] Associating the periodical essay with a reprieve from the "busiest scenes of life," his sentence also acknowledges that the busy world and the literary devices through which it can be read necessarily consist of "small and unconnected parts."

Samuel Johnson identified this resistance to systematic analysis as the key to the power and popularity of Addison's work, which was read "not as study but amusement."[20] Johnson's own *Rambler* observes that the peculiar methodology of the periodical essayist makes it especially suitable to represent economic fortuity. Comparing the practices of the periodical essayist's "careless glance" and "transient survey" with that of the "compiler of a system of science" or a "relator of feigned adventures," Johnson distinguishes the essayist by his haphazard procedure.[21] His unsystematic method is not, however, a consequence of compositional negligence, and instead Johnson proposes that the essayist, unlike the philosopher or novelist, purposefully gives expression to the contingency of human action. "It is not commonly observed...how much, even of actions, considered as particularly subject to choice, is to be attributed to accident, or some cause of our own power, by whatever name it be distinguished."[22] While the novelist (the "relator of feigned adventures") erects his characters within a structure by which "the great events [are] regularly connected," the essayist strives to represent the irregular and random articulation points of human action, thereby giving mimetic expression to continuity but not causality. Which is to say, while the novel strives to manage and delimit the complexities of modernity by arranging contingency into plot, the periodical essay bears witness to the infinite number of stories that might never be told.

As my definitional forays into Addison and Johnson suggest, there is nothing particularly distinctive about the American version of the periodical essay. Indeed, American periodical essayists routinely extol the excellences of their British ancestors, and allude specifically to the *Tatler* (1709–11), the *Spectator* (1711–14), and the *Guardian* (1713) as exemplary models whose generic patterns they wish to follow faithfully. One of the longest running periodical series published in the *Columbian Magazine*, The Retailer (1788–89) begins, for example, by establishing himself as heir to British essayists from the first half of the century. Invoking his forefathers, "Addison, Steele, Johnson, Hawksworth" in the first entry, the Retailer claims that they have established the utility of the genre for subsequent readers and thereby legitimated his own practice.[23]

Like the British periodical essayist, the American author introduced himself as a solitary figure—the Meddler, the Correspondent, the Friend, the Retailer, Robert Slender, the Man at Home, the Gleaner—before turning the series over to other correspondents, establishing the essayist, as was the case of Mr. Spectator, as a member of a public club. The American periodical essay also adopted other stylistic and thematic formula of the earlier British versions, which included providing an imaginary dream or vision, offering essays narrated from the perspective of foreign visitors (often from the "East"), spinning allegorical narratives, and relaying moral anecdotes. The typicality of these generic choices is evidenced in the Retailer's third essay, which records the frequency with which periodical essays utilize the dream device. Noting "the *Spectator* snores in less than a week, the *Rambler* soon wanders in nocturnal adventures, and the *Observer*, by the time he is author of seven numbers," his own series does likewise, and he provides his readers with a somnambulant visit with Addison, Johnson, Pope, Young, and Hume.[24] His next essay includes another standard feature, as he relays an Orientalist tale about the young prince of an Ottoman court. The Retailer later remarks on the typicality of this kind of essay when one of his own correspondents describes a trick played on a relative who insists that there has been no good English prose writers since "the days of Pope, Addison, and Johnson." Substituting a periodical "tale in the eastern style" from the *Columbian Magazine* for one in his relative's volume of the *Spectator*, the correspondent triumphantly reports that his cousin praised the American essay, unable to distinguish it from its predecessor.[25]

The utterly stereotypical features of the periodical essay were so familiar to its practitioners that many self-consciously satirized them, even as they also participated in their conventions. The Dreamer, for example, explains the rules that will secure his literary fame:

> Those who write for the innocent diversion of the publick, should make it a rule to pursue every hint which may be useful to the community—to make known every epidemical vice, and publish every uncommon virtue... [He] ought not to spare his animadversions on the extravagance of luxury, the impertinence of the coxcomb, nor hesitate to reprimand whatever contradicts good manners, civility and decorum.[26]

The frequency with which American periodical essays wrote about the dangers of luxurious consumption and dissipation as pro forma themes is laconically summarized in the introduction to Washington Irving, William Irving, and James Kirke Paulding's *Salmagundi*: "Our intention is simply to instruct the young, reform the old, correct the town and castigate the age."[27] Perhaps it is because they are so self-consciously derivative that this crucial genre of early national letters has been largely ignored. Although it is "the most nearly representative type of prose written in the eighteenth century" and saturates the American magazine, it has generated relatively little scholarly attention.[28] Because there seems to be nothing particular to the American deployment of the genre, Americanist scholarship that traditionally devoted itself to mining the archives for examples of literary nationalism, found little worthy of attention.

The periodical form's disinclination towards national or partisan factionalism is a typical feature of the form—and perhaps another likely reason for the critical lack of attention. Dealing primarily in the generalities and relatively uncontroversial terrain of social manners, serial essayists represented themselves as transcending the fray of partisan politics.[29] The Worcester Speculator, for example, who regularly wrote on behalf of Constitutional Federalism, also proclaimed his own virtuous disinterest: "Next to the sword of the duelist, or the dagger of the assassin, I abhor the envenomed pen of ill natured satire and malignant revenge." His ambition, he insists, is to be "at least inoffensive."[30] This directive to cause no offense affords no small degree of political inconsistency within periodical essays. The Worcester Speculator, for example, offers a fairly conventional argument on behalf of American agricultural interests, outlining the dangers of relying too heavily on foreign trade. But only a few entries later, this position is reversed when the essayist advocates for a more liberal trade policy with Europe. Given this mutability it is not surprising that the Addisonian essays that filled eighteenth-century American magazines have not provided critics, whose focus often centers on the partisan divide of the early national period, an especially fertile form to investigate.

I propose that the refusal of the periodical essayist to hold fast to a political position ought not be taken as a sign of disinterested virtue, but as part and parcel of a merchandising strategy. The periodical essayist does not rise above the partisan fray, but rather diversifies his or her textual goods to appeal to a wide consumer market. The metaphor of the essay as commodity is ubiquitous in the genre, and in fashioning essays that speak to manifold tastes and political persuasions, the essayist represents him or herself as a savvy merchant. The *Massachusetts Magazine's* Essayist, for example, praises his chosen genre for its delivery of a wide variety of goods, affording his readers abundant pleasure in the necessarily limited hours they can devote to reading. This is why, he explains, the *Spectator* has been so much "more efficacious in promoting the interests of virtue and true piety," because even "ten minutes…devoted to one of Addison's numbers might be sufficient to communicate much pleasure and lasting instruction."[31] In his validation of the moral economy of the periodical essay, the writer explicitly invokes a comparison to the marketplace: those readers who "relish a plain disquisition on some branch of ethics…without ornament or disguise" *and* those "who choose to survey the fair face of virtue through the transparent veil of fiction" will both find material to please their respective tastes. Indeed, he summarizes, whether one is "politician, philosopher, sentimentalist," or whether one is "attached to any particular species of writing, as history, biography, romance, satire, or anecdote," they will "find something in the olio adapted to their peculiar taste."[32]

Joseph Dennie and Royall Tyler likewise adopt the marketplace metaphor in the title of their longstanding series, "From the Shop of Messrs. Colon and Spondee." One advertisement for the series reads, "Messrs. Colon and Spondee would now inform their kind customers, that they brighten the dullest compositions in prose and verse, by the apt and judicious insertion of capital letters, italics, dashes, asterisks…with notes of interrogation, obnubulation, and admiration, by the gross or dozen."[33] If their tone suggests irony in representing textual objects as if they could be sold by the dozen, then this is not always the case. The Retailer, for example, seems quite sincere in his self-fashioning as an essayist who will bring diverse "wares" to his "customers." And in his very first essay, he asserts that one way he can provide this variety is by employing the task of authorship to other essayists, thereby avoiding "the dull monotony of a single writer."[34] He thus identifies himself as both manufacturer and merchant: he produces his own writing, but also sells the work of others. Later he publishes a scolding letter from a "satirical gentleman" who castigates the Retailer for "degrading [his] store to a huckster's shop," but in so doing he repackages the criticism as just another diverse ware on his shelf.[35] Other periodical essayists give prominence to the diversity of their goods through the titles. Joseph Dennie does so in his earlier periodical series, *Farrago* (1792–97), as does Washington Irving in *Salmagundi* (1807–8). The mixed fodder referenced in Dennie's title and the chopped antipasto in Irving's also provides a culinary metaphor that is frequently found in the genre. The periodical essay serves different pleasures to consumers of many different tastes. In the first *Farrago* published in *The Table*, Dennie compares the essays that will follow to a Spanish soup, "Olla Podrida, a dish formed by a motley mixture of many ingredients," and contrasts it with any kind of systematized "lenten entertainment."[36] Implicitly gesturing towards the metaphor Addison draws between "Mental Taste" and "Sensitive Taste" in *Spectator* 409 (1712), Dennie suggests that his literary dish will appeal to many because it will give expression to the range of "different Flavour that affect[] the Palate." Dennie's essayist worries that his own products will be censured for "sameness of sentiment," and he complains that unlike "in the periodical publications of Great Britain," where "the papers are usually furnished by the members of a literary society, who assemble at some coffee-house or tavern, and club their genius to amuse the public, as they club their cash, to discharge their reckoning," he is a *"lone author"* and always at risk of both "lenten" blandness and bankruptcy.[37]

This correlation between solitary authorship and economic insolvency is one that the Retailer also invokes when another correspondent accuses him of financial malfeasance. Commenting on the Retailer's repeated advertisement of his "display of a general assortment of European, East-India and West-India goods," a correspondent speculates on the likelihood of the essayist's financial ruin. Labeling The Retailer an "adventurous trader" who has demonstrated a proclivity towards "adulterat[ion]" and "take[ing] goods on commission," he anticipates the Retailer "will soon become bankrupt."[38] The Retailer counters with the simple observation, "I do not trade beyond my capital," an assertion that he confirms by appropriating his correspondent's letter into his own merchandise. The Retailer writes, "when that day arrives in which some ingenious printer shall republish these lucubrations...I wonder if [my correspondent] would not wish his epistle to be united in the volume."[39] The salvo asserts what the Retailer has maintained all along, which is that because his series has been able to "diffuse variety," it will be a financial success. Some ingenious printer will continue to market his work, which includes the letters from his critics, precisely because they are motley. The Retailer thus avoids bankruptcy because he makes himself dependent on other people and relies on their goods for his commission.

The recurrent stress in periodical essays on what Joseph Dennie terms "motley miscellany" showcases the diverse commodities found in the market and the diffuse number of persons trading in them. This formal stress on miscellany also seems to give the periodical essayist license to an unsystematic method. Dennie's essayist announces he will adopt the haphazard stance of his "renowned predecessor, the Spectator," providing his observations as he "roams from object to object, as caprice inspires."[40] The Trifler proclaims his task as dedicated to "irregular studies and imperfect acquisitions" and observations on "various and unconnected literature."[41] The General Observer extols the virtues of the periodical essay by remarking on how amenable its hasty style is for readers who "either through want of inclination, or being engaged in the business and active scenes of life... will be more likely to read a short essay on any subject, than to set down and peruse in course a lengthy differentiation."[42] The Friend insists that "miscellaneous essays" are especially pleasing because the reader's mind "is not cloyed by prolixity, nor wearied by that close attention, which long treatises, intimately connected in their parts necessarily require."[43] This imperative towards digression and the suggestion that the formal emphasis on "small and unconnected parts" will be the best mechanism to illustrate the small and unconnected nodes that constitute modern socio-economic relations are the major hallmarks of the form, and one that is featured by Freneau, Murray, and Brown.

### Weaving with Philip Freneau

Although he is primarily remembered as the "poet of the Revolution" and as an editor, Philip Freneau was also a prolific essayist who, following in the footsteps of the writer he termed "godlike Addison," published periodical essays throughout his long career.[44] Beginning in 1782, Freneau published as the Pilgrim in the *Freeman's Journal*; later in the decade he added Tomo-Cheeki (a Creek Indian) and Robert Slender (an itinerant weaver) to his repertoire of essayists. Like other Addisonian essayists publishing in North America, Freneau invoked the conventions familiar to the genre as it had been practiced by their British predecessors, and perhaps it is because Freneau so carefully follows these generic paradigms that scholars have deemed his work in this mode uninventive, as "clothed in tatters from transatlantic cousins familiar to almost any reader of Addison or Goldsmith."[45] Freneau also adopts the stylistic convention of his British counterparts by presenting his essayists as politically neutral, and no doubt it is because this posture of political moderation is so strongly at odds with the highly partisan persona of "that rascal Freneau," as George Washington called him, that scholars have also had very little to say regarding these periodical essays.[46]

Freneau was a vituperative critic of the Washington administration, assuming the editorship of the Jeffersonian *National Gazette* and devoting its pages to attacking Hamilton's financial policies. And, as such, it may seem counterintuitive to identify his periodical writing as exemplifying what I am describing as a Hamiltonian narrative of economic explanation. But Freneau was personally invested in commercial trade, which gave him first-hand knowledge of its complexity. After 1785, he became the captain of a forty-ton ship, purchased by his brother, from which he would secure partial profits in the coastal trade between North America and the West Indies. Many of these voyages would find expression in the works of one of

Freneau's most prolific essay personae, Robert Slender, and in tracking Slender's career, we can see how Freneau uses the literary form of the periodical essay to represent the commercial economy that ultimately becomes a subject of his political critique.

When scholars discuss Freneau's Robert Slender, they typically refer to the essays in the *Philadelphia Aurora* between 1799 and 1800, but these later texts are very atypical in that they reflect the highly partisan environment in which they were published. However, Slender first comes to life much earlier as the "author" of a dramatic poem, *A Journey from Philadelphia to New-York by way of Burlington and South-Amboy* (1787). The poem is framed by the conceit that an editor, Adam Buckskin, has discovered the manuscript "amongst the papers" of his recently deceased friend Slender, a "stocking weaver."[47] Freneau gives further expression to his stocking weaver in a collection published the following year, *The Miscellaneous Works of Mr. Philip Freneau* (1788).[48]

*Miscellaneous Works* is a patchwork affair that includes essays and poems, some reprinted from earlier newspaper and magazine publications and others taken directly from manuscript. While the printer's advertisement that introduces the book suggests that the volume is designed to preserve Freneau's writing from the impermanence of the periodical venue, there is no attempt to systematize or organize the ninety-three individual titles the volume contains. The table of contents lists the individual titles without any taxonomical or chronological organization, and so the effect of the volume is somewhat paradoxical. The leather bound book makes permanent the ephemera of the periodical press and manuscript hand, but the volume's deliberate refusal of editorial method makes it read like a commonplace book, almost as if Freneau designed the volume with an emphasis on miscellaneous disorder. For example, several of Freneau's Pilgrim essays that were originally published in *Freeman's Journal* are revised and presented in the book under the new title, "The Philosopher of the Forest," which would seem to indicate his dedication to the work as a discrete codex. Yet eleven of these essays are interspersed with other poems and essays, as if to reconstruct the experience of diversified reading associated with the original periodical publication.

The essayist most prominently displayed in this volume—and whose work is even more explicitly associated with this imperative towards miscellany—is Freneau's pseudonymous Robert Slender. He emerges in the fifth title in the collection, "Advice to Authors by the late Mr. Robert Slender." Here an unnamed "editor" introduces the posthumous weaver with roughly the same biographical story as was provided a year earlier in *Journey*. Slender, we are told, was "a stocking and tape weaver by trade" and an occasional author who left a "strong-box" filled with a "bundle of manuscripts, penned in a very antiquated, obscure and perplexing hand" (42). The editor announces that he shall "now and then present thee with an essay, a paragraph, a sentiment, or a poem" from this "miscellaneous collection of original papers" (43). But he also criticizes Slender for traveling "the American continent and islands" instead of following the more lucrative pattern of his "brother weavers [who] were more profitably employed at home at their looms" (42).

Although the editor presents the weaver as a profitless dilettante, insisting that both his writing and weaving constituted "amusements" rather than "serious occupations" (43), this is not how Slender represents himself. After all, the very fact that his first essay offers advice to authors as to how they can best get their work into print belies the editor's assertion of Slender's accidental authorship. Slender does not characterize his textual or textile vocations as amateurish, instead advertising the coupling of the two trades as a primary means by which other authors might subsidize their writing. "Graft your authorship," he advises his compatriots, "upon some other calling" (44). Freneau is making a familiar argument about the fiscal precariousness of the early national author who needs another vocation for material support. This argument also explains his advocacy on behalf of a proposal that imported British books be charged an excise tax, the collection of which could be used to support "real American writers, when [they] become old and helpless, and no longer able to wield the pen to advantage" (45).[49] In asserting the benefits of this Hamiltonian protectionist strategy, Slender also asserts a symbiotic relationship between the two trades. He further draws an analogy between Slender's labors by proposing that essays are like the other commodities Slender constructs (ribbons and socks) and by suggesting that his essayist possesses the skill of twining together myriad strains of both fiber and tales.

Like all other periodical essayists, Slender writes on many topics and genres, but Freneau even more emphatically stresses his eclectic production by collecting his essays into discrete "books." While the "Philosopher of the Forest" essays are scattered throughout the entirety of *The Miscellaneous Works*, Freneau organizes the Slender essays into smaller collections, which he provides with separate titles, as if to suggest that they had earlier been published in book form, although none of them had. Twelve of the essays are collected under the title, "Tracts and Essays on Several Subjects by Mr. Slender"; nine are clustered in the collection, "Essays, Tales, and Poems by Mr. Slender," which comprises another sub-collection of miscellany titled, "Narratives, Observations and Advice on Different Subjects"; and finally another set of essays are located in "Reflections, Narratives and Ideas of the late Robert Slender." Freneau thus emphasizes Slender as a manufacturer of miscellanies and the writer of numerous topics and genres. We read, for example, orations on the splendors of rum, meditations on the privations of employment as a private tutor, and discourses on the plights of an Incan astronomer. His characterization of Slender as an author capable of writing about varied topics using various literary forms reflects Freneau's own literary ambitions, and also stresses the unique method of the periodical essayist: an imperative towards social observation that is not organized towards any particular narrative plot or philosophical system. And even as Freneau packages his periodical essayist in a book volume, he stresses the refusal of such order in the titles' emphases on "different" and "several subjects."

Through the persona of Slender, Freneau also establishes a strong correlation between the formal emphasis on variety and a representation of the commercial marketplace. Slender not only expends much of his narrative labor in describing the complexities of commercial transactions, but his own presentation of topics and genres reproduces the complex structure of his primary subject. The term "complex," etymologically related to *plectere* (to weave, braid, or twine), is particularly apt since it is linked to Slender's own trade as a weaver. Slender plaits stories of commercial transaction into a tapestry that documents the miscellany. It would seem then that Freneau makes his periodical essayist a weaver precisely because this vocation is metaphorically aligned with the form he adopts. And both form and metaphor are especially well suited to talk about the tangle of economic relations that frequently served as its subject. In fact, Slender's first "book" is haunted by the financial precariousness that is inextricable from commercial practice. Slender makes the dialectic transparent when he offers a pair of texts that he calls two sides of one "medal" (95). One depicts "The Man in Business," and the other, his counterpart, "The Man out of Business." The latter probably more prominently occupies Slender's sensibilities since the very next essay, "The Debtor," describes the somatic symptoms that emerge in the face of Slender's own financial liability: "a deadly tremor pervading all my limbs, a cold sweat forcing its way through the pores of my skin, a dreary discomposure of mind, and a total inability to act, think, or speak with the vigour and assurance...I can command upon other occasions" (96). The terrifying unmanning of the debtor is caused by the creditor who Slender describes as "a monster in human shape with features horribly distorted; an everlasting frown on his countenance, and a jail with iron windows engraven on his forehead!" (97).

Slender compensates for the "discomposure" that threatens the integrity of his textual product in the very next essay, which entirely changes both its form and style, providing "Rules and Directions, How to avoid Creditors, Sheriffs, Constables, &c." submitted by Slender under the auspices of his position of treasurer of an imaginary Debtor's Club (97). Playfully invoking the literary clubs of his predecessors—and again appealing to a standard feature of the periodical essay—Freneau makes Slender a member of a club that is devoted not to literary production but the evasion of creditors. Written two years before he was hired by Jefferson to pillory the establishment of public credit, Freneau offers a recognizably Jeffersonian position in his satirical portrait of a club designed to thwart creditors. But the essay does not represent debt as an immoral betrayal of civic virtue, but as an inevitable consequence of any marketplace. The only advice the club can offer, after all, is to avoid all economic exchange.

Slender thus renders tales of personal fiscal disaster with typical appeals to sentiment, but rather than stressing the emotional costs of ruin, he explicates the larger socio-economic systems from which these losses stem. In one particularly revealing tale, "The Inexorable Captain," Slender takes his readers to the Barbados. This geographic shift literalizes a central fact of modern commerce, which is that the Philadelphian weaver is as enmeshed in global trade as any merchant or ship captain. Slender also underscores economic precariousness as he explains how a substantial change in circumstances has left the formerly fertile and wealthy island in poverty and distress. Because of a scarcity of food, when the ship arrives carrying grain it is greeted with numerous supplicants: "everyone wished to become a purchaser" (129). One woman begs the captain to sell her two bushels of grain for the price of one-third of a bushel, but the "inexorable captain" of the tale's title rejects the sale. The captain is similarly hard-hearted when a farmer requests that the captain sell him grain in exchange for futures on the coffee and cotton that will ultimately be harvested from his own plantations. Given the callous refusal to aid characters that Slender draws with considerable pathos, the story seems primed to deliver a moral about the need to value human charity beyond monetary profits.

Yet this is not the moral that Slender dispatches. Instead Slender justifies the captain's refusals. In the case of the woman, Slender protests against the demands of "pity and compassion," arguing that both the woman and the captain were agents in a transaction in which each attempted to secure their respective best interests. After all, Slender explains, the compassion that would supply the woman with a better bargain will not mitigate the captain's custom fees nor appease the owners of the boat who take a portion of the captain's profits (130). So conventional are the condemnatory portraits of financial avarice that we might be inclined to read Slender's argument as satire. Yet the tale underscores the sincerity of Slender's critique, hard-hearted though it may be. For example, the first person to attempt purchase from the captain is an "engrosser" who tries to negotiate for the entire stock but fails because he will only buy if he receives some abatement in price. The representation of the engrosser is clearly pejorative, since he would be attempting to profit on his own speculative investment, but crucially, the story presses at the structural similarity between the positions of the speculator and the woman. Her situation might be more pathetic, but both are attempting to bargain for a transaction that will yield more profit.

The tale offers a similar argument in a subsequent encounter between the captain and a farmer. The captain here offers more detail in explaining why he will not be persuaded by the farmer's plaintive story. Representing their encounter as a random intersection of two narratives of necessity, he tells the farmer, "You and I are two beings that have this day met by accident, and could reciprocally spend a month in relating the story of our mutual wants and difficulties" (132). Abridging his own strand of the story, the captain explains that his mercantile journey has been punctuated by countless hardships: "I have risqued the cruelty of enemies, the horrors of shipwreck; have patiently endured the beating shower, long, dreary nights, and cold, pinching winds! – and a thousand difficulties and mischances may yet attend me on my way to my native land" (132). The captain is unwilling to extend credit to the farmer because he is not in a financial position to risk the losses that might accrue if the farmer should default on his promissory notes. Given the motif of debt that has circulated in so many of the other essays, the captain's insensibility must be read as the means by which he keeps himself out of financial misery.

Slender concludes the tale by articulating the explicit moral he wants his readers to harvest: "necessity alone renders one half of the world insensible to the miseries and wants of the other" (133). Slender's lesson stresses the ways that individual privation disrupts sympathy, but it just as importantly also explains why storytelling—and the arrangement of stories—becomes a particularly fraught affair in a world of increasingly elaborate relationships of economic dependence. "The Inexorable Captain" depicts an economic and narrative competition in which tales of deprivation are mobilized so as to secure better access to a commodity that is in short supply. Even as each storyteller (the Captain, Slender, the engrosser, the woman, the farmer) is embedded in an extensive economy, their respective appeals to sympathy refuse to acknowledge this larger weave of economic dependence. The farmer, orienting his appeal around the hungry family and starving animals he has left at home, requests charity and credit: credit because he is asking the captain to allow him time to repay the purchase, and charity because he is asking the captain to waive the costs of the captain's own risk. But his request does not acknowledge that in requesting this transaction, the captain would inevitably become less solvent and therefore less able to repay his own creditors. And so on. Despite their appeals to compassion, these supplicants do not acknowledge that the merchant captain is himself the protagonist of his own economic tale.

While each individual storyteller in the narrative is unable to imagine her integration into the network of economic exchange, the tale itself (which is said to be a fragment from "Slender's Journals") emphasizes the incomplete quality of the discrete perspectives. Indeed the almost hyperbolically miscellaneous quality of the contained "books" of Slender, reflected by the haphazard organization of Freneau's volume, similarly reveals the inadequacy of any one narrative to take account of these various supply chains. In other words, the self-conscious emphasis on generic and topical variety not only represents the plenitude of modern commerce, but also serves as a constant reminder of the inability of one plot to capture the myriad causalities of the market. Emerging only a decade after the invention of a classical political economic theory that espoused the necessary coincidence between self-interest and market efficiency, Freneau's story of scarcity and inequality clearly exposes a crack in the logic.

Freneau also explicitly stresses miscellany in the second of Slender's "books," which provide its readers with a motley arrangement of subjects: an interview with an impoverished American poet who claims he has transmigrated between the bodies of a Persian king, a Jamaican slave, and a British sailor (199); some documents from an Otaheite exploration of North America that characterizes the "savage" customs of white people who are "intolerably proud, selfish, vain, malevolent, and lazy" (211); a "fragment" that details a phantasmagoric visitation of classical philosophers; and a maudlin seduction story that "may possibly please such as have a true taste for modern Novels" (251). As if to further insist on this topical and generic heterogeneity, the final essay, "Narratives, Observations and Advice on Different Subjects" (269) itself comprises nine sundry sections. The only coherence between these miscellaneous texts is that they are all the product of Slender's pen: his imaginary persona is what holds the assortment together. But rather than portray Slender as an accomplished editor, as someone who can unify, and weave together, his textual products, Freneau renders the volume more like a patchwork assemblage that exposes the seams drawing people together into economic relations.

"Narratives, Observations and Advice" puts this social assemblage at the center of one story's plot, which relays another voyage that Slender takes to the Barbados. His fellow passengers on this "unlucky and disastrous" journey include a wealthy "Creolian family" returning home to their sugar plantation (273). When the ship encounters a storm that seems likely to kill them, the widowed mother of the family determines to write a will. But when she awards the entire plantation and all of her slaves to the eldest daughter, the youngest child balks: "you always promised *Sue* to me in your life time, and I shall take it very hard if you will not allow me one choice out of so many now you are d__d—dead!" (278). The intended humor of the sketch, such as it is, is found in the fact that the mother, focused on her imminent destruction, is deeding her human property to a daughter who will drown with her, and that the younger daughter is railing against her dispossession forgetting that she too will perish in the shipwreck. The target of the satire is clearly human venality but, as in the case of the "Inexorable Captain," Freneau also draws attention to human myopia: the inability for an individual to see another's ruin. That these women are trading in human lives, which they judge as nothing other than property, is accentuated when the next paragraph records that another passenger aboard the same ship is sailing with a slave he intends "to dispose of to the highest bidder" (278). Also aboard is an "Indian priest" who argues against slaveholding.[50] Freneau shifts his narrative focus to that of the enslaved man: after surviving the storm, we follow the slave to the prison in which the man is bound and impounded with "a cargo of newly imported Africans" (279). Ravaged by the journey and the conditions of his imprisonment, the man dies overnight, and the essay concludes with the slave owner announcing this death: he "told us with *tears in his eyes*, that the negro was dead!" (281). This conclusion thus reorients the narrative chain to the perspective of the slave owner who sobs because of his financial loss. Insofar as Slender and the Indian priest reflect on a correlation between "cruelty and avarice" (280), the essay gestures towards an abolitionist argument.[51] But because the narrative ends by picking up the first stitch of the slave owner's story of ruin, the stress is not on the amorality of slavery but the tension that inheres within the weave of tales that link all the passengers aboard the ship.

Freneau's use of Robert Slender suggests the suitability of the periodical essay to describe the complex texture of commercial relations, but it also points to an essential paradox. The best way to depict mimetically the vicissitudes of modern commerce is through Slender's miscellaneous method. But efficiency in the modern marketplace requires specialization. Slender seems to recognize precisely this paradox when he observes, the "great advances which the moderns have made in the walks of art" do not arise from superior talents but from the modern emphasis on specialization in which "the whole attention of a man's life is bestowed upon the formation of a pin or a needle" (352), a reference that clearly alludes to Adam Smith's analysis of pin manufacturing and the increasing efficiency that emerges when labor is focused on specialized tasks. Acknowledging that "society at large has profited by this regulation" (352), Slender also waxes nostalgic for an earlier time when an individual could perform an array of different tasks. Given Freneau's own versatile literary practices, it is easy to imagine that he is suggesting that his own devotion to the miscellany is a rebuke to the imperative towards specialization under capitalism. As an example of the atavistic economic ideal, Slender references Odysseus: "Homer...gives the hero of the *Odyssey* several different trades, so that when he was cast ashore on the solitary island where *Calypso* afterwards detained him, he was not at a loss how to build and rig a vessel with his own hands....What a pitiful figure would a modern of the same rank exhibit on a similar occasion!" (352–53). In offering the story of the marooned sailor, Slender suggests Robinson Crusoe, who survives only because he can salvage the numerous goods aboard the wrecked ship, and does not therefore represent economic self-sufficiency. By contrast, Odysseus, as a jack-of-all-trades, is economically independent. Slender implicitly draws a similarity between the diversified talents of Homer's hero and his own vocational range as a stocking and tape weaver as well as an author who can write in numerous genres about manifold subjects.

But Slender also seems to suggest that he might be like the marooned sailor, a specialized laborer. After all, as both a weaver and an author, his economic health depends on the costs of his raw material and the spending habits of consumers. In meditating on the opportunity costs between efficient specialized labor and diversified production, Freneau clearly has his mind on the economic status of the author. On one hand, the miscellanist who tries her hand at numerous topics and genres will inevitably be less efficient and therefore will receive less remuneration. On the other hand, this same writer is more likely to find success since she improves the odds of finding an audience. Given Freneau's own eclectic generic output, it seems he makes the choice for diversification over specialization. But the risks of this choice are revealed through Freneau's avatar Robert Slender whose success in the literary market is substantially tempered by the central conceit behind his essays, which is that they are all published posthumously.

The choice between efficiency and diversification is challenged even more dramatically when Freneau resurrects Robert Slender a decade later as a correspondent to the *Aurora* and substantially transforms the project, style, and trade of his initial persona. This new Slender has become a cobbler, and he is neither a keen observer of human variety nor a producer of generic heterogeneity. He instead advertises himself as one of the "swinish multitude."[52] In adopting the phrase first used by Edmund Burke in 1790 and then coopted by

English radicals, Freneau reinvents his miscellanist as a Jacobin democrat.[53] No longer does Slender write as a periodical essayist, but rather as a political naïf turned polemicist. His first letter, for example, "replies" to a letter Freneau had himself written and published in the *Aurora* as "A Monarchist," which disingenuously articulated support for the Alien and Sedition Acts. Here, as will be the case in all subsequent letters, Slender describes himself as a timorous reader of Federalist propaganda. Following the rhetorical strategy that began in response to Hamilton's Report on Public Credit, Freneau represents Slender as a credulous victim of Federalist literary machinations, a dupe desperately in search of the explanations provided by the *Aurora's* "plain tales."[54]

The shift in Slender's vocation also marks a significant revision. Not only does Freneau eliminate all the metaphorical resonances of weaving, but Slender's new employment as cobbler seems a likely reference to a major labor action by Philadelphian journeymen cordwainers in 1799, a strike that one economic historian identifies as the "earliest struggle of capital and labor on American soil."[55] The journeymen were protesting what they saw as wage fixing on the part of the master cordwainers, who were transitioning into shoe merchants by purchasing the labor of the journeyman and selling the product to a broader marketplace. In this way, the Philadelphia shoe trade epitomized an increasing cleavage between labor and capital. Freneau is thus drawing a strong distinction between the two vocations of his essayist. The earlier weaver Slender, who both manufactures and sells his goods, emblematized the unity of labor and capital within the identity of his singular body, and his texts thus could give expression to the supply chains of Atlantic capital and commodity circulation. Conversely, the credulous cobbler, divested from anything other than selling his labor, can only give simplistic and singular expression to his marginalization. Thus he enumerates the familiar set of Hamiltonian institutions as responsible for his mystification: "when I heard so much about *funding systems, and banking systems*, and *public debt* being *a public blessing*; O, said I to myself, my poor head can't understand this—I wonder what it means?"[56] And although he is a cobbler, Slender routinely apostrophizes farmers—"Ye honest, ye independent, ye virtuous farmers"—thereby aligning himself with the well-established political rhetoric that pitched the conflict as one neatly drawn between agrarianism and commerce.[57]

Freneau thus transforms his itinerant periodical essayist into an author whose primary task is to sketch cautionary tales about financial seduction. By adopting the style of authors like George Logan and John Taylor, the cobbler also condemns the Hamiltonian style of his earlier persona. Whereas the weaver's work drew its potency from its detailed illustrations of the commerce of everyday life, the partisan cobbler asserts that any attempt to represent the complexities of this everyday commerce constitutes a coercive strategy of obfuscation. And so, even though Freneau retains the title of his earlier periodical essayist, he abandons the *genre* of the periodical essay precisely because it was so poorly suited to the simple story that the Jeffersonians wanted to tell.

## Gleaning with Judith Sargent Murray

Like Freneau, Judith Sargent Murray was versatile in her literary composition, publishing poetry, political essays, drama, and narrative fiction. She was also enmeshed in early American periodical culture. Indeed, the essay for which she is best known, "On the Equality of the Sexes" (1790), a significant work of early American feminism, was originally published in Isaiah Thomas's *Massachusetts Magazine*. This periodical was also the location for two of Murray's long-running Addisonian essay series, The Repository and The Gleaner. Murray also published as The Reaper in *The Federal Orrery*, a semi-weekly Federalist newspaper. As such, a considerable amount of Murray's literary output is devoted to the genre of the periodical essay. In this section, I want to focus especially on her Gleaner series, which dedicates itself to a formal reproduction of the extensive and dependent strands of commercial and financial capitalism.

Murray publishes thirty-two essays as "The Gleaner" between 1792 and 1794. In 1798, she repackages these original essays, adding seventy-odd more installments to make a book, entitled *The Gleaner: A Miscellaneous Production*. The subtitle manifestly underscores the formal continuity to the essays' original publication in the *Massachusetts Magazine*, a magazine that likewise dedicated itself to miscellany, announcing in its subtitle that it was a repository for "The Literature, History, Politics, Arts, Manners, [and] Amusements of the Age."[58] It is difficult not to marvel at the formal heterogeneity offered by Murray's three-volume book, which is divided into 100 different entries of roughly equal length that offer epistolary narratives, sketches, moral parables, two plays, as well as political, pedagogical, and literary essays. From his very first essay, the Gleaner depicts himself as devoted to this miscellaneous production, explaining that he is motivated to write because he felt the magazine's editors wanted to "increase the number of...miscellaneous correspondents" (15). Murray also secures this emphasis on diversity through her rather complex manipulation of pseudonyms and authorial voices. Following the conventions of the periodical essay, Murray introduces her pseudonymous Gleaner to the public with the conceit that her writer is a man of leisure offering his keen and desultory observations from his daily wanderings around the city. But readers soon learn that the Gleaner who wanders in public also has a private life and another name, Mr. Vigillius. The narrative persona is further complicated in the book publication when the title page identifies the author of all the letters as "Constantia," and then represents Constantia "unmask[ing]" herself as the author in the final essay of the volume (804). This proliferation of implied authors corroborates Murray's dedication to "Miscellaneous Production": not only will her writing provide a farrago of generic styles, but she will construct it as the product of numerous and miscellaneous authorial masks. Murray is the sole author of the essays, but she wants her readers to consume them as if they are an aggregate production.

Nina Baym argues that Murray engages in this virtuosic display of genre and authorial impersonation so as to evidence the considerable range and versatility of her literary talent—and the performance is indisputably masterful.[59] Nevertheless I want to propose that Murray's emphasis on variety is designed to obscure the author's individuality and instead to call attention to the network of commercial and financial exchanges that comprise the broad world in which the Gleaner's various characters are embedded. Recognizing that a woman in Boston in 1790 has better access to global goods than ever before, but also that her relationship to these goods and to the people that produce and distribute them is more remote, Murray uses the form of the periodical essay to illustrate the strands of this economic market and to explicate the systemic interdependence between the market's far-flung participants. Murray similarly represents the relationship between her periodical essayist and the audience as one of interdependence—a textual economy that requires the postponement of interest for some and repayment for others. Perhaps this argument seems belied by the series' title, since gleaning implies labor that evades an economic system that calibrates production and consumption. Gleaning involves a very different relationship between labor and property than would reaping, speculating, or retailing (all activities referenced by other periodical essayists from the age). A gleaner neither buys nor sells, instead consuming property that has been abandoned: she has customary, but not legally propertied, rights to the produce of a certain parcel of land.[60] This is why the possession of such goods was understood not as trespass or robbery, and why gleaning is associated with usufruct and philanthropy, and not commerce.

It is not surprising, therefore, that the pseudonym has led readers to emphasize Murray's literary product as associated with the antimonetary economies of either patronage or pastoralism. Kirstin Wilcox, for example, argues that the Gleaner's name is meant to intimate the essayist as either an impoverished woman, like Ruth gleaning in Boaz's field, or as a man of leisure, a refined gentleman who offers his periodical contributions as generous gifts to readers.[61] This assessment is corroborated by the Gleaner's self-portrait as a literary amateur, as a writer who has an "itch for scribbling" (15). But this literary itch does not remove the Gleaner from the commercial economy in which he circulates, and instead Murray repeatedly draws attention to this networked economy. According to Michael T. Gilmore, Murray chooses the pseudonym "to disarm accusations of plagiarism and to lay a modest claim to the overflowing granaries of the opulent."[62] Yet the essays seem rather to emphasize the arduousness of authorial labor and distribution, both of which require "penury and hardship" (14). Even Mr. Vigillius, who introduces himself as amateur scribbler, immediately renders his leisure activity as a productive and commercial economy when he declares that the essays he distributes to his readers are "piece-meal commodities" (18). In so doing, Murray makes clear that far from being exterior to, or alienated from, the literary marketplace, the Gleaner is a cunning practitioner who can translate discoveries into literary wares that will be consumed (hopefully with relish) by an audience. Gleaning will resuscitate what would otherwise be wasted, and the Gleaner will reintroduce what he "industriously collects" (17) into the marketplace.

The Gleaner immediately introduces us to one such hungry consumer, his adopted daughter, Margaretta. We meet the young woman in the second essay of the series as the Gleaner establishes an elaborate *mise en abyme* in which he describes the girl combing through the pages of the *Massachusetts Magazine* trying to find a poem written by the "American Sappho" (a reference to Sarah Wentworth Morton who, like Murray, published in the magazine under the pseudonym, Constantia) only to discover in their stead an essay "entitled the Gleaner" (24). Margaretta is thus both consumer and "piece-meal commodit[y]": both a character crafted by his pen and a customer who combs through the magazine looking for entertaining reading material. As it turns out, however, Margaretta is a disappointed consumer, chagrined to find her father's gleanings instead of the desired poetry by Morton. As a recurrent character in the essays, Margaretta is a privileged example of this particular combination of product and consumer, but her position is one that all readers occupy. When the Gleaner cites Margaretta's response to seeing her own name in the magazine ("Bless me!"), he also reproduces his magazine reader's similarly surprised response to her appearance, "But pray, it may be asked, who is Margaretta?" To answer this question—one that might be asked about any character introduced onto a narrative stage—the Gleaner travels into his own past, tempted to describe "many scenes novel and interesting, prospects extensive and views truly picturesque" (18). This encounter between reader and writer is illustrative. Readers do not typically demand explanations for the existence of characters, nor are writers compelled to justify them, but Murray wants to draw attention to the negotiation in order to highlight the ample store from which the Gleaner sketches his scene—and the necessary selectivity that any such composition entails. And because the Gleaner has declared himself to be a miscellanist, he also feels at liberty to abandon this new character and the narrow confines of the domestic scene by turning his vision to the vast storehouse located in "prospects extensive" and "views truly picturesque."

We might imagine that this commitment to diversified production would be cause for celebration: following the economic logic of Slender, the Gleaner speculates that a range of textual goods will appeal to a wider constituency of buyers. We instead learn that his choice has caused considerable displeasure. His readers want to read the tale of Margaretta and her possible seduction by the nefarious Sinisterus Courtland, her marriage to the noble Edward Hamilton, and ultimately Hamilton's ruin and redemption. And they are unequivocally and unanimously piqued by the Gleaner's abandonment of the romance plot for the other topics and sketches that comprise the miscellany of his presentation. One such reader complains that Margaretta was introduced too abruptly, accusing the Gleaner of having "popt her upon us," but then lambastes the essayist for abandoning the character just as she proved interesting: "whip, in a moment, she was gone" (48). A novel-loving young woman says that she is "one of a great many ladies, which is absolutely dying to see something more about Margaretta" (53). Another woman confesses that Margaretta's absence from his pages has caused her to "read your numbers under this cloud of disappointment" (54). Even his male readers articulate their displeasure that the Gleaner has abandoned his evident promise to make Margaretta his principle commodity. "I think you have conducted your matters devilishly oddly...What, to raise our curiosity, leading us to expect the history of a fine girl, and then to sob us off with your *musty morals*," one complains (55).

In giving voice to the grievances of these readers, Murray makes several important arguments. She reveals a crucial paradox of the commercial marketplace, which is that despite the clamor for diversified goods, tastes can be remarkably homogeneous. Consumers may enter stores, and magazines, with the expectation of diverse choices, and yet they gravitate to particular objects in mass. Murray also identifies a very specific market tendency of the 1790s: a fondness for the sentimental romance novel. She is not disavowing the novel, since she continues to include Margaretta's domestic plot within her own periodical essays, but she is suggesting a formal difference between the novel's dedication to a limited cast of characters on one hand and the periodical essay's imperative for multiple genres, numerous characters, and a repudiation of any singular plot line on the other. The formal distinction is emphasized when the Gleaner recontinues Margaretta's story. The return may seem a capitulation to his audience's tastes, but he insists that he will only provide "sketches" and that he will retain "the privilege of discontinuing and resuming them, as shall suit my convenience" (56–57). He will tell the story of Margaretta, but not as an integrated narrative. This preference for the miscellaneous sketch over the integrated narrative is confirmed when Murray chooses to retain the essayistic form in the book publication instead of combining all of the Margaretta sections into one coherent narrative.

When his readers express their dissatisfaction with anything other than the story of Margaretta, they articulate their displeasure as an economic, and not aesthetic, critique. The Gleaner, they insist, does not repay them for their time since he so often strays away from the primary reason they read his column. The Gleaner counters that he will "compensate the reader for the trouble he may take in travelling through these pages" (139), but despite such promissory notes, his readers perpetually protest his paper; and the Gleaner painstakingly records these complaints by circulating the letters that express them. One angry correspondent lambastes the columnist for providing a "scanty pittance" that "ill repays the labour of travelling through the dull pages he is so studious to multiply" (278). The Gleaner's relationship to his readers and correspondents is one in which he is constantly in "arrears" (277). Although we might think of gleaning as an essentially efficient operation (since it transforms what would otherwise be waste into a consumed product), Murray's essays instead characterize gleaning as a kind of extravagance. Without any clear end point or agenda, the Gleaner meanders through his topics, assuming that someone will ultimately take pleasure in any given commodity that he provides. Conversely, the narrative economy associated with Margaretta's tale is one whose trajectory is always towards moral example, romantic resolution, and consumer satisfaction. Murray thus seems to contrast the profligacy of the periodical essay with the sentimental novel that serves as a paradigm for narrative and moral economy. Despite the conventional attack on novel reading as a waste of time, her text makes clear that the novel is a literary form that delivers its goods to market with very little waste. Murray later writes, "The pecuniary fund of the novelist is...inexhaustible" (334). And the contemporary reader's taste for the novel, Murray suggests, is a consequence of this desire for narrative efficiency.

Even contemporary Murray scholars have indicated their preference for the novelistic tale embedded in the Gleaner essays. In her edition of Murray's writing, Sharon M. Harris identifies the Margaretta sections as an "important early American novel," and she has canonized this apprehension by doing what Murray's book did not: isolating Margaretta's story from its larger context and giving it a separate title, "A Story of Margaretta."[63] The title page of the Union College reprint of *The Gleaner* similarly advertises the Margaretta tale as something discrete, referring to it as the "novella of Margaretta" even though there is no similar heading in the 1798 edition of the book. It is no surprise, then, that Jennifer Baker refers to what she titles "The Story of Margaretta" as a "novel," and identifies Murray as a novelist.[64] Wilcox similarly argues that *The Gleaner* is didactic fiction, reading the book as a prototype for the nineteenth-century realist novel.[65] These modern critics do not of course condemn the Gleaner for his failure to satiate their novelistic tastes, but they do reproduce their predecessors' generic predilections insofar as they attend almost exclusively to the narrative of Margaretta, and it is as novelist that they celebrate Murray.

Yet neither the Gleaner nor Murray embrace the novel as the ideal form, and the Gleaner explicitly disclaims his identity as novelist.[66] Overhearing one of his readers propose that he "withholds" Margaretta "from the fear of giving to his productions the air of a novel," he responds with ebullience: "I could hardly forbear taking my advocate in my arms." The Gleaner is thrilled that his "advocate" recognizes that he wants to be esteemed as an essayist and not "a mere annalist of brilliant fictions" (49). Because early American writers so frequently repudiated the novel on moralistic grounds, we might assume that this is what motivates the Gleaner's response. But while conceding that novels are sometimes "licentiously luxuriant," this is not why the Gleaner resists classification as a novelist, since he acknowledges that it would be easy enough to write one that would "be more serviceable to the interests of virtue" (49). Instead, Murray suggests that the novel is inferior because of the claustrophobic focus on a limited cast of characters, set in small domestic space, and organized in chronological time. The role of the essayist is preferable to the "mere annalist," because it offers a greater range of topics and without the constraint of either linear chronology or embodied characters. This is why, for example, Murray insists on a distinction between the Gleaner and Mr. Vigillius: while Mr. Vigillius is an embodied character (a father and a husband) motivated by his private economic concerns, the Gleaner is a person without a body who can travel effortlessly across the globe into other people's interests. One angry reader, in fact, indicts the Gleaner as a Lovelacian rake, referencing him as a "perfect Proteus" and a "heterogeneous figure" who by "becoming stationary in no one respectable character" ingeniously manages to insinuate himself into the private recesses of the letter writer's own domestic life (278). The rhetoric of his impeachment invokes the seduction we associate with novels, but the force of the attack is instead that the Gleaner does not possess the consistent identity that we associate with novelistic characters. For this reader, then, the problem with the Gleaner is not so much that he behaves like a rake in a novel, but that he does not behave enough like one.

What is so curious about the Gleaner's commitment to the miscellaneous essay, however, is that his consistent representation of this particular generic economy as profligate stands in such stark opposition to the economic homilies that comprise these selfsame sketches. That is, even as the economic lessons emphasized in the Gleaner's pages are orthodox ones—to live within your means and to be generous in forgiving other people's debts when they are in financial tumult—the textual economy that Murray practices is one that is aligned with the excesses of commercial capitalism. Thus Murray's generic experiment reveals the waste that lies in the heart of commercial culture. For example, one of the sketches the Gleaner provides, and about which his readers complain, is a little parable about two merchants, Ernestus and Crastinatus. As his allegorical name implies, Ernestus is organized and efficient: although he has an expansive and complicated business, because he manages his accounts so well, he also has plenty of time for amusement. Conversely, Crastinatus's bookkeeping is so confused and tangled that he will, the Gleaner speculates, doubtlessly leave his wife and children bankrupt. Given that the Gleaner offers this homily as part of a larger Franklinian refrain on the need to ration time as if it were a good— "the wonder is, that we are so little attentive to [time's] waste that in its regulations and distribution we economize so little" (26)—it would seem the Gleaner means to make the case for efficient and ordered writing. We might likewise suppose that the Gleaner means to identify his own literary strategies as similar to Ernestus's. According to such an analogy, the Gleaner would have time to scribble precisely because he manages his other affairs so skillfully.

But even as the parable preaches efficient time management, the Gleaner's rendering of the story is deemed profligate by both his readers and himself. His narration bears a remarkable similarity to the incoherent bookkeeping for which Crastinatus is taken to task. He writes:

When Crastinatus hath paid the great debt of nature, his affairs will lay open to the inroads of fraud, his widow and his orphan children will be the sufferers, and the probability is, that an insolvency will take place. Whereas, had he—But it is time that I recollect myself; it may be thought that I encroach too far upon a department, which may be considered as already filled.    (29)

In his counsel to "recollect" himself, the Gleaner reveals that, like Crastinatus, he strays from the main path of his business; we cannot help but wonder if his own writing might leave his own wife and child destitute. After all, just as Crastinatus's meandering books render him indebted to countless creditors, so too does the Gleaner default on what his readers feel he owes. And by consistently referencing his relationship to his readers and correspondents as one in which he is in "arrears" (277), he confesses that he engages in a narrative economy based on the extension of credit.

We ultimately learn that one reason that the Gleaner offers this digressive story of Ernestus and Crastinatus is that he means to divert Margaretta's inquiries about the identity of the author whose essays she is reading in the *Massachusetts Magazine*. As his daughter reads the Gleaner's essays, she recalls that her father had always proposed the "Gleaner "would be his pen name were he "ever to appear[] in the world as an author" (24). The Gleaner thus offers his parable about procrastination so as to misdirect Margaretta's attention, a divagation that continues for the next several entries in which he takes on a series of miscellaneous topics. But, as we have seen, his successful distraction of Margaretta irritates his other readers. Thus one crucial revelation Murray makes is that textual economies are not dyadic. Murray does not represent her author as writing for one reader, or even writing for a readership whose interests and needs are commensurate. Instead she figures readership as a diverse chain of obligations and competitive attachments: to repay one is always potentially to defer the interest of another. Murray is implicitly disputing the fantasy most readers have about their reading in which there is an unmediated and fully compensatory relationship between a producer-author and a consumer-reader. While every reader knows, of course, that a book is not written for her alone, the act of reading—book in hand, eyes on pages—provides a fantastically simple metonymy of exchange in which one author delivers one reader a single product.

Instead of cultivating this fantasy, Murray ruptures it by stressing the dependent and competitive relations of the literary and commercial

market. She does this is by subtly intimating that the Gleaner's
debt is at least partially a consequence of his willingness to incorporate his readers' disappointments into his column. It is, then, a splendid
irony—and clearly one that Murray intended—that the denuncia-
tions made against the Gleaner by his readers constitute a prime
example of his essays' seeming profligacy: that is, the publication of
correspondence testifying to his readers' disapproval also delays
their satisfaction by deferring the Margaretta tale. One of his more
frequent correspondents, Mr. George Seafort, rebukes the Gleaner
for precisely such inefficient narrative piloting: "I have been plaguily
puzzled to know at what you were driving" and warns that if the
Gleaner continues to "[contrive] matters, as to run every invalid of
us fast aground the lee shore of conjecture," and if he "does not
resume…plain sailing," then Seafort will stop reading his work
(306). But while the "old sea commander" challenges the Gleaner's
style, he also replicates it since he likewise interrupts himself by
imagining his own readers growing impatient with his digressions:
"But what is all this to the purpose? avast a moment, and you shall
hear" (51). And this long letter, included in its entirety, has postponed
any further discussion of Margaretta for yet another month.[67]

The incorporation of real and fictional correspondence was a
familiar stylistic technique in the eighteenth-century magazine, and
this at least partially explains Murray's emphasis on readers' letters
in her own columns. But Murray also includes these letters to emphasize the topic central to her work, which is the analogy between
social, textual, and monetary economies. More than perhaps any
other genre, correspondence emphasizes writing as an exchange: the
letter writer provides a text to her recipient and she immediately is
owed a letter, but as soon as her correspondent replies, the original
writer assumes the position of debtor. This is why so many letters
begin with a reckoning of who owes what to whom, castigating the
other for either failing to write enough or for writing too much,
thereby disturbing the equilibrium that is the ostensible ideal of any
given correspondence.[68] When the Gleaner apologizes to his audience for his delayed responses, he makes it clear that this basic
economic structure characterizes public letters as much as it does
private ones, and Murray's emphasis on correspondence in the
Gleaner essays signals her overarching argument that both textual
and monetary relations necessarily involve debt and deferral. For
this reason, although critics have tended to see Murray's incorporation

of correspondence into her columns as testifying to her desire to use the *Massachusetts Magazine* as the space to model a participatory democracy, such a reading does not recognize the fundamentally agonistic relationship that exists between the writer and readers.[69] Nor does Murray depict this conflict as something to resolve, but instead as evidence of the dependencies that exist within the literary marketplace. "Stories," the Gleaner writes, "seem naturally to produce or grow out of each other" (474), indicating the generative economy of this textual model.

But Murray also acknowledges that the productive capacity of credit networks poses considerable risks and conflicts. The Gleaner himself is rather dissatisfied with what his own consumers bring to their side of the exchange, expressing annoyance that his readers' focus is almost entirely on uncovering his identity and not on the quality of the textual products in question. "[T]his hunting after names," he opines, is "descriptive of the frivolity of the human mind" (105). Even more damning, he believes this obsession with ascertaining the identity of the anonymous author confirms his readers as both poor consumers and businesspeople: "The business of the reader is to scan the *intrinsic value* and *general tendency* of the composition; if that is considerable...he ought to leave the author to announce himself under what auspices he shall judge proper" (105). Here, however, he lambastes his readers for abiding by the very logic of the market: for passing judgment not on the basis of his work's "real" worth, but only on the reputation of the supposed author. Nevertheless, when he overhears another group of critics who do estimate the value of his products without attention to his name, he is disheartened by their unceremonious rejection of his essays. One of these readers makes the economic resonances of her appraisal quite clear, judging "his essays in general much *below a mediocrity*...depreciated as rapidly as the paper currency of insolvent memory" (105–6). This critic, then, does judge the "intrinsic value" of the Gleaner's paper goods, and she finds them as worthless as the depreciated bills of exchange that funded the Revolutionary War. Her dismissal offers a timely reminder to the Gleaner that the value of his produce is determined not primarily by his labor and talent, but by those who credit and consume it. As if in response to this realization, the Gleaner's next column provides an installment of Margaretta's tale, recognizing that value is secured when he supplies his readers' demands. He repays his debt to readers by describing the birth of Margaretta's first child, but he also takes out another loan, promising his readers: "if thy acquaintance with me continuest, we will occasionally peep in upon her, and thus learn, from time to time, how matters go on" (113). The Gleaner thus negotiates a contract in which his audience must continue to accept his depreciated essays so as to receive in the future the product they covet. If they abide by the promissory notes of his "mediocr[e]" essays, they will be rewarded with stories of Margaretta (106).

Of course, while his readers come to remarkable consensus in clamoring for Margaretta, their respective investments in her story are very different. While one young female reader begs the Gleaner to "let us know something of her dress, and if she wears a head as high as Miss Sycamore" (55–56), adult readers entreat the Gleaner to use Margaretta as a moral exemplum for their daughters. The Gleaner abides by a wish from one reader, Mrs. Aimwell, that he provide educational essays, and for several months his column transcribes the pedagogical letters Margaretta's mother writes her daughter. When the Gleaner finally stops providing this veritable correspondence course, he apologizes to other consumers, "Possibly, the number of letters, which my solicitude to comply with the wishes of Mrs. Aimwell hath engaged me to furnish, may not have been in unison with the feelings of the generality of my readers" (444). In giving expression to this incessant negotiation between the constituents of this textual marketplace, Murray reveals her keen understanding that even as the market may seem to speak with one voice, it is necessarily composed of individual participants whose investments do not necessarily align.

As Jennifer Baker argues, Murray clearly understood credit and debt as a necessary entailment of modern life.[70] And there is considerable biographical justification for this conviction, since we know that Murray's first husband was a perpetually insolvent merchant. Attempting to restore his ruined credit, her husband traveled to the West Indies trying to build up a storehouse of goods to sell, but he instead died in a St. Eustatius jail for outstanding debts to new creditors. In the aftermath of his death, Murray was responsible for payment to her husband's numerous creditors.[71] Murray thus had first-hand knowledge of the ways that financial attachments, like debt, transcend corporeality: long after the person of her husband was gone, she was affected by his imbrications in a wide net of financial dealings. Unlike Jefferson, who responded to the interpersonal hauntings of debt by crafting the metonymic "generation" that could be neatly excised from the social fabric, Murray tells the stories of the debt's multifarious effects. Baker argues that Murray comprehended this interdependent structure of debt in terms of sympathetic attachments: that she vindicated a credit economy by detailing the affective relations that linked economic participants together. Certainly such affective and financial attachments are portrayed throughout the Gleaner: when Margaretta's husband is financially ruined, he turns to his father-in-law for assistance, and numerous sketches describe parents who manage their children's future so that they might avoid ruin. Baker focuses her analysis on Murray's play, *Virtue Triumphant*, included in the book version of *The Gleaner*, which also portrays its characters as entangled through financial borrowing. And in many of these cases, individuals are willing to lend money not from a profit motive, but because their sympathetic nature leads them to want to restore another's financial rectitude. Thus Baker argues that Murray advocates on behalf of credit because the extension of credit, confidence, and faith testify to generosity and philanthropy.

While this account of Murray's argument on behalf of a credit economy is not wrong, it does neglect a crucial slippage between charity and credit on which Murray herself focuses. While *Virtue Triumphant* makes manifest the analogy between affectionate relations and pecuniary ones insofar as its plot revolves around a marriage between a wealthy gentleman and an unpropertied young woman, it does not efface the differences between social and monetary relations. For example, when one insolvent character turns to his aunt for money, she provides her nephew the loan, but not from her own capital reserves. She explains that instead of selling her own bank stocks, she will borrow the necessary funds from a wealthy friend who provides them, insisting the loan is a "mere bagatelle," which she should "never mention" (562). At first glance, this fiscal arrangement appears to be based on intimacy and affection: the nephew borrows from his aunt, who borrows from a friend, who fashions the credit as courtesy. Their fiscal intercourse looks like transactions of the heart and not the pocket. And yet, the aunt later also tells her nephew that she has "procured the money on common interest" (562). As such, while her creditor may characterize the loan as a "mere bagatelle," Murray's text makes it clear that it is an advance for which she must pay interest. And the aunt is an equally ambiguous creditor: when her nephew tells her that his "obligations are unreturnable," she calls the loan merely a "common action" and declares that if the monies help his "convenience," then her "reward will be more than proportioned to my merit!" (563). But insofar as her nephew is obliged to repay the loan lest his aunt be in arrears to her own creditor, her "reward" cannot consist only of his pleasure. Moreover, given that his aunt has decided to borrow under "common interest" instead of selling her own bank shares, we can presume she made a calculated decision as to which was the fiscally more prudent strategy. As such, for all the ways that the participants in this highly mediated debt structure tender their affair as one based on sentimental bonds, Murray makes it patently clear that they also owe money in addition to affection.[72]

Rather than seeing Murray's text as using sentiment to compensate for the alienations of the marketplace, we should instead understand the play as demonstrating once again Murray's attempt to formalize these alienated relations. This formal strategy is evidenced in part because of the play's own meandering plot. Murray identifies this rambling quality as a defect in the introduction to the play, which records a sarcastic remark by earlier audiences that her play might be improved if someone had "the goodness to bestow on the paltry production…nothing more nor less than a plot!" (544). Murray's emphasis on the play's discontinuities is also signaled by the way she incorporates the text of the drama into the book volume of *The Gleaner*. The play had existed as an independent work and was performed by the Federal Street Theater in Boston under the title *The Medium*. Because it was a complete text, we might expect Murray to include it as a separate work in *The Gleaner*. But Murray instead frames the play as a gift made to the Gleaner by a correspondent, "Philo Americanus," who announces that his donation should be included in the Gleaner's heterogeneous array of literary goods: "Your work is confessedly a Miscellany; and, as there can be no impropriety in your admitting, among the variety it contains, dramatic performance, you may probably find it convenient to give it a regular continuation through the numbers of the Gleaner" (545). Murray further emphasizes the disjointed quality of the drama by literally publishing it "through the numbers of the Gleaner," dividing the play into shorter numbered essays. We read the play as "Letters 70-75," and therefore with the sense that it is a textual product that has been trafficked through numerous hands. And so, even though Murray chooses a title (*Virtue Triumphant*) and a marriage plot characteristic of didactic and sentimental fiction, she disseminates it to us through the medium of the periodical essay that necessarily rewires the economy of sentiment we associate with the novel.

If, as Joseph Fichtelberg has so nicely phrased it, sentimental fiction is constructed to "render[] Adam Smith's 'immense and infinite system' in comforting human terms" then Murray's text has the opposite effect.[73] Her work gives constant expression to this "immense and infinite system," but not so as to make it more comforting. The one-hundred texts that constitute the Gleaner's work are not arranged to mollify or manage the reader's terrible recognition that they are a merely a tiny gear in the engine of global capitalism. Instead they consistently highlight how the various textual goods the Gleaner brings to his readers are themselves the products of numerous other people, themselves linked to countless other communities of production and distribution. Murray's chosen literary vehicle reveals a commercial system that is composed of individuals and yet so extensive as to dwarf the significance of these individuals. The Gleaner himself acknowledges this worldview:

> Man is a limited being [and] his movements are circumscribed within narrow bounds; his eye can take in, at a single view, but a small portion of our world: If he would transport himself from place to place, his progress, impeded by a variety of incumbrances, must be gradual; and if he could traverse the globe, he must devote to the arduous enterprise the revolution of many succeeding months. Every individual is necessarily descended from a particular family. (690)

Murray here gives expression to the cognitive and affective limits of individual human bodies, of our "narrow bounds," in comparison to the transcendent vision of the "Deity" who can "at a single glance" see "the universe outspread before him" (690). Murray's Gleaner can see more because, as periodical essayist, he is not confined by eyes or limbs. But he cannot see "at a single glance," nor can he convey what he sees outside of narrative time. Far from transcending the minutiae that makes up the commercial world, the Gleaner tries to offer partial expression to it. Murray's periodical essayist provides something like a bird's-eye perspective that also descends into random individual lives so as to briefly capture the local attachments that bind the multitude.

By emphasizing the Gleaner's own writing as entailing the credit of his readers, Murray imagines her own author as caught within this reticular structure. This enmeshment becomes a crucial topic when the Gleaner recounts the financial travails of Margaretta's merchant husband, pointedly named Hamilton. Although the Gleaner never specifies precisely how Hamilton loses his fortune, readers would likely have assumed that he was damaged by the same events that were hurting many United States merchants, namely the increasing tendency of British privateers to seize the cargo of American ships en route to one of the French colony islands in the West Indies. Boston newspapers from the Spring of 1794 were filled with stories of such seizures.[74] Murray gives expression to this economic catastrophe in the Gleaner's column for April 1794, which describes the "melancholy pause, and extreme dejection which…pervades every order of citizens," a destitution that reverses the economic prosperity that had characterized the previous years in which "our navigation is extensive" and "our commerce, wafted by the breezy gale, hath accumulated riches upon the far distant shore" (207).

The Gleaner does not, however, focus on the "deranged state of Mr. Hamilton's affairs" caused by these seizures, and instead meditates on the peripheral consequences for himself. The Gleaner has become so "much occupied and greatly exercised" that he has lost his ability to choose his own literary topics and is no longer "at liberty to pursue…[his] accustomed avocations" (175). Because of this discomfiture, he is forced to "substitute" the topic on which he "intended to expatiate" with a reproduction of "a folded paper I lately picked up," which contained an insipid prose "eulogy" to the month of December. The Gleaner thus brings his own readers into the disrupted supply circuit: because American trade has been interrupted, a man has been ruined, and this man's failure has caused the Gleaner to fail to produce original work, forcing his own readers to have to settle for a discarded essay. And lest we imagine that in recirculating this found document, the Gleaner is attempting to demonstrate his capacity for efficiency, Murray instead draws our attention to the profligacy of the text. Like all the Gleaner entries, it begins with a poetic epigraph, but in this case an especially long one comprising sixteen heroic couplets, the argument of which merely repeats the text of the "folded paper" that the Gleaner has purportedly discovered. Both poem and prose describe the cold harshness of December with its "hoary" winds, before realizing that because it is the month in which Jesus was born, it becomes (according to the poet) the "blest harbinger of light" or (as the prose writer writes) a "blest period, most illustrious in the order of time" (175, 177). By merely offering a paraphrase of the poem, the gleaned text exemplifies an especially inefficient textual economy: two texts perform the work of one.

This profligate essay illuminates the ambitious project in which Murray is engaged. While she follows the conventional agenda of the periodical essayist, which is to "promote ... the interests of rectitude" (807), she also demands that her readers see themselves as making ethical, aesthetic, and financial decisions that have far-ranging consequences and whose own decisions are themselves affected by countless other remote agents and actions. The Gleaner writes, "The world is a vast, an ample theatre, and its inhabitants are an audience to each other—we are alternately actors and spectators" (491). Yet the Gleaner also registers his displeasure at the perils of this structured dependency. He must circulate the worthless essay because the financial collapse of his daughter's husband has affected his own productivity. Similarly, he must provide the Margaretta story because his audience demands it. While the periodical essayist may position himself as a man of leisure, at liberty to discourse on what he pleases, Murray's work routinely belies this fantasy of autonomy.

Given the emphasis on debt throughout these essays, we might anticipate that Murray would make some explicit reference to the subject of public debt that was so central to political disputes throughout the 1790s. She does allude to the controversy when the Gleaner chides those citizens who "never see a tax-bill, or attend to the requisitions of government" without complaining that such "exorbitant demands" far exceeded the British demands that yielded the Revolution (29). This critique is to be expected since Murray was aligned with the Federalist party, dedicating her book to President John Adams in 1798; but the terms by which the Gleaner criticizes the opponents of the excise tax are notable. The protestation against taxation is motivated by a "fond predilection for ... the ancients" (34) and not premised on sound economic or political policy. This assertation that opponents of Hamilton's financial proposals are old-fashioned echoes the familiar critique of Jeffersonian economic policy, but the Gleaner further suggests that this "predilection" for the old is also associated with "local affection," a preference for the location of one's birth and childhood. By contrast, the Gleaner declares his own project as devoted to digressive trespass: "quitting a field, in which the Gleaner had not intended at this time to have wandered, I proceed to say...that all things are in a state of progression...[and] that at no period since the lapse of Adam, was the world in so high a state of improvement as it is at this very instant" (34).[75] Through the persona of her meandering Gleaner, Murray explains a fundamental paradox of modern economic life: there is no private property without trespass and debt.

## Scribbling with Charles Brockden Brown

Like those of Freneau and Murray, Charles Brockden Brown's career was shaped by his participation in magazine culture. Indeed, his first prose publication was in the pages of *The Columbian Magazine* where he wrote as "The Rhapsodist" in 1789. While Brown's novelistic production occupies only a fraction of his abbreviated literary career (all six of his novels were published in a four-year period), he writes as a periodical essayist throughout his life, beginning as "The Rhapsodist" and concluding as "The Scribbler" in 1809, a year before his death. Even during his most prolific period of novel composition, he continues to publish as a periodical essayist. But critics have largely approached Brown's work in this genre as secondary since it is his novels that are celebrated as pioneering examples of the transparent narration and psychological realism that eventually became the hallmark of novelistic fiction. But although many of Brown's novels accommodate our modern taste for individual characters at the center of their limited world (consider Clara Wieland, Edgar Huntly, Arthur Mervyn), Brown also strives to represent the intersections of manifold characters and plots as if to capture, however inadequately, the limitless horizon of modernity and its multiplicity of possible worlds. Indeed it is this scattershot approach that so often is responsible for the pejorative judgments of Brown's style as haphazard and chaotic. This tendency towards diffusive narrative is inextricably linked to Brown's attempts to represent the large-scale and highly mediated systems that defined modern life in 1790s Philadelphia. And so we see the paradoxical morphology of Brown's writing, which simultaneously constructs the individual as a totality with which to organize meaning while also subsuming this individual in a narrative structure that rigorously refuses to end. The second of these projects will be my focus in this section, which will study Brown's work as a periodical essayist as a counterpoint to his novelistic writing. Like Murray, Brown suggests that there may be better ways to represent a world characterized by economic interdependence than either the bildungsroman or the sentimental novel.

We see Brown's interest in social entailments in his very first Rhapsodist essay, which opens with a recognition that to enter the world of print is to engage in a dependent relationship with others. In submitting his essay to the public, the Rhapsodist concedes that he has "voluntarily parted with his ancient liberty and becom[e] the general vassal."[76] Characterizing writing as a contract that costs him "freedom," he also establishes the relationship as feudal. Brown's periodical essayist is therefore not the desultory man of leisure frequenting coffee shops and public streets but a vassal "slave." Willing to concede his loss of autonomy, the Rhapsodist seems therefore reluctant to depict his entrance into the magazine in terms of a commercial economy. He distinguishes his writerly ambitions, which he hopes will be immune from the contamination of the market, from those of his fellow essayist, The Retailer, whose popular series was located in the same magazine—a pseudonym the Rhapsodist declares to be necessarily associated with a "despicable idea."[77] As Jared Gardner notes, the Rhapsodist thus presents himself to his audience in precisely the way that Brown would be "celebrated for generations... [as] the ideal romantic man of genius in a culturally threadbare world of merchants and clerks."[78]

But even as the Rhapsodist establishes himself as antithetical to the commercial economy that is paradoxically epitomized by his chosen medium (magazine) and genre (periodical essay), he cannot help but give expression to his imbrication in its fabric. As Gardner observes, although critics have largely accepted this portrait of the Rhapsodist as romantic hermit at face value, Brown encourages a different reading.[79] After all, the Rhapsodist admits that ever since he abandoned his refuge "on the solitary banks of the Ohio" for the "thronged streets" of Philadelphia, he is "little more than a Rhapsodist in theory."[80] While he frames this theoretical turn as a deterioration, stating that only in his rural enclave could he write as he ought—with "purity and vigour," he also gives us some hints as to the products he generated from this place where the "joys of social life were scarcely known."[81] We learn, for example, that he occupied his time incessantly babbling to himself in a "language unintelligible," and so the "purity" of his expression is defined by its incommunicability. In this way, the Rhapsodist points to a fundamental contradiction between his purported desire for social isolation and his vocation as periodical essayist. The same contradiction is expressed when he tells his readers that he is an "enemy to conversation," but nonetheless "derives half of the materials of his thoughts from intimate acquaintance with the world."[82] Here he admits that his literary product depends on the stock of others, and so he is much nearer to the Retailer in occupation than he would care to admit.

The contradiction between the Rhapsodist's proclaimed fondness for social isolation and his literary practice is so apparent that it seems we should read the entire series ironically. What does it mean for our Addisonian essayist to tell us that were "he not compelled...he would withdraw himself entirely from the commerce of the world"?[83] The irony becomes more obvious when our essayist turns his column over to another correspondent. Confessing that the decision is a "flagrant violation of these established rules by which I regulate my conduct," he nonetheless relinquishes his own column to "print" a letter from a reader rebuking the Rhapsodist for his insincerity and subterfuge. In so doing, Brown's essayist literally enacts the conditions of what he declares as his limited "sovereignty over my own person and actions."[84] Here, then, in one of his earliest texts, Brown portrays some of the central tensions that will inform the financial disputes of the 1790s: an individual wants simultaneously to renounce and embrace a commercial economy, and she will do so by asserting economic autonomy even as the material conditions of both labor and produce reveal her to be entangled in the market. Even the chosen title signals Brown's emphasis on this socio-economic imbrication and not isolation. While the word "Rhapsodist" no doubt conveys an emotional interiority and individual expression, its etymology suggests something else. The word derives from the Greek, *rhaptein* (to stitch) and *oide* (song): and thus the Rhapsodist is one who stitches or sutures songs (a rhapsode is a person who recites epic poems). Despite then all the pretenses towards solitude, Brown's Rhapsodist, like Freneau's Weaver and Murray's Gleaner, cannot help but express how deeply interwoven he is into a broad social tapestry, a pervasive theme in all of Brown's work.

Brown returns to the theme ten years later in his longer periodical series, "The Man at Home," where he renders his essayist in exactly the same fashion as he had depicted his early Rhapsodist: as both isolated individual and voluble correspondent. The Man at Home initiates his correspondence with a disregard for audience to which Brown draws our attention through the exaggerated use of the first-person pronoun, "I." The first essay begins:

> I know not whether my pen will afford me any amusement in my present condition. I have been little accustomed to the use of it, but I have nothing else to do....I am without books....I have...no alternative....I cannot consent to pass a life of inactivity. But what shall I write?[85]

By opening the series with a singular concern for his own pleasure, Brown's essayist defies the standard decorum and practice of the periodical essayist, which is to be solicitous of the reader's desires. The Man at Home instead represents himself as fully in command of his authorial and financial destiny, and his narrative begins to follow the basic pattern of an economic bildungsroman. He details his commitment to cautious and "moderate" economic development, explaining that his investment strategy was always to invest a "little property in funds, which appeared to me safest and most productive." He describes his economic status as lying in that perfect middle-class equipoise between not needing "to borrow, and...not rich enough to lend" (1).

His financial independence, however, is ruptured before the series even begins as he tells the story of how a former business partner inveigled him into endorsing several promissory notes. When this man defaults, the Man at Home becomes financially responsible for the debt, an amount so large it would consume his entire fortune. In the face of this bankruptcy, he refuses his obligation: he will neither pay the debt nor submit to the law that would imprison him for default. He has instead exiled himself "at home," the space from which he writes the essays. The essay series thus expresses exactly the same tension as did Brown's earlier Rhapsodist, between a fantasy of economic autonomy and recognition of social ecology. But the terms by which Brown considers this dynamic are very different than we might suppose. Brown's tale of economic distress seems to offer the conventional setup for a lecture about the prudence of fiscal solvency, autonomy, and responsibility. When, in recollecting his partner's request for endorsement, the essayist asks, "Should I superscribe or not?" readers would rightly anticipate cautionary stories explicating why his decision to endorse the notes was fatally flawed or detailing his moral responsibility to repay.

This is not, however, the way the story goes. Instead, the Man at Home confirms the soundness of his original calculation to supply the loan. Because his old partner was a successful merchant who was in possession of real capital and not merely "floating planks," and because he had a reputation of "integrity" and "punctuality," he had every reason to believe his partner was a reliable risk (2). Even more crucially, he insists there is no way to avoid the kind of hazard he encountered in his decision to endorse. Even though the Man at Home describes himself as a "safe" man, he also asserts the potential dangers of any choice:

> We must, in the business of human life, confide in foregoing calcula-
> tions. We must act on the supposition that events will come. We
> cannot postpone our resolutions till they have actually arrived    (2).

What he articulates here in some ways is entirely self-evident: we base our decisions on a past that we know and a future about which we can only guess. We cannot avoid this kind of speculative calcula-tion because to do so would be to escape time. The passage also offers a remarkably plain statement about the inevitable contingencies entailed in the "business of human life"—one that absolutely contra-dicts the moralistic imperative we expect to find in stories of finan-cial ruin. The Man at Home is not extolling the virtues of fiscal autonomy or charity; he is not advocating for the cautious practice of risk management or for the advantages that might come from risky speculations. His task is to explain how he arrived at his present po-sition "at home" by locating this event as the consequence of a series of earlier episodes. And he will not characterize these earlier actions as inevitable or regrettable since they could not be made with fore-knowledge of their effects; additionally, each of these "causes" was itself a consequence of an earlier action that abides by the same rules of contingency. Admitting that any series of events occurs in chrono-logical progression, the Man at Home also explains that we cannot trace their causality. Because "we cannot postpone our resolutions till they have actually arrived," the business of human life is necessar-ily speculative, its causes and effects forever just out of reach.

With hindsight he might believe that his decision to aid his former business partner caused his insolvency, but this causality is only circumstantial and only known after-the fact, or by experience. The essayist's logic roughly follows David Hume's analysis in that he posits cause and effect as entirely discrete events. Indeed he even seems to echo Hume's example of the billiard balls. Hume writes, "When I see... a billiard ball moving in a straight line towards another; even suppose motion in the second ball should by accident be suggested to me, as the result of their contact or impulse; may I not conceive, that a hundred different events might as well follow from the cause?"[86] Hume turns to the billiard ball because humans are only willing to accept that "experience" is required to ascertain cause and effect when contemplating "an intricate machinery or secret structure of parts." By contrast, when we look at "the simple qualities of objects," like, for example, billiard balls, "[w]e are apt to imagine that we could discover these effects... without experience."[87] To assert that the Man at Home should not have endorsed the note would also be to presume that economic causality is simple: that, in the absence of experience, it would be easy to calculate the effects of endorsing the note. The Man at Home understands that his decision to enter into a financial relationship is proximate to his insolvency; he also insists that such causes "may be equally asserted on a thousand other occasions" (2). As evidence, the essayist describes his biweekly visits to the market in the winter in which he always opts to venture the "sunny side of the way," even as this path takes him under hanging scaffolds. He takes this risk, he says, because the benefits of a warmer journey outweigh the dangers of an accident in which a brick might strike him on the head, and because any number of events are possible regardless of which side of the street he chooses. In the case of his endorsement of his partner's notes, his decision becomes serially linked to his present predicament: "the period elapsed, my friend was incapable of making good his engagements, the law has been resorted to, and a writ is issued for arresting me" (3). But this does not controvert the grounds on which he made his decision: there are, after all, many other actions that are temporally proximate to his present predicament. He offers the story of his debt not in order to locate the original cause of his location in the lodging house but because this is the contiguous serial event that most recently preceded his present position.

As if to emphasize the inadequacy of one narrative plot to capture the various episodes that brings The Man at Home to his predicament, the essayist turns his pen to topics that seem to bear no relationship to his economic circumstance. It is not until the very last essay in the series when the sheriff summons him to debtor's prison that his refusal to repay once again becomes important. The twelve intervening essays instead consist of multiple narrative lines about characters who are only tangentially connected to the essayist's own story of debt and imprisonment. His essays take us across the globe and include the history of his landlady recounting her childhood in Ireland, the story of her original employer and his immigration to Philadelphia, the biographies of the previous occupants of his room, including a French émigré from Santo Domingo and his daughter, a meditation on the factional conflict of the regions of southern Italy through a recollection of two friends, a portrait of the devastation of Philadelphia by yellow fever epidemic, etc. The Man at Home's experience is thus much like that of the Rhapsodist whose introspective essays were hijacked by his correspondent: despite his isolated setting and solipsistic imperative, he does not long remain the focus of his own letters.

Brown instead emphasizes the weave of intersecting tales by spinning several of his stories from his essayist's meditations on the physical objects that he finds in his small twelve-square-foot room: an "old and feeble" pine table, a bed, a chair, and a chest. Interrogating the history of the table allows him, for example, to speculate on table's past: "What pity that it cannot tell tales!" (66) he exclaims. But he nonetheless indulges the conceit and imagines the table was "wrested" from its previous owner from "pressure of necessity, or claim of a landlord" (66). Further supposing that his own landlady, Kate, had cheaply purchased the table at some "constable's sale," he makes the rather remarkable assertion that since he had earlier loaned her money to help capitalize her boardinghouse business, "It follows then that the table is my property" (66). His claim, of course, has no legal justification since the terms of his original loan to Kate have been completed; moreover, he has already admitted that all his property is held in arrears for his endorsed note. His imaginative appropriation of the table, thus, epitomizes his pretensions at economic autonomy even when absolutely contradicted by his own encounters in the market. He believes he can escape his financial obligations by squirreling himself away in the tiny room, but he simultaneously asserts that his own loan is inalienable. After all, he is not claiming he owns the table through squatter's rights, which would suggest that his possession is a consequence of his occupation of the room in which it sits; rather, his claim is based on the assumption that he has rights to everything that his money purchased, even when he was not party to the transaction. His letters however, belie the very assertion he makes, since he is indebted to Kate not only for the home but also the substance of his own essays, since her story and property become the primary subjects of the series.

Something similar happens when he focuses his gaze on the locked chest in his room, a rumination that extends over several essays.[88] He begins with a romance, dreaming that the chest might be filled with "English guineas, or Mexican dollars" (66) that could provide his economic rescue. Although he has earlier acknowledged that "the property contained in [the chest] may be [Kate's]," once he contemplates the possibility it could hold gold bullion, the essayist again imaginatively appropriate its contents: "here am I on the verge of poverty, and in danger of a gaol, yet thousands are within my reach" (67). But he cannot maintain possession over his own fantasy let alone the contents of the chest, as his meditation is interrupted by a flood of other speculative possibilities. He cannot stop thinking about the likelihood that an earlier occupant might have already discovered and taken the hidden treasure, and then this meditation is diverted by imagining the stories that might have been invented to explain and justify the newfound wealth of these earlier tenants. The essayist is practically overwhelmed by the infinite number of stories surrounding the chest. To his question, "What may be here concealed?" he rhapsodizes, "A man may exhaust the whole catalogue of his conjectures, and yet be wrong" (66). As if suddenly recognizing that in trying to follow the various hands in which the imaginary coins have been passed, he has lost his claim to their contents, he rewinds his plot, asserting that he is in full command of his "train of reflections" (100). He also tries to restore himself as the protagonist of his tale by recollecting his own adventures as a supercargo that led to a longtime stay on Île Amsterdam. The narrative here gives us every indication of becoming a Robinsonnade, as the Man at Home describes his tendency towards a "certain romantic adventuresomeness" that leads him to the "sterile and desolate spot" from which he hopes to make a fortune by hunting seals and selling their skins.[89] But instead of pursuing this narrative path, the essayist abruptly returns his story to the lodging house and tales that might "spring from this chest" (100).[90]

Just as Brown's essayist earlier expressed the impossibility of calculating causality, so too here does he stress the infinite magnitude of possible stories that might be teased out from his locked box: "The world of conjecture is without limits. To speculate on the possible and the future, is no ineligible occupation" (101). Reiterating his earlier claim that in the "business of human life," we must "confide in foregoing calculations" and also "act on the supposition that events will come" (2), the essayist embraces contingency as a speculative enterprise. It is, moreover, an endeavor that provides considerable pleasure: "Me thinks," the Man at Home muses, "I could sit here, occasionally glancing at [the box], and find employment for years, for my mind and pen, in revolving and recording the ideas which it furnishes" (101). Brown also makes it patent that he associates his essayist's mental exercise—in which, from the confines of his tiny room, he can "ransack[] every corner of the world"—with his own work as periodical essayist when he labels these imaginative excursions as a "new series" (101). The term "series" self-consciously identifies the periodical essayist's work as a series delivered in successive installments. The term also calls attention to Brown's insistent stress that the "business of life" can only be conceived as a chain of actions that interconnects with the aggregate material surrounding any one object or person. The essays do not emphasize the integrity of the individual stories that orient themselves around the man, his debts, his table, his landlady, or his box, instead focusing on the fact that they are serially stitched to another.

Not surprisingly, the essayist uses economic language to describe these serial connections. As we have seen, the Man at Home is indebted to Kate not only for providing him his asylum from debtor's prison but also for generating material from which he can produce his speculative fantasies about the box. And so, despite the intimation that he is something like an imaginative alchemist conjuring his infinite stories from his inexhaustible mental store, he cannot help but credit his landlady. He sends her out to ask questions about the room's earlier tenants, and then expresses gratitude that she returns able to "to retail[] to me all that she could glean" (101). His use of the term "retail" highlights the intrinsic relationship in all periodical essays between storytelling (retelling) and selling (retailing). The words are, in fact, etymologically linked. To describe selling, the word originates in the fourteenth century, from French, *retailler* (to cut or clip), referring to the ways goods would be cut or clipped to sell again. To describe retelling, the word has a later origin (the first OED entry is 1597 from Shakespeare's *Richard III*) and likely derives from Old Saxon, *talon* (to reckon or enumerate). Brown chooses "retail" to capture both meanings, thereby conveying that his essayist is as deeply enmeshed in a world of narrative retail as any reader of the *Weekly Magazine*. Brown also uses the term "gleaning" to describe Kate's narrative collection, thereby self-consciously associating his Man at Home series to Murray's earlier series. And like Murray, although the use of the term "glean" seems to invoke a non-commercial and agrarian economy, this extra-economic fantasy is ruptured almost immediately since, even if we accept the premise that Kate is harvesting stories that no one else wants, she is not herself consuming them but "retailing" them back to our essayist, who likewise retails them to his readers in the form of the magazine. As such, we must understand Kate as something like a middleman or wholesaler in a longer supply chain into which we are also bound.

This supply chain is the real subject of Brown's series. Its links are constructed out of manifold connections: causal (one thing is temporally proximate to another), categorical (one thing is like or unlike another), and associative (one thing engages another). They involve any number of attachments: economic, affectionate, casual, voyeuristic. But in all cases, Brown's essayist means to retail them, to recount "the slender contingencies on which the momentous revolutions in human life depend" (136). Late in his series, for example, we are introduced to a new stock of characters, including a young man, Wallace, who has survived the 1793 Philadelphia yellow fever epidemic. While in the aggregate, the fever killed many, Wallace announces that the epidemic "was, to me, the most fortunate event that could have happened" (322). Before the fever, he was a poor and indebted shopkeeper, but because he left Philadelphia early, he not only was spared the ravages of the disease but fortuitously was able to meet "a young lady, who added three hundred pounds a year" to his fortune (322). For Wallace, "A lovely wife, a plentiful fortune, health, and leisure are the ingredients of my present lot, and for all these am I indebted to the Yellow Fever" (323).

We could read this response as indicating narrow self-interest—that we are meant to critique Wallace for valuing his own fortune above those of his fellow Philadelphians. This moral is not, I would suggest, Brown's primary agenda. The letter begins with the essayist posing a rhetorical question, "What a series of calamities is the thread of human existence" (320), a formulation that echoes the earlier statement about "the slender contingencies on which the momentous revolutions in human life depend," reframing "revolutions" as "calamities." In the recognition of these threads that interweave human lives together, the essayist remarks, some people are "driven to suicide": "They employed their imagination in running over the catalogue of human woes, and were so affected by the spectacle, that they willingly resorted to death to shut it from their view" (320). Most people, the essayist continues, are not driven to self-destruction but rather are "generally prone...when objects chance to present to us their gloomy side, to change their position, till we hit upon the brightest of its aspects" (320). It is in this context that we are asked to read Wallace's evaluation of the yellow fever epidemic. His selfish perspective illustrates a cognitive, rather than moral, incapacity. In the face of "slender contingences," he will identify the fever as the *singular* cause of his own "momentous revolution." He is simply unable to contemplate complex causality. And in the face of other people's suffering, he will tell a story that excises himself from the global consequences of the fever. Instead of considering the various agents to whom he owed money before the disease devastated the city, he declares himself only "indebted" to the fever which provided his insulated domestic economy: "[a] lovely wife, a plentiful fortune, health, and leisure." Although his position is decidedly less pleasant, Brown's essayist begins with a similar narrative gambit—holing himself up in his tiny room, he abdicates his responsibilities for any financial and social debts. His essays, however, ultimately belie his assumed autonomy: they disprove the simplistic causality that allows Wallace, for example, to treat the yellow fever as a clear social benefit. Brown uses the periodical essay to showcase how the individual tale cannot be seamlessly extricated from a broader social fabric. Which is not to say, that the essayist wants to describe the yellow fever as an unalloyed evil: part of the reason he provides Wallace's story is to reveal the positive consequences that could also grow from the epidemic. The periodical series is thus designed to show the infinite scale of consequences that descend from even the most horrible of calamities.

This same imperative to represent systemic interdependence also explains, at least in part, what Brown saw as so difficult and dynamic about the epistolary form. While narrative renders a world plotted around the unified subject position of a protagonist, epistolary writing provides a series of exchanged retellings. It emphasizes not only *what* is told, but the formal reticulation that links writers and readers together. As Deirdre Lynch notes, despite the claims that epistolary fiction allowed access to "the otherwise hidden psychology of characters," the "action" in epistolary writing "pivots on the mediation of characters in the semiological sense of the term."[91] Brown tries out the shared affordances of the epistolary mode and periodical essay in his "Series of Original Letters," which he begins to publish simultaneously with the conclusion of "The Man at Home." Brown offers what appears at first to be a conventional epistolary novel consisting of letters between a young man, Henry, and his sister, Mary. The language of their letters is novelistic in its emotional volatility. Henry describes his extreme melancholy and "growing regrets," accusing his sister of gloomy solitude. She, in turn, rebukes her brother for his emotional outbursts. But despite all these expressions of intimacy that seem to lay the ground for a romance plot, the letters are decidedly not introspective. They instead tell stories about the cast of characters that Henry finds in his new boarding house: about Mary's recent birthday party and the relative merits of practicing law. And after several installments, the series abruptly concludes. Brown writes an epistolary fiction that articulates no plot and that provides no rationale for the sequence of events and characters described. In so doing, he reveals how each letter writer is embedded in other social systems of which this correspondence is only one node. Brown's abrupt conclusion and the introduction to minor characters about which we have no obvious reason to care allow Brown to highlight the necessary limitations of fiction to represent the broadloom of social intercourse.

It is almost as if Brown is using this fragment to reveal what Alex Woloch describes as a "jost[ling]" for space that is essential to the "character-system," or the "arrangement of multiple and differentiated character-spaces...into a unified narrative."[92] Woloch depicts the author as negotiating economies of scarcity: novelists cannot adequately represent "the interior life of a singular consciousness" while simultaneously "casting a wide narrative gaze over a complex social universe."[93] According to Woloch, this scarcity becomes a crucial problem for the realist novelist for whom the imperative was to represent both psychological and social systems. But we can see this negotiation at work much earlier in Brown's fictional projects, which are designed to showcase the necessary costs the protagonist bears when the author casts his "narrative gaze over a complex social universe." In both "The Man at Home" and "Original Letters" series, Brown gives us every indication that his plots will orient themselves around protagonists—the fiscally insolvent "Man" and the emotionally overwrought siblings. Instead, however, he turns his pen to the plotlines of numerous minor characters, and their tales are not limited to their convergence with those of the purported protagonists. In the jockeying for narrative space, these minor characters prevail and our major characters become the satellites. In this way, Brown uses both the epistolary and periodical forms to reproduce the broad scale and density of the social world, but also to register the limitations of any plot to represent adequately the complex matrix of this world. As Roland Barthes puts it, "There would always be a corner, a detail, an inflection of space or color to report."[94]

Brown thus clearly conceives of these periodical essay series as engaged in a different kind of representational project than that which we typically associate with the novel. We expect the domestic novel to provide us with a cast of characters (some major and some minor) whose actions, thoughts, and responses are sequenced in time and place. We will know if someone is a major character because the plot will be arranged around their person: their perspective will organize the sequence of actions, and it will be through their lens that causality will be judged. This is not Brown's project, which instead offers us a form of world building, a term I take from science fiction where it is used to reference the requirement that authors invent the species, landmasses, technologies, languages, customs, institutions, and all the other stuff that composes their speculative worlds built in imaginary places and times. Brown's speculative world is not fantastic since almost all of his fiction is set in late eighteenth-century Philadelphia and, despite the occasional ghost or spontaneous combustion, we wouldn't call it science fiction. Yet Brown describes the literary artist's project as one of speculation: "To speculate on the possible and the future, is no ineligible occupation."[95] His fictional work reveals an assemblage of characters and objects whose interaction constitutes any number of plots that might, or might not, be recorded. Which is also to say, any individual (real or fictional) is necessarily a character in multiple plots and any one plot involves an infinite number of possible characters.

This understanding of Brown's project can also help make sense of a notable feature of his larger corpus, which is to reuse characters that appeared other places. For example, sections of "The Man at Home" were excerpted and republished as the seventh chapter in *Ormond* and reworked into a major plot line of *Arthur Mervyn*.[96] It is tempting to read these choices as economical recycling: Brown decides that he might as well reuse earlier writing about the yellow fever epidemic. Critics have tended to follow this line, reading for example the chapter in *Ormond* as disruptive and anomalous.[97] Brown seems aware of the disruptive possibility of the chapter, advising his readers: "however foreign [the story] may at present appear...there will hereafter be discovered an intimate connection between them."[98] In deciding to relocate an incident and characters from one narrative into another, Brown is indeed emphasizing the "intimate connection[s]" that traverse imaginative worlds, but so accustomed have we become to reading novels as totalizing worlds that even when the settings they represent are realistic (say, the summer of 1793 in Philadelphia), we do not believe they coexist. *Ormond* and *Arthur Mervyn* are set in roughly the same place and time and yet we do not think the characters from one novel can wander into the other because we understand them as two fundamentally distinct spaces. Brown challenges this assumption, suggesting that individual texts should be read as an aggregate, parts of a boundless textscape. By repositioning the scene from "The Man at Home" into his later novel, Brown shows the interlay of human action: that any incident can be woven into multiple narratives. Brown's investment in serialized narrative—the two parts of *Arthur Mervyn*, or the continued story of *Wieland*'s Carwin in *Memoirs of Carwin the Biloquist*—are a consequence of this larger theory of storytelling. That is, they should be read less as sequels or prequels and more as attempts to narrate the boundless territory that actually constitutes the social systems Brown means to represent. The critical tendency to read Brown's work in terms of moral agency and sentiment (is Carwin legally responsible for the murders? Is Arthur Mervyn a treacherous mountebank?) presupposes that novels orient events around the actions and consciousness of the individual characters who occupy the center of their fictional worlds. By contrast, I am suggesting, following Woloch's terminology, that Brown is more interested in representing character systems. Brown attempts a narrative that does not try to condense or epitomize the complex social world, but strives instead to reproduce mimetically its stochastic patterns.

Brown self-consciously meditates on the intersection between the periodical form and social contingency when he returns to the periodical essay genre, writing as the "Scribbler" in 1800 in the *New-York Commercial Advertiser* and then again in 1809, a year before his death, in the *Port Folio*.[99] The first "Scribbler," published in a daily newspaper, signposts the key generic features of the periodical essay. Declaring his work to be a casual affair, the Scribbler offers his product by allowing his readers the option to accept or reject what he provides: "If therefore they have not time nor patience to peruse a mere scribble, let them overlook my lucubrations, and pass on to the next column, where...their curiosity and taste will be amply gratified."[100] As Gardner notes, the terms "lucubrations" and "scribbler" were exceedingly popular ones used to describe the miscellaneous and occasional musings of periodical essayists, and so Brown's employment of both words suggests his intention to deliver a sequence of essays in the Addisonian fashion.[101] Yet this expectation is challenged in only the second installment, which begins *in media res* with a disorienting address to a heretofore unmentioned sister: "Ah! Jenny! these are hard times, but ours is no extraordinary lot."[102] In so doing, as with "A Series of Letters," the text settles into a plot that seems more novelistic than essayistic. But while "A Series" provided a story of brother and sister that dilated beyond their dyadic epistolary relationship to survey their other social interactions, the "Scribbler" is relentlessly introspective and focused on its eponymous narrator.

Indeed, the essays seem almost designed to reveal the aesthetic limitations of literary projects devoted to social autonomy. In the essays that follow, we discover that the siblings were once wealthy, but have recently immigrated to New York, where they find themselves alone and penniless. This material condition also makes the Scribbler poorly equipped to provide the necessary heterogeneous wares of an Addisonian essayist, since he lacks the leisure to wander and collect subjects about which to write. Although he declares his irresistible itch to "scribble" for pleasure, he also works ten hours each day as a scrivener, and this occupation leaves him no time to glean subjects about which to write. One essay, for example, primarily consists of the essayist rebuffing his sister's requests that they take a stroll on the battery because he wants to devote his limited free hours to his scribbling. When he finally assents to his sister's request for a walk, the essay notably shifts to verse as if to formally mark the transition from enclosed domicile to public walkway. But the pleasant footfall of his iambic tetrameter lines provide nothing picturesque or beautiful, instead describing the urban habitat as stifling, colorless, and noisy:

> But long dead walls and narrow street,
> Shop-window-lights and homeward cars,
> And brawling tongues and shuffling feet
> And smoky airs and winking stars;
> Are all that we shall find, dear sister Jane.[103]

Whereas Brown's earlier periodical essayists could generate myriad plots from their limited spheres, the Scribbler maintains his limited gaze even when he wanders. He has nothing to write about in or outside the house, and his essays are almost hyperbolically dull: as if Brown means to make an analogy between his essayist's impoverished style and the siblings' material insufficiency. We get a recipe for hasty pudding ("Indian meal sprinkled in boiling water, in a wooden dish and a couple of pewter spoons") that is as dull as Joel Barlow's mock-epic on the same subject is whimsical. Another extended passage involves a disquisition on hats: reflecting on the shabby state of his and his sister's haberdashery, the Scribbler indulges a fantasy in which an anonymous gentleman learns of their need and delivers a hat to their lodging room.

The consequences of the Scribbler's purported autonomy becomes very clear when the entire series comes to an abrupt conclusion in the fifth essay, as the Scribbler is interrupted by a stranger who, having read the previous four essays in the newspaper, has tracked him down and now promises to provide economic stability for both siblings. It might seem that Brown has provided a highly efficient narrative of economic mobility—an economic bildungsroman in five columns. Yet there are details in the arrangement that substantially undercut this interpretation. For example, although the Scribbler has described himself as devoted to his sister, the new arrangement will physically separate them: he will join the household of his new benefactor, while Jenny will live with their benefactor's widowed sister. Additionally, although Jenny's position in this new household is described as being like a "daughter and a friend," she is also being asked to "take charge of [the] family." And so one cost of their ostensible economic emancipation is that his sister becomes a domestic laborer. Likewise, although the Scribbler enthusiastically assents to his new position in which he will have "as much independence as easily and well-earned wages can afford," he does not offer any specifics by which we can gauge the difference between this new position and his last. Presumably, he will receive higher wages, but the only thing he makes explicit about the new employment is that he must "drop this scribbling." He justifies the sacrifice, maintaining that he had previously only "took up the pen only to amuse myself" and that he "no longer need[s] to seek amusement in scribbling." This rationalization, however, reads as insincere since he had earlier refused his sister's suggestion that he stop writing that "[it] profits you nothing [and] enlarges not, by the bulk of a cent, the days scanty earnings."[104] Now, however, he reconstructs his relationship to scribbling as one of compulsive servility. Confessing that he is "loath to part" with his pen, he also announces that all who love to write "are slaves to a very potent fascination [and] passion" that adheres neither to the dictates of "reason" or "discretion." It is in these terms, that he triumphantly concludes, "'Tis done, and I am thy slave no longer."[105] His expression is one of liberation, but he has been emancipated into the position of a hired hand, presumably to serve as a scrivener for his new employer. Returning to the theme with which he began in "The Rhapsodist" essays, Brown sketches the presumptive autonomy of his author, but in so doing establishes a sequence of events that translates the Scribbler into a minor (and silent) character in someone else's plot.

Nine years later Brown returns to the "Scribbler" in the pages of the *Port Folio* magazine. Given the ubiquity of the name, there's no reason necessarily to assume that Brown intended any continuity between the two series, and yet the *Port Folio* "Scribbler" appears to reference his younger self when, in his first essay, he remarks on the state of American letters in which "many a stripling is tempted to write by the facility which newspapers afford of publishing his lucubrations."[106] Presenting himself as wiser, the older Scribbler provides his own "lucubrations" with the recognition that he is not in command of his textual effects and that there will always be a disequilibrium between the value that authors assign their work and that assigned by its readers. To illustrate the point, he even references the topic of a walk: "I am sure that my favourite walk, would be equally thorny, dreary, and irksome, to some others, as theirs is to me."[107] Like the earlier Scribbler, he adheres to the fundamental premise of the diversified market, that "however trivial or worthless" any particular topic may seem, it will appeal to "readers whose tastes and inclinations coincide."[108] But instead of blithely assuming he could both participate in and transcend this marketplace, the older Scribbler thinks of little other than his imbrication into an economy of uneven exchanges.

The *Port Folio* "Scribbler" also recycles an earlier work, "Thoughts on American Newspapers," which Brown had published in his *Monthly Magazine* in 1800 and in the *Literary Magazine and American Register* in 1806. His evident interest in the piece, signaled by its repeated republication, was motivated by its central topic, which was the unique affordance of newspaper publication. The essay involves a dispute between the Scribbler and an interlocutor who stages an invective against American newspapers as entirely partisan affairs "in which the two factions, who divide the nation, perpetually fight their battles."[109] Although he begins with this standard accusation about party factionalism, the core of their quarrel is about the compass of the newspaper's vision. The Scribbler's disputant argues that most of any newspaper's content is irrelevant to the daily lives of American citizens. He claims, for example, American readers, who "cannot very materially benefit" from international news, should limit their "attention…to family affairs…and the understanding by writings that explain to us our personal duties."[110] He also disclaims against the economic information (prices current, shipping schedules, exchange rates, discount rates) that filled much of the daily newspaper's pages, rhetorically asking,

> What have I, a plain farmer…or a man of some studious vocation, physician, lawyer, or divine, or a country shopkeeper or city artisan,— what has such a one as I to do with this long history of shipping—this catalogue of sloops and brigs to be sold or freighted—these lists of goods, wet and dry, to be found at such a corner or in such an alley? These things occupy three out of four huge and overflowing pages which I daily receive, and are absolutely of less use to me than blank paper.[111]

His opprobrium against the newspaper assumes that unless something is directly secured through its consumption, then the news has no value: it might as well be "blank paper." Although he is railing against the same media in which Brown's first Scribbler was published (the *New-York Commercial Advertiser* was a four-sheet newspaper

primarily devoted to mercantile information), both "authors" are
making very similar assessments about information economies:
each assumes a highly specialized reader whose taste and consumption is regulated by immediate needs. In the first "Scribbler" series,
Brown offers a parodic version of the product generated from his
author's narrow self-interest: dull essays that ultimately conclude in
the cessation of writing, or literal blank paper. The *Port Folio*'s
Scribbler states the case even more plainly announcing, "nothing is
more unreasonable than for any one man, or one class to expect that
his benefit or pleasure shall be solely consulted."[112]

The *Port Folio*'s Scribbler mounts his defense of the newspaper in
terms that are strikingly similar to the world building project that is
characteristic of Brown's periodical writing. He extols the newspaper's ability to link individual readers to topics, events, and people
from across the globe: "The scene cannot be so remote but we have
an eye to it: and Napoleon the emperor, and Charles the archduke
are people with whom every American, the meanest and most laborious among us, is as intimately acquainted, as with his next door
neighbor."[113] The Scribbler is not only praising the newspaper as a
technological invention that can carry the news across long distances, but he is also suggesting that this technology establishes the
conditions for grasping a new conception of social solidarity. Because
we see our next door neighbors and because our property is contiguous, we clearly fathom the ways that their actions will affect us. If
their chickens stray onto our land, we see it as trespass; if their house
turns to squalor and then burns down, the fire might consume our
own. We do not make similar assumptions about Napoleon only because his actions are remote—the causal links that attach his actions
to our own are indirect. Yet the attachment exists and the newspaper,
the Scribbler explains, provides the tools by which to comprehend
the longer and more disconnected causal chains that link our individual lives to events and actors across the globe.

In precisely the same terms, the Scribbler controverts his opponent's claim about the irrelevancy of economic data. His adversary
characterizes the minute financial details that occupy so much of
commercial newspapers as trivia: as inconsequential to him as the
"legers and receipt books" of "some obscure taylor." "What are the
bales of dry goods, or the bags of prime green coffee, to be sold
tomorrow by an auctioneer to me who lives an hundred miles off,

or whose pursuits have nothing in them of a mercantile cast?" he demands. The newspaper is useless, he continues, because its pages consist of "connexion[s] . . . perfectly incongruous and irrational and unnecessary."[114] Against this denunciation, the Scribbler articulates the congruity of the heterogeneous data located in the newspaper's pages: "Every merchant and townsman is a citizen . . . though every citizen is not a merchant, or inhabitant of a town; and while one is contented to receive (for he need not read) the salesman's catalogue for the sake of the literature or politics connected with it, the trader is prompted to extend his view beyond his professional concerns by the vicinity of other topics."[115] Brown's Scribbler presents the periodical press as a repository of accumulated data, and his own practice as periodical essayist displays the genre as uniquely suited to explain how this data directly and vicariously affects individuals. Brown engages the periodical precisely the way Hamilton approached Postlethwayt's and Rolt's economic encyclopedias: as texts that give expression to the massive scale of economic affairs. And it raises similar narrative challenges: how to construct a story of economic agency and a theory of economic causation amid the din and chaos of modern facts.

It is from precisely such questions that classical economic theory was born. Recognizing the complex interdependence of various economic sectors, actors, and regions, the discipline of economics that emerges in the nineteenth century was also motivated by the need to offer predictive judgments about the consequences of adjustments made to these constituent parts. Economic science thus established narratives that relied on huge pools of heterogeneous data but that simplified this data with models or synecdoches—as we saw, for example, in Chapter 2's discussion of Quesnay's *Tableau*. These explanatory models do not try to capture all the details and nuances of the real economic forces they set out to explain and schematize, but instead are based on fictional principles—that individuals make decisions with a goal towards maximizing utility or that markets offer perfect and equitable competition. These presumptions then become the basis for predictions regarding an unknown future. The periodical essays of Freneau, Murray, and Brown are engaged in a similar speculative project in that they likewise trace the many possible consequences that descend from specific moments of production, consumption, and exchange. But without the imperative that drives both the economist and the novelist to construct a plot organized around a limited set of characters who occupy the center of narrative focus, the periodical essay is given license to follow the circuitous paths of capital: it can represent the long strands of global supply, the precarious matrix of economic dependence, and the tumultuous ricochet effects of capital markets.

# The Slave as System

My first chapter described the vociferous debates over Hamilton's proposal to fund the public debt in the winter of 1790. During those same weeks Congress was also debating another controversial subject that involved many of the same issues, including the ambiguous language of the Constitution, the limits of Federal authority, the importance of property rights, and the dangers of fluctuating value. The subject was slavery. Having received three antislavery petitions (two from Quaker assemblies and one from the Pennsylvania Abolition Society), Congress was forced to return to a conversation that had been uneasily resolved three years earlier with the constitutional clause stipulating that there was no federal power to regulate the foreign slave trade until 1808. And thus, at the same time the rafters of the Congressional hall were filled with spectators and speculators listening to the long and heated debates about public finance, they were also hearing long and heated debates about American participation in the slave trade.

As with the controversy that would soon surround the Bank of the United States, much of the discussion circulated around the ambiguous language provided in the Constitution. At issue was the "clumsy and obscure phrasing" of Article 1, Section 9, Clause 1 of the Constitution: "The Migration or Importation of such Persons as any of the States now existing shall think proper to admit, shall not be prohibited by the Congress prior to the Year one thousand eight hundred and eight, but a tax or duty may be imposed on such Importation, not exceeding ten dollars for each Person."[1] The sentence emerged as a compromise crafted out of the schisms that divided regional economies from one another: the taxation of export goods, navigation acts, the importation of slaves, capitation taxes, and import taxes on human property. As the familiar history goes, the constitutional delegates from New England made an accommodation

*Speculative Fictions: Explaining the Economy in the Early United States.* Elizabeth Hewitt, Oxford University Press (2020).
© Elizabeth Hewitt.
DOI: 10.1093/oso/9780198859130.001.0001

with those from the deep South so as to secure their own requirement that the navigation acts would require a simple majority vote (and not the two-thirds that the Carolinas and Georgia wished). As the Maryland delegate Luther Martin wrote, "the *eastern* States, notwithstanding their *aversion* to *slavery*, were very willing to indulge the southern States, at least with a temporary liberty to prosecute the *slave* trade, provided the southern States would in their turn gratify them, by laying no *restriction on navigation acts*."[2] The ultimate compromise position yielded the sentence that clearly authorized the United States' (or at least some states') participation in the Atlantic slave trade, but also allowed for the possibility of future federal regulation. It was on the basis of this Constitutional ambiguity that the petitioners approached Congress in early 1790.

Or rather, it was on the basis of this Constitutional ambiguity that they justified their petitions. The resounding theme of each text was not oriented towards the details of constitutional policy, but to state in plain and unambiguous terms their objection to "the gross national iniquity of trafficking in the persons of fellow-men."[3] The appeal was for Congress to use "the full extent of your power, to remove every obstruction to public righteousness," further suggesting that despite the "seeming impediments," it was "within your power to exercise justice and mercy [that]...must produce the abolition of the slave trade."[4] As the petition from the Pennsylvania Society for Abolition, signed by Benjamin Franklin, phrased it, "you will devise means for removing this inconsistency from the character of the American people...and that you will step to the very verge of the power vested in you for discouraging every species of traffic in the persons of our fellow-men."[5] This language became crucial because the immediate response on the part of southern representatives was to reject the petitions entirely. A representative from South Carolina asked the petitions "be thrown aside," as they "contained an unconstitutional request," and this claim about the petitions' unconstitutionality was repeated consistently.

In reply, those advocating for the petitioners insisted that there was no trespass of Federal authority in the request since it only asked "that Congress should exercise their constitutional authority to abate the horrors of slavery, as far as they could." One possible exercise of this limited power, it was proposed, would be to implement the "small duty of ten dollars."[6] Charging the duty, it was implied, would serve as a small financial disincentive for participation in the slave trade. The duty had been proposed only a few months earlier by a Virginia representative who suggested amending a tariff bill with a proposed ten dollar duty on each imported slave, a tax that he hoped would reduce "the irrational and inhuman traffic."[7] Perhaps more significantly, those aligning themselves with the petitioners argued that even though the Constitution obviously limited their ability to outlaw the importation of slaves altogether, it also articulated their power "to regulate this business."[8] Clearly intending provocation, Elbridge Gerry thus hypothetically proposed that Congress had "a right, if they see proper" to purchase southern slaves in the United States worth, he estimated, ten million dollars with the "resources in the Western Territory." Gerry admitted that "he did not intend to suggest a measure of this kind," but in entertaining the possibility he set out to establish Congressional authority over the trade.[9] And by a vote of forty-three to eleven, the House ultimately recommended a special committee to consider the range of these powers.

The committee's final report did little to nourish the hopes of the American abolitionist community, as it explicitly stated that Congressional authority did not extend to the prohibition of importation nor "from interfering in the emancipation of slaves...or to the internal regulations of particular States, relative to the instruction of slaves in the principles of morality and religion, to their comfortable clothing, accommodation and subsistence; to the regulation of their marriages, and the prevention of the violation of the rights thereof...to a comfortable provision in cases of sickness, age, or infirmity, or to the seizure, transportation, or sale of free negroes."[10] Instead they merely recognized Congressional authority to levy a tax, to regulate the conditions of this foreign trade (perhaps responding to the widely circulated image of the slave ship that had originally been published by Thomas Clarkson in 1789), and to prohibit foreign slave ships from using the New York City harbor.[11] Nevertheless, the southern representatives reacted with hostility, launching into hours of vehement proslavery apologias.[12] Their filibustering was either successful or proved unnecessary since, as historian Howard A. Ohline describes it, "No prominent New England or Middle Atlantic congressman assumed leadership in defending the report on the floor of the House."[13] The reasons for this disinterest undoubtedly included both apathy and racism: there were no strong antislavery advocates in Congress at this time. But Ohline proposes that the apathy was at least partially motivated by the concurrent discussions surrounding the funding of the public debt. Once again the northeastern states had made a tacit bargain with their fellows in the south, trading reservations about the slave trade for southern support of their own regional economic interests. As one of the Quaker petitioners, James Pemberton, phrased it, "The funding system is so much their darling...that they want to obtain the favor of those from Carolina and Georgia."[14] Thus even those who claimed sympathy with the abolitionist cause were willing to abandon the moderate language of the subcommittee report in the hope of appeasing the representatives from Georgia and South Carolina into voting for Hamilton's proposal for debt assumption.

There is, of course, no reason to believe that there would have been a different outcome to this moment of "federal consensus" had the Congressional debate about the slave trade not coincidentally happened to occur simultaneously with the disputes about public debt.[15] Nothing in U.S. history would suggest that Congress was eager to take up the topic of slavery, let alone legislate against it. But the coincidence does bring into relief the necessary relationship between the economic development of the United States and the perpetuation of legalized slavery. I refer here not to the fact that American capital wealth was fueled by the labor of enslaved peoples, a subject that has been rigorously interrogated in recent historical analyses.[16] Instead I want to focus on how the Constitution protected slavery on the basis of an economic argument about the relative value of slave labor. When we reference the "American Paradox," we gesture at the political contradiction written into the Constitution that appeals to natural liberty even as it explicitly authorizes the holding of human property. But we should also identify an economic paradox in the fact that the Constitution accepts a premise about the relative unproductivity of slave labor even as it simultaneously legitimizes the importance of this unfree labor force to the nation's economic development by sustaining it within the founding document of the United States. I refer, of course, to the federal ratio, or three-fifths compromise that provided slave-holding states with partial representation for their human property.

Although the compromise was an explicitly political one designed to appease the discrepant state interests regarding legislative representation, the discussion was fundamentally about wealth. The vulgarity of the compromise is that it fractionalized individuals, establishing in plain numbers an inequality between white and black persons.

But the conversation that surrounded the compromise, which translated unfree laborers into partial people, was based on an assumption that individual bodies generated wealth and that unfree bodies generated less wealth. We have largely lost sight of this conversation, perhaps because the popular history of the Constitution emphasizes a story in which the "American paradox" is resolved by the Thirteenth and Fourteenth Amendments. The effectiveness of this solution, however, is contradicted by the striking economic inequities between black and white Americans that persist well into the twenty-first century. In the 2016 census report, for example, the median income of a black household was 39,490 dollars; that of a white household was 81,431 dollars.[17] The ratio here is not even three-fifths. Perhaps this signals the need to return to conversations about slavery, race, and American wealth that are located in the political economic writing that shaped American economic development in its earliest decades.

In this chapter, I consider the ways the three-fifths compromise emerged from an economic assumption that became gospel in the eighteenth century: that slave labor was necessarily inefficient. As we will see, the writers whose work influenced the fiscal feuds between the Hamiltonians and Jeffersonians—including Malachy Postlethwayt, David Hume, Pierre de Nemours Du Pont, Marquis de Mirabeau, and Adam Smith—found consensus in their assessment of institutionalized slavery as antithetical to the virtues of capitalism. This doxa of economic liberalism begs a crucial question, however, which is how these same theorists account for the maintenance of slavery as a labor system in *spite* of its ostensible inefficiency. For the most part, these eighteenth-century liberal economic theorists present us with an early instance of what Jeanne Morefield describes as the "deflective impulse...drawing critical attention away from the liberal empire's illiberalism."[18] In other words, they exile a crucial mode of production from their analysis of wealth generation and distribution. Chapter 2's analysis of Thomas Jefferson, George Logan, and John Taylor provides exemplary cases of this deflection through simplification. But, as in Chapter 3, I propose that there are other narrative strategies that attempted to capture the complex circuits of global capital, including the trade of human persons, more accurately and fully. Black Atlantic captivity narratives offer one such literary strategy, and in the second half of this chapter, I focus on the work of James Albert Ukawsaw Gronniosaw, Venture Smith, and Boyrereau

Brinch, reading each text not as autobiography or liberation narrative, but as economic treatise, an explanation of the long chains of economic interdependence and the construction of value.

## Calculating Worth

In 1796, Albert Gallatin, who would become the Secretary of Treasury in 1800 under Thomas Jefferson, published *A Sketch of the Finances of the United States*. The text was written at the behest of Jefferson, who conveyed his desire to James Madison that Gallatin "present us with a clear view of our finances, and put them in a form as simple as they will admit.... The accounts of the United States ought to be, and may be made as simple as those of a common farmer, and capable of being understood by common farmers."[19] Gallatin had become a hero to the Democratic-Republicans with his announcement that the public debt had increased by five million dollars, thereby corroborating the worst fears of Hamilton's opponents.[20] Jefferson clearly hoped that Gallatin would expose the fiscal chicanery of his enemies, yielding a text that could combine the rhetorical force of Logan and Taylor with a command over economic theory. It is difficult to believe that the 200-page volume that mostly comprises statistics about revenue would have appealed to the "common farmer," but Gallatin does buttress his text with the simple argument that Jefferson wanted to cultivate, which is that the public debt was principally responsible for sowing rancor between the states: "who can doubt that the jealousies, the apprehensions, the discontents excited by the public debt have been more injurious to our domestic peace, have gone farther to weaken our real union, than any other internal cause."[21]

Gallatin offers what he posits as an easy solution to the problem: eliminate the national debt by selling western land. The financial advantages, he argues, would be threefold: the purchase monies could be used to pay down the national debt; land could be purchased with the exchange of current debt securities; and the purchased land would be settled and cultivated, resulting in tax payments that would further support national revenue.[22] He thus posits westward expansion as an economic cure for national discord without acknowledging that this territorial growth would inevitably bring the conflicting interests over slavery to the surface. Gallatin, who was himself a member of the Pennsylvania Society for Promoting the Abolition of

Slavery, certainly would have understood that new American territories would inevitably also increase the number of slaves in the nation. Yet his gambit in *Sketch* is to act as if a conversation about a national economy can happen without talking about slave labor by simply ignoring the fact that American wealth is predicated on slavery. Gallatin thus provides an illustrative example both of Morefield's "deflective impulse" and, more specifically, what Robin Einhorn characterizes as a crucial early American political project of "how to avoid talking about slavery."[23] Gallatin here sketches American finance by erasing the fact of slave labor.

Gallatin, however, is not entirely successful in his erasure. In describing the possible revenue to be generated from taxation of this newly cultivated territory, Gallatin concedes that the terms of taxation will raise the hackles of those geographically smaller states with larger populations, since taxation, like representation, was apportioned to population. But in a rebuttal to those who "will think themselves aggrieved by a species of tax which must reach their lands, not in the ratio of their value, but in that of the whole number of inhabitants," Gallatin counters that "Labour [is] the only source of wealth."[24] Because he insists that value comes from labor, population becomes the "best" basis on which to apportion taxes. This assertion, however, leads Gallatin unwittingly to the issue of slavery as he recollects the rationale behind the three-fifths clause in the Constitution:

> Nor does it appear that any better criterion [than population] could have been adopted, in order to ascertain that annual produce of labour, than the number of inhabitants, making the same allowance with the Constitution, by estimating the net produce of the labour of five slaves, (after deducting that part necessary for their sustenance) equal to the net produce of the labour of three freemen.[25]

Here, then, Gallatin provides an economic arithmetic that justifies the three-fifths clause not in terms of political expediency or compromise, but as a statistical assessment about the relative unproductivity of slave labor. Gallatin's *Sketch* therefore reveals precisely the same economic paradox as is located in the Constitution: he extols the riches to be secured by the combination of American labor and American land, while tacitly admitting that this wealth is necessarily diminished when slave labor is used to harvest this land. Gallatin's negation of any other viable outcome also serves to make the compromise seem an inevitable conclusion, a solution that emerges from an indisputable mathematical calculation.

The three-fifths ratio first emerged as a standard by which to evaluate the comparative wealth of black and white labor during deliberations about public debt and tax apportionment in 1783. The original determination, as articulated in Article 8 of the Articles of Confederation, that war debts be funded "in proportion to the value of all land within such State" was replaced with the provision that the basis for taxation would be on population. The first version proposed that the proportion should be calculated on "the whole number of white inhabitants, and one half of the number of all other inhabitants of every sex and condition," and this was emended in March as "the whole number of free inhabitants, and three-fifths of the number of all other inhabitants of every sex and condition."[26] This phrasing was changed yet again in the final version as: "the whole number of white and other free citizens and inhabitants of every age, sex and condi-tion, including those bound to servitude for a term of years, and three fifths of all other persons not comprehended in the foregoing description."[27] There are several things to observe about these tex-tual variations. First, we see the struggle to collapse the categories of economic and political freedom, such that even an indentured serv-ant could be labeled "free." Second, the language stitches this "free" status to a racial color, to whiteness, thereby establishing race as a both a political and economic condition. Third, by explicitly stipu-lating that the "whole number" would reference "every age, sex and condition," so long as one was either "white" or "free," freedom is explicitly unfastened from political agency or suffrage. Fourth, the ease by which "one half" is replaced with "three fifths" suggests the flexibility of the calculation. And finally, as always in the case of American founding documents, even as the manifest subject is slavery, the text refuses to pronounce the word, choosing instead to designate labor that is neither free nor indentured as simply "other."

We can see a visual record of this silence in John Dickinson's first draft of the Articles of Confederation, in which he suggests using a population census to propose payment into the "Common Treasury" by the "several Colonies in proportion to the number of     in each Colony." The gap in Dickinson's manuscript signals both his admis-sion of the dangers of the calculation and his unwillingness to articu-late them. What followed from this lacuna was a discussion that brought together race and economic theory, one that ultimately became the basis for the Constitution's three-fifths clause. It was the Maryland delegate in 1776, Samuel Chase, who first insisted that "white" be used to describe the people who would count as whole bodies and conversely to assert that the number of "negroes" did not serve as a useful "barometer" by which to gauge wealth.[28] In reply John Adams insisted that there was no meaningful distinction between "the labouring poor" and "slaves" since they required exactly the same provisions to sustain their labor and yielded no greater output. "Suppose," he hypothesized, "by any extraordinary operation...of nature or of law one half the labourers of a state could in the course of one night be transformed into slaves: would the state be made the poorer or the less able to pay taxes?" According to Adams, while a "slave may indeed from the custom of speech be more properly called the wealth of his master, than the free labourer might be called the wealth of his employer; but...as to the state both were equally it's [sic] wealth, and should therefore equally add to the quota of it's [sic] tax."[29] Although Adams's point was to equate the productive capabilities of free and slave labor, his rather remarkable statement also declares the difference to be simply a matter of nomenclature because in both cases the productive value is appropriated by someone else, be it a "master" or an "employer." The first mention of any fractionalized enumeration was by Benjamin Harrison, who replied "that two slaves should be counted as one freeman," explaining he "doubted if two [slaves] effected more than one [freeman]." As evidence of the supposition, he turned to empirical data: "the hire of a labourer in the Southern colonies [was] from 8. to £12, while in the Northern it was generally £24."[30] He takes his linguistic notes from Adams by conflating both slave and free wage labor as "the hire," but using labor cost as an index of productivity he makes "Northern" workers twice as efficient. We might observe, of course, that this wage differential could just as readily be used to confirm a higher level of exploitation: that the unique coercions of slavery lowered labor costs and therefore raised profits.

This supposition about reduced productivity became the grounds for the 1783 legislation, which, in calculating slaves at three-fifths, accepted the fundamental premise that their labor was worth less and also equivocated the issue of whether the apportionment was based on population or property. This 1783 text ultimately became the basis for the compromise effected four years later at the Constitutional Convention.[31] Charles Pinckney, a South Carolina slaveholder, was the first to suggest the idea and he explicitly invoked these earlier discussions, saying "the productive labor of inhabitants was the best rule for ascertaining their wealth."[32] As the debate continued, other delegates demanded full representation for slaves, entirely revising early assessments of the relationship between wealth and population now that representation and not taxation was at issue: "the labour of a slave...was as productive & valuable as that of a freeman."[33] The hypocrisy of this position was not lost on other participants, one of whom noted, "it was urged by the Delegates representing the States having slaves that the blacks were still more inferior to freemen" during discussions of taxation, but that "At present when the ratio of representation is to be established, we are assured that they are equal to freemen."[34] But northern delegates were also accused of self-interested posturing since during discussion of the Articles some had advocated that black slaves be counted as whole bodies in calculating taxation, and only now that the conversation had shifted to representation did they instead demand that black slaves not be counted at all.

The fact that the positions could shift so drastically and that pro-slavery and antislavery advocates could entirely revise their calculations of productive labor might seem to undermine the pretensions of an emerging discipline that set out to calibrate with some precision how labor was materialized in national wealth. And these computations were crucial to the first generation of anti-mercantilist political economic writers whose work laid the infrastructure for economic liberalism's orthodox position about the inherent efficiency of "free" labor. These were the selfsame writers who so deeply influenced American political debate during the 1790s. Consider, for example, Postlethwayt, whose *Universal Dictionary,* as we saw in Chapter 1, was so influential to Hamilton's own economic knowledge. Employed by the Royal African Company, Postlethwayt had written prolifically in the 1740s on behalf of English participation in the slave trade, stressing it as a critical component in sustaining British wealth. A decade later, however, he advocated for the superior economic advantages that could come from a commercial trade in nonhuman African commodities. Although his rationale was exclusively pecuniary, his work nevertheless had a substantial influence on the Anglo-American abolitionist movement. Anthony Benezet, for example, uses several uncredited passages by Postlethwayt in the conclusion of *Some Historical Account of Guinea* (1771) when he advocates for a prosperous commodities trade as preferable to "skimming a trifling portion upon the sea coast of Africa."[35] Postlethwayt's work continued to be widely used and cited by other antislavery writers including James Dana, James Swan, and Arthur Lee.[36] He is identified as one prominent branch in Thomas Clarkson's "Map of Abolition of Slave Trade," which served as the frontispiece for *The History of the Rise, Progress, and Accomplishment of the Abolition of the African Slave-Trade* (1808). Thus we see an early suturing of antislavery argument with economic liberalism.

In her study of the intersections between French economic writing and French abolitionism, Madeleine Dobie posits that "the economic discourse was not just *an* important facet of abolitionism but rather *the* principal conceptual register in which slavery and emancipation were discussed."[37] Her attention to the French liberal economic tradition is useful because, as I proposed in Chapter 2, that work was so instrumental to Jeffersonian economic theory in the 1790s. And in the physiocrats we can see some of the earliest analyses about the relative productivity of slave labor. Unlike Postlethwayt, whose attention was on the commercial wealth that England could capture from securing a dominant position in Atlantic trade, the physiocrats turned their eyes to the best way to manage large-scale agricultural production. Although the primary subject of their inquiry was agricultural production in the metropole, colonial sugar plantations were, in many ways, an ideal test case for physiocratic theory, a real world example of the maximum net product that might emerge from the unencumbered or "natural" circulation of capital and labor that Quesnay modeled in his *Tableaux*. The issue then turned on whether enslaved labor could be part of this natural system.

Mercier de la Rivière, who served as an administrator on Martinique, employed Quesnay's economic terms but also proposed an additional category, "produit net des nègres," which he conceived as an exclusive form of wealth to be generated from West Indian slaves.[38] Michel-René Hilliard D'Auberteuil made very similar claims from his perspective on Saint Domingue. Although Hilliard's work isn't as clearly indebted to physiocrat terminology, his antimercantilist perspective puts him squarely within the ranks of eighteenth-century French liberalism.[39] And as with Mercier, Hilliard extols the tremendous economic gains that accompanied slave labor: "there is no country in the universe that offers wealth in such a proportion" as Saint-Domingue.[40] With effective management, he proposed, slaves could be accommodated to an "exact and invariable discipline" that would yield produce far greater than the costs of the labor.[41]

Mercier and Hilliard were, however, exceptional, and the preponderance of the French Économistes determined enslaved labor to be archaic and corrupt. In his extremely popular *L'ami des hommes* (1756), Mirabeau condemns the practice in general terms as degrading the occupation of farming that should be the most noble of all arts.[42] He also directs his remarks toward the very pragmatic consequences of colonial reliance on an enslaved labor force, saying that the conditions of West Indian slavery yielded a "constant loss of labor," a loss so great that it would lead to "the eventual ruin of the state."[43] Anne Robert Jacques Turgot made similar claims: "The slaves have no motive to carry out the work which is forced upon them with the intelligence and care which could ensure their success; as a result this work is hardly productive at all."[44] Mirabeau and Turgot were both influenced by Benjamin Franklin's "Observations Concerning the Increase of Mankind" (1751), a text that was especially important to Mirabeau's own study of population growth in *L'Ami des hommes*, the subtitle of which was *Traité de la population*. In "Observations," Franklin asserts that it is "an ill-grounded Opinion" that American slaves are more efficient than British free labor, an opinion that he sets out to disprove with an economic calculation, he maintains, that "Any one may compute." The computation proves, he says, that "the Labour of Slaves can never be so cheap here as the Labour of working Men is in Britain."[45] Du Pont explicitly acknowledged Franklin's work in his own study and expands on his calculations with pages of political arithmetic that lead him to the similar conclusion that the average per annum cost of owning a slave was substantially more than the average yearly wage of most European laborers. Du Pont thus reasons that it would be fiscally advantageous for plantation owners to hire free laborers.[46]

These declarations about the relative unprofitability of slave labor became much more widely known in the English-speaking world after Adam Smith provided a similar analysis in *Wealth of Nations*, asserting that "work done by slaves . . is in the end the dearest of any."[47] Smith couples Franklin's and Du Pont's attention to capital expenditures of slave ownership with Turgot's focus on "motive," and explains that because the slave had nothing personally to gain from his labor, his only "interest" is "to eat as much and to labour as little as possible."[48] Smith thus establishes what came to be an increasingly orthodox position in economic liberalism about the incompatibility between a free market economy and the employment of slave labor. And, as in the case of Postlethwayt, these passages from *Wealth* became an integral component of abolitionist argument. In fact, Clarkson's map draws Adam Smith as another abolitionist tributary, one that intersects directly with Postlethwayt's branch.

This economic argument becomes veritable canon for antislavery writing, even when it doesn't take an explicitly economic focus. John Ramsay, an Anglican minister, condemned American slaveholding on religious and moral grounds and was especially concerned with the violation of the Sabbath: that, in their cupidity, slave owners demanded seven-day work weeks. Yet he produced copious economic statistics to prove that the slaveholder "sins, not only against heaven, but his own immediate interest."[49] Antislavery writers in the United States made similar claims: Noah Webster stresses the moral argument but also references the labor ratio as support for abolition: "It is said by gentlemen, well informed on this subject, that three blacks will not perform more than one free white in the northern states."[50] Webster specifically links his antislavery position to his political economic theory, saying that slaveholding is antithetical to private ownership and minimal taxation, which are necessary to economic growth.

We see a similar argument by David Hume who, having briefly served as a clerk for a Bristol sugar merchant, had extensive knowledge of the central role of slavery in supporting the large influx of capital that was passing with increasing speed and ease across the Atlantic world.[51] Much of Hume's commentary on slavery is relegated to footnotes, the most infamous of which is located in "Of National Characters," where he muses, "I am apt to suspect the negroes to be naturally inferior to the whites."[52] Although Hume sounds the note of modern racism, he does not find any economic justification for slavery, and in another footnote he declares modern chattel slavery to be "as little advantageous to the master as to the slave." His analysis is strictly economic: "It is computed in the West Indies that a stock of slaves grow worse five *per cent.* every year, unless new slaves be bought to recruit them."[53] According to Hume, the high mortality rate of West Indian slaves makes "the price of the first purchase...so much loss" to the owner. And it is a loss that is compounded, according to Hume, because the threat of physical punishment is less of an inducement to productive labor than "the dread of being turned off, and not getting another service," which motivates the free laborer.[54]

The examples of Postlethwayt, Turgot, Mirabeau, Du Pont, Smith, and Hume epitomize the paradox I noted at the beginning of the chapter: the insistence on the incompatibility between slave labor and free market capitalism even as the two social systems are seen to be working in perfect synchronicity. If capitalism works because one buys cheap and sells dear, and if chattel slavery yielded the inverse condition, then why was the latter sustained for so long? One obvious answer would be to reject the presumption that unfree labor is inefficient. One South Carolinian congressman, William Smith, made precisely this argument during his almost four-hour long filibuster in opposition to the abolitionist petitioners in 1790. Smith entertains all the familiar arguments made on behalf of American chattel slavery—that abolitionists were hypocrites and traducers, that there was no possibility of social harmony between free white people and free black people, that black people were inferior (and here he directly cited Jefferson's statements on the subject from *Notes on Virginia*), that emancipated slaves expressed a preference for their former condition, and that slavery was sanctioned both by the Bible and human history—but the culmination of his argument was an economic one. South Carolina, he insisted, "can only be cultivated by slaves," because "the climate, the nature of the soil, ancient habits, forbid the whites from performing the labor" required to make the land valuable. "If the slaves are emancipated," he declares, "all the fertile rice and indigo swamps will be deserted, and become a wilderness."[55] There are several remarkable things to note about his comments. First, he shifts the distinction between free and unfree work to one about race: a difference between the capabilities of black and white bodies. Second, although his analysis seems to posit black bodies as more productive—the only laborers able to secure profits from the swampy wilderness—he also conflates blackness and servitude, suggesting that the only reason black labor is more productive is because it is not voluntary: "If the slaves are emancipated, they will not remain in that country." And thus, even as he is testifying to the significant economic gain to be secured from indigo and rice, he also confesses that there is no economic incentive for free individuals to labor for these commodities.

Smith's proposal about the lucrativeness of slave labor was predictably met with disapproval—and not only by those opposed to slavery. His argument, after all, contradicted one of the emerging truisms of economic science, which was that slavery was "doomed" to fail under the self-correcting conditions of capitalism. It is an argument that has had remarkable durability over the centuries. I take the term "doomed," for example, from a sentence in Eric Hobsbawm's *The Age of Capital*, where he interrogates the "possible compatibility" between Southern slavery and "the dynamically expanding capitalism of the North," and concludes, "Of course slave societies, including that of the South, were doomed," and "It is difficult to envisage the survival of the South as a slave society into the twentieth century."[56] More recently in the work of historians like Edward Baptist, Walter Johnson, and Matthew Karp, we have seen sustained analysis of the mutualism between capitalism, financialization, and slavery, but even now their work is met with considerable antagonism, so pervasive is the assumption about the inefficiency of slave labor.[57]

Rather than entering the waters of this contemporary debate, I want to consider how eighteenth-century political economists explained the durability of slave labor even as the system was proclaimed as economically deleterious. The earliest theorists of economic liberalism blamed the cognitive limitations of economic agents: they argued that because individuals were unable to comprehend the scale of the market, they were also unable to recognize the ways slavery drained wealth. Consequentially, these myopic economic agents perpetuated an economically irrational system. Turgot, for example, while admitting the universal disadvantages of slavery, also confesses "there is an advantage to having slaves…for the owner," because his profits from the "costly commodities" compensates him for his high labor expenses. As he expresses it in a letter to Du Pont, in the case of individuals the evaluation of slavery involves "a totally different question." For Turgot, the difference lies in the scale of the reckoning: the slave owner who is capturing extraordinary profits from labor cannot be persuaded that the labor system on which he reaps his profit is unsustainable.[58]

Adam Smith makes the very same assessment. Even as he asserted the manifest economic disadvantages of chattel slavery, he did not anticipate the disappearance of the institution, explaining instead why human beings would continue to perpetuate an economic system that ultimately drained wealth. Striking a distinctly Hobbesian note, Smith describes a human propensity towards tyranny: "The love of domination and authority over others, which I am afraid is natural to mankind, a certain desire of having others below one, and the pleasure it gives one to have some person whom he can order to do his work rather than be obliged to persuade others to bargain with him, will forever hinder [emancipation] from taking place."[59] Like Turgot, Smith proposes that individuals are incapable of thinking beyond their personal and short-term gain. Far from experiencing slave labor as a financial drain, slaveholders conceive of their human property as doubly valuable. Not only do they reap the rewards of slave labor (however inefficient), but slaves also compose their liquid capital since there is a ready market in which they can be exchanged for money and other commodities: "To abolish slavery...would be to deprive the far greater part of the subjects...of the chief and most valuable part of their substance....If he set a slave at liberty this was robbing his master of the whole value of him."[60] Smith also illustrates another paradoxical fact about modern slavery, which is that as societies become wealthier and their governments more liberal, the conditions for slaves grow worse.[61] He declares the conditions of North American slavery as preferable to those in the West Indies, but also explains that this relative betterment is a consequence of "merely th[e] poverty" of the North American colonies. Disputing Mirabeau's claim in *L'Ami des hommes* that free trade (which included not regulating slavery) would encourage economic growth, which would ultimately lead slave labor to wither on the vine, Smith anticipates slavery's perpetuation of brutality in the face of economic prosperity.[62]

So, even as Turgot and Smith theorize slaveholding as antithetical to self-interest, they also posit that the individual lacks the imaginative power to speculate into the future or to see beyond the limited borders of his domestic economy.[63] Emancipation yields a loss of both power and property that feels immediate, tangible, and therefore intolerable. But we must also see the cognitive limitations of Turgot's and Smith's own analysis: slavery is a blind spot in their tidy theorization of the spontaneous efficiency of free market capitalism. Either slave labor is productive, in which case "the simple system of natural liberty" does not "establish[] itself of its own accord"; or, alternatively, slave labor is unproductive, in which case its durability signals the fallacy of the assumption that myriad selfish interests of individual market participants will spontaneously fall into efficient order under the conditions of the free market.[64] And so these early writers must exile the subject of slavery to enable their description of the market economy as a benevolent and productive system that maximizes social welfare.[65]

## Plotting Objects

The intellectual achievement of eighteenth-century political economic science, as Jacob Viner phrases it, was to bring coherence and order "to the wilderness of economic phenomena."[66] The conundrum of the discipline is that this imperative towards systematic order often yields a distortion of the very "wilderness" it sets out to map. The distortions frequently take the shape of simplification, and one form this simplification took was the elision of slave labor from the narratives that described capital accumulation in the free market. And paradoxically, those most likely to narrate the interpenetration between a "free" market economy and slavery included those who advocated for its continuation. During discussion of the antislavery petitions in 1790, for example, proslavery advocates railed against abolitionism as a threat to their own personal property, but they also insisted that the whole national economy depended on their ownership of slaves. One congressman speculates that any legislative restrictions to the slave trade will cause "a blow" to the economies of South Carolina and Georgia, "which will immediately recoil on yourselves."[67] He offers precise figures to flesh out the realism of his economic story:

> one hundred and forty thousand slaves ... require annually five yards of cloth each, making seven hundred thousand yards at half a dollar a yard, this makes three hundred and fifty thousand dollars, besides the articles of linen, flannel, Osnaburgh, blankets, molasses, sugar, and rum, for the use of the negroes; now, either the Eastern and Middle States will supply us with all these articles, or they will receive the benefit of the impost on them. . . . If you injure the Southern States, the injury would reach our Northern and Eastern brethren; for the States are links of one chain: if we break one, the whole must fall to pieces.[68]

The detailed political arithmetic does not enumerate the profits that would be captured from the cultivation and sale of indigo and rice, and instead showcases the substantial profits the northern states will make from selling the various commodities required to sustain the labor necessary to *produce* this indigo and rice.

This explanation of the ways that northeastern and mid-Atlantic regional economies depend on the perpetuation of chattel slavery is plotted in much the same way that the periodical essay described the long supply chains and remote social relations that characterized the economic world of the late eighteenth century. As I argued in Chapter 3, without the imperative of a plot organized around a limited set of characters who occupy the center of narrative focus, the periodical essay is given license to follow the circuitous paths commerce takes—and this would include following the path of the Osnaburgh (whether manufactured in Scotland or New England) that would clothe southern and Caribbean slaves.[69] The periodical essay was particularly well-suited to these narrative divagations because the essays were serialized and inconstant, the serial essayist frequently transformed his own column into a textual market by handing over its property to other producers, and the magazine itself served as a synecdoche for the commercial marketplace.

Similarly well-designed to tell the stories of currency and goods that linked human beings together in commercial trade and exchange were "it-narratives," or novels of circulation, in which bank notes, coins, clothing, and children's toys became the protagonists of their own adventures. Extremely popular in the early history of the English-language novel, the subgenre continued into the nineteenth century, although more often marketed towards children readers. And in recent years, there has been increasing scholarly interest in this relatively short-lived literary form, precisely because it seems to witness a moment of cultural production that was highly cognizant of the signal power of objects in shaping human lives and their stories. As Liz Bellamy explains, these texts patently demonstrate "the mechanisms of exchange and the rapidity of circulation."[70]

Like the periodical essay, the plots of it-narratives depict both the enormity of a commercial world (by describing how an object can move across the globe) and its minutiae (by acknowledging that commerce solely consists of countless short moments of impersonal contact between human beings and their objects). And not surprisingly the representational project yielded a literary form that strongly resembles the periodical essay: a motley and unsystematic text.

Bellamy, for example, describes the "loose discursive form of the circulation novel, with its evasion of narrative closure, [which] presented a world that was diverse and inconsequential, lacking any structural or thematic coherence."[71] She further adds that this unsystematic representation of the world was "increasingly measured against a fictional tradition that emphasized a narrative form that could present an ordered and meaningful picture of the social system."[72] But before the tradition of the novel was fully established, periodical essays and it-narratives provided plots that emphasized the contingency of transit, and not the teleology of possession that would come to define modern capitalism.

Periodical essays and it-narratives also share a common infancy, as literary historians often identify Joseph Addison's "Adventures of a Shilling" (1710), first published as *Tatler* 249, as one of the earliest it-narratives. This nascent example presents its specie narrator as a picaresque hero who begins by revealing his own location of origin:

> I was born, says he, on the side of a mountain, near a little village of *Peru*, and made a voyage to *England* in an Ingot, under the Convoy of Sir *Francis Drake*. I was soon after my arrival, taken out of my *Indian* habit, refined, naturalized, and put into the *British* Mode, with the face of Queen *Elizabeth* on one side, and the Arms of the Country on the other. Being thus equipped, I found in me a wonderful inclination to ramble, and visit all the parts of the new world into which I was brought.[73]

Addison's coin thus also tells a particularly American story: an abbreviated tale of colonial dispossession, as the Peruvian ingot takes off his "Indian habit" and becomes "refined" and "naturalized" as a British shilling. But because the protagonist is a coin, and not an indigenous Peruvian, once landed in this "new world" of England, he can move into "every corner of the nation," and fulfill his destiny as a circulating unit of value: "we Shillings love nothing so much as travelling." When he is not moving—when he falls into the hands of hoarders and misers—the Shilling experiences "unspeakable grief." The coin's story is only interesting (it only has value and only deserves to be told) when he can narrate his rapid movement between owners: "I was sent to the Apothecary's shop for a pint of Sack. The Apothecary gave me to an Herb-woman, the Herb-woman to a Butcher, the Butcher to a Brewer, and the Brewer to his Wife, who made a present to me to a Non-conformist Preacher." Written sixty-six years before Adam Smith's own story of the butcher, the brewer, and the baker, Addison's coin narrates the human motivation that sustains the commercial market, but from the vantage of the object that the butcher and brewer covet, and for which they labor.

Much of the scholarship about the subgenre of the it-narrative suggests that the form offers either a critique of this emergent world of commodity capitalism or accommodation to it. Bellamy exemplifies the former in explaining, "for most of the eighteenth century the circulation format was primarily used to provide a satirical vision of the atomized and mercenary nature of society within a commercial state."[74] By contrast, Christina Lupton asserts, "It-narratives license our complacency about the sovereignty of objects."[75] Lynn Festa offers a somewhat similar reading in that she sees the talking commodities of the eighteenth-century it-narrative as designed to "fend off that day" when "commercial society has allowed [these objects] to supplant the humans that own them."[76] In this way, the prevailing critical emphasis has been on the social relationship between people and things, and on the assumption that people are not things. The "narrative energy" of the it-narrative, Markman Ellis argues, derives from "an essential incompatibility between the narrator's animal (or even inanimate) point of view and its human comprehension of the things around it (the peg top is not only human but English, Christian, pious, and so forth)."[77]

My interest in it-narratives is not on the relationship between people and things, but on its explanatory capacity—on the fact that the genre is motivated by the same imperative as political economic writing to explain the magnitude (the "wilderness," to use Viner's term) of a system that strains the limits of any one person's cognition. It-narratives depict the market economy as an integration of the heterogeneous interests of atomized individuals. By tracing the movement of a singular object as it is exchanged, it explains how people are brought into social relations, even when they are unaware of these relations. The genre thus represents what economic theorist, F.A. Hayek will famously call a "spontaneous system"—a social order that emerges from uncoordinated human action. For Hayek, social theory "begins" with the recognition that "there exist orderly structures which are the product of the action of many men but are not the result of human design."[78] According to Hayek, the first text to represent the spontaneous structure of a modern economy was not

Smith's *Wealth of Nations*, but Bernard Mandeville's *Fable of the Bees* (1714), which "for the first time developed all the classical paradigmata of the spontaneous growth of orderly social structures."[79] Hayek's analysis calls particular attention to the moment from *Fable of the Bees* that describes the manufacturing of a crimson cloth:

> What multiplicity of Trades and Artificers must be employed! Not only such as are obvious as Wool-combers, Spinners, the Weaver, the Cloth-worker, the Scowrer, the Dyer, the Setter, the Drawer and the Packer; but others that are more remote and might seem foreign to it; as the Millwright, the Pewterer and the Chymist.[80]

Mandeville's narrative is very much in keeping with Addison's "Adventures of a Shilling" in that it registers the "multiplicity" of human agents who are brought together in the manufacturing and exchange of a singular object.

For Hayek, Mandeville's insight is to realize the productive capacity of a spontaneous system—an assumption that is foundational to economic liberalism, which asserts that an unregulated market is more efficient. Indeed, Mandeville's tale of the crimson cloth was a crucial inspiration for Adam Smith, who spun his own kind of it-narrative about a woolen coat:

> The woollen coat…which covers the day-labourer, as coarse and rough as it may appear, is the produce of the joint labour of a great multitude of workmen. The shepherd, the sorter of the wool, the wool-comber or carder, the dyer, the scribbler, the spinner, the weaver, the fuller, the dresser, with many others, must all join their different arts in order to complete even this homely production. How many merchants and carriers, besides, must have been employed in transporting the materials from some of those workmen to others who often live in a very distant part of the country! how much commerce and navigation in particular, how many ship-builders, sailors, sail-makers, rope-makers, must have been employed in order to bring together the different drugs made use of by the dyer, which often come from the remotest corners of the world![81]

Smith's rhapsodic tale unravels the coat to explain how its construction incorporates laborers from across the globe. The limited perspective of the wool-carder might allow her to see her relationship to the sorter and even to the weaver, but she cannot comprehend her attachment to the ship-builder—nor to the various laborers who generate the goods necessary to manufacture the ship. Smith's account of the uncoordinated market interactions that go into manufacturing and selling the coat resemble both the narratives of Mandeville's crimson cloth and Addison's shilling. But we also should recognize a deep similarity between Smith's story and the commentary with which this section began, which described how it was that workers from across the nation produced the "linen, flannel, Osnaburgh, blankets, molasses, sugar, and rum" that went into the production of another crucial commodity to the eighteenth-century capital market: the slave.

## Narrating Slavery

Because it-narratives obscure the difference between people and things, many scholars have remarked on the awful similarity between the genre and another eighteenth-century narrative form, Black Atlantic captivity narratives. Festa acknowledges the similarity as a "grotesque gathering," but also notes that "both sets of texts display and enact a disturbing confusion of subject and object, person and thing."[82] Jonathan Lamb points to the "superficial resemblances," which include the similarities of titles (most it-narratives and slave narratives include some variation on the phrase, "interesting narrative" or "adventures of") and the paratextual apparatus that establishes the authenticity of the narrator. As he further observes there is a crucial difference since in the case of an it-narrative, this apparatus "advertises a fiction" while "its counterpart in a slave narrative affirms the opposite."[83] And of course, it is this essential difference— that the slave is a person but a coin is not—that makes the comparison grotesque.

Despite all the crucial differences between the genres, I want to suggest that both performed a remarkably similar function, which was to represent and describe the wilderness of the eighteenth-century global economy. Like the it-narrative, the autobiographies of captured slaves draw attention to the otherwise invisible chains that linked the consumption of goods to the labor of their production. This task was fundamental to antislavery writers who strove to draw direct links between slave labor and the consumption of the commodities derived from that labor. Anti-saccharite campaigns, for example, asserted a direct causal relationship between the consumption of sugar and the victimization of black people. This was the pointed emphasis of William Fox's *An Address to the People of Great Britain*, an anti-slavery pamphlet that saw over twenty different editions and circulated in both Britain and the United States: "A family that uses 5 lb. of sugar per week...will, by abstaining from the consumption 21 months, prevent the slavery or murder of one fellow creature."[84] Fox also signals this argument on the cover, by citing lines from William Cowper's "The Negro's Complaint" as the epigraph:

> Think, ye masters iron-hearted,
> Lolling at your jovial boards,
> Think how many backs have smarted
> For the sweets your cane affords.

Ventriloquizing the toiling Caribbean slave, Cowper's poem demands its readers listen to the person who cultivates and refines the sugar with which they sweeten their tea: "Sighs must fan it, Tears must water, / Sweat of ours must dress the Soil." The rhetorical project in Cowper and Fox is partially to compel sympathy through an attenuated bodily identification. The tea drinker will prove not to be "iron-hearted," and will be unable to sip because she has been made cognizant of the pain (the "sighs," "tears," and "sweat") that metaphorically fill her cup. And the reluctance to consume is also achieved through gustatory manipulation, or what Timothy Morton calls the "blood sugar topos," in which coffee and tea become "nauseating by the notion that they are full of the blood of slaves."[85] A similar project was at work in the decision to decorate sugar bowls with Josiah Child's Wedgwood medallion that portrayed the supplicant slave and the motto, "Am I not a Man and a Brother." Here then the chained slave adorns the very commodity that comes from his labor. Some of these bowls explicitly advertised that the sugar they contained was sourced from East Indian sugar, thereby inoculating their produce from the contamination of slavery.[86]

The anti-saccharite campaign thus depended on narrative and visual strategies designed to telescope the long supply chains that made it otherwise easy for the British consumer to forget how sugar arrived at his table. As Fox puts it, "The slave-dealer, the slave-holder, and the slave-driver, are virtually the agents of the consumer, and may be considered as employed and hired by him to procure the commodity." Collapsing the distance between the slave driver and the consumer, Fox attributes equal moral culpability ("virtual" agency) to every person along the production and supply chain of sugar production. Indeed the campaign established a narrative paradigm that is still used by commercial boycotts over 200 years later, which likewise strive to shorten the chain between production and consumption so as make consumers acknowledge that their purchases cause direct harm. But if these narrative and visual strategies produce a conceptual map that more clearly illuminates the economic interdependence between a London household and a Jamaican plantation—or between an American Target store and a Bangladeshi garment factory—then such narratives also work to cultivate a tale that supports a simple fantasy that one can disentangle him or herself from the cruelties of slave labor (in the eighteenth or twenty-first centuries) by abstaining from one singular commodity. In other words, even as the purpose is to de-fetishize the commodity by forcing the consumer to register the good as a product of human labor, the practice also offers a distorting portrait of the market insofar as it necessarily suggests that the production of any one commodity can be teased out of the larger commercial system. But in an economic landscape in which objects trade at an astonishingly fast rate—in which a hogshead of refined sugar might be exchanged for any number of objects (lumber, grain, cloth, coin) between the time it leaves the Jamaican shore and before it is purchased by an English retailer—then how does one keep one's hands free of the blood?

The premise of the anti-sugar campaign was to elide this kind of question and instead to postulate an absolute distinction between the brutalities of the slave trade and a civilized, and civilizing, global commerce. In his study of eighteenth-century anti-slavery writing, Philip Gould designates a particular genre, the "commercial jeremiad," as the construction of this particular rhetorical strategy. As Gould persuasively explains, in emphasizing the moral depravity of commercial enterprises that are closely associated with the enslavement of Africans (which included not only the slave trade, but the sugar and rum trades), writers established by contrast the moral legitimacy of other trade commodities.[87] It was precisely such a fantasy that some proslavery advocates set out to belie when they highlighted the profits that emerged for those who sold commodities not as obviously linked to slave labor as sugar and rum, like Osnaburgh and flannel.

We typically read slave narratives, which testify to the personal harms that come from the global enterprise of chattel, as examples of the commercial jeremiad. Both Quobna Ottobah Cugoano and Olaudah Equiano, for example, explicitly follow Postlethwayt's suggestion that Africa could be more profitably incorporated into European colonial commerce by abandoning the slave trade and cultivating Africa as a source of raw materials and consumers.[88] Such narratives are influenced by abolitionism and classical political economy, which assumes a radical difference between the barbaric traffic of slavery and the free trade of global capital. But we should also attend to the ways slave narratives break with these doctrines and narrate the complexity of economic entanglement.

This is not, however, how scholars have typically approached writing about the transatlantic economy by enslaved Africans. The slave narrative, as Henry Louis Gates Jr. explains, is a "testimony of defilement: the slave's representation and reversal of the master's attempt to transform a human being into a commodity, and the slave's simultaneous verbal witness of the possession of a humanity shared in common with Europeans."[89] Gould describes a similar process, in which the ex-slave author must "autobiographically claim an individuated identity from the anonymity of slavery."[90] Even for those critics, like Gould, who conceive of Black Atlantic writing outside of "the constraints of ethnicity and national particularity," as Paul Gilroy phrases it, there has nonetheless been a sustained focus on personal agency and identity.[91] Nor is it surprising that literary critics have tended to approach the eighteenth-century slave narrative as autobiography given the importance of self-articulation to the political work of abolitionism. Because human individuality was said to develop only through the acquisition of Christianity or capital, these are the two plots through which the slave narrative has tended to be theorized: the conversion narrative and the economic bildungsroman.[92] Both approaches are similar insofar as they are oriented around a person who testifies to his human individuality as either faithful Christian or as savvy capitalist, and this is why we tend to think of the slave narrative according to a fairly simple binary. Either the slave is property (not in possession of his self or his labor) or he is free (in possession of his own person, and therefore choosing to labor and secure property).

I propose we consider Black Atlantic captivity narratives outside this paradigm in which the person acquires both self and property.[93]

In doing so, I am following the lead of scholars who have described how the imperatives of possessive individualism had pernicious effects on black subjectivity both before and after emancipation. As Saidiya V. Hartman demands, we must recognize "the ways that the recognition of humanity and individuality acted to tether, bind, and oppress."[94] My project is somewhat different, however, in that my ambition is not to calibrate the ways that black life writing indexes submission and resistance to liberalism. Instead, I counterintuitively propose that we read these autobiographical texts with absolutely no concern for matters of subject formation or personal autonomy. While it is certainly true that by the early decades of the nineteenth century, there was a suture between political liberalism and the genre of the personal narrative, in the earlier texts on which I focus in the rest of this chapter, the association between autobiography and liberalism is not yet firmly established. And if we do not put our interpretive emphasis on the ways Black Atlantic writers reveal the torturous pursuit of self-possession, we can begin to unpack how these authors instead use narrative to describe the complex economy that necessarily integrated capitalism and slavery.

Like periodical essays and it-narratives, captivity narratives explain the dependencies that link their titular protagonists to other people and other goods along a supply chain that cannot be comprehended from the position of autonomous individual. Writing from the perspective of commodity, of commodified labor, and of commodity holder, the ex-slave depicts economic relations according to various vantages, providing a multi-faceted cartography of commerce. The slave narrative thus accomplishes something similar to what we saw Jean le Rond d'Alembert proclaim was the project of Diderot's *Encyclopédie*. It yields a birds-eye map that explicates the interdependence between remote regions, objects, and people; but it also draws the concrete details of those lost within the economic wilderness. If the seamless integration into capital life requires, as Marx argued, an inability to recognize the essence of social relations, then the ex-slave narrator is not afforded the luxury of the wage slave: he or she has been cast into the roles of labor, capital, commodity, consumer, and producer in a way that the "free" laborer is not.

In what follows, I will focus on three captivity narratives that explain the complex intersections between capital and slave markets: *A Narrative of the Most Remarkable Particulars in the Life of James Albert Ukawsaw Gronniosaw* (1772); *A Narrative of the Life and*

*Adventures of Venture* (1798); and *The Blind African Slave, Or Memoirs of Boyrereau Brinch Nicknamed Jeffrey Brace* (1810). The narrator of each was born in Africa and was captured into slavery at a young age; each man was ultimately emancipated; and in each case their story is recorded by an amanuensis. All three lived in North America and all three books were published in the United States. There are, however, crucial differences. For example, because it represents the benefits of Christianity as more than compensatory to the injuries of his exile from Africa and enslavement, Gronniosaw's *A Narrative* is often read as a paradigmatic text of religious conversion. By contrast, *A Narrative of the Life and Adventures of Venture* is taken as an exemplary case of capital acquisition. The much less familiar narrative, *The Blind African Slave, Or Memoirs of Boyrereau Brinch*, eschews both of these paradigmatic plots, giving testimony to the ways an individual life is subsumed into a capital economy that relies on the exploitation of Africans. But in all three cases, the narrators conduct their readers through the wilderness of the global economy.

## Weaving with Ukawsaw Gronniosaw

*A Narrative of the Most Remarkable Particulars in the Life of James Albert Ukawsaw Gronniosaw* is probably best known to readers today because it provides the original example of what has come to be a vital generic convention of the earliest slave narratives, the "talking book." Eve Tavor Bannet has argued that the text exerted this influence on subsequent black autobiographers because Gronniosaw's narrative was so widely read.[95] First published in Bath in 1772, the book was reprinted numerous times in both England and the United States. But, as Bannet admits, although Gronniosaw's text had substantial influence on subsequent black autobiographers, it has generated considerably less interest among twenty-first-century scholars, in large measure because it does not include many of the other features we expect from narratives about American slavery: accounts of the Middle Passage, of the slave auction, or even of his experiences laboring as a slave. Gronniosaw glosses over these episodes too quickly for the modern reader's expectations.

One likely reason his work provides so little detail is that even as the book aims to humanize and individualize Gronniosaw, thereby fulfilling the essential generic mandate of the slave narrative, the text was neither produced nor disseminated as an abolitionist text, despite the fact that it is frequently classified alongside works that were. Instead, the cluster of white Englishmen and women who brought the book to press—Selina Hastings (to whom it is dedicated), George Whitefield (mentioned in the text, and another patron of Gronniosaw), Walter Shirley (who wrote the introduction), and Mary Marlow (who is probably the "young lady" who records Gronniosaw's story)—were all proslavery Calvinists. Whitefield, for example, used slaves as the primary labor force at his Georgia orphanage. Like many slaveholders, he insisted that the land in the deep south required the labor of black slaves, asserting "that hot countries cannot be cultivated without negroes."[96] Upon Whitefield's death, the Countess of Huntington, Selina Hastings, inherited both the house and the human property, the latter of which increased during her tenure as owner. Thus while Hastings and Whitefield were patrons of prominent black writers like Gronniosaw and Phillis Wheatley, their ambition was to convert people of African descent and not to emancipate them.[97] No wonder Gronniosaw's emphasis is on his conversion to Christianity.

He begins his narrative by telling an origin story that identifies him as exceptional in that he possesses a preternatural desire for monotheism that predates his knowledge of Christianity.[98] Gronniosaw asks spiritual questions that his family cannot answer and consequentially they "disliked" him and he is left "always dissatisfied" (34). This almost typological rendering of his spiritual development is central to the book's larger project made explicit in Walter Shirley's preface to the narrative, which is to present the "benighted Parts of the World where the Gospel of Jesus Christ hath never reached" as "foreknown," thereby establishing Gronniosaw's captivity as an act of Providence and not "mere Chance and accidental Circumstance" (33). Choosing a verse from Isaiah, "I will bring the Blind by a Way that they know not, I will lead them in Paths that they have not known," as the epigraph to the narrative, Shirley establishes the text as a map of Gronniosaw's movement into a Christian world in which he was preordained to travel. Gronniosaw uses this very same structure to craft his own narrative, characterizing himself as "frequently lost in wonder at the works of the Creation," "afraid, uneasy and restless," and desperately wanting "to be informed of things that no person could tell me" (34). Indeed, this spiritual restlessness is ultimately what causes him to be enslaved. Because he feels a "secret impulse…which I could not resist," Gronniosaw agrees to accompany a merchant to the "Gold Coast" where he is sold and placed on a Dutch slave ship to make the Middle Passage. In this way, he plots his enslavement as the necessary price for his conversion to Christianity, offering an argument roughly commensurate to Wheatley's "On Being Brought from Africa to America."

The emphasis on religion in Gronniosaw's account of his life might make it appear that his text has no particular concern for what he describes as "temporal comforts," or the economic system into which he finds himself once sold to the Dutch slaver. And critics frequently act as if temporal and spiritual concerns are separate domains in our reading of eighteenth-century Black Atlantic autobiographies, as seen for example in the critical dispute about whether Equiano's narrative is best read as economic bildungsroman or conversion narrative. But these are not mutually exclusive genres, and Gronniosaw describes his conversion to Christianity and capitalism as a tandem exercise: both demand his faith in an immense system ordered by an invisible hand.

The theological questions that leave Gronniosaw so uneasy and dissatisfied at the beginning of his life and the narrative are about the large cosmos in which he is located, and the questions he poses that serve to exile him from his friends and family are those that would also be asked by a natural philosopher. They are the very same questions that Adam Smith identifies as eliciting wonder in his "History of Astronomy." What is the "superior power" that organizes the arrangements between "the sun, moon and stars" (34)? What causes "the very heavy rain and thunder"? "Who made the *First Man*?" "where does the fly come from, as no one can make him?" (35). Gronniosaw's spiritual inquiry takes the form of a desire to know first causes, to fathom the temporal and spatial edges of the enormous world in which he resides, and to comprehend the invisible chains that link seemingly disconnected objects. Gronniosaw continually emphasizes intellectual and imaginative agitation in the face of these concerns: he is "uneasy," and the disequilibrium leaves him "labour[ing] under anxieties and fears that cannot be expressed" (34). This anguish is calmed when the Pennsylvanian Dutch Reformed minister who purchases him explains that his integration into the universe is shaped by an invisible hand that belongs to a Christian God:

He told me that God was a GREAT and GOOD SPIRIT, that He created all the world, and every person and thing in it, in Ethiopia,

Africa, and America, and every where. I was delighted when I heard
this.   (39)

So delighted is Gronniosaw that he expresses his desire to possess
"wings like an Eagle" and to "fly to tell my dear mother that God is
greater than the sun, moon, and stars; and that they were made by
him" (39). Even as this early lesson in Christianity asserts the sovereignty of God, it also leads to a feeling of empowerment in which
Gronniosaw imagines himself, God-like, as encircling the entire globe.

This equipoise that allows him imaginatively to take flight, returning both to mother and motherland, is disrupted, however, as soon
as he begins to read—first the Bible, then John Bunyan's *The Holy
War* and Richard Baxter's *A Call to the Unconverted*. Each text returns
him to his earlier tumult. Gronniosaw describes, for example, his
"agonies," his "grief and distress" that comes from a passage from
Revelations 1.5: "Behold, He cometh in the clouds and every eye shall
see him and they that pierc'd Him." As was the case with his earliest
spiritual anguish, he feels exiled from the community, and instead of
imagining that he is included in the "every eye" that might see Christ,
he is convinced that the passage marks him as exceptional in not
being able to see. He is certain that the verses are "directed…to me
only," that no other person "besides myself [was in] such grief and
distress as I was," that "my master hated me," and "that if God did
come…He would be sure to be most angry with *me*" (40). While
Gronniosaw now understands a Christian God to be author and first
cause of the universe, he also believes the logic of Christian salvation
to exclude him from this universe. Since Gronniosaw's owner (who
the text identifies as "Mr. Freelandhouse") was Theodorus Jacobus
Frelinghuysen, a minister who sparked a sectarian controversy when
he refused to grant communion rites to those would could not testify
to a sincere conversion experience, Gronniosaw's spiritual anxieties
make a good deal of sense.[99]

But Gronniosaw is ultimately incorporated into the community of
the faithful, and he describes his moment of revelation in which he
"seemed to possess a full assurance that my sins were forgiven me" (42).
The scene of his salvation occurs under an oak tree, a "large remarkable fine Oak-tree, in the midst of a wood," where he "often lamented
my own wicked heart, and undone state" (42). The tree provides both
setting and conduit for Gronniosaw's spiritual development: "It was
the greatest pleasure I ever experienced to set under this Oak, for

there I used to pour out my complaints to the LORD: and when I had any particular grievance, I used to go there and talk to the tree, and tell my sorrows, as if it were to a friend." It is also during one of his frequent visits to the tree that he first is "fill'd and awed by the Presence of God that I saw (or thought I saw) light inexpressible dart down from heaven upon me" (42). The solitary and naturalistic land-scape of his revelation is typical in the Dutch Reform tradition of which he was a member, but his emphasis on the oak tree also has the effect of recalling the significance of another tree, the palm that he was forced to leave behind in Africa.[100]

In the first pages of his narrative, as Gronniosaw describes the religious practices of his people in Bournou, he also offers extensive commentary about palm trees. Indeed, he goes into so much scrupu-lous detail that he apologizes to his readers for "the digression" (35). Gronniosaw recollects that people in his city had worshipped "under a large palm tree," which was both "high and majestic" (34). Like the American oak, the palm had been the location for religious devo-tion. But unlike the oak, which perfectly served his spiritual needs, the palm tree was not large enough "to cover the inhabitants of the whole City" (34), and as a result, the community is divided into "con-gregations." It might seem as if he indulges the digression in order to describe the spiritual inferiority of the Bournou palm to the American oak. Yet Gronniosaw instead celebrates the plenitude that he associates with the palm species as a whole, about which he says, "the beauty and usefulness of them are not be described" (34).

In asserting the palm tree as something so beautiful and useful as to beg description, he establishes a parallel between his wonder at the tree and his wonder at the larger "works of the Creation." But in the case of the palm, Gronniosaw finds himself equal to the task of description and he recounts how the tree provided satisfaction to his community:

[T]hey supply the inhabitants of the country with meat, drink and clothes; the body of the palm tree is very large; at a certain season of the year they tap it, and bring vessels to receive the wine, of which they draw great quantities, the quality of which is very delicious: the leaves of this tree are of a silky nature; they are large and soft; when they are dried and pulled to pieces it has much the same appearance as the English flax, and the inhabitants of BOURNOU manufacture it for cloathing &c. This tree likewise produces a plant or substance

which has the appearance of a cabbage and very like it, in taste almost
the same: it grows between the branches. Also the palm tree produces
a nut, something like a cocoa, which contains a kernel, in which is a
large quantity of milk, very pleasant to the taste: the shell is of a hard
substance, and of a very beautiful appearance, and serves for basons,
bowls, &c.   (34–35)

There are several ways that we might be presented with this enthusiastic record of economic products that come from one tree. Perhaps
Gronniosaw means obliquely to suggest the palm as an alternative
resource that might be extracted from Western Africa. In describing
the versatile products that can be manufactured from the plant,
including an explicit comparison to English flax, Gronniosaw might
be making an argument similar to one made by Postlethwayt,
Equiano, and Cuguando, which is that England would find superior
economic profit in an African trade that did not involve human
property. But although Gronniosaw hints at the commodification of
the palm's many products, the economy he actually describes is neither commercial nor capitalist. The community does not trade the
wine, fruit, and cloth that come from the palm, but consumes them.
Additionally, the palm provides all their necessities and so there is no
need for any other goods: it offers a self-sufficient and closed economy. The palm provides something like Jefferson's pastoral fantasy.

The economic system that organizes itself around the palm is
therefore very different from that of the American oak. Gronniosaw
discloses fewer details about the economic uses of the oak, but we do
know that the reason he finds himself "in the midst of a wood" where
he discovers his special tree is that he "often used to be employed
there in cutting down trees, (a work I was very fond of)," and that
this timber work was "a great part of my business" (42). We thus
learn that a substantial part of his labor as slave was to hew lumber,
and this timber business would have been a capitalized one. Because
he is a slave, he cannot sell his own labor power, but Frelinghuysen
does sell it, thereby commodifying Gronniosaw's labor. We also
know that Frelinghuysen is a minister and therefore he is not using
the wood for his own business, but rather selling it on the market as
lumber for building, ship construction, or barrel manufacturing.
And, since it is not clear that Frelinghuysen actually owns the property on which the woods sit, it is also possible that he has actually
hired out Gronniosaw's labor to the property owner, offering yet

another link in this long strand of commodity exchanges. In this way, the narrative makes Gronniosaw's conversion to Christianity and capitalism simultaneous. Gronniosaw even articulates his conversion experience in distinctly economic terms, announcing "I was now perfectly easy, and had hardly a wish to make beyond what I possess'd" (43). This is both an expression of economic and spiritual equilibrium ("perfectly easy") but also of marginal growth, since the formulation, "had hardly a wish," implies that he did have a wish, albeit a small one, to make just a little bit "beyond what I possess'd."

His religious awakening is followed immediately in the narrative by Gronniosaw's emancipation. But far from celebrating his freedom, he describes it as a loss: "my temporal comforts were all blasted by the death of my dear and worthy Master" who "left me by his will ten pounds, and my freedom" (43). Now legally free and in possession of his own labor, Gronniosaw's spiritual doubts reemerge and he recalls being "unhappy by the clouded and perplex'd situation of my mind...with doubts, fears, and such a deep sense of my own unworthiness" (43). And so he returns "into the wood to prayer" and his faith is restored—a faith that depends on a "helpless" submission to God's sovereignty (43). The text consistently works to accentuate both Gronniosaw's spiritual and economic helplessness. His spiritual equipoise seems to depend on his incorporation into an economic system that he must accept with faith and not knowledge. This is why, I think, there is so much emphasis on his economic ignorance. At various moments Gronniosaw tells us: "I never knew how to set a proper value on money" (45), "I never regarded money in the least" (45), and "I did not understand the real value of [money]" (47).

These assertions about his financial illiteracy are, however, substantially contradicted by numerous moments in the narrative that seem to evidence both his comprehension of capitalism and his ambition to explain the mechanics of his movement in a world entirely established by currency and commodity exchanges.[101] Like Addison's Shillling, Gronniosaw presents his life as a series of episodes in which he is traded between owners. We thus learn that he is first purchased "for two yards of check," later for "fifty dollars," then "£50." Typically we read these moments in slave narratives the way Gates prescribes, as scenes of degradation: not only is the person converted into a dollar value, but even though the narrator is now nominally free, he or she is forced to recall and rehearse this valuation at a monetary price. But if we shift our focus from reading the narrative as designed to present the self as autonomous, and instead recognize that Gronniosaw's task was also to diagram the economic system in which he is caught, the passages yield a very different effect.

When Gronniosaw describes his first sale to the captain of a Dutch ship, he demonstrates that the exchange is all about supply and demand. Recognizing himself as physically "little," Gronniosaw is convinced that "no person would buy me" (38). This assessment indicates that he enters a market that he already understands values the human body for its capacity for labor: as a smaller child, he will be less productive and therefore yield less profit to any purchaser. Terrified that if he isn't purchased he will either "be treated very ill, or possibly murdered," he begs the Dutch captain to buy him, albeit in a language that the captain does not understand. God becomes an intercessor in this transaction, providing his services as both translator and slave trader, and thanks to divine "influence . . . on my behalf" Gronniosaw is purchased and makes his way into the Middle Passage. We could read Gronniosaw's representation of divine intervention two ways: either as confirmation that Christian conversion is worth the cost of enslavement, or as a sly critique of the cooperative logic of chattel slavery and Christianity. Given the framing of the narrative by his sponsors and patrons, there is every reason to believe both readings are correct. But in addition to characterizing the sale as providential, Gronniosaw's detailed account of this first sale also yields considerable insight into the non-religious elements of this commodity exchange. The Dutch captain buys Gronniosaw "for *two yards of check.*" Textiles were a crucial component of Atlantic traffic, and pieces of fabric, along with guns and rum, frequently served as a forms of currency in the slave trade. Although Gronniosaw is somewhat vague in his designation of the fabric type, the word "check," as well as the fact that the ship is Dutch, would seem to indicate the textile in question was a cotton cloth (often checkered in pattern) manufactured in India and traded through the Dutch East India Company. And so in this first purchase, Gronniosaw does not merely depict an exchange of two commodities—his body for the two yards of fabric—but also a much more intricate trade network: the Dutch captain will purchase his body (which could ultimately produce value through its labor or, as it turns out, be traded as a commodity that stores labor to be produced later), and he will pay with cloth that itself comprises the congealed labor from the Indian workers who wove it. The exchange of child for cloth is also a global one, since it required transport between the Netherlands, India, and now the West Coast of Africa. Gronniosaw thus indirectly suggests the many reasons why East Indian sugar may not be so "pure."

Gronniosaw also insists that his English readers know that the value of this cloth fluctuates. He observes that the fabric for which he was exchanged "is of more value *there*, than in England" (38). Gronniosaw's use of the present tense is somewhat curious, as he is describing a transaction that happened sixty years earlier. But in insisting that his contemporary readers should reckon the exchange rate that made an African child equivalent to two yards of cloth in contemporary monetary rates, he highlights his own attentiveness to the fact that value fluctuates according to multiple variables. The value of the cloth is not the same in England as on the Gold Coast; it is likewise not the same in 1710 and 1777. This is not the only moment in the narrative where Gronniosaw is keen to demonstrate the importance of currency exchange; he does so again in recounting the second time he is sold: "I was sold for fifty dollars (*four and six-penny pieces* in English)" (38). Here too he wants to make clear that the language of trade requires the translation of currency. The child is made equivalent to fifty dollars, and we can presume that the unit is a Spanish dollar. To make the value meaningful for his British audience, Gronniosaw offers the standard currency exchange, in which a Spanish dollar was equivalent to four shillings and a six-pence. Gronniosaw does not perform the multiplication that would establish the total value of the sale in pounds sterling, because the point of noting the rate is not to establish his worth in monetary terms, but instead to convey that all value is determined by the contingency of the exchange.

Even in a scene that appears explicitly designed to prove Gronniosaw's economic illiteracy, there are strong suggestions that the narrative instead expresses his keen comprehension of capitalist traffic. Gronniosaw observes that when he is first bought by the Dutch captain, his purchaser receives not only his body in exchange for the fabric but also the "large quantity of gold" he was wearing (38). Instead of remarking on the fact that the gold would have been an important part of the captain's calculation to purchase the boy, Gronniosaw instead forces a distinction between this exchange of gold and the exchange of his body. He does this by creating a parable about the corruptions of wealth. Gronniosaw describes the gold as "rings" that "were linked one into another, and formed into a kind of chain, and so put round my neck, and arms, and legs" (38). And he describes his dispossession of these "chains," which would also constitute a considerable source of wealth, with pleasure, saying he "was glad when my new Master took it from me." Here Gronniosaw establishes wealth, in its classic form as gold, as enslavement and represents his entrance into the Atlantic slave economy as liberation from the burdens of gold. This moral nicely accords with the larger ambitions of the book, which is to characterize Gronniosaw as a subject for charity and as a romantic "savage" who doesn't understand the value of money. It allows a convenient fantasy of cheerful submission to slavery, as the African prince gives up his gold, which he feels as a burden, so as to take up his new position as slave. Moreover, in exchange for the gold, he receives clothing "in the Dutch or English manner" (38), and donning the fabric spun from a global capitalist economy, he is brought into sartorial "civilization." But the scene does not only evidence his submission, since it also proves that Gronniosaw comprehends how exchange value works. Gold constitutes wealth and is extremely valuable as a medium for exchange for the Dutch captain, but it holds no value for the slave who has just been made into a commodity. As with Robinson Crusoe, the young Gronniosaw can do nothing with his ample reserves of gold, and so he trades it for something that, at that moment in time and place, is more useful for him.

He describes a similar moment of calculated cost-benefit analysis when he recalls his experience on a privateer ship, the narration of which elucidates the long strands of financial dependence linking human society. Gronniosaw is compelled to join the privateering venture "in Character of Cook" in order to repay a white man to whom he was indebted for three pounds (44). Although he is legally free, his indebtedness leaves him vulnerable since as a black man he can easily be recommodified. Thus when his creditor threatens to sell him illegally, Gronniosaw agrees to the terms of the voyage. Gronniosaw narrates this part of his career by calculating the profit he makes, revealing that his share of the pillage of the French merchant ships offshore of St. Domingo was 135 pounds and a hogshead of sugar. His possession of this money is short-lived, however, since his creditor takes it all from him, claiming the total is necessary to repay the debt. He presents a scene that will be repeated in numerous slave narratives, in which the legal precariousness of free people of color allow them to be victims of fraud and larceny. But there are two other things to note about Gronniosaw's narration of the incident. First, Gronniosaw tells a harrowing story about the origins of the money, recalling how the captain of his ship takes more than 4,000 pounds from one prisoner, and echoing the scene of Gronniosaw's initial captivity, the prisoner gives up "several valuable rings" in order to bargain for his life. Gronniosaw knows that the captain intends to kill the man, but because they do not speak the same language, he cannot "let him know his danger" and the man is murdered (44). Gronniosaw thus acknowledges that the 135 pounds stolen from himself was itself taken by force. And so, even though he conveys his pathos for the murdered man and his plight, the explicit echoing of his own captivity, as well as the fact that the money comes from a French merchant ship outside of St. Domingo, also signals that the 135 pounds cannot be disentwined from the wider routes of Atlantic slave traffic. Second, Gronniosaw does not describe his capitulation to the theft as either naiveté or cowardice, instead articulating it as a calculated decision. Because his creditor was "one of the Principal Merchants in the city," there are substantial financial risks in opting "to quarrel with him" (45). Indeed, even when another merchant wishes to recover the money for him, Gronniosaw declines the offer, saying "I wou'd rather be quiet" (45). He congratulates himself on this decision, revealing that his larcenous creditor later experiences a series of "losses and misfortunes" and ultimately drowns. It is certainly possible to read this as confirmation of divine providence, as evidence that God has punished the man for his avarice. But Gronniosaw does not credit God, instead implying that the episode justified his own economic decision to let the matter go.

His faith in the market may seem misplaced given that Gronniosaw remains in relative poverty for the duration of his life, and the story of economic hardship and life among the working poor in England dominates the second half of the narrative. This portrait of poverty serves the broader ambitions of those who helped him publish the narrative, which was to showcase how salvation was extended to people of all ranks and conditions. This was a crucial argument for Whitefield, Hastings, Frelinghuysen, and Benjamin Fawcett, Gronniosaw's own minister when he lived in Kidderminster, England. Fawcett had published *A Compassionate Address to the Christian Negroes in Virginia* in 1756, a text that demands its audience "be patient, be submissive and obedient…even when some of your masters are most unkind," justifying the temporal suffering of enslavement as the necessary price of deliverance from "the Frauds of Mahomet, or Pagan Darkness, and Worship of Dæmons."[102] Fawcett acknowledges that "there is much Difference of outward State and Condition, between high and low, rich and poor, prosperous and afflicted, *bond and free*," but explains that "such Differences are small and inconsiderable...[because] Christ is *all* for Salvation, and *in all* Persons, of whatsoever Rank and Condition in Life provided they be such as receive and obey him."[103] Gronniosaw provides his life as a case study of Fawcett's mandate, demonstrating his faithful submission to both chattel slavery and wage slavery, explaining that he will take his ultimate reward in the promise of eternal salvation. Yet Gronniosaw also devotes a considerable portion of his text to explicating how the "free" worker sells his labor in the marketplace.

Consider, for example, how much the textile industry dominates Gronniosaw's life story. As we have seen, the first transaction that turns him into commodity is when he is exchanged for yard of a cotton fabric, likely manufactured in India and imported by the Dutch East India Company. In providing this detail, Gronniosaw not only reveals the importance of fabric to the Atlantic slave trade, but also gestures at the importance of the trade wars that surrounded textile imports throughout the eighteenth century. His readers would recognize, for example, that the fabric for which he was first exchanged was also banned from import to England by the Calico Acts in 1721, legislation explicitly designed to "Preserve and Encourage the Woollen and Silk Manufactures of this Kingdom, and for more Effectual Employing the Poor" by prohibiting London merchants from importing fabric but allowing a continued export trade to her colonies.[104] Included among the ranks of "the poor" that such legislation was purportedly designed to aid was the woman Gronniosaw ultimately marries. And thus the second half of his narrative describes these woolen and silk manufacturing trades at considerable length, thereby also mapping the intersections between various commodities—human and textile—crossing the Atlantic.

When he first meets his future wife, Betty, sometime between 1764 and 1767, she is weaving silk on Petticoat Lane, one of the major hubs of silk production in London's Spitalfields neighborhood.[105] Although silk manufacturing came relatively late to England, and only after the large influx of Huguenot weavers in 1685 (after the revocation of the Edict of Nates), it quickly emerges as a significant national industry. But the industry also became a case study in protectionist economic policy.[106] From the latter part of the seventeenth century on, Parliament enacted a variety of laws, including tariffs, bounties, and prohibitions, designed to protect domestic silk manufacturing and trade.[107] In fact, the Spitalfields silk weavers had been instrumental to the passage of the Calico Acts, in part because the Weaver's Company put legislative pressure on Parliament, but also because the weavers were principal actors in the infamous riots and assaults against calico-wearing London consumers.[108] And so, for much of mid-century, the English silk business thrived, as is evidenced by the fact that when Gronniosaw first meets Betty, she is making, as he puts it, "a very good living by weaving" (49). Although there were regulations prohibiting female silk weavers, the high demand for silk goods required more laborers, and women increasingly entered their ranks. And because the trade was organized around master weavers who employed journeymen weavers, women could labor at home and get paid by the piece.[109] Since Gronniosaw tells us that Betty is working on a loom on the top floor of their lodging house in Spitalfields, we can presume that these are the conditions of her employment.

But the economic situation for London silk weavers was also highly volatile since England was entirely dependent on imports for their raw silk; when the silk supply was disrupted, the impact was immediately felt by the journeyman weavers. This was the situation in the 1760s when Gronniosaw and Betty are living in Spitalfields. Weavers took to the streets to protest, becoming increasingly organized in their resistance and forming "clubs" that met in pubs and taverns.[110] The demonstrations come to something of a head in 1769, when a huge crowd attacked the Duke of Bedford's house in retaliation for his proposed legislation to reopen the British market to French silk imports; this is perhaps what Gronniosaw references when he recalls, "there was great disturbance among the weavers" (49).[111] He does not make explicit his wife's involvement in the labor disputes except to mention that he was "afraid to let my wife work," lest they "should insist on my being one of the rioters" (49), thereby articulating his anxiety that he will be compelled into a radicalism that would have been particularly dangerous as a black man.[112] It is also distinctly possible that as a female weaver, Betty could have been the object of protest, as some of the violence was directed at women and more recent immigrants who were accused of depressing wages.[113] The protests ultimately lead to the Spitalfields Weavers Act of 1773, which effectively established a set labor price for the weavers, but long before this, Gronniosaw and Betty had abandoned the silk industry.[114]

They abandon silk manufacturing, but each of the cities to which they travel—Colchester, Norwich, and Kidderminster—were significant locations in British textile manufacturing.[115] Gronniosaw's narrative depicts life in these cities as one of hardship and poverty. In fact, while he is notably silent in describing the material conditions of his life as an American slave, in this section of the narrative, he goes into painful detail about his depravations. He recalls, for example, how he and his family almost starve to death, and that his wife is forced to chew their only food, raw carrots, in order to sustain their infant child. As was the case in Gronniosaw's account of his life as a chattel slave, he nevertheless represents himself as faithfully submitting to his condition and gratefully receiving the gifts of Christian charity. But he also showcases a deep comprehension of the mechanics of economic exchange that leaves his family destitute.

Gronniosaw first finds employment with a wealthy Quaker merchant, Osgood Hanbury, in Colchester.[116] The source of Hanbury's wealth was directly linked to North America slavery, for he had inherited his father's business, one of the largest and most successful importers of Virginia tobacco.[117] George Washington used the firm to export his tobacco, and his extensive correspondence with Hanbury records annoyance at the volatility of the commodities market. Remarking on the depressed prices for tobacco in 1774, an exasperated Washington threatens Hanbury, "it will not be worth continuing the business of Planting any longer."[118] Gronniosaw does not detail the nature of his work for Hanbury, saying only that "There were several employed in the same way with myself," but he does tell a story of his wages that indicates a clear-sighted vision into what Marx will later designate as surplus value. Again evidencing his attention to economic detail, Gronniosaw recalls, "I was allowed but eight-pence a day, and found myself" (49). That is, he was required to provide his own food and shelter with the daily eight pence wage he received from Hanbury. Gronniosaw does not complain about the wage, declaring himself to be "thankful and contented though my wages were but small" (49). But he does explain that when he meets his employer, Hanbury insists that the income is "too little," and he orders an increase to "eighteen pence a day" (49). At one level, this scene is probably designed to represent Hanbury as a philanthropic benefactor. This generous portrait is revised, however, when Gronniosaw also mentions that at the beginning of the winter, having "no further occasion for me" (50), Hanbury dismisses him from his employ. As such, we should read this account of his changing wage as a recognition of the highly fungible price of free labor. After all, if his wage can fluctuate almost six shillings per week, then what are the grounds on which his employer has chosen to value his labor? The anecdote would seem to imply that labor is like any other commodity in that its price is variable. And the fact that Gronniosaw doesn't specify the type of work he performs would also seem to indicate the issue is not whether he is engaged in productive labor (like weaving) or unproductive labor (like valeting), but that all labor prices are an index of what the market will bear. This market will bear whatever is requisite to reproduce labor. Hanbury's insistence that eight pence is "too little" is not a concern for Gronniosaw's comfort, since he is quick to dismiss him as soon as winter comes, but instead recognition that the laborer requires more than a daily eight pence to sustain his capacity for work.

One reason that Gronniosaw provides such an extended portrait of his family's poverty is to lay bare the most basic fact of capitalism, which is that workers' lives can only be sustained if they trade their labor for wages. But he describes a system in which "we could not get our living in a regular manner" (52). The family travels to Norwich, which had been the capital of English wool production, and his wife rents a loom in an effort to sustain the family. But Gronniosaw enumerates the various causes that make it so they are unable to "support a family" (52). He characterizes the boom and bust cycle of textile production in which "sometimes she could get nothing to do," while at other times when they "had orders from LONDON they were so excessively hurried" (52). Irregular employment and irregular payment of wages leads to debt and threats of eviction and starvation. Gronniosaw once again explicitly uses the story of his misery to credit God's grace, a grace that takes the form of a wealthy Quaker providing charity. Gronniosaw recalls that Mr. Henry Gurney "heard of our distress" and "hired our room of, paid our rent, and bought all the goods, with my wife's loom, and gave it us all" (52).[119] The Gurney family were important figures in English woolen manufacturing. In fact, Henry Gurney's father had spoken in Parliament on behalf of the Calico Acts, arguing that the failure to protect British woolen manufacturing would cause "many hundred thousand families [to] perish."[120] By mid-century, the firm had become the exclusive supplier of wool to Norwich weavers, and also began to loan money to purchase equipment and labor. The lending business proved so lucrative that they ultimately left the woolen trade for banking exclusively, forming the original Norwich Bank in 1770.[121]

These facts are pertinent to Gronniosaw's narrative because they significantly change our understanding of his financial encounter with Gurney. While his family was certainly rescued from a dire financial predicament when Gurney pays their rent and purchases all their belongings, it is also clear that Betty will be expected to produce in kind labor for the exchange. And the inconsistency by which weavers receive orders for products makes her income impossible to predict, and so even with the purchase (or rent) of the loom, Gronnisow confesses that it was impossible for the family to "get our living in a regular manner" (52). To augment their income, Gurney purchases a tool for Gronniosaw so that he can find "the employment of chopping chaff" (52). Chaff cutting was recommended to farmers as a way to feed their animals more efficiently, as sheep and cattle could more quickly eat straw and hay that was cut into smaller pieces.[122] Gronniosaw describes his pleasure at the business, which made him "easy and happy" (52). But he also explains that his "comfortable state" was sustained only when he was only one of the "few persons in the town that made this their business." Once other people disrupt the oligopoly, they ruin him by working "under price on purpose to get my business from me" (52). Even as his narrative condemns his competitors as "envious and ill-natur'd," his description also necessarily raises the question as to what is the proper price at which his labor ought to be sold. Gronniosaw had determined a price (which he does not identify) at which to sell the chaff that would yield both happiness and comfort. When others sell their labor more cheaply, the price he had set is no longer competitive, and he becomes "again unfortunate" (52). In this brief account of the chaff chopping industry, Gronniosaw articulates the precarity of free trade.

And so Gronniosaw and his family travel to yet another English city dedicated to textile manufacturing. Kidderminster had been the site of British textile production for centuries and was known for the manufacture of a worsted broadcloth called "Kidderminster Stuff." By the time Gronniosaw moves there, because of the volatility of the global textile trade, the city was beginning to shift to the manufacture of a carpet that was likewise called Kidderminster. But Gronniosaw and his wife continue in the older industry, employed by John Watson, a prominent stuff manufacturer.[123] Betty "by hard labor at the loom, does everything that can be expected from her towards the maintenance of our family," and Gronniosaw is employed "in twisting silk and worsted together" (53). Spinning together raw materials taken from domestic sheep and imported silk, Gronniosaw manufactures a thread, which Betty will weave into a fabric that will enter into the very same trade network through which Gronniosaw first became a commodity: a boy for two yards of check.[124] These final images of the narrative thus provide a snapshot of the warp and woof of the economic story Gronniosaw tells—a story that, as we have seen, patiently explains the entwinement of chattel slavery and the free market.

## Reckoning with Venture Smith

In its tone and style, Venture Smith's narrative account of his captivity and life in slavery couldn't be more different than Gronniosaw's. Whereas Gronniosaw shapes his narrative as a story of spiritual redemption and represents himself as humble supplicant to Christian charity, Smith narrates his life story as one of physical and material perseverance in the face of betrayals and injury. And much of the scholarship on Smith's narrative has tried to make sense of the way that he depicts the value of his life, and his family's life, around pecuniary terms, as if his autobiography was a ledger book.[125] A good deal of attention, for example, has been paid to Smith's expression of loss at the death of his son: "In my son, besides the loss of his life, I lost equal to seventy-five pounds."[126] Critics have tended to see his strict accounting of dollar value as submission to the impersonal and mercenary logic of slaveholding and capitalism and have tried to rationalize it.[127] But rather than trying to redeem Smith from his balance sheets, I want to read it as a strategy with which he explicates the economic logic by which human beings are given value. Smith's scrupulous accounting is designed to illustrate the economic system into which he and his audience are implicated.

His story of captivity begins as a tale of economic betrayal: his father promises to pay a "large sum of money, three hundred fat

cattle, and a great number of goats, sheep, asses, &c." to his enemies
in exchange for his people's "liberties and rights," but "their pledges
of faith and honor proved no better than those of other unprincipled
hostile nations" (372) and his family and community are taken captive. His father quickly dies at the hands of an enemy who tortures
him in an attempt "to make him give up his money" (373). Other
scholars have written about the significance of this early incident, as
it offers a psychological explanation for the intense focus that Smith's
narrative puts on capital acquisition. His dedication to economic
solvency becomes a compensatory exercise not only for his own
experience as slave, but also for his defeated and betrayed father. But
the scene also reveals Smith's conception of economic exchange
more generally: instead of seeing economic contracts as the epitome
of free exchange, he sees them as a power struggle in which one side
inevitably takes advantage of the other. For Smith, the "market" does
not operate according to a *doux commerce* thesis in which, as Thomas
Paine said, the "pacific system" of commercial exchange would "cor-
dialise mankind" but is based instead on a zero-sum game.[128] Smith
describes economic exchanges not in terms of use value—people
acquire things that they desire to use and consume—but in terms of
exchange value: purchasers will convert their commodities (including, of course, human property) into other commodities that they
hope will prove more lucrative in a highly diversified marketplace of
buyers and sellers.

Like many African-born slave narrators, Smith describes the
financial transaction that initiates his passage over the Atlantic: he
recalls that he was purchased by the slave ship's steward, Robertson
Mumford, "for four gallons of rum, and a piece of calico," further
explaining that he received his name, Venture, "on account of
[Mumford] having purchased me with his own private venture"
(374). Like other ex-slave autobiographers, Smith provides the terms
of the purchase in order to highlight the fact that chattel slavery
values a human child in terms of rum and cloth, but the details, as
with Gronniosaw, reveal much about the economics of the slave
trade. We learn that Mumford's purchase is a "private venture," an
investment he is making in addition to the income he would expect
to receive as a percentage of the profit netted by the voyage. In
exchanging his rum and calico for Smith, Mumford is taking an
individual risk in betting that the child will reap him more profit
than the sale of the rum and calico. He is making a calculated specu-

lation about the future value of objects, and in naming his property "Venture" he describes his gamble to purchase a boy that, unlike rum or cloth, could die.

Smith's specifications about the terms of the exchange also provide a highly condensed representation of the global reach of Atlantic traffic. In referencing rum and calico, two commodities that were often used as currency in the Gold Coast slave trade, Smith allows readers to see the deep connections between slave trading and other commercial enterprises. For example, Mumford probably acquired the gallons of rum with which he made his purchase from one of the thirty existing Rhode Island distilleries that served as major sources of rum production in the early eighteenth century. Rum constituted the primary form of payment between Rhode Island merchants and Gold Coast slaving ports like Anomabu, from which Smith himself began the Middle Passage.[129] The rum was distilled from the molasses that emerged as a byproduct of sugar refinement in the West Indies, an industry almost exclusively dependent on slave labor. And so Smith establishes his own purchase price as a synecdoche for the larger Atlantic traffic that exchanged sugar, molasses, rum, and human beings. In this way, he also signals that he is necessarily linked to West Indian plantation production even as he himself only passes through Barbadoes en route to New England.

The purchase price of the piece of calico, as we saw in Gronniosaw's narrative, reveals another interconnected market, reorienting the geography away from the Atlantic world of North America and the West Indies and towards the eastern Atlantic and the trade between England and India, where almost all calico cotton was woven and printed. Like New England rum, which was called Guinea Rum, Indian-made cloth, often called Guinea cloth, was a primary commodity currency with which merchants paid for African slaves and was a crucial link in the economic relationship between England and her North American colonies. Mumford's ownership of a piece of the cloth identifies him as a very minor player in this export trade. But, as in the case of the four gallons of rum, the detail also allows Smith to present this singular transaction by which he is enslaved as epitomizing a larger circuit of economic relations linking Calcutta textile mills to London offices of the East India Company, to Barbados sugar plantations, to Rhode Island rum distilleries.

Even after Smith lands in New England and seemingly enters a much more localized economy, his narrative draws our attention to the myriad ways New England plantation life was incorporated into the expansive reach of Atlantic trade.[130] In his descriptions of his time on Fishers Island, Smith reveals how his labor on the remote island in the Long Island sound was linked to the Caribbean economy. He explains that he was required "to pound four bushels of ears of corn every night in a barrel for the poultry" and "to card wool until a very late hour" (375). He conveys how his labor was used to make the corn digestible for the poultry that will reproduce his labor, which is valuable to his owners because it is used to produce the wool and sheep that constituted the primary export from Fishers Island. Since we know that the Mumford family leased the Island for 1,100 pounds a year (they did not own the land), we have some indication of just how lucrative this trade was.[131] Given that 78 percent of New England's export trade at mid-century was with colonies that relied on slave labor, either in North America or the West Indies, we can see that much of the produce on Fishers Island is circulating to other economies powered by slave labor.[132] And so, in his brief references to poultry and sheep, Smith gestures towards an agricultural market that extends its reach to the West Indies and by extension also to Africa, Britain, and the East Indies.

Smith's description of his labor on Fishers Island also makes careful reference to his long hours, as he explains that "every night" he was required to pound the corn, and that he carded wool "until a very late hour" (375). Certainly part of what is at stake here is Smith's desire to testify to ways that enslaved children were abused, and his recollection perhaps also serves as a moment of pride in which he marvels at what he was able to perform even as a young child. We might register something similar when Smith later recalls being ordered to carry a "barrel of molasses" for two miles, or to carry seven bushels of salt the distance of "two or three rods" (377). But in each case, Smith is also implicitly making an argument about the efficiency of slave labor. In other words, instead of accepting the widely held premise that forced labor was necessarily less productive than free labor—for example, to use the familiar formulation, that the labor of five slaves was equal to the labor of three free persons—Smith insists that the threat of physical punishment proves incentive to highly productive work. He continues to work late into the night and he transports absurdly heavy objects, because he wants to avoid being "rigorously punished" (375). The fact that he is carrying barrels of molasses and salt, commodities that came from the West Indies and were produced and harvested from slave labor, also serves to represent how he is attached to a commercial system that extends throughout the Atlantic world. Hefting the commodified form of slave labor on his shoulders, Smith provides a tidy visualization of how New England and the West Indian landowners and merchants work in cooperation to secure the wealth that comes from his work.

In making this economic argument, Smith echoes Olaudah Equiano's similar claim from his narrative, in which he specifically disputes the contention "that a negro cannot earn his master the first cost."[133] Equiano and Smith are engaged in two projects: the first is to contradict the racist assumption that black bodies required non-pecuniary incentives to labor, and the second is to elucidate how slavery accommodated itself to capitalized labor. Equiano observes that many of the specialized trades—mechanics, coopers, carpenters, masons, and smiths—are occupied by slaves, thereby revealing that slave owners appropriate the value of what his readers would typically understand as both skilled and free labor. Equiano further observes, "I have known many slaves whose masters would not take a thousand pounds current for them," thus plainly displaying the considerable profit that could be taken from the work of slaves."[134] The danger is that by identifying the productivity of unfree labor, Equiano threatens to contradict a presupposition of antislavery writing, which is that there is a fundamental distinction between slavery and free labor, between a commercial market that compels work through economic incentive and one that compels it through brute force. Such considerations are at work in Equiano's recollection that during his tenure as a slave driver, he was able to improve the productivity of his workforce by ameliorating their treatment: by providing more food and rest, his slaves "did more work by half than by the common mode of treatment they usually do."[135] He advocates for improving the conditions of enslaved persons in the West Indies through an explicitly economic argument: there is more profit to be gained from healthy slaves than impoverished ones. He does so, I would suggest, at least partially because he wants to represent the economics of slave trading, slave owning, and slave labor as in a continuum with other enterprises that generated wealth in the eighteenth century.

Smith provides his own life as an illustration of a similar point in his detailed accounting of how he secured the funds to purchase his manumission. He tells this story through two intertwined narrative threads. Emphasizing himself as an article of exchange, he presents his life as determined by the men who hold him; but he also asserts himself as an owner, as someone who will secure objects of value. We see this counterpoint structure when Smith recalls being sold after a failed escape:

> I was sold to a Thomas Stanton, and had to be separated from my wife and one daughter.... He resided at Stonington-point. To this place I brought with me from my late master's, two Johannes, three old Spanish dollars, and two thousand of coppers, besides five pounds of my wife's money. This money I got by cleaning gentlemen's shoes and drawing boots, by catching musk-rats and minks, raising potatoes and carrots, &c. and by fishing in the night, and at odd spells. (377)

The scrupulous record of his savings allows us to see the heterogeneous currencies through which North American colonists engaged their commercial affairs, as well as the various occupations through which Smith secured his capital. He received a wage for cleaning and drawing footwear, but also would have sold the produce of his hunting, farming, and fishing. In both cases, he found time for these private ventures only "in the night" and in "odd spells," when his labor was not being used to improve the property of his owners. Five pounds also comes from wife—and Smith's sentence registers the fact that although he is separated from her body, he retains possession of the money she herself has acquired through her additional labor.

Although Smith itemizes his holdings by referencing various mediums of exchange, he also translates the amount into another medium, observing "All this money, amount[ed] to near twenty-one pounds York currency" (377). He provides the sum in this denomination because, he explains, this is the amount "my master's brother, Robert Stanton, hired of me, for which he gave me his note" (377). This loan, which Smith entered with the presumption that his capital would be returned with interest, ends up exemplifying the fiscal perfidy of white colonists, as later Stanton "broke open my chest containing his brother's note to me, and destroyed it" (379). The significance of the capital loss is registered formally as the event constitutes a rare example of narrative disruption in a story that Smith otherwise tells according to a strictly linear chronology: "It may here be remembered, that I related a few pages back, that I hired out a sum of money to Mr. Robert Stanton, and took his note for it" (379). As he treats so many losses in his narrative, Smith represents this one unsentimentally, taking it as an occasion to reconsider basic tenets of capitalist economics. Refusing to abide by the moral of the Parable of the Talents that espouses the basic dogma of capitalist accumulation, Smith explains his decision to bury his money "in the earth" as it would be "safer than to hire it out to a Stanton" (379). In other words, Smith determines that the only way he can keep his money safe is to take it out of circulation even as he recognizes that this also effectively makes his money worthless.

By contrast, Smith emphasizes just how much money his owners make by circulating his body as capital. He recounts, for example, how one man, Hempsted Miner crafts a strategy in which Smith should appear "discontented...and unreconciled," and by adopting this posture, Miner anticipates he will be able to "bargain" a reduced price to purchase Smith. Miner then tries to sell Smith, hoping to secure a quick profit. When his speculation fails, Miner instead opts to pawn Smith for ten pounds, thereby borrowing money using Smith's body as debt collateral. Smith shrewdly observes that Miner's intention is "to convert me into cash, and speculate with me as with other commodities" (379). Indeed Smith reveals that Miner is still in arrears for his purchase and, thus, is not only trading with Smith but also engaged in leveraged trading: as a white man, Miner can secure both Smith's exchange value and use value even though his own ownership of Smith is mortgaged.[136]

When Smith recounts his strategy to purchase his own freedom, he thus describes himself as engaged in a direct competition with his owners over who will appropriate the profit that emerges from his status as both cash commodity and productive laborer. Although, like Gronniosaw, Smith claims he has an "ignorance of numbers" (383) that allows him to be "cheated," his painstakingly precise descriptions of his fiscal affairs suggests his acute comprehension of the myriad ways the market economy expropriates his value. Further, Smith's description of how he finances his manumission also demonstrates how white colonists were able to profit from their capacity both to hold and emancipate slaves, thereby shattering any illusions about a clear dichotomy between slave and free labor. Smith begins his attempt at self-purchase by reinvesting in the possibility of capital circulation as he digs up the "money which I some time since buried" (380). But, having learned the deep risks of engaging in any economic contract as a slave, he asks a "free negro man" to serve as his proxy for the trade. In many ways, this triangulated exchange seems relatively straightforward: his new owner, the merchant Colonel Oliver Smith, "consent[s]" to Smith's desire to buy his freedom, and Smith "engage[s]" a freeman to initiate the exchange. Yet the terms that Smith uses to describe the transaction suggest a very complicated financial relationship between Venture Smith and Colonel Smith. The free black man agrees to "take [Colonel Smith's] security" because Venture Smith "could not safely take his obligation myself" (380). Because Smith has told us that the transaction involves his manumission, we are led to assume that the "security" and the "obligation" refer to the receipt of purchase price, but neither term typically is used to depict the receipt of property, and instead are used to reference credit exchanges: a debtor provides some form of security indicating his obligation to repay. Thus it seems that Smith's payment serves as both a down payment on his self-possession and an extension of credit to his owner. Smith makes this clearer when he explains that he received "some interest accruing on my master's note to my friend the free negro man above named" and that he uses this interest to accumulate more funds by which to buy his freedom. Smith notes that he did not have sufficient funds to pay for his entire purchase price, but that "my master agreed to wait on me … until I could procure it for him" (380). Here, then, Smith represents his owner as the creditor and himself as indebted—as mortgaged to Oliver Smith—even as he is also receiving his owner's interest payments.

But Smith makes it clear that unlike a mortgage, which implies both debt and ownership (I am the legal owner of my house although I still owe over half its value), his own purchase payments do nothing to change his status: no matter how much he pays, he is still the legal property of Colonel Smith. We see this as Smith explains that he was required to ask permission to "go[] out to work" and in his detailed enumeration of the conditions of this labor. We learn that Colonel Smith allows him to labor on his own behalf (which is to say, to secure the profits from his own labor), but only if he pays 25 percent of these earnings. After one season under this arrangement, Colonel Smith renegotiates the terms even more to his advantage, demanding Smith pay two pounds per month for the "privilege" of earning his own money as a laborer. Smith observes that of the twenty pounds he earned that season, only six pounds and fourteen shillings could be used "for my freedom," while the remaining "thirteen pounds six shillings…my master drew for the privilege" (380). This time, then, Smith must pay his owner 66 percent of his earnings. The financial details are crucial because they allow Smith to showcase just how profitable slaveholding and slave emancipating is for white owners. Even as he is ostensibly allowing Smith an opportunity for autonomous labor and self-ownership, Colonel Smith secures 100-hundred percent of his profits both in the fee for the "privilege" and the payment for himself. And thus there is nothing for Smith to celebrate in his emancipation beyond the realization that he has "made considerable money with seemingly nothing to derive it from" and that he has "paid an enormous sum for my freedom" (381).

It is in the aftermath of this anti-climactic self-purchase, in the final chapter of the narrative, where Smith provides the passages that, as Jennifer Rae Greeson observes, "have given recent commentators most pause."[137] Readers are "discomfit[ed]" when Smith extends his scrupulous bookkeeping to tally the people he himself purchased. He explains, for example, that he "lost all" when the "negro man" he bought runs away (382). Even more troubling is when Smith reckons the purchase of his son, who ultimately dies during a whaling voyage, as a monetary loss: "In my son, besides the loss of his life, I lost equal to seventy-five pounds" (382). Indeed, he monetizes all his family members: for his pregnant wife Meg, he "gave forty pounds" (382), for each son he "paid two hundred dollars" (385). Greeson argues that such moments are not evidence of Smith's assimilation into the logic of possessive individualism, but rather signal a rarely acknowledged fact about liberal self-possession, which is that a "precondition" of ownership is alienation or objectification.[138] Simply put, I cannot imagine owning myself unless I already conceive of myself (my body, my labor, my consciousness) as something to own, and therefore also alienable. By theorizing the economy as a system in which all components (seller, buyer, good) find equivalence in another form of representational value, Smith highlights this paradox of self-possession.

But because the captivity narrative has historically been read as a genre exclusively designed to represent the triumph of economic emancipation, we have been unable to read Smith's reckonings as anything beyond capitulation to economic liberalism. Indeed, even Greeson, who rightly sees in Smith's work a demonstration of the mutualism between the tenets of free trade capitalism and the Atlantic slave trade, nonetheless frames his project as a "struggle to acquire the already alienated self."[139] That is, she sees the plot of Smith's narrative as exclusively one of property ownership. Yet given the stunning bathos of Smith's description of his emancipation, we might read his book according to another plot. He presents his life story in order to reckon the many transactions across supply chains spanning the Atlantic, and his text thus offers a pertinacious analysis of the intersections between the slave trade and free market capitalism. In doing so, he also levels an implicit rebuke to those who imagine that they can free themselves from the atrocities of the slave trade by, say, reading an abolitionist text.

## Mapping with Boyrereau Brinch

Published in Vermont in 1810, *The Blind African Slave, or Memoirs of Boyrereau Brinch, Nicknamed Jeffrey Brace* provides a story of a life that in its basic contours resembles the narratives of other eighteenth-century African-born men stolen into slavery. Taken captive while in his teens, Brinch made the Middle Passage in 1758 on a British slave ship. Soon after his arrival in Barbados, he was purchased by an officer of the English Navy, and he sailed between the West Indies, North America, and Europe during the Seven Years' War. At the war's conclusion, he was carried to Connecticut, where he was bought and sold numerous times. He was finally emancipated at the end of his service for the American side during the Revolutionary War, after which he settled in Vermont. Like Gronniosaw and Smith, Brinch recorded his memoir through amanuensis—in his case, the white abolitionist, Benjamin Prentiss.[140] Prentiss arranged publication with a local newspaper printer, but sales of the book were not good, and it was not until Kari J. Winter edited a scholarly version in 2004 that the book was reprinted.[141]

There are a variety of reasons why *The Blind African Slave* did not achieve the popularity of similar narratives directed at an abolitionist audience. The publisher that printed it went out of business soon after the release of the book, and Brinch's emphases on northern racism in his portrait of his life as free man of color in Vermont would not have been especially appealing to the New England abolitionist readers serving as the primary market for the book.[142] But neither of these explanations account for why *The Blind African Slave* still remains in relative obscurity in the twenty-first century. Besides

Winter's extensive introduction to her edition of the text, there is only one full-length essay on Brinch.[143] This lack of attention is all the more curious given the numerous features of the narrative that would seem to make it a compelling text for twenty-first-century readers. Brinch provides, for example, a relatively rare detailed portrait of the horrors of the Middle Passage, Barbados slave markets, and slave-breaking prisons.

In her consideration of the reasons for the text's "disappearance...from scholarship and history," Winter posits one explanation: "no one until now has undertaken...the historical research necessary to 'authenticate' [Brinch's] story and indeed his existence."[144] Her diagnosis is astute: the key generic requirement of the slave narrative—even in our own time—is that it gives authentic expression to an individual life. This imperative explains why his narrative continues to receive such limited attention, even sixteen years after Winter has provided the rigorous archival work to corroborate the facts of his life. But the formal features of Brinch's narrative diminish the expected emphasis on authentic autobiography—on the narration of an individual self. Prentiss, for example, consistently identifies Brinch as the "narrator" of the text and himself as the "author," thereby establishing a distinction between authorship and narration that most slave narratives work to obscure. The book also incorporates a range of other texts (sometimes with attribution and sometimes not) into its pages, producing a text that often feels more like an encyclopedia than a memoir. Moreover, even as Prentiss's title identifies the narrative as a "memoir" that he has transcribed "from [Brinch's] own mouth," it is also the case that Prentiss's voice occupies a more significant presence in the text than is typically the case. Consequentially, contemporary critics may find the narrative uncompelling precisely because it diminishes the feature most valued in slave narratives: a personal testimony of individual experience and perseverance under systematic subjugation.

But, as we saw with both Gronniosaw and Venture Smith, we do these texts a disservice if we insist that the only vehicle through which the former slave can narrate opposition to slavery is through a story of economic liberalism. The extensive explanations and descriptions of commodity exchange offered by Black Atlantic writers are designed not only to demonstrate the human degradations under chattel slavery, but also more basically to explain how a modern economy works. The point is not to describe an escape from an oppressive economic system, but to explain how *everyone* is tied to this economic system. A very similar project, I argue, is at work in Brinch's narrative. Instead of beginning as do most slave narratives— with the African narrator employing a singular first-person pronoun to identify the location of his birth—*The Blind African Slave* begins from the vantage of the non-African seeking knowledge of the continent from an atlas: "Few indeed have been the travellers who have penetrated into the interior of Africa, as far as the kingdom of Bowwoo, which is situated between the 10th and 20th degrees of north latitude, and between the 6th and 10th of west longitude."[145] The first three chapters proceed in similar fashion, sketching Brinch's life according to generic conventions more typical of travel narratives and geographies, even excerpting long passages from popular books, including William Guthrie's *A New Geographical, Historical, and Commercial Grammar* (1770) and Jedidiah Morse's *Universal Geography* (1796).

The consequence, not surprisingly, is that these opening chapters have been credited to Prentiss and not to Brinch, and the authorial relationship between the two men is cast as competitive—as a struggle in which Brinch strives to "assume[] narrative agency from ... Prentiss."[146] Winter characterizes the relationship as more cooperative, as a "blending," but she too assumes a schism between Brinch's "stories" and Prentiss's "research" (6). And certainly the literary history of slave narratives has given us many reasons to be suspicious of the ways white editors shaped and disfigured the words of ex-slaves to accommodate their own literary and political projects. No doubt Prentiss's own agenda is at play in his publication of *The Blind Slave*. Prentiss describes his ambitions for the project in his "Introduction," asserting that the book will "contain a general narrative of an African slave" (89). His use of the indefinite article suggests that he wants to submit Brinch's life story as metonymy for the life of any enslaved African. He even articulates his regret that a "simple narrative of an individual African cannot possibly compass all the objections to slavery" (90). We could then understand the opening chapters as a strategy to widen the aperture—to force the "simple" Brinch to stand in for all the complexities of imperialist exploitation of West Africa. And because this project would seem to eclipse Brinch's story of self-possession, we might be inclined to read the schism that Winter describes. Prentiss uses his research to sketch the general contours of an abolitionist argument, while Brinch wants the opportunity to speak as a free person—as "Boyreau Brinch, nicknamed Jeffrey Brace," and not as "*an* African slave" or even "The Blind African Slave."

But there is no reason to assume that the panoramic scale of these first chapters contradict Brinch's own narrative ambitions.[147] Neither should we assume that the more encyclopedic sections of the text are solely the design of Prentiss. Indeed we can even locate textual evidence to suggest that Brinch had his hand in the idiosyncratic opening in the patronizing "Apology," written by Prentiss, with which *The Blind Slave* concludes. Identifying himself as both "writer" and "author," Prentiss apologizes for the inadequacies of Brinch's narration. Prentiss complains that "not speaking plain English, it was extremely difficult to get a regular chain of [Brinch's] ideas" and that he "would frequently recollect circumstances, which he had omitted in their proper places" (183). In other words, he accuses Brinch of possessing a digressive narratorial style. It is a strange accusation since the more autobiographical sections of the text are arranged according to a quite regular chronological narrative—and, indeed, the most digressive sections are located in the opening chapters that have typically been credited as the product of Prentiss's pen and not Brinch's voice. We might thus read the apologia as indicating that Brinch was himself at least partially responsible for these sections. And rather than view this digressive style as Prentiss does—as evidence of artistic incompetence—let us instead comprehend the stylistic choice as a strategy by which Brinch attempts to explain the broader economic system that ensnares him.

Prentiss blames Brinch for not maintaining a "regular chain," using a metaphor that cannot help but bring to mind a tool that was used to subjugate his memoirist. This is not, however, the figure of linearity emphasized by the text itself. Brinch's early life is rather organized around a motif of divagation that traces the pathway of the Niger River. *The Blind Slave* emphasizes the Niger River's navigability from the very first paragraph, explaining that the only reason readers are able to "penetrate[] into the interior of Africa" is because Europeans travelled by waterway. The second paragraph extends the thesis by offering a plethora of citations from European geographers, explorers, and encyclopedists illustrating attempts to locate the source waters of the Niger and speculating on the economic value the river provides: the Niger "fertilizes the country, and has grains of gold in many parts of it" (92).[148]

This expansive sketch of the river is suddenly narrowed in the opening sentence of the third paragraph, when the narrator announces that the same river that fertilizes the valley and circulates gold fragments is also the vehicle by which Europeans trafficked in slaves: "In the year 1758, an English vessel, engaged in the slave trade, sailed up this river to the head of navigation and came to anchor before the town of Yellow Bongo" (92). This particular English vessel is also the one that captures Brinch, and so the sentence does double-duty: it emphasizes the beautiful river's cooperation in extending European economic conquest over northwest Africa, and it narrows our perspective onto the life of one of the millions of people stolen into slavery. It is at this moment that the "account" is said to be "taken from the narrator's own mouth who was only 15 or 16 years of age when he was taken and borne away from prosperity, affluence and ease into ignominious slavery" (93). Yet the narrative also here deflects the focus on Brinch's autobiography when it announces, "Here we will leave these dealers in human flesh and blood, and give some account of the kingdom of Bow-woo" (93).

In the pages that follow, which are typically credited to Prentiss (although they are also identified as coming from Brinch's own "mouth" and "memory"), we take a narrative digression away from the scene of Brinch's kidnapping and into a more expansive portrait of the region from which Brinch is captured. The emphasis turns to geography and the commercial riches that will flow from "this most luxuriant part of the world" (98). Combining Brinch's own recollections with citations from geographies and travel narratives, the book enumerates the many "commodities" that could be harvested from the region: fruit, grain, saltpeter, wine, timber, etc. This narrative strategy is of course coupled to the familiar abolitionist argument that advocated for the economic value located in African natural resources. But it is also crucial that the book is fashioning Brinch's story as one that cannot be extricated from political economy: readers cannot understand the story of the man without understanding the story of the economic system that has controlled his life. To make sense of this broader system, the narrative dilates its lens further to include not merely the Niger valley, but the region further to the north, "the whole empire of Morocco and Barbary states" (98).

Confessing that this perspective is an excursus, the narrator also justifies it: "it may not be improper to digress so far from the narrative as to give a short sketch of the history of these states, although the kingdom of Bow-woo does not partake much of the general history of them" (100). This digression, which resembles the meandering path of the Niger River, is acceptable because it provides an origin (a sort of source water) to explain the military and commercial contact between Europe and Africa that ultimately leads us back to 1758 and the English slaver travelling up the Niger.

The broader history of the Moroccan Empire is also important to Brinch's autobiography because we learn that it was in 1758 that Brinch's father was "summoned to attend the King on a tour to the city of Morocco to visit the Emperor" (109). It is there that his father has his first encounter with Europeans, returning from the visit having made two significant purchases of "European and India manufacture": "a pair of pistols and [a] piece of purple silk" (109). As we have seen in the narratives of both Gronniosaw and Smith, guns and textiles were crucial vehicles of exchange in the slave trade. Thus Brinch's narrative implicitly links the father's purchase to the extensive paths of global traffic, which would also include the slave trade. The European pistols and Indian silk have moved through various hands and ships—and may have been exchanged for human beings—before they finally make their way to the interior of West Africa to be admired by Brinch's father and his family.

The narrative even more explicitly emphasizes the significance of these commodities associated with the Atlantic slave trade when it locates the recollection of the objects as a moment at which the text shifts to the first-person:

> While my Father and Mother had some gentle dispute about the quality of the silk (for here the writer takes the language of the narrator) I was busy snapping and observing the beauties of the pistol. As soon as an opportunity offered I asked my father where the pistols came from, and where he had obtained them, he said, they came from the white people, who lived on the waters and came to our shores and landed at Morocco, where he purchased them.   (109)

Until this moment, the narrative has followed a third-person voice (which is why readers have assumed the earlier sections are narrated by Prentiss and not Brinch), but here encountering the foreign objects his father has brought back from Morocco, the text adopts the grammar of the memoir ("*my* Father and Mother," "*I* was busy"), which is retained for the remainder of the book. The young boy recollects his admiration for the pistols—a technology of European provenance that also symbolizes the violence used to subjugate people. And the child also wants to know how his father came to possess the pistols. Brinch's father narrates the supply route: the guns come from "white people" who have traveled across the ocean to trade with merchants in the Moroccan Empire, who then trade with him. The father's purchase thus provides a synecdoche of the political geographical overview with which the book began. The objects remain at the narrative focus when Brinch recounts with vivid detail how his father adorned himself to celebrate the feast day that proved to be the last time Brinch would see his family. Having only recently returned from Morocco, his father attires himself in clothing manufactured from the Indian silk, he carries the pistols, and he dresses his "African horse" with other articles he "had procured at Morocco" (110). At the end of the feast, following "custom," his father gives Brinch some of his clothing and his son travels with other boys to bathe in the Niger River. It is on the river that Brinch is taken captive. After a day of "delightful sport" in which he and his friends "plunged into the stream, dove, swam, sported and played in the current," the "white Vultures" descend and seize most of the boys (118).

Brinch's story has finally returned its readers to the English slaver anchored on the Niger River from which the narrative had wandered away in the first chapter so as to provide an expansive illustration of the economic system that determined the rest of Brinch's life. On that day in 1758, the "dealers in human flesh and blood" (93) take the boy out of the Niger River and transform him into a commodity that travels "down the stream like a sluice" (119). The river that had earlier been described as fertilizing the soil and carrying gold to support a population is now the conduit by which human beings are sluiced to the Atlantic Ocean to be sold. And it is while sailing down the Niger that Brinch recollects "here to my sorrow I learned what the white men came to Morocco in, which my father had so imperfectly described to me" (124). Notably, from this point of captivity on, Brinch's narrative adopts the "regular chain" that Prentiss deprecates him for lacking. The peripatetic style associated with the beautiful river becomes the narrative chain that shapes and binds Brinch's movement.

It is also on the cusp of his capture that the book offers another excursus on scripture. As is the case with many abolitionist texts, *The Blind Slave* wants to dispute biblical justification for the enslavement of Africans. To prove that Africans are not the descendants of Cain, Brinch cites passages from Genesis confirming that all humans are the progeny of Seth. And he further traces scriptural lineage to argue that his own family are ancestors of Jethro, Moses's father-in-law. Europeans may not be able to find the source waters of the Niger River, but members of his own family, including his Grandmother, could "trace [their] origin . . . to the days of Noah" (116).

Brinch uses this same narrative excursion to wrestle with the theological issue of prelapsarian free will. His meditation begins with a rhetorical question about scripture: if Adam and Eve are the ancestors of all human beings, then "where is the distinction" that authorizes the enslavement of Africans. But he next turns to a metaphysical problem that he cannot so easily resolve. Adam and Eve, he says, were "irresistibly drawn" by God's will "to partake of the forbidden fruit," but they also were "perfectly free," and so it was also with "the volition of their own wills that they did thus partake of the forbidden fruit" (112). With this answer Brinch accedes to conventional Christian doctrine that original sin was an act of free will; but he also entertains the much more controversial claim that original sin was "irresistible." Brinch raises this thorny theological issue in an effort to draw a moral distinction between those actions undertaken when free and those that are "involuntary." He reframes the same issue in secular terms when he asks "whether a person or any other property, which is sold by any person, who has no other right save that he gains by stealth or theft can be valid, or . . . rendered binding by the laws of this or any other civilized nation" (139). Here, however, there is no ambiguity, as Brinch asserts, "I wish not to attempt to legalize or moralize any transaction that has happened to me since my captivity, as I consider all to be illegal and immoral" (139). He is doing more than saying that slavery is immoral, and therefore that it ought to be illegal. He is suggesting that any enslaved person should not be subject to legal authority: as property, a slave does not possess free will and therefore cannot not be a subject of human governance.

That Brinch intends a relationship between this claim about civil law and his earlier analysis of original sin is evidenced when he describes his own temptation by fruit. He remembers being led from his first prison on Barbadoes to the home of a slave driver and spotting "an orange tree, where the oranges covered the ground" (139). Because he is famished, he desperately wants to eat one of the fallen oranges. But he has no free will: "for fear of being whipped, although hunger that is indescribable...urged, yes, almost forced me to partake of the forbidden fruit," Brinch does not eat the orange. Although he is tempted like Adam and Eve, he does not "partake" because he is not free: if he eats the fruit, he will be beaten with a whip. Brinch thus rewrites the Edenic myth from the experience of slavery: having been transformed into chattel, his obedience cannot be virtue and his transgression cannot be a sin.

The same logic pertains to his experience as an economic subject. Once captured and transformed into commodity, Brinch has no free will, and he refuses to pretend he has any economic agency over his future. Unlike most ex-slave narrators, for example, Brinch does not provide his readers with a detailed accounting of his purchase prices. While Gronniosaw and Venture Smith painstakingly enumerate the exchanges that made them equivalent to fabric, guns, rum, and sterling, Brinch withholds the terms by which he is exchanged. He makes clear that he was exchanged as property—that he was sold, bartered, or "descended like real estate, in fee simple" (158), but he steadfastly does not identify the purchase price.[149] His silence on this subject should be read as an unwillingness to legitimate the contractual nature of the exchanges. Since his labor is compulsory, he does not wish to "legalize...any transaction that has happened to me since my captivity" by itemizing the price at which he provides it (139). We must also observe that his use of the present perfect tense ("has happened") repudiates the legitimacy of contracts even *after* his emancipation.

This is not to say that Brinch equates the experience of being a slave to that of being a free person. Indeed he demarcates the distinction in specifically economic terms when he articulates the moment of his emancipation with the following sentence: "for the first time I made a bargain as a freeman for labor; I let myself to a Mr. Elisha Osborn for one month, at the price of five dollars" (166). Here is the first time in the narrative that Brinch references currency—the vehicle by which objects are supposedly made equivalent under a system of free trade. And as he continues to transcribe his life story, he similarly provides the exact terms of these financial transactions. He next "let[s] himself" to a Vermont landowner "for the sum of thirteen pounds ten shillings, for six months" (166). Soon after he tries to purchase twenty-five acres of land for which he promises "to work six months," contracting with the landowner that he will be paid 250 dollars if he does not receive title. The fact that Brinch offers these details reveals by contrast how little he conveys about the economic arrangements of his enslavement. On one hand, then, Brinch sets out to mark an essential difference between involuntary and voluntary labor: he will only use the language of capital to talk about his labor after emancipation. On the other hand, however, he identifies the numerous contract violations that occur after he is free. Time and again, his labor is devalued and he does not receive the value afforded by the letter of the law.

Even as a freeperson and a landowner, Brinch has only precarious control of his own labor or that of his family. Brinch tells the story of a neighbor who lodges a "complaint" against him in order to seize his stepson as an indentured servant: "As [my son] was about twelve years of age...and could earn more than his living, it was sufficient to induce almost any honest selectman to procure a complaint...that he might have the profits of his labors" (170). Brinch expostulates, appealing first to scriptural law and then to economic fairness. He recognizes that the neighbor's motivation is solely pecuniary: the child becomes profitable when the costs of reproducing his labor are less than the value he generates. And so Brinch explains that he requires his stepson's labor to help clear his own land, the result of which would be to fulfill the Jeffersonian ideal of economic autonomy. But even in Vermont—the first state to prohibit slavery—Brinch "could get no redress" because he is "an old African Negro," and his stepdaughter is likewise indentured despite his protestations (171). Years later, another neighbor makes a similar attempt to indenture his biological children: and while this time the attempt is unsuccessful, it nevertheless exemplifies the fragile status of Brinch's "freedom." No wonder, then, that Brinch uses the present perfect tense: he wants to make it clear that even after he has secured his legal freedom, his destiny is still shaped by the moment in the Niger river in which he enters the economy as human commodity.

The text is bifurcated at this moment of captivity: the systematic illustration of Africa's position in a global economy is reined in by the shift to tell the story of one of slavery's victims and survivors. While Gronniosaw and Smith use their own individual lives to explicate the complex mutualism between the free market economy and the slave trade, Brinch presents a picture of their cooperation in his encyclopedic portrait of European contact with Africa and then tells the life of an individual who will never be free even after his emancipation into the privileges of the market. And so even as his book concludes with familiar abolitionist gestures, including a story of his conversion experience and an expression of hope that his words will soften the hearts of slaveholders, it does not sing the virtues of economic liberalism. Brinch's work does not possess the censorious tone of Venture Smith's narrative, but the effect is much the same: he challenges the supposition that his readers can so easily evade their implication in the economic system of slavery.

One imperative of abolitionist literature was to tell stories that would make remote connections proximate: to stitch the life of an individual person to the larger system that brought sugar to the tea table. We can see how this literature worked in tandem with the emerging discipline of economic science. In mapping the wilderness of economic phenomenon, both the political economist and the ex-slave explained how goods came to market. But, as we have also seen, the economic theorists who most vociferously articulated the essential difference between free and slave labor also presented a theory that assumed its participants would be unable to achieve the perspective necessary to recognize the incompatibility. Economic subjects could only make their decisions on the basis of narrow self-interest and not the macroeconomic analysis that asserted the reduced efficiency of physically coerced labor. The economic irrationalism of the slaveholder was thus a considerable blind spot in classical political economic thought.

Despite their protestations of economic illiteracy, Gronniosaw, Smith, and Brinch provide detailed descriptions of the manifold components of the commercial economy so as to illuminate this spot. Their analysis does not merely showcase the limitations of the individual economic subject, but instead uses their experiences along the long commodity chains of global capital to repudiate the easy distinctions other political economists made between doux-commerce and the slave trade. The detailed economic analysis of these captivity narratives thus tries to force its readers to see with a much wider lens and to recognize, as Paul Gilroy will later put it, that slavery is not the "special property" of black people, but is instead "a part of the ethical and intellectual heritage of the West as a whole."[150] Their work provides a similar illumination of historical capitalism, thereby achieving what Immanuel Wallerstein demands: "We must rid ourselves of the simplistic image that the 'market' is a place where initial producer and ultimate consumer meet."[151] While the dominant narratives of both historical slavery and capitalism have cultivated these "simplistic image[s]," these early transatlantic African captivity narratives provide us with a very different narrative template. Forced to occupy so many roles in this immense system, the ex-slave is not afforded the luxury to read according to the Jeffersonian narrative mode and instead provides a multi-perspective map of capitalism as a world system.

# { Conclusion }

## EXPLAINING THE ECONOMY IN THE TWENTY-FIRST CENTURY

I first began work on this project in 2008, just as the magnitude of the Great Recession was beginning to become apparent to someone like me, living on what felt like the remote edges of highly leveraged finance and derivatives markets. As a fixed-rate mortgage-holding professor in Ohio, whose retirement funds were primarily held in index funds, I paid scant attention to the vicissitudes of the stock market and none at all to credit default swaps—until, that is, the bottom dropped out in September of 2008 with the collapse of Countrywide Financial and Lehman Brothers, and the Federal government's takeover of Freddie Mac, Fannie Mae, and AIG. Then it was all anyone could think about.

Maybe it was simply the coincidence of reading Jeffersonian screeds from the 1790s while also listening to the rising hysteria from the media reporting on the fiscal collapse of 2008, but I was immediately struck by the similarity of the rhetoric. Just as Hamilton's opponents had condemned his fiscal proposals as narrative chicanery—as purposefully abstruse and designed to confuse and dupe the average American farmer—so too, in the wake of the collapse, the argument was that the crisis was at least partially a consequence of language. The housing bubble, so the reasoning went, was caused by the hocus pocus of financiers and hedge fund managers who created and marketed all sorts of new-fangled financial instruments that were too byzantine to be comprehended by ordinary bankers and regulators, let alone regular folk. Following in Hamilton's footsteps, these twenty-first century fiscal wizards and shadow bankers could hoodwink everyone because the instruments they used were designed to

*Speculative Fictions: Explaining the Economy in the Early United States.* Elizabeth Hewitt, Oxford University Press (2020).
© Elizabeth Hewitt.
DOI: 10.1093/oso/9780198859130.001.0001

not be understood. And just as was the case in 1790, many seemed to suggest that the solution to the opacity that made good capitalism turn bad would be found in narrative simplicity.

When the National Commission on the Causes of the Financial and Economic Crisis in the United States in their 2011 report attempted to locate causes and assign blame, they laid much of the responsibility on a hermeneutics that was inadequate to the complex signification of the new financial instruments in which the global economy was vested. Financial institutions "made, bought, and sold mortgage securities they never examined"; financiers created "complex" derivatives with "little documentation"; mortgage purchasers did not read the fine print and did not "understand the most basic aspects of their mortgages"; and regulators, even when they were "warned of this toxic mix…were not on the same page."[1] The report thus identifies bad reading at all sectors of the market. A Goldman Sachs vice president confesses that he "was standing in the middle of all these complex, highly levered, exotic trades he created without necessarily understanding all the implications of those monstrosities." The report drolly observes that the Goldman executive chooses a third-person pronoun to describe his involvement in both the authorship and miscomprehension of these instruments.[2] It lays the same charge at the feet of regulatory agencies, when it cites the president of the Federal Reserve Bank of New York musing, "I don't think people…had a full understanding of the complexity of the shadow banking system."[3] He too tries to relocate responsibility by referencing the ignorant in his own office as anonymous "people."

The commission's emphasis on misinterpretation also explains why the authors present their own 500-page report as an example of narrative lucidity. Having "reviewed millions of pages of documents," "interviewed more than 700 witnesses," and analyzed "a large body of existing work about the crisis," they present their text as a way "to explain in clear, understandable terms how our complex financial system worked, how the pieces fit together, and how the crisis occurred."[4] The appeal to clarity and "understandable terms" does not, however, translate into an attempt to identify a singular cause for the Great Recession since the authors distribute blame widely, pointing to, for example, failures of federal regulatory agencies, malfeasance in corporate governance, and irresponsible debt management at both the household and corporate levels. In fact, the report's latitudinarian approach to apportioning responsibility was the subject of much criticism. A reviewer in *The Economist* offered tepid praise for the report's "comprehensive" coverage, but found considerable fault in the inability to locate "definitive" culpability through its "confusing narrative."[5] These same terms appear in other reviews, which characterize the report as "comprehensive but not definitive."[6] Thus while the report "was a minor hit at the bookstore," having spent two weeks on the *New York Times* bestseller list, it also "faced nearly universal criticism."[7] Having identified its mandate to be the clear identification of *how* the crisis had occurred, the report failed its readers by not locating a singular culprit.

Not surprisingly, one feature that was said to vitiate any possibility for definitive judgment was the inclusion of two "dissenting views," a feature that points to the partisan eyes through which the crisis was judged. Both dissenting opinions were written by Republican-appointed members of the commission, and each rejected the narrative of complex causality that the report had established. The first dissent proceeds by selecting a different cause—a worldwide credit bubble—as a more necessary and sufficient cause, but actually places much more rhetorical stress on narrative weakness in the "majority's approach to explaining the crisis."[8] Castigating the majority authors for not constructing a clear causal narrative, the dissent complains about the report's worthless prolixity: "The majority's almost 550-page report is more an account of events than a focused explanation of what happened and why. When everything is important nothing is."[9] Tellingly, they take their stylistic notes from the lexicon of corporate jargon. The mantra, "When everything is important nothing is" was coined by a corporate management guru to express succinctly the need for employees to prioritize their deadlines. The problem with the 550-word report, in this estimation, is that its argument cannot be printed on a motivational poster. Just as Hamilton's opponents demanded writing that any ordinary farmer could understand, the critics of the 2011 report want narrative explanation so effortless that anyone can grasp it at a glance.

The second dissenting statement displays its partisan hand even more apparently, beginning with the title page that identifies the affiliation of the author, Peter J. Wallison, with the American Enterprise Institute. Predictably, Wallison accuses the Commission of simply being wrong in identifying regulatory incompetence as a necessary cause of the crisis. But, as with the first dissenting opinion, he also complains about the report's attempts at comprehensive explanation: "the majority's report turned out to be a just so story *about* the financial crisis, rather than a report on what *caused* the financial crisis" (444). He condemns the story for its diffusiveness— for offering too much description of setting and not enough plot. His own report, by contrast, will locate a singular cause—"U.S. government housing policy"—as the *"sine qua non"* of the nation's financial collapse (444). But he also characterizes the majority's report as a "just so story," which is to say a fantastical tale that invents a causal explanation. According to this logic, then, the Commission failed both by not pinpointing a clear cause and by insisting on the wrong one. Wallison doubles down on this paradoxical argument later publishing two books—*Bad History, Worse Policy: How a False Narrative about the Financial Crisis Led to the Dodd-Frank Act* (2013) and *Hidden in Plain Sight: What Really Caused the World's Worst Financial Crisis and Why It Could Happen Again* (2015)—that offer a potent cocktail of metaphoric excess and simplistic narrative worthy of John Taylor of Caroline himself. In both books Wallison reprises the argument he had made in his dissent, but with the added flourish of claiming President Barack Obama as the mastermind behind this "dominant narrative" that will undermine the very principles of free trade.

The fact that there is such a tidy analogy to be drawn between Wallison's twenty-first-century condemnation of the Dodd-Frank Act, legislation intended to rein in the excesses of corporatism and financialization, and Taylor's denunciation of Federalist financial policy in the 1790s as legislation designed to expand corporatism and financialization serves to confirm Bray Hammond's thesis about the labile relations between economic policy and political ideology. Like "Hamlet and Laertes," our contemporary politicians have "switched weapons," and Obama can thus step into the role of Alexander Hamilton in this new American tragedy.[10] Of course, as in the 1790s, opposition came from across the political spectrum, with many on the left claiming that the Commission's majority report had been far too gentle in its analysis of regulatory oversight, with the consequence that their long-winded text would effect no meaningful financial reform.[11] But what all these readers found lacking in the *Financial Crisis Inquiry Report*, a document that in many ways stylistically resembles the major reports authored by Hamilton, was the very thing that the Jeffersonians had provided to their readers in the 1790s: a plot that would provide a seamless narrative of economic causality.

This imperative to tell a simple and transparent story of American capital motivates two prominent Hollywood films produced and released as a direct response to the 2008 crisis: Martin Scorsese's *The Wolf of Wall Street* (2013) and Adam McKay's *The Big Short* (2015). Although the historical context for *Wolf of Wall Street* is an earlier moment of financial collapse, both movies were inspired by anger in the aftermath of the crash of 2008 and the subsequent bailout. Scorsese explicitly announced his desire to excoriate modern finance, saying "The film came out of frustration over the unregulated financial world....I kept saying that I wanted to make a ferocious film."[12] McKay vents his spleen in the conclusion to *The Big Short*, which asserts that the guilty financial industries survived the crash unscathed—without adequate punishment or regulation. Both films were also adapted from non-fiction texts that likewise advertised themselves as exposés in which an "insider" author would provide a detailed explanation of the economic subculture that deviously misled and fleeced the average American. Jordan Belfort's memoir, *Wolf of Wall Street* (2007) comprises more than 500 pages of braggadocio narrating Belfort's life from Wall Street "pond scum" to "wolf" to prison inmate, with the avowed purpose of providing "a cautionary tale...to anyone who thinks there's anything glamorous about being known as a Wolf of Wall Street."[13] Michael Lewis's *The Big Short* (2010) took its readers "inside the doomsday machine" of the financial crash by telling the story of the clearsighted insiders who knew it was coming. Lewis does not offer his book as a cautionary tale: having attempted this project with his first book, *Liar's Poker* (1989), a memoir of his experiences as Wall Street bond trader in the 1980s, he knew just how badly Americans read stories about capital accumulation. He recalls his naïve wish that "some bright kid at Ohio State University who really wanted to be an oceanographer would read my book, spurn the offer from Goldman Sachs, and set out to sea." This fantasy did not materialize, and he instead found himself "knee-deep in letters from students at Ohio State University who wanted to know if I had any other secrets to share about Wall Street." They didn't read his life story as a cautionary tale, but as a "how-to-manual."[14]

It was perhaps in anticipation of this American penchant for misreading that the directors of both adaptations opted to be so explicitly meta-fictive in their respective films. Each draws attention to *how* it will tell its story with the seeming ambition to ensure the audience will read it correctly. Both films, for example, are narrated by a diegetic character: Belfort (played by Leonardo DiCaprio) narrates *Wolf of Wall Street*, while the *The Big Short* is narrated by a minor character, Jared Vennett (played by Ryan Gosling). Both films make lavish use of voiceovers by these characters, and both films repeatedly break the fourth wall. Scorsese's decision to have Belfort narrate his film is an obvious allusion to his earlier *Goodfellas* (1990). Echoing Henry Hill's opening voiceover from that movie, "I always wanted to be a gangster," Belfort commences his own tale, "I always wanted to be rich." When *The Big Short* has Vennett rehearse the history of American mortgage securitization by delivering a monologue directed at the camera, McKay is clearly paying homage to both Scorsese films and self-consciously making a similar argument that Wall Street is organized crime that doesn't recognize itself as such.

Yet there are some key differences revealed by these opening monologues. The *Wolf of Wall Street* is narrated by its protagonist and, thus, is plotted like many a story of American business: an autobiography of the fat cat and his ruinous greed. Which is to say, even as the film tells us a little bit about the larger financial ecology in which Belfort operates—about "pumping and dumping" and fake IPOs—the movie is not really about this socio-economic world.[15] It is, instead, an extended character sketch of one individual player in this world. The film may despise its protagonist, Jordan Belfort, even more than many of Scorsese's famous sociopaths, but its story is nevertheless fundamentally Belfort's. One reason Scorsese probably chose his then current muse, Leonardo DiCaprio, for the part was to underscore this fact: the star is the star. By contrast, McKay's *The Big Short* is an ensemble film—one in which, for example, A-lister Brad Pitt plays an entirely ancillary role. Even more crucially, the star of McKay's film is not a person. Instead, the film purports to be about an institution: about the mortgage bond market that fueled a global financial crisis. Vannett's narrative that begins the film emphasizes this point: he will tell a coming-of-age story in which "boring old" banking becomes the "number one industry" of the United States. McKay's emphasis on institutions and not people, on actions and not agents, would seem to convey a very different project from Scorsese's. While both want to offer a furious indictment of American finance and banking, they will do so through different means. *Wolf of Wall Street* condemns its protagonist by associating his financial speculation with corruption, sexual dissolution, and moral turpitude. By contrast, *The Big Short* indicates that it will offer its critique through a comprehensive examination of the system that almost destroyed a global economy. What *Wolf of Wall Street* will accomplish through metonymic association, *The Big Short* will accomplish through exegesis.

The distinction is important because, at first glance, it appears as if the two films model the explanatory modes I have described in this book. Scorsese follows the Jeffersonian template in his portrait of the wolf wreaking havoc in the American garden. By contrast, McKay's film attempts an ambitious reimagining of storytelling and capital exchange: instead of trading in the symbolic currency that lines Wall Street's coffers, it will explicate it. The film is censuring the financial and banking systems associated with Hamilton's legacy, but its own formal structure appears Hamiltonian insofar as it works to elucidate the complexity of the economic vehicles and relations that are also said to cause the financial catastrophe. Indeed, the movie, like Lewis's original book, was lauded by critics for its explanatory density and clarity. Almost all reviewers, for example, called attention to three moments in which the film cut away from diegesis to showcase celebrities defining the financial instruments that were essential components of the crisis. Luxuriating in a bubble bath, Margot Robie explains mortgage backed securities (MBSs); Anthony Bourdain explicates collateralized debt obligations (CDOs) from a restaurant kitchen; and Richard Thaler (the "father" of behavioral economics) and Selena Gomez join forces to explain synthetic CDOs. These moments are essential to one argument *The Big Short* tries to make, which is that the crisis was caused by the inability of economic actors to understand the very objects they were trading. Accordingly, the movie self-consciously presents itself as a Rosetta Stone translating economic gibberish.

This pretense towards narrative clarity is fundamentally different than *Wolf of Wall Street*'s stress on unreliable narration. Much like F. Scott Fitzgerald's "Babylon Revisited" (1931), the movie recollects tales of excess, but it also depicts its protagonist as perpetually forgetting the crashes and cruelties perpetrated while consuming this excess. The most obvious example is when Belfort recounts his short drive home while high on an especially potent form of Quaaludes. According to Belfort's version, the journey miraculously happens without incident. We see him driving his car cautiously before pulling into his driveway with the voiceover: "somehow I made it alive, not a scratch on me or the car." Only the next morning, when Belfort is confronted by the police and discovers the car completely destroyed, does the narration change: "Maybe I hadn't made it home okay." And the film then offers us the "real" vision of the previous night in which Belfort smashes and crashes his way home. The two scenes are played for pure comedy, but the theme of amnesia is one the movie takes quite seriously. Consider, for example, that Belfort begins his career as a stockbroker on Black Monday (October 19, 1987), the day in which the American markets shed 22 percent of their value. But only five years later, in 2002 (the year in which Belfort is arrested), Black Monday was no longer designated a "crash," but merely a "correction." Scorsese's film implicitly argues that this recursive disregard for past losses is as necessary to fuel American financial bubbles as are capitalism's insatiable appetites.

Yet, even as the film seems designed to expose how amnesia perpetuates financial markets, its own narrative strategy depends on obfuscation. In one scene where Belfort speaks directly into the camera, for example, he begins to detail the logistics of his fraud and explain how his firm was able to profit from manipulating the prices of an initial public offering. But he stops himself in mid-sentence to proclaim, "You know what, you're probably not following what I'm saying." This assumption about the audience's ignorance and limited attention span is repeated at the very end of the film in which, after Belfort has served his short prison sentence, he speaks to a sellout crowd who have paid to hear him dispense business advice. The camera positions us to see Belfort through his audience's perspective and, like them, we are seduced into accepting his renewed credibility. We seem to be no wiser now than we were at the beginning of the movie.

The basic problem for Scorsese, as it seems to be for almost any cultural artist who aims to give expression to global finance is that the film is hamstrung between a wish to present a "realistic" portrait of an economic subculture and a conviction that familiar narrative methods are inadequate to the representational task. And thus the film oscillates between two forms: a standard Robinsonnade about Belfort's capital accumulations and losses, and a meta-fictive account about the unnarratable financial market in which he operates. These two aesthetic options are described by Leigh Claire LaBerge in her trenchant literary history of financial fiction of the 1980s (the same time in which *Wolf of Wall Street* is set). She identifies two fictional

forms by which authors tried to represent finance in this period: the
"digestible" postmodern novel and "revanchist realism."[16] The former
is motivated by the assumption that "aesthetic rupture" is required to
represent the "radical newness of finance," and the latter insists that
a "simple" narrative form is the best way to make finance legible.[17] So
committed is *Wolf of Wall Street* to its excoriation of American financial crimes that it tries out both representational strategies, presenting us with both a Tom Wolf-style satirical exposé and postmodern
cognitive estrangement.

*The Big Short* appears to operate with a different aesthetic play-
book, stitching its most postmodern moments—the non-diegetic
celebrity cameos—to a project manifestly aimed at elucidating financial complexities. The lesson of the film is that when we listen to
Bourdain compare the CDO to a seafood stew made from four-day
old cod, we will finally understand this obscure financial object and
therefore be inoculated from future financial harm. The movie likewise proposes that its protagonists' superiority lies in their ability to
read and comprehend what is illegible to others. And the manifest
argument of both the book and movie is that those who foresaw the
ultimate housing crash did so because they actually read the original
subprime mortgages on which the whole bubble was propped. Dr.
Michael Burry, the head of Scion Capital (whose fund in real life
realized profits of 720 million dollars on shorting the housing
market), instructs his employee to find information about every
single individual mortgage that is packaged in the top mortgage-
backed securities. The film likewise implies that acute reading is the
key to the success of Mark Baum, the hedge fudge manager whose
firm in real life doubled its value to 1.5 billion dollars because of its
short positions.[18] Giving us a glimpse of Baum's childhood, the
movie reveals that he was an excellent yeshiva student and scholar of
the Torah, but his rabbi worried that the only thing that motivated
Baum's indefatigable study was his pursuit of "inconsistencies in the
word of God."

This hermeneutic is also the paradigm for the film's critique of
Wall Street, which argues that the fiscal crash was caused by lazy
investors and rating agencies who failed to comprehend the opaque
financial instruments they were trading and grading. The merry
band of outsiders who serve as the film's protagonists, by contrast,
are clever and disciplined enough to unravel the complexity. They
are Talmudic scholars whose rewards will be found in billion dollar

profits. But the film further suggests that they will take their profits in moral purity since it also posits its heroes as a virtuous counterpoint to the behemoth banks. Good reading thus indemnifies its scholars from all the derogations of capitalism. The film represents Baum, a hedge fund manager working under Morgan Stanley, as a Robin Hood whose half a billion dollars of profit are righteous salvos against a corrupt market. When, for example, Baum travels to Florida to investigate the stability of the real estate market and realizes the financial precariousness of most of the subprime mortgage customers, he proclaims, "it's time to call bullshit." Yet Baum follows his declaration with the purchase of millions of dollars of credit default swaps. Which is to say, here calling bullshit is an act of both interpretation and speculation as he places an asymmetrical bet that shit is indeed shit.

Indeed, for all its pretenses towards explanatory transparency, *The Big Short* systematically misrepresents the financial actions of its protagonists by suggesting that they somehow transcend the very market in which they are participating. Admittedly, the film sets out to represent the wonderous system by which a solid real estate market could be sliced and diced into unrecognizable parts, and in a Hamiltonian fashion it plots the story as an intricate sequence of contingent actions. But ultimately this ambition is defeated by the conviction that explanation is simply a matter of exposing the pure artifice of financial representation.

Nowhere is this more apparent—and yet also cleverly obscured—than in the film's portrait of Baum's interaction with a CDO manager he meets at the American Securitization Forum in Las Vegas. At this meeting Baum realizes the magnitude of the CDO market and, once again, the film turns to non-narrative exegesis to explicate the financial mania generated from the subprime mortgage market. Thaler and Gomez analogize the CDO market to a blackjack game on which there are countless side bets for and against the original hand. Yet their lucid explanation significantly misrepresents the transactions in one crucial way: it depicts everyone at the table as losing money. When Gomez doesn't win her hand, the crowd erupts in sorrowful groans, and Thaler intones, "They all should have known the odds they could lose." What the film elides is that there would necessarily be winners in this mob of speculators. The scene thus offers something of the inverse of what we witnessed in Logan's economic explanations in Chapter 2, in which he insisted that economic exchanges made everyone a winner. In both cases, their chosen metaphors cannot capture the fact that economic exchanges are sequenced across time and dispersed among countless players. Moreover, as with Logan, the elision here is critical to the populist argument the film wants to make: the narrative alchemy transforms the hedge fund speculators in toxic assets into working-class heroes.

More precisely, while boasting its expository clarity, the film deliberately obfuscates the role its protagonists played in creating the bubble. The synthetic CDOs comprise the very same credit default swaps the protagonists are purchasing—a fact that Lewis's book makes explicit when the CDO manager, Wing Chau, details how his own business depends on these swaps, "I love guys like you who short my market. Without you I don't have anything to buy. . . . The more excited that you get that you're right, the more trades you'll do, and the more trades you do, the more product for me."[19] But while the book identifies the credit default swaps as the building blocks of the speculative mania and depicts the real-life Baum admitting his complicity in the system (he says, "That's when I realized they needed us to keep the machine running"), the film does not.[20] Instead the movie offers a moralizing story about a wise and good Baum (whose indefatigable reading has allowed him to see there is no liquidity in the market) and the stupid and evil Chau (who, so long as he is making fees from the transactions, will not consider the consequences of the illiquidity). And thus even as this meeting concludes with Baum ordering his team to "short everything that guy has touched" and purchase half a billion more in swaps, it emphasizes his righteous indignation as he mournfully snaps, "I am going to try to find moral redemption at the roulette table."

The movie occasionally gives voice to the ways the protagonists' gains are tethered to other people's losses—as, for example, when the two young founders of the hedge fund, Brownfield Capital, are scolded by their wise elder for their over-exuberant celebration after purchasing millions of credit default swaps from Goldman Sachs, Merrill Lynch, and Bear Stearns. "You just bet against the American economy," he pronounces, "If we're right it means people lose homes, jobs, retirement savings, pensions." The admonishment offers some acknowledgment that the winners of the "big short" are necessarily implicated in the financial catastrophe, but for the most part the film conceals the connection between their profits and the market collapse, depicting its protagonists as a moral vanguard against the dissolute greed of Wall Street.

In an especially illustrative scene, we see a cast of characters awaiting the ground transportation that will take them to the airport. Baum and his team depart in a sensible Lincoln Town Car and the boys from Brownfield take a yellow cab. By contrast, the nefarious CDO manager, Chau, takes a long black stretch limousine. The moralizing becomes even more apparent when we see the departure of an SEC employee, played by one of the few women in the film. The movie had introduced her earlier primarily to convey the news that the SEC provided no regulatory oversight for the mortgage market, and that she traveled to the American Securitization Forum in Vegas with the hopes of securing a job at one of the big banks. When we watch her leaving the Vegas hotel, she embraces and kisses a Bear Stearns broker, mouthing "call me," before stumbling into her own cheap taxi while he enters his black SUV. The character thus neatly allegorizes the endemic corruption of the finance industry: she isn't regulating the industry, she is having sex with it. The hotel vignette epitomizes the very simple argument this movie ultimately makes about finance—one that uses the most old-fashioned of novelistic plots, a seduction tale. The biggest banks are lascivious rakes who prey on the easily seduced: immigrants, women, and governmental bureaucrats who are too stupid to see the deception or too venal to resist it.

The movie's ostensible argument on behalf of laborious and patient reading is also belied by its own visual syntax, which frequently offers a barrage of images in sequences of fast cuts. One of these highly abbreviated montages occurs in a scene in which Burry is being chided by a major investor for purchasing over a billion dollars' worth of credit default swaps. The screen flashes with the manifold texts that surround Burry: computer screens, prospectuses from Fannie Mae, posters, books (including a volume of Adam Smith's writing). McKay's visual style seems to exemplify the cinema of complexity, inviting us to pause our screens, and imitate Burry by trying to make sense of the cacophony of images. And yet no amount of pausing or rewinding is going to make these images tell a story, as the directions in the screenplay attest. The scene depicts Burry sitting in front of his monitor absorbing the details of individual subprime mortgages, and the script describes the shot as a "[closeup] of a COMPUTER SCREEN showing THOUSANDS OF COMPLICATED LINES OF MORTGAGES from a MORTGAGE BACKED SECURITY. The lines are almost indecipherable, but we see Michael Burry is reading them intently like it's a page turning mystery novel." The script thus marks the audience's necessary inadequacy to the task at hand: Burry will be able to read the "thousands of complicated lines" as if they are a best-selling mystery, but they will be "indecipherable" to the rest of us.

When *Wolf of Wall Street* was first released, it was widely criticized for celebrating the wolves and failing to acknowledge the victims of Belfort's crimes. Scorsese may have wanted to make a movie that ferociously attacked the endemic and pathological greed of American finance, but much like Lewis's *Liar's Poker*, it was read as an indulgent glorification of, and instruction manual for, late-twentieth-century conspicuous consumption. By contrast, *The Big Short* was almost universally praised for explicating the monstrous complexity and linguistic arcana of shadow banking and the derivatives market— and for depicting the real consequences of the collapse. But, as I have tried to explain, McKay's film only simulates explanation: in the guise of exegesis, it ultimately offers a moralistic fairy tale about the socially awkward hedge fund managers who could not protect us from greedy banks and incompetent federal regulators. Which is to say, even a film seemingly motivated by a sincere desire to provide a detailed explanation of our modern financial system and of the byzantine interrelations and causalities that led to a global economic crisis, ultimately falls back on a plot that identifies individuals as the nefarious villains responsible for the catastrophe.

I offer this reading not because I want to accuse the filmmakers of bad faith, but to pose a more basic question: why does *The Big Short* fall so far from its ambitions? One possible answer might be found in the argument I suggested about *Wolf of Wall Street*: that our cultural forms are inadequate to the demand and that there are no available "cognitive maps," to use Fredric Jameson's familiar metaphor, with which to represent "the ensemble of society's structures as a whole."[21] Responding to Jameson's diagnosis, twenty-first-century scholars interested in cultural representations of late capitalism either stress the limitations of existing imaginative forms to index and reveal what Jameson identifies as the "increasing abstraction and deterritorialization" of finance capital, or they propose that new imaginative genres are up to the task.[22] McKay opts for a genre that some critics have proposed is very well-suited to narrating the movement of twenty-first century capital—the "network narrative," sometimes also called "hyperlink cinema," the characteristic features of which include multiple protagonists across multilinear plotlines.[23] The critical assumption is that the disaggregated plot structure is particularly adept at showing how individuals are embedded into imbricated economic and social networks.[24]

But, as we have seen in the case of *The Big Short*, this structure is finally put in the service of simple explanation: a conspiracy theory. In interviews, for example, McKay often asserted that his ultimate ambition was to indict the essential fraudulence of Wall Street: "I thought, 'This is bullshit. These guys are making this more complex than it really is to cover up what happened.' And that was my central thesis of the movie... [H]alf of economics and finance... is bullshit. I think it's designed to protect the money to keep it in the rich people's hands."[25] Again, we should observe how much the director's critique of twenty-first-century finance here sounds like the Jeffersonian critique of Hamilton. And like his eighteenth-century polemical ancestors, McKay couples his indignation with an explanatory project that is shaped by the imperative to contradict the linguistic machinations of high finance. For all the seeming sprawl and intricacy of its network narrative, its argument ultimately hinges on the supposition that economic systems should be drawn very simply lest imaginative authors reproduce the malfeasance of financiers. *The Big Short* thus points to the durable appeal of the explanatory narrative crafted by the Jeffersonians in the 1790s.

In returning to the economic disputes of the first decades of the United States, my goal was to show that there are many ways to tell stories about the immense social system that we call the "economy." The morphology of these narratives—whether conveyed by economists or novelists, by realists or postmodernists, by Keynesians or Hayekians—necessarily shapes what is otherwise an infinite constellation of contact points between economic agents. This is why economist Deirdre McCloskey stresses the importance of narrative to economic science: "Storytelling offers a richer model of how economists talk and a more plausible story of their disagreements."[26] And this is also why, when Marx ridicules classical economists for their partiality for *Robinson Crusoe*, he is condemning both their scientific and aesthetic practice. In a similar fashion in the 1970s, G.L.S. Shackle evaluated the limitations of the economist's "art," which he says "consists largely of the devising of means to give to essentially and incurably imprecise notions an air of exactness and rigour."[27] Economics is thus, he summarized, "the art of heroic simplification, the art of the Gordian knot, carefully tied up in advance...by the very man who is going to cut it."[28] Twenty years later, Ronald Coase similarly lamented, "Existing economics is a theoretical system which floats in the air and which bears little relation to what happens in the real world."[29] This assessment is fundamental to the work of Tony Lawson, probably the most vociferous critic of current economic science. For Lawson, the basic flaw of orthodox economic theory is that it assumes the economy as a closed system and its mathematical models are thus formally incapable of depicting the dynamic causal relations between its various objects of inquiry. "Modern economics," he writes "is not very successful as an explanatory endeavor."[30] In like manner, Richard Bronk argues that economic study could be significantly improved by a shift away from the presumed homology between economics and physical sciences and towards economics and aesthetics: "social interaction is often better modelled according to the organic and biological metaphors favoured by Romantics than the mechanical equilibrium metaphors used by neoclassical economists."[31]

The crucial point I mean to draw by referencing these self-critical analyses of contemporary economic writing is that they articulate something very similar to Jameson's argument about imaginative writing. It would seem that scholars from various disciplines are dissatisfied with the representational capacity of writing about the economy whether it takes the form of a mathematical formula or a Hollywood film. At the start of this book, I proposed that one reason to return to a moment before the generic divide between imaginative and economic writing had solidified is to resist an analysis that is born from the presumption that the two genres have a necessarily different disposition towards the object of their inquiries. But the crux of the difference, I have tried to show, is not located in genre—neither in the difference between imaginative and economic prose, or between a slave narrative and a policy report. Nor is it found in economic ideology—for example, the difference between a liberal trade policy and an interventionist one. Instead the early debate over American economic policy points to two different explanatory methods—two ways to translate uncertainty into causality.

In the aftermath of the most recent financial crisis, literary artists, cultural critics, and economists told stories about how the global crash came to happen. Because the crisis involved so many sectors of the economy, so many nations, and so many obscure financial instruments, it would seem complex explanation would be requisite. But narratives that establish simple causality have considerable charm in both art and science. And it appears we are still constrained by the aesthetic responses that Adam Smith outlined in "History of Astronomy": either to take solace in the economy as a "simple machine" or to experience "wonder" at the unfathomability of our economic landscape. The broad ambition of this book, then, was to return to the archives of early American literature and political economy to discover other kinds of narrative strategies with which to describe the geographically vast and microscopically infinitesimal components of both a capitalist infrastructure and the cargo that moves through it. The global economy of 1800 was certainly very different than that of today, but an aesthetic appreciation for the speculative, digressive, and unsystematic plotlines of these earlier narratives has the capacity to generate new imaginative projects with which to make sense of our increasingly difficult economic world. Alexander Hamilton, arguably the most influential author of American capitalism, might also provide the speculative fictions whereby we might begin at last to reimagine it.

# { NOTES }

## Introduction

1. Franklin Delano Roosevelt, "Address at the Groundbreaking for the Thomas Jefferson Memorial," December 15, 1938, *National Archives.* https://catalog.archives.gov/id/197846. Andrew Burstein explains that Roosevelt was largely responsible for the twentieth-century refashioning of Jefferson as egalitarian democrat and "liberal humanist." See *Democracy's Muse: How Thomas Jefferson Became an FDR Liberal, a Reagan Republican, and a Tea Party Fanatic, All the While Being Dead* (Charlottesville: Univ. of Virginia Press, 2015). Burstein offers a rousing account of Jefferson's protean political legacy.

2. Roosevelt writes the review for New York's *Evening World* at Bowers's request. See David E. Kyvig, "History as Present Politics: Claude Bowers' *The Tragic Era,*" *Indiana Magazine of History* 73 (March 1977): 29n.30.

3. Ronald Reagan, "Remarks Announcing America's Economic Bill of Rights," July 3, 1987. https://www.reaganlibrary.gov/research/speeches/070387a. While figures about national debt are somewhat controversial, I took the number from a journal with a decidedly "free market" and pro-Reagan bent. See "The Sad Legacy of Ronald Reagan," *The Free Market* 6.10 (October 1988): 1. There are, of course, substantial differences between Hamilton's public debt and Reagan's—not least of which is that Hamilton demanded provisions be made for its extinguishment. See Max Edling, "Hamilton and the Restoration of Public Credit," *William and Mary Quarterly*, 3rd series, 65.2 (April 2007): 287–326 for an extensive description of Hamilton's understanding of public credit and the funding act.

4. Quoted in Stephen F. Knott, *Alexander Hamilton and the Persistence of Myth* (Lawrence: Univ. of Kansas Press, 2002), 6. Will's formulation is not unique. A *Wall Street Journal* essay takes the title, "We Worship Jefferson, but We Have Become Hamilton's America," February 4, 2004. A *Fortune Magazine* article is titled, "Why Hamilton—Not Jefferson—Is the Father of the American Economy," February 16, 2016.

5. Charles A. Beard, *An Economic Interpretation of the Constitution of the United States* (New York, NY: Macmillan Company, 1921), 100.

6. Vernon Louis Parrington, *Main Currents in American Thought: an Interpretation of American Literature from the Beginnings to 1920,* vol.1 (New York, NY: Harcourt, Brace & World, 1927), 292.

7. Parrington, *Main Currents*, 292 and 342.

8. An excellent survey of the debate over the Beardian thesis can be found in the first chapter of Robert A. McGuire's *To Form a More Perfect Union: A New Economic Interpretation of the United States Constitution* (Oxford: Oxford Univ. Press, 2003), 15–32. Joyce Oldham Appleby provides a different account of historiographic responses to Beard in her "The Vexed Story of American Capitalism," *Journal of the Early Republic* 21.1 (Spring 2001): 1–18.

9. Eric Slauter, "Revolutions in the Meaning and Study of Politics," *American Literary History* 22.2 (2010): 325.

10. Ed White, "The Ends of Republicanism," *Journal of the Early Republic* 30 (Summer 2010): 180. White explicitly references Parrington's assessment of the correspondence between nineteenth-century romanticism and liberal individualism: "There is no more fruitful source of romantic hope than a fluid economics that overflows all narrow preemptions and sweeps away the restrictions that hamper free endeavor" (180).

11. I have in mind here not only Pierre Bourdieu's formulation that the "field of cultural production" is "the economic world reversed" (see the first chapter of *The Field of Cultural Production* [New York, NY: Columbia Univ. Press, 1993], 29–73), but also Appleby's assertion of the "anticapitalist bias" that has shaped the study of American political thought. Referencing "the cohort of social historians working in the 1960s and 1970s," she observes, "they followed the Beardians in depicting capitalism as an exogenous force, thrust into the lives of unwary folk by profit-maximizing outsiders" (Appleby, "The Vexed Story," 4).

12. White, "The Ends of Republicanism," 180.

13. The popularity of Chernow's biography of Hamilton and, even more significantly, of Lin-Manuel Miranda's musical have certainly increased Hamilton's stock. But much of the critical literature on him has focused on biographical issues—that he was an immigrant, for example—and not on his economic writing. See, for example, Sean X. Goudie's *Creole America: The West Indies and the Formation of Literature and Culture in the New Republic* (Philadelphia: Univ. of Pennsylvania Press, 2007).

14. *Debates in the Congress of the United States on the Bill for Repealing the Law for the more convenient organization of the courts of the United* States (Albany: Whiting, Leavenworth, and Whiting, 1802), 624.

15. Jacob Viner, *Essays on the Intellectual History of Economics*, ed. Douglas A. Irwin (Princeton, NJ: Princeton Univ. Press, 1991), 44 offers a brief history of this "doctrine," explaining how it fundamentally revised both an older Christian tradition that vilified commerce and the predominant economic theory that preceded it, namely mercantilism.

16. These are three of the crucial economic theories identified by Farhad Rassekh as essential to the history of Western capitalism in his *Four Central Theories of the Market Economy* (Abingdon, UK: Routledge, 2017). The fourth is Say's Law, or The Law of Markets, which was only emerging as a theory in the 1790s and that I take to be a source of dispute between the two parties.

17. Viner, *Essays*, 198.

18. Many of canonical texts of early American criticism consider this partisan divide: See Cathy Davidson, *Revolution and the Word: The Rise of the Novel in America* (Oxford: Oxford Univ. Press, 1986); Christopher Looby, *Voicing America: Language, Literary Form, and the Origins of the United States* (Chicago, IL: Univ. of Chicago Press, 1996); Jane Tompkins, "What Happens in Wieland," in *Sensational Designs* (Oxford: Oxford Univ. Press, 1986), 40–61; and Michael Warner, *The Letters of the Republic: Publication and the Public Sphere in Eighteenth-Century America* (Cambridge, MA: Harvard Univ. Press, 1990).

19. This is how Stanley Elkins and Eric McKitrick begin their chapter, "Finance and Ideology," which explains the economic disputes of the two founding party. See *The Age of Federalism: The Early American Republic, 1788–1800* (Oxford: Oxford Univ. Press, 1993), 77.

20. Much of this work took place in the schism that emerged in the 1970s surrounding the "republican synthesis" thesis. The canonical texts of this debate include J.G.A. Pocock, *The Machiavellian Moment: Florentine Political Thought and the Atlantic Republic Tradition* (Princeton, NJ: Princeton Univ. Press, 1975); Lance Banning, *The Jeffersonian Persuasion:*

*Evolution of a Party Ideology* (Ithaca, NY: Cornell Univ. Press, 1978) and his more recent *Conceived in Liberty: The Struggle to Define the New Republic, 1789–1793* (Oxford: Rowman & Littlefield Publishers, 2004); Drew R. McCoy, *The Elusive Republic: Political Economy in Jeffersonian America* (Chapel Hill: Univ. of North Carolina Press, 1980); Joyce Appleby, *Capitalism and a New Social Order: The Republican Vision of the 1790s* (New York: New York Univ. Press, 1984) and "Commercial Farming and the 'Agrarian Myth' in the Early Republic," *The Journal of American History* 68 (1982): 833–49; and Isaac Kramnick, "Republican Revision Revisited," *American Historical Review* 87 (1982): 629–64.

21. Mary Poovey, *Genres of the Credit Economy: Mediating Value in Eighteenth- and Nineteenth-Century Britain* (Chicago, IL: Univ. of Chicago Press, 2008).

22. For examples of the former see Jennifer Jordan Baker's *Securing the Commonwealth: Debt, Speculation, & Writing in the Making of Early America* (Baltimore, MD: Johns Hopkins Univ. Press, 2005), which sees the sentimentalism of the early American novel as instrumental to the project of sympathy and credit necessary to the development of the American commercial and financial markets. Joseph Fichtelberg's *Critical Fictions: Sentiment and the American Market, 1780–1870* (Athens: Univ. of Georgia Press, 2003) and Karen Weyler's *Intricate Relations: Sexual and Economic Desire in American Fiction, 1789–1814* (Iowa City: Univ. of Iowa Press, 2004) also fall under this critical camp insofar as they explain how novels adapt their readers into the radical social transformations brought about by the new market order. Stephen Shapiro's *The Culture and Commerce of the Early American Novel: Reading the Atlantic World-System* (State College: Pennsylvania State Univ. Press, 2008) adopts the second critical strategy, claiming that Charles Brockden Brown sought "to craft a new relation between literary production and social transformation [that could] intervene within a world that is rapidly altering toward conservative and capitalist predicates" (259–60). Timothy Sweet's *American Georgic: Economic and Environment in Early American Literature, 1580–1864* (Philadelphia: Univ. of Pennsylvania Press, 2002), which takes on a much larger historical archive, provides readings of the contact points between economic and imaginative literature that exemplify both positions. Other accounts especially focused on literary representations of the commercial market include David Anthony's chapter on Washington Irving in *Paper Money Men: Commerce, Manhood, and the Sensational Public Sphere in Antebellum America* (Columbus: Ohio State Univ. Press, 2009), 41–69; Michelle Burnham's *Folded Selves: Colonial New England Writing in the World System* (Hanover, NH: Univ. Press of New England, 2007) and her *Transoceanic America: Risk, Writing, and Revolution in the Global Pacific* (Oxford: Oxford Univ. Press, 2019); Philip Gould's *Barbaric Traffic: Commerce and Antislavery in the Eighteenth-Century Atlantic World* (Cambridge: Harvard Univ. Press, 2003); and David Shields, *Oracles of Empire: Poetry, Politics, and Commerce in British America, 1690–1750* (Chicago, IL: Chicago Univ. Press, 1990). We associate the phrase "cash nexus" with Thomas Carlyle and his indictment of a social culture increasing mediated through industrial capitalism, but it was Elizabeth Gaskell who first coined the expression in *North and South* (1855). The genealogy of the term is explained in Steven G. Marks, *The Information Nexus: Global Capitalism from the Renaissance to the Present* (Cambridge: Cambridge Univ. Press, 2016), x.

23. Adam Smith, *The Theory of Moral Sentiments*, ed. D.D. Raphael and A.L. Macfie (Oxford: Clarendon Press, 1976).

24. Adam Smith, "The Principles which Lead and Direct Philosophical Enquiries; Illustrated by the History of Astronomy," *Essays on Philosophical Subjects* (London: T. Cadell

and W. Davies, 1795), 20. The essay was probably written in the 1750s, but was published posthumously in 1795. For more on the significance of this essay to Smith's economic theories, see Warren J. Samuels, "Adam Smith's 'History of Astronomy' Argument," *History of Economic Ideas* 15.2 (2007): 53–78.

25. Smith uses the phrase "invisible hand" when he observes that "the invisible hand of Jupiter" was never credited to explain mundane causal sequences like burning wood or quenching thirst with water ("Astronomy," 25).

26. Smith, "Astronomy," 16.

27. Smith, "Astronomy," 18.

28. Smith, "Astronomy," 42.

29. Smith, "Astronomy," 76.

30. Charles Brockden Brown "The Difference between History and Romance," *The Monthly Magazine and the American Review*, April 1800, 251.

31. Shapiro, *The Culture and Commerce of the Early American Novel*, 220.

32. Brown, "The Difference between History and Romance," 251.

33. One of the first literary scholars to consider the fictionality of economic science, Kurt Heinzelman describes the economist as "a poet, a maker of fictions." See *The Economics of the Imagination* (Amherst, MA: Univ. of Massachusetts Press, 1980), 50.

34. The most lucid explication of actor-network theory is provided by the scholar most associated with the approach: Bruno Latour's *Reassembling the Social: An Introduction to Actor-Network Theory* (Oxford: Oxford Univ. Press, 2005). My understanding of the significance of actor-network theory to the study of economic markets has been largely shaped by Michel Callon's introductory essay, "Introduction: the Embeddedness of Economic Markets in Economics," in *The Laws of Markets,* ed. Callon (London: Blackwell, 1998): 1–57. Although I do not take up Callon's larger thesis, which is that the discipline of economic science has formed the object of its inquiry, his work has been crucial to my understanding of the study of markets. See also Mark Granovetter, "Economic Action and Social Structure: The Problem of Embeddedness," *American Journal of Sociology* 91 (November 1985): 481–510.

35. Callon, "The Embeddedness of Economic Markets," 8.

36. Antoine Destutt de Tracy, *A Treatise on Political Economy*, trans. Thomas Jefferson (Georgetown: Joseph Milligan 1817), iv. Jefferson's praise for Tracy is interesting because the French economist explicitly contrasts his project with the early French physiocrats who were so influential to Jefferson's own education in political economy.

37. I'm thinking here of classical accounts of the novel by Ian Watt, *The Rise of the Novel: Studies in Defoe, Richardson and Fielding* (Berkeley: Univ. of California Press, 1957) and Deidre Shauna Lynch, *The Economy of Character: Novels, Market Culture, and the Business of Inner Meaning* (Chicago, IL: Univ. of Chicago Press), 1998.

38. Georg Lukács, *The Theory of the Novel* (Cambridge, MA: MIT Press, 1974), 56.

39. Walter Benjamin, "The Storyteller," in *Illuminations*, trans. Harry Zohn, ed. Hannah Arendt (New York: Schocken Books, 1968), 56.

40. See Baker's *Securing the Commonwealth* and Weyler's *Intricate Relations*. See also Kristina Garvin, "Corporate Ties: *Arthur Mervyn*'s Serial Economics," *Early American Literature* 50.3 (2015): 737–61; Sean X. Goudie, "On the Origin of American Specie(s): the West Indies, Classification, and the Emergence of Supremacist Consciousness in *Arthur Mervyn*," in *Revising Charles Brockden Brown: Culture, Politics and Sexuality in the Early Republic*, ed. Philip Barnard, Mark Kamrath, and Stephen Shapiro (Knoxville: Univ. of

Tennessee Press, 2004); Elizabeth Hinds, *Private Property: Charles Brockden Brown's Gendered Economics of Virtue* (Newark: Univ. of Delaware Press, 1997);, and Carl Ostrowski, "Fated to Perish by Consumption: The Political Economy of *Arthur Mervyn*," *Studies in American Fiction* 32.1 (2004): 3–20.

41. Leah Price reads this passage from *Middlemarch* as exemplifying a deep concern for Eliot "about the power of parts to misrepresent a whole" (143). Although Price is discussing the construction of literary anthologies, the conceptual problem is fundamental to economic science. See Leah Price, *The Anthology and the Rise of the Novel: From Richardson to George Eliot* (Cambridge, UK: Cambridge Univ. Press, 2000).

42. Immanuel Wallerstein, *Historical Capitalism* (London: Verso, 1983), 31.

43. Fredric Jameson, "Future City," *New Left Review* 21 (2003): 76.

## Chapter 1

1. Knott, *Alexander Hamilton & the Persistence of Myth*, 7.

2. Cited by Knott, 38.

3. Alexander Hamilton to Lafayette, in *Alexander Hamilton: Writings*, ed. Joanne B. Freeman (New York, NY: Library of America, 2001), 521. All subsequent quotations located in this collection will be cited parenthetically within the text.

4. Representative George Clymer, from Philadelphia, expressed this anxiety. For both quotations, see *The Debates and Proceedings in the Congress of the United States*, vol. 1 (Washington, DC: Gales and Seaton, 1834) 1:1080.

5. *Debates and Proceedings*, 1:1081.

6. *Debates and Proceedings*, 1:1080.

7. *The Gazette of the United States*, January 20, 1790, 322.

8. This commentary is printed under "National Intelligence," in *The Federal Gazette*, February 3, 1790, 2.

9. For a splendid study of the ways this logic worked one hundred years later, see David A. Zimmerman's *Panic!: Markets, Crises, and Crowds in American Fiction* (Chapel Hill: Univ. of North Carolina Press, 2006).

10. There is no small degree of irony in the fact that Hamilton's enemies, by prolonging the debate over public credit, actually aided the cause of speculation, since the lack of clarity over policy made the price of outstanding certificates so volatile. Perhaps it was this fear that motivated Andrew Brown, editor of the *Federal Gazette*, to beg his readers' patience for having postponed publication of several letters he had received until *after* his paper had printed the Secretary of Treasury's original report, explaining that since the report "contains a full refutation of the principles advanced in favor of a discrimination," any effort on the part of its opponents to foment controversy in the newspaper might have "dangerous consequences to the credit, and therefore to the continuance of the Union" (*The Federal Gazette*, January 26, 1790, 3).

11. *The Journal of Willliam Maclay* (New York: Frederick Ugar Publishing Co., 1965), 173.

12. Maclay writes that Hamilton's "price was communicated in manuscript as far as Philadelphia" (*Journal*, 183). Maclay does not make clear precisely what he is accusing Hamilton of perpetrating, but Charles Beard surmises that "doubtless" Maclay is accusing Hamilton of divulging the policy described in his Report to friends (*Economic Interpretation*, 108).

13. *Journal*, 194. It must be noted that while it appears that this accusation is directed at Alexander Hamilton, it immediately follows Maclay's angry remarks on James Madison

(who had just proposed his own plan for debt discrimination). Maclay is no fan of Madison's proposal either, since he says it does nothing to reduce the tax burden, although it does "afford[] some alleviation as to the design the tax will be laid for" (194).

14. Margaret Schabas, "Temporal Dimensions in Hume's Monetary Theory," in *David Hume's Political Economy*, ed. Carl Wennerlind and Margaret Schabas (New York, NY: Routledge, 2008), 128 (emphasis added).

15. Elkins and McKitrick, *Age of Federalism*, 107.

16. David Hume, *Essays: Moral, Political, and Literary*, ed. Eugene F. Miller (Indianapolis: Liberty Classics, 1987), 155.

17. Hume, *Essays*, 155.

18. Hume, *Essays*, 155.

19. Hume, *Essays*, 156.

20. Hume, *Essays*, 124.

21. Hume, *Essays*, 125.

22. Hume, *Essays*, 126.

23. Hume, *A Treatise of Human Nature*, ed. David Fate Norton and Mary J. Norton (Oxford: Clarendon Press, 2000), 315.

24. In his analysis of the apparent contradiction in Hume's monetary theories, Carl Wennerlind observes that Hume "was not philosophically opposed to non-metallic money." See "An Artificial Virtue and the Oil of Commerce: A Synthetic View of Hume's Theory of Money," in *David Hume's Political Economy*, 108.

25. Hume, *Essays*, 206.

26. Hume, *Treatise of Human Nature*, 138.

27. Annette C. Baier, *A Progress of Sentiments: Reflections on Hume's Treatise* (Cambridge, MA: Harvard Univ. Press, 1991), 103.

28. C. George Caffentzis, "Fiction or Counterfeit? David Hume's Interpretations of Paper and Metallic Money," in *David Hume's Political Economy*, 155.

29. Caffentzis, "Fiction or Counterfeit," 158.

30. In his study of American debates over public debt, Richard Vernier argues that Hamiltonian fiscal plans departed from the orthodoxy of Hume, Smith, and Steuart, and that, as a consequence, they effectively ceded the work of the Scottish political economists to their Jeffersonian opponents. See "The Fortunes of Orthodoxy: The Political Economy of Public Debt in England and America during the 1780s," in *Articulating America: Fashioning an a National Political Culture in Early America* (Lanham, MD: Rowman & Littlefield Publishers, 2000): 93–130.

31. Ron Chernow, *Alexander Hamilton* (New York: Penguin Books, 2005), 298. E. James Ferguson claims that discovering such owners would not, in fact, have been that difficult. See *The Power of the Purse: A History of American Public Finance, 1776–1790* (Chapel Hill: Univ. of North Carolina Press, 1961), 303. But he also argues that James Madison's campaign on behalf of discrimination was primarily motivated as a political calculus (298).

32. Robert E. Wright, *One Nation Under Debt: Hamilton, Jefferson, and the History of What We Owe* (New York: McGraw Hill, 2008), 130.

33. The first quotation is taken from Robert Ferguson, *Reading the Early Republic* (Cambridge: Harvard Univ. Press, 2004), 157 and is used to describe the rhetoric of the *Federalist Papers*, although Ferguson is referring to John Jay and not Hamilton specifically. The second passage is taken from Trish Loughran's *The Republic in Print: Print Culture in the Age of U.S. Nation Building, 1770–1870* (New York: Columbia Univ. Press, 2009), 247.

34. The line, of course, comes from Lin-Manual Miranda's "Aaron Burr, Sir."

35. Chernow, *Alexander Hamilton*, 110.

36. *Alexander Hamilton's Pay Book*, ed. E.P. Panagopoulos (Detroit, MI: Wayne State Univ. Press, 1961), 6. Panagopoulos notes that Hamilton had cited directly from Postlethwayt's *Dictionary* as early as 1775, in "The Farmer Refuted" (7).

37. *The African Trade, the Great Pillar and Support of the British Plantation Trade in America* (London: J. Robinson, 1745) and *The National and Private Advantages of the African Trade Considered* (London: Published for John and Paul Knapton, 1746). See Jack P. Green, *Evaluating Empire and Confronting Colonialism in Eighteenth-Century Britain* (Cambridge: Cambridge Univ. Press, 2013), 159 for more on Postlethwayt's writing about Africa and the slave trade. Eric Williams's *Capitalism and Slavery* (Chapel Hill: Univ. of North Carolina Press, 1944) also extensively discusses Postlethwayt's work. For an account of Williams and Postlethwayt, see William Darity, Jr., "Eric Williams and Slavery: A West Indian Viewpoint?" *Callalloo* 20.4 (1997): 800–16.

38. Postlethwayt is much better known for the former position, and Christopher Leslie Brown observes that "[o]nly a handful of studies have been alert to the way Postlethwayt's published views shifted over time" (97 n9). See "Empire without America: British Plans for Africa in the Era of the American Revolution," in *Abolitionism and Imperialism in Britain, Africa, and the Atlantic,* ed. Derek R. Peterson (Athens: Ohio Univ. Press, 2010).

39. Karl Marx, *Capital: Volume 1* (New York: Penguin Books, 1992), 385–86. Marx also describes Postlethwayt as a "defender of the workers" (386).

40. Joseph Schumpeter, *History of Economic Analysis* (New York: Routledge, 1994), 351–52 n15.

41. Hamilton's opinions on African American slavery has been a source of considerable scholarly dispute—one that was amplified in the wake of the enormous success of Lin-Manual Miranda's musical, which tacitly represented Hamilton as an abolitionist. We know that Hamilton was a founding member of the New York Manumission Society, which explicitly articulated the natural rights of slaves and the need to "endeavor by lawful ways and means, to enable [slaves] to Share, equally with us in that civil and religious Liberty." Yet what is less clear is how far Hamilton was willing to go to support the natural rights of black slaves in favor of the rights to human property on the part of slave holders. See Michael D. Chan, "Alexander Hamilton on Slavery," *The Review of Politics* 66.2 (2004): 207–31.

42. What is more, Postlethwayt argued in later editions of his *Dictionary* that the economic livelihood of England depended entirely on the economic production to be found in their American and Caribbean colonies.

43. Malachy Postlethwayt, *The Universal Dictionary of Trade and Commerce*, 2 vols. (London: John and Paul Knapton, 1751), 1:576.

44. Postlethwayt, *Dictionary*, 1:875.

45. Postlethwayt, *Dictionary*, 1:875.

46. It must be noted that Hamilton is somewhat circumspect in making this claim, since he continues, "Yet he is so far from acceding to the position . . . in which it is sometimes laid down, that 'public debts are public benefits,' a position inviting to prodigality, and liable to dangerous abuse" (569).

47. Postlethwayt, *Dictionary*, 1:ix.

48. Postlethwayt, *Dictionary*, 1:xi.

49. Postlethwayt, *Dictionary*, 1:xiii.

50. Panagopoulos reprints the extant notes, which he speculates were probably recorded between 1776 and 1779 (*Hamilton's Pay Book*, 3n4).

51. Panagopoulos observes that Hamilton uses these notes later in his Report on Manufactures when he argues for the potential profits to be made from glass production in the United States (*Hamilton's Pay Book*, 24n3).

52. *Hamilton's Pay Book*, 25.

53. Postlethwayt, *Dictionary*, 1:344.

54. Postlethwayt, *Dictionary*, 1:345.

55. *Hamilton's Pay Book*, 28; and Postlethwayt, *Dictionary*, 1:345–46.

56. *Hamilton's Pay Book*, 28–9.

57. Postlethwayt, *Dictionary*, 1:347.

58. *Hamilton's Pay Book*, 30.

59. Postlethwayt, *Dictionary*, 1:v.

60. Postlethwayt, *Dictionary*, 1:v.

61. Richard Rolt, *A New Dictionary of Trade and Commerce* (London: T. Osborne and J. Shipton, 1756), 1.

62. Rolt, *New Dictionary*, 3.

63. Rolt, *New Dictionary*, 2.

64. Rolt, *New Dictionary*, 3.

65. *Hamilton's Pay Book*, 36–9.

66. *Federal Gazette*, June 2, 1790, 2.

67. *Fallacy Detected by the Evidence of Facts* (Philadelphia: s.n., 1790), 6.

68. "Letter the First," *New-York Daily Gazette*, February 6, 1790, 3.

69. [George Logan], *Letters Addressed to the Yeomanry of the United States* (Philadelphia, 1793), 5.

70. While no one publicly admitted authorship, it seems likely that the author was Jeremiah Wadsworth, a prominent Connecticut businessman and friend of Hamilton, since he wrote Hamilton in December 1789 (while the Treasury Secretary was still working on his Report) to ask if he had read the essays by "The Observer": "I wish you would read them & if you find nothing which you disapprove say so." *The Papers of Alexander Hamilton*, vol. 6, ed. Harold C. Syrett (New York: Columbia Univ. Press, 1962), 15.

71. "The Observer, No. 3," *Gazette of the United States*, November 7, 1789, 237.

72. "The Observer, No. 4," *Gazette of the United States*, November 11, 1789, 241.

73. "The Observer, No. 4," 241.

74. "Letter the First," *New-York Daily Gazette*, February 6, 1790, 3.

75. "Letter the Second," *New-York Daily Gazette*, February 10, 1790, 3.

76. *The Federal Gazette*, January 26, 1790, 2.

77. [Equity], "From the Independent Chronicle, printed at Boston," *The United States Chronicle: Political Commercial and Historical*, January 7, 1790, 1.

78. *Virginia Independent Chronicle*, April 7, 1790, 2.

79. *Pennsylvania Gazette*, February 10, 1790, 2.

80. *Pennsylvania Gazette*, January 27, 1790, 3. This issue publishes Hamilton's report on its front page and also includes the "Observer 13."

81. *Pennsylvania Gazette*, January 27, 1790, 3.

82. *Pennsylvania Gazette*, January 27, 1790, 3.

83. *Pennsylvania Gazette*, January 27, 1790, 3.

84. Colin Nicholson observes that the "representation of Credit as an inconstant, often a self-willed but sometimes a persuadable woman gained a certain cross-party currency" (*Writing and the Rise of Finance: Capital Satires of the Early Eighteenth Century* [Cambridge: Cambridge Univ. Press, 1994], xi). The metaphor of sexual misconduct was frequently used to attack Hamilton. Opponents who saw his renegotiation of interest rates as a tacit repudiation of public credit accused Hamilton of both prostitution and hypocrisy: "The virtuous will not excuse a prostitute, and give her their confidence and friendship, because she pleads with tender eloquence her actual necessities, as an excuse for her loss of honor" (*New-York Journal*, April 15, 1790, 2).

85. *Pennsylvania Gazette*, February 17, 1790, 2.

86. Quoted in Vernier, "Fortunes of Orthodoxy," 120.

87. *Pennsylvania Gazette*, February 10, 1790, 2.

88. *Pennsylvania Gazette*, February 10, 1790, 2.

89. *Pennsylvania Gazette*, February 17, 1790, 2.

90. *The Cambridge History of English and American Literature*, 18 vols., ed. A.W. Ward, et al. (Cambridge: Cambridge Univ. Press, 1907–21) refers to Webster as one of the "two ablest writers" on the subject of economics (18:x).

91. Pelatiah Webster, *Political Essays on the Nature and Operation of Money, Public Finances and Other Subjects* (Philadelphia, PA: Joseph Crushank, 1791), 48–9.

92. Webster, *Political Essays*, v.

93. Selections from the pamphlet were reprinted in the *Federal Gazette*, the *New-York Daily Gazette*, and the *New-York Packet*, and it was also advertised widely in newspapers.

94. Webster, *Political Essays*, 341.

95. Webster, *Political Essays*, 312.

96. *Federal Gazette*, January 20, 1790, 2.

97. Webster, *Political Essays*, 348.

98. Webster, *Political Essays*, 329.

99. Webster, *Political Essays*, 348–49.

100. Webster, *Political Essays*, 349.

101. *Debates and Proceedings*, 1:1137–38.

102. *The Independent Chronicle*, March 4, 1790, 2.

103. *The Independent Chronicle*, March 4, 1790, 2.

104. *Fallacy Detected*, 44.

105. For a useful discussion of Portia's legal position in relation to questions of equity, see Peter Platt, *Shakespeare and the Culture of Paradox* (Burlington, VT: Ashgate Publishing Company, 2009), 112–15.

106. *Fallacy Detected*, 44.

107. "For the Pennsylvania Gazette," *Pennsylvania Gazette*, February 17, 1790, 2.

108. *National Gazette*, May 7, 1792, 219.

109. *The Daily Advertiser*, March 10, 1790, 2.

110. *Independent Gazetteer*, March 3, 1789, 2.

111. Webster, *Political Essays*, 318.

112. Webster, *Political Essays*, 318.

113. *Independent Gazetteer*, March 10, 1790, 4. The focus of this particular letter is on the realization that George Washington was planning to assent to Hamilton's plan. The old veteran learns that Washington "is now in the hands of fine folks, who do not like to admit

any body who has not new shoes." Many of the essays written in the first months of 1790 focus on what was thought to be Washington's perfidy. For example, the dialogue between the soldier and the tax-gatherer concludes with certitude that "Immortal Washington" will sign an order telling his "poor soldiers to pay no more funding tax for the support of speculators—Jew Brokers—Quarter Masters, and British Subjects" (*Independent Gazetteer*, March 3, 1789, 2). Webster likewise assumed Washington would reject Hamilton's finance plan: that an "immense sum of money due to his companions and supporters" was not paid, he says "would be too much for his mighty fortitude to sustain (*Political Essays*, 326). In a later footnote Webster confesses he had "not the least idea that any possible consideration could have induced general Washington to sign any act, which…would cut his soldiers out of their pay" (326).

114. *The Federal Gazette*, January 16, 1790, 2.

115. *The Daily Advertiser*, February 22, 1790, 2.

116. *Gazette of the United States*, January 23, 1790, 327.

117. *Gazette of the United States*, February 3, 1790, 339.

118. *Gazette of the United States*, February 3, 1790, 337. This same issue includes a section from Hamilton's Report and several essays written on its behalf.

119. *The Gazette of the United States*, February 3, 1790, 337.

120. *James Madison: Writings*, ed. Jack N. Rakove (New York, NY: Library of America, 1999), 198.

121. Bray Hammond, *Banks and Politics in America from the Revolution to the Civil War* (Princeton, NJ: Princeton Univ. Press, 1957), 118–19.

122. Charles Austin Beard, *Economic Origins of Jeffersonian Democracy* (New York: Macmillan Company, 1915), 157–58.

123. Adam Smith, *An Inquiry into the Nature and Causes of the Wealth of Nations* in *The Glasgow Edition of the Works of Adam Smith*, 2 vols. (Oxford, UK: Clarendon Press, 1976), 1:26 (I.ii).

124. See Stuart Leibiger, *Founding Friendship: George Washington, James Madison, and the Creation of the American Republic* (Charlottesville: Univ. of Virginia Press, 2001), 133–37, for a detailed account of Madison's response and rationale to the proposed bank.

125. *Gazette of the United States*, February 23, 1791, 2. A more complete, and annotated version, of Madison's response is located in *The Papers of James Madison*, vol. 13, ed. Charles F. Hobson and Robert A. Rutland (Univ. of Virginia Press, 1981): 372–82.

126. *The Gazette of the United States*, February 23, 1791, 1. Although this is the first printed version of the speech, Madison's argument had already begun to circulate since the very same page of the newspaper contains an article, "On the National Bank," written by "A Constitutionalist," which specifically endorses the constitutionality of the Bank Bill.

127. *The Papers of James Madison*, 13:373.

128. *The Papers of James Madison*, 13:375.

129. *The Papers of James Madison*, 13:376.

130. *The Papers of James Madison*, 13:376.

131. *James Madison: Writings*, 198.

132. Walter Dellinger and H. Jefferson Powell, "The Constitutionality of the Bank Bill: the Attorney General's First Constitutional Law Opinions," *Duke Law Journal* 44 (1994): 112.

133. Thomas Jefferson, "Opinion on the Constitutionality of a National Bank," in *Thomas Jefferson: Writings*, ed. Merrill D. Peterson (New York: Library of America, 1984), 416.

134. Jefferson, "Constitutionality of a National Bank," 416.

135. Jefferson, "Constitutionality of a National Bank," 420.

136. Edmund Randolph, "Opinion on the Constitutionality of the Bank," in *The Papers of George Washington, Presidential Series*, ed. Jack D. Warren, Jr. (Charlottesville: Univ. Press of Virginia, 1998): 8:332.

137. "To Alexander Hamilton from George Washington, 16 February 1791," *The Papers of Alexander Hamilton*, vol. 8, ed. Harold C. Syrett (Columbia Univ. Press, 1965), 51.

138. Gerald Stourzh describes Nos. 23–35 of *The Federalist* as "among the most impressive statements of what has become known as the doctrine of implied powers." See *Alexander Hamilton and the Idea of Republican Government* (Stanford, CA: Stanford Univ. Press, 1970), 161.

139. Umberto Eco, *From Tree to the Labyrinth: Historical Studies on the Sign and Interpretation* (Cambridge, MA: Harvard Univ. Press, 2014), 3.

140. Eco, *From Tree to the Labyrinth*, 4.

141. Eco, *From Tree to the Labyrinth*, 4 and 18.

142. Umberto Eco, *The Limits of Interpretation* (Bloomington: Indiana Univ. Press, 1990), 143.

143. Jean Le Rond d'Alembert, *Preliminary Discourse to the Encyclopedia of Diderot*, trans. Richard N. Schwab (Chicago, IL: Univ. of Chicago Press, 1995), 4.

144. D'Alembert, *Preliminary Discourse*, 5.

145. D'Alembert, *Preliminary Discourse*, 5.

146. "From Alexander Hamilton to -------," *The Papers of Alexander Hamilton*, vol. 2, ed. Harold C. Syrett (Columbia Univ. Press, 1961), 242.

147. Robert McNamara argues that because Hamilton rejected such "abstract calculations," he should not be conceived as an economic theorist. See *Political Economy and Statesmanship* (DeKalb: Northern Illinois Univ. Press, 1998), 97. McNamara notes that Hamilton's argument here is reminiscent of James Steuart's own critique of the French économistes: "what the French call Systèmes . . . are no more than a chain of contingent consequences" (99).

148. In comparing Hamilton's economic analysis to that of behavioral economists, I am not suggesting that Hamilton was especially interested in human psychology. But insofar as behavioral economics has become the mainstream subfield most dedicated to explaining how, as Richard H. Thaler puts it, "people depart from the fictional creatures that populate economic models," it seems a useful analogy. See Thaler, *Misbehaving: The Making of Behavioral Economics* (New York, NY: Norton Books, 2015), 6.

## Chapter 2

1. As a point of comparison, while Shenstone is cited fourteen times, Pope receives six, and Milton eight citations.

2. Kevin J. Hayes notes that Jefferson's purchase is made only one week after the death of his sister, and that Shenstone's melancholic elegies may be have been the motivation for the purchase. Hayes observes that the "inscription for [Jefferson's] sister's tomb . . . echoes one of the memorial inscriptions at Leasoews." *The Road to Monticello: The Life and Mind of Thomas Jefferson* (Oxford: Oxford Univ. Press, 2008), 87.

3. *Thomas Jefferson: Writings*, ed. Merrill D. Peterson (New York: Library of America, 1984), 623. Unless noted, all citations from Jefferson are from this Library of America collection.

4. Thomas Whatley, *Observations on Modern Gardening* (London: T. Payne, 1770), 162.

5. Whatley, *Observations*, 162.

6. Cited in Ann Leighton, *American Gardens in the Eighteenth Century* (Amherst: Univ. of Massachusetts Press, 1976), 350. See also Christopher Gallagher, "The Leasowes: A History of the Landscape," *Garden History* 24.2 (Winter 1996): 201–20.

7. Samuel Johnson, *The Lives of the Poets* (Oxford: Oxford Univ. Press, 2009), 127–28.

8. Raymond Williams, *The Country and the City* (Oxford: Oxford Univ. Press, 1975), 18.

9. Cited in Leighton, *American Gardens*, 350.

10. Johnson, *Lives of the Poets*, 129.

11. Sandro Jung offers an extended analysis of Johnson's censure of Shenstone as improvident, indolent, and selfish in "Idleness Censured and Morality Vindicated: Johnson's 'Lives' of Shenstone and Gray," *Étude Anglais* 60 (2007): 80–91. Johnson's assessment largely confirms his commentary on pastoral verse more generally from the *Rambler* 36, where he posits pastoral verse as a "species of poetry" whose "narrow" lens almost always renders it inferior.

12. *The Dictionary of National Biography*, ed. Sidney Lee, vol. 52 (New York, NY: The Macmillan Company, 1897), 50.

13. Jack McLaughlin refers to Shenstone as "one of Jefferson's favorite poets." See *Jefferson & Monticello: The Biography of a Builder* (New York, NY: Henry Holt and Company, 1988), 450.

14. Shenstone uses the word "verdure" frequently throughout his poetry.

15. Leo Marx, *The Machine in the Garden: Technology and the Pastoral Ideal in America* (Oxford: Oxford Univ. Press, 1964), 118.

16. John C. Shields has written substantially about Wheatley, but this brief description of her generic mode is in his classic essay, "Phillis Wheatley's Subversion of Classical Style," *Style* 27.2 (1993): 255.

17. There is an edition of *The Works, in Verse and Prose, of William Shenstone, Esq.* (London, 1773), inscribed "Mary Everleigh to Phillis Wheatley Sept. 24, '74" in the Schomburg collection of the New York Public Library. Caretta's biography indicates that Shenstone was one of the English-language poets who influenced Wheatley, albeit less of an influence than Milton, Pope, or Cowper, in *Phillis Wheatley: Biography of a Genius in Bondage* (Athens: Univ. of Georgia Press, 2011), 167. The fact that the volume is dated after the publication of Wheatley's own poems raises the possibility that she read him after her own work was composed, but he was popular enough that it seems likely she had an earlier familiarity with his verse.

18. Carretta notes that Wheatley befriended Sharp while she was in England, and one letter describes her visiting the Tower of London with him (*Phillis Wheatley*, 118).

19. Granville Sharp, *An Essay on Slavery* (Burlington: West Jersey, 1778; London: reprinted, 1776), 39.

20. Shenstone, "Elegy I," *The Works, in Verse and Prose*, 3 vols. (London: H. Woodfall, 1768), 1:30.

21. Phillis Wheatley, *Complete Writings*, ed. Vincent Carretta (New York: Penguin Books, 2001), 36.

22. Although my reading of the argument about pastoralism is different, my analysis of Wheatley's verse is indebted to John Shields. He provides a detailed description of the allusions that Wheatley is making to Virgil and Horace in "On Imagination," arguing that

Wheatley's strategy is to "carv[e] out her own property, the property of her imagination, in a realm inviolable by the ravages of slavery." See Shields, "Phillis Wheatley's Subversion," 261.

23. Wheatley, *Complete Writings*, 32.

24. Eric D. Lamore provides an extensive study of Wheatley's relationship to Virgil's *Georgics*. He proposes that she would have been familiar with the distinction between an "optimist" and "pessimist" school as to whether labor is capable of sustaining the land in the face of political and natural catastrophe in "Wheatley's Use of the Georgic," in *New Essays on Phillis Wheatley*, ed. John C. Shields and Eric D. Lamore (Knoxville: Univ. of Tennessee Press, 2011), 111–58. By contrast, Shenstone's verse, even when it alludes to the *Georgics*, reverses its logic, taking its "pleasures" in the fact that the land only produces beauty.

25. Wheatley, *Complete Writings*, 32.

26. Caroline Wigginton has revealed that one pastoral poem that had been attributed to Phillis Wheatley, "Elegy on Leaving," was in fact written by Mary Whately, an English poet who lived near William Shenstone, who served as a mentor. See "A Chain of Misattribution: Phillis Wheatley, Mary Whately, and "'An Elegy on Leaving,'" Early American Literature 47.3 (2012): 679–84.

27. William C. Dowling, *Literary Federalism in the Age of Jefferson: Joseph Dennie and the Port Folio, 1801–1811* (Columbia: Univ. of South Carolina Press, 1999), 20.

28. Dowing, *Literary Federalism*, 20.

29. Stuart Curran, *Poetic Form and British Romanticism* (Oxford: Oxford Univ. Press, 1986), 85.

30. Paul Alpers, *What Is Pastoral?* (Chicago, IL: Univ. of Chicago Press, 1997), ix.

31. Curran, *Poetic Form*, 85.

32. Annabelle M. Patterson, *Pastoral and Ideology: Virgil to Valéry* (Berkeley: Univ. of California Press, 1987).

33. Lawrence Buell, "American Pastoral Ideology Reappraised," *American Literary History* 1 (1989): 14.

34. Curran, *Poetic Form*, 86.

35. Alpers, *What Is Pastoral*, 35. Williams locates the doubleness a little bit later, with Hesiod in 9 BCE (*The Country and the City*, 14). See also Terry Gifford, "The Environmental Humanities and the Pastoral Tradition," in *Ecocriticism, Ecology, and the Cultures of Antiquity*, ed. Christopher Schliephake (Lantham, MD: Lexington Books, 2016): 159–74.

36. Curran argues that in the classical pastoral the idyll is found in the past and in the Christian pastoral, it is found in the future, and in both there is a recognition that the present "cannot embody the pastoral." He argues that this realization yields the anti-pastoral form (*Poetic Form*, 92).

37. I am using the term "pastoral" and not the georgic, because I take seriously Timothy Sweet's argument that the georgic functions differently in this early colonial moment. As he explains, the representation of nature in some of the earliest colonial texts about North America do not necessarily have the monetarist focus on which critics have exclusively focused.

38. James Madison, "Population and Emigration," *National Gazette*, November 19, 1791, 1.

39. Mercy Otis Warren, *Poems, Dramatic and Miscellaneous* (Boston: I. Thomas and E.T. Andrews, 1790), 229–34.

40. Timothy Dwight, "Columbia," in *The Beauties of Poetry, British and American* (Worcester, MA: Mathew Carey, 1791), 126.

41. David Humphreys, "Future state of the western territory," in *The Beauties of Poetry*, 131–33.

42. Alpers, *What Is Pastoral*, ix.

43. Alpers, *What Is Pastoral*, xi.

44. For a useful and synthetic study of pastoral criticism see Terry Gifford, *Pastoral* (New York: Routledge, 1999), especially chapter one, "Three kinds of pastoral" (1–12).

45. Buell, "American Pastoral Ideology," 4.

46. One exception is Roxanne M. Gentilcore, "Ann Eliza Bleecker's Wilderness Pastoral: Reading Virgil in Colonial America," *International Journal of the Classical Tradition* 1.4 (1995): 86–98.

47. Allan Kulikoff, *The Agrarian Origins of American Capitalism* (Charlottesville: Univ. of Virginia Press, 1992), 74.

48. The phrase is located in Robert W. Tucker and David C. Hendrickson, *Empire of Liberty: The Statecraft of Thomas Jefferson* (Oxford: Oxford Univ. Press, 1990), 30.

49. Throughout the 1790s, we see references to Jefferson as embodying a pastoral literary mode. A self-styled "Farmer in the County of Plymouth" remarks on the allegiance between agricultural practice and literary tributes: "Poets, in all ages and countries, have taken from rural life and rural scenes, their finest and most perfect descriptive images. Thomson in his Seasons, and Mr. Jefferson in his Notes on Virginia, furnish beautiful instances of the two last observations. "On the Importance and Profits of Agriculture," *The Massachusetts Magazine*, July 1790, 409.

50. Pocock, *The Machiavellian Moment*, 531.

51. Joyce Appleby, "What is Still American?" *William and Mary Quarterly* 39 (1982): 302.

52. Joyce Appleby, "Commercial Farming," 836.

53. Sweet, *American Georgics*, 97–121.

54. Joseph H. Harrison, Jr. "*Sic et Non*: Thomas Jefferson and Internal Improvement," *Journal of the Early Republic* 17.4 (1987): 335. Lance Banning argues that the "republican synthesis" argument has been misrepresented as positing a fundamental antagonism between commerce and virtue, and that there is not much difference between the two versions of Jefferson since both agree that Jefferson was invested in commerce and that his party mobilized a rhetoric that condemned mercantilism, luxury, and speculation. See Banning, "Jefferson Ideology Revisited: Liberal and Classical ideas in the New American Republic," *William and Mary Quarterly* 43 (January 1986): 3–19. Robert Shalhope has described this debate between "advocates of republicanism and those of liberalism" as tediously "sterile": See Shalhope, "Anticipating Americanism: An Individual Perspective on Republicanism in the Early Republic," in *Americanism: New Perspectives on the History of an Ideal*, ed. Michael Kazin and Joseph A. McCartin (Chapel Hill: Univ. of North Carolina Press, 2006), 54.

55. Kulikoff, *Agrarian Origins*, 74n33.

56. Marx, *Machine in the Garden*, 104.

57. Marx, *Machine in the Garden*, 107–8. Marx's reading of both texts are inadequate. After all, Crèvecoeur's later chapters famously complicate, and even flatly contradict, the agrarian fantasy that the farmer James offers in the first three letters of the volume. How can we not read the "swarm of insects" that descend on the South Carolinian slave to "feed on his mangled flesh and to drink his blood" as a grotesque parody of Virgil's description of the magnificent honey to be found in bodies of putrid bulls (chattel) from Book IV of the

*Eclogues.* For sophisticated accounts of the anti-pastoral logic of Crèvecoeur, see Sweet's *American Georgic* and Teresa A. Goddu's *Gothic America: Narrative, History, and Nation* (New York, NY: Columbia Univ. Press, 1997). Goddu focuses on the gothic underbelly of the pastoral fantasy found in the "Letter from Charlestown." Sweet focuses on the story of Andrew the Hebridean.

58. Marx, *Machine in the Garden*, 5.

59. Marx, *Machine in the Garden*, 7 and 26.

60. Marx, *Machine in the Garden*, 125–26.

61. Since *Machine in the Garden* was first published, numerous critics have revised and repudiated the argument it makes about American pastoralism. Marx himself commented on the "severe attacks" the book received in the 1970s in a later essay (from 1992). He accepts the critique that his scholarship generalized key categories and provided a hegemonic account not only of American literature, but Americanism. See Marx, "Afterword: The Machine in the Garden," *The Massachusetts Review* 40.4 (Winter 1999): 483–96. Some of the most important of the critical responses include Annette Kolodny's *The Lay of the Land* (Chapel Hill: Univ. of North Carolina, 1975) and *The Land Before Her* (Chapel Hill: Univ. of North Carolina Press, 1984); and Myra Jehlen, *American Incarnation: The Individual, the Nation, and the Continent* (Cambridge, MA: Harvard Univ. Press, 1986). Two excellent overviews of Marx's legacy include Buell's "American Pastoral Ideology Reappraised," and, more recently, Gordon Sayre's "The Oxymoron of American Pastoralism," *Arizona Quarterly* 69.4 (Winter 2013): 1–18.

62. Buell, "American Pastoral Ideology," 4.

63. J.G.A. Pocock, *Politics, Language, and Time: Essays on Political Thought and History* (Chicago, IL: Univ. of Chicago Press, 1960). Pocock locates this realization as the "origins of America historical pessimism" (100).

64. William Empson, *Some Versions of Pastoral* (New York: New Directions, 1935), 23.

65. Empson, *Some Versions*, 11.

66. Marx, *Machine in the Garden*, 125.

67. Alpers, *What is Pastoral*, 22. Alpers takes the phrase from Kenneth Burke.

68. Herbert E. Sloan, *Principle & Interest: Thomas Jefferson and the Problem of Debt* (Charlottesville: Univ. of Virginia Press, 1995), 51.

69. Sloan, *Principle & Interest*, 22.

70. Hume, *Essays: Moral, Political, and Literary*, 259.

71. Manuela Albertone, *National Identity and the Agrarian Republic: The Transatlantic Commerce of Ideas between America and France, 1750–1830* (Burlington, VT: Ashgate Publishing Co., 2014), 139.

72. Paul Cheney, *Revolutionary Commerce: Globalization and the French Monarchy* (Cambridge, MA: Harvard Univ. Press, 2010), 141.

73. Cited in Cheney, *Revolutionary Commerce*, 144. Others translate the phrase, "abyss of confusion."

74. Du Pont de Nemours, *De l'origine et des progress d'une science nouvelle* (Paris: P. Geuthner, 1910), 5. The full text is: "Que cela depend d'une infinite de circonstances variables, difficiles à démêler & à évaluer."

75. Ronald L. Meek, *The Economics of Physiocracy: Essays and Translations* (London: George Allen & Unwin Ltd, 1962), 370.

76. "Extract from 'Rural Philosophy,'" in Meek, *Economics of Physiocracy*, 57.

77. Schumpeter, *History of Economic Analysis*, 230.

78. Max Beer, *An Inquiry Into Physiocracy* (New York: Russell & Russell, 1939), 105 and Schumpeter, *History of Economic Analysis*, 230. Schumpeter notes that Louis XV is said to have corrected the page proofs for Quesnay (230,n8).

79. The "Introduction" to Meek's *The Economics of Physiocracy* offers an exceptionally clear and readable account of the history of physiocracy and its fundamental precepts.

80. Marquis de Mirabeau, *The Oeconomical Table, An Attempt towards Ascertaining and Exhibiting the Source, Progress, and Employment of Riches* (London: Printed for W. Owen, 1766). Du Pont also published versions the *Tableau* in his own work. Because Quesnay's name was never mentioned in either the Mirabeau or Du Pont reprintings, Quesnay was only later credited as the author of the table.

81. Le tableaus "est un dérivé des deux autres, et les complete également en perfectionnant leur object" (Mirabeau, *Philosophie Rurale ou économie générale* [Amsterdam, 1766], 52).

82. Smith, *Wealth of Nations*, 2:679 (IV.ix).

83. Peter C. Dooley, *The Labour Theory of Value* (New York: Routledge, 2005), 65–6.

84. Smith, *Wealth of Nations*, 2:672 (IV.ix).

85. Meek, *Economics of Physiocracy*, 108.

86. Smith, *Wealth of Nations*, 2:674 (IV.ix).

87. Meek, *Economics of Physiocracy*, 108.

88. Schumpeter, *History of Economic Analysis*, 231.

89. Meek, *Economics of Physiocracy*, 117.

90. Meek *Economics of Physiocracy*, 117.

91. It seems worth noting that Mirabeau clearly did not find the table as pellucid as Quesnay. In a letter to Mirabeau, Quesnay writes that he has been told "you are still bogged down in the zigzag" (quoted in Meek, *Economics of Physiocracy*, 115).

92. Karl Marx, *Theories of Surplus Value*, trans. G.A. Bonner and Emile Burns, vol. 1 (London: Lawrence & Wishart, 1951), 44.

93. Marx, *Surplus Value*, 44. For an illuminating analysis and explanation of Marx's reading of the Physiocrats and the *Tableaux économique*, see Christian Gehrke and Heinz D. Kurz, "Karl Marx on Physiocracy," *The European Journal of the History of Economic Thought* 2.1 (1995): 53–90.

94. Marx, *Surplus Value*, 44.

95. Karl Marx, *The Poverty of Philosophy* (New York: Penguin Books, 1995), 97.

96. Gehrke and Kurz, "Karl Marx on Physiocracy," 58.

97. Marx, *Surplus Value*, 48.

98. Meek, *Economics of Physiocracy*, 115.

99. Marx, *Surplus Value*, 343–44. Michel Foucault expressed a similar admiration for the table's ability to compress the numerous exchanges of goods and specie transpiring across time and space into the single year visually encoded into one static image. See Liana Vardi, *The Physiocrats and the World of the Enlightenment* (New York: Cambridge Univ. Press, 2012), 13–14.

100. Marx, *Surplus Value*, 50.

101. Marx, *Surplus Value*, 50.

102. Marx, *Surplus Value*, 51.

103. Marx, *Surplus Value*, 53.

104. Charles Eisinger, "The Influence of Natural Rights and Physiocratic Doctrines on American Agrarian Thought in the Revolutionary Period," *Agricultural History* 21 (January 1947): 17. Robert E. Shalhope, *John Taylor of Caroline: Pastoral Republicanism* (Columbia: Univ. of South Carolina Press, 1980), 45.

105. Albertone, *National Identity*, 99.

106. Albertone, *National Identity*, 140.

107. Albertone, *National Identity*, 231.

108. "To the Public," *Independent Gazetteer*, January 9, 1790, 3.

109. [George Logan] *Letters, addressed to the yeomanry of the United States. By a farmer.* (Philadelphia: Eleazer Oswwald, 1791). The following citations will be located parenthetically in the text, and are to this book volume and not the original newspaper publications.

110. Frederick B. Tolles, "George Logan and the Agricultural Revolution," *Proceedings of the American Philosophical Society* 95 (1951): 589.

111. Albertone, *National Identity*, 141–42.

112. Quesnay writes, "Let us assume, then, a large kingdom whose territory, fully cultivated by the best possible methods, yields every year a reproduction to the value of five milliards." Gianni Vaggi argues that this passage assumes that "large-scale cultivation has been extended to all lands, which, in turn, are exploited by rich farmers. These farmers, acting as capitalist entrepreneurs, make large investments in agriculture" (*The Economics of François Quesnay* [Durham, NC: Duke Univ. Press, 1987], 28).

113. George Logan, *Fourteen Agricultural Experiments to Ascertain the Best Rotation of Crops* (Philadelphia: Bailey, 1797), 32.

114. He is not isolated in this reading since, as one economic historian notes, "It has become fashionable to represent [Quesnay's *Tableau*] as an input-output table." See Dooley, *The Labour Theory of Value*, 72.

115. Meek, *Economics of Physiocracy*, 289. See also Vaggi, *Economics of François Quesnay*, 28–31.

116. Occasionally Logan's pamphlet gives expression to the differences between a household and national economy, when he registers that heterogeneous and contradictory economic interests constitute the nation, as for example when he claims that merchants are "citizens of the world, and…know no country but their coffers of gold" (34) or when he describes bankers as "living upon the blood of their fellow-citizens" (36–7). We might understand this as a tacit acknowledgment that Quesnay's model can only represent an idealized system, one in which there are neither merchants nor bankers, and in which landowners transmit all surplus back into the economy and do not retain wealth in the form of money or gold. Yet by designating merchants and bankers as metaphoric vampires and cancers who parasitically sap the nation's body, Logan instead reestablishes the key premise, which is that a healthy national economy is formally indistinguishable from a well-managed small-scale farm.

117. "A Farmer," *National Gazette*, February 27, 1792, 2.

118. "A Farmer," *National Gazette*, February 27, 1792, 2.

119. [George Logan] *Letters addressed to the Yeomanry of the United States, containing some observations on funding and banking systems* (Philadelphia: Childs and Swaine, 1793), 21. Logan first publishes the letters included in this pamphlet in the *National Gazette*. Subsequent citations will be located parenthetically in the text.

120. The metaphor is a common one, but it seems worth mentioning that James Madison had used the same phrase to describe some of the difficulties of implementing a policy of discrimination to treat American debt. Referring to people who purchased debt on the secondary market and subsequently sold it, Madison says, their "pretensions…will lead us into a labyrinth, for which it is impossible to find a clue." "Discrimination between Present and Original Holders of the Public Debt," *Papers of James Madison*, ed. Charles F. Hobson and Robert A. Rutland, vol. 13 (Charlottesville: Univ. of Virginia, 1981), 34.

121. J. Hector St. John de Crèvecoeur, *Letters from an American Farmer and Sketches of Eighteenth-Century America*, ed. Albert E. Stone (New York: Penguin Books, 1981), 67.

122. Garrett Ward Sheldon and Charles William Hill, *The Liberal Republicanism of John Taylor of Caroline* (Madison, NJ: Farleigh Dickinson Univ. Press, 2008), 79.

123. Scholars who have employed the term pastoralism include Loren Baritz, *City on a Hill: History of Ideas and Myths in America* (New York: John Wiley, 1964), 159–203 and Shalhope's *John Taylor of Caroline*. Albertone devotes a chapter to explicating the fundamental physiocratic principles that informed Taylor's work (even as she also acknowledges his deviation from them). Duncan Macleod is exceptional in claiming that Taylor did not embody "some republican, romantic vision of a pastoral society" (389) and that "Taylor and the physiocrats had different and incompatible agendas" (391). Macleod, "The Political Economy of John Taylor of Caroline," *Journal of American Studies* 14.3 (December 1980): 387–405.

124. Taylor is identified as the author in a letter from Madison to Jefferson, August 11, 1793. The correspondence between the two men also indicate that Taylor had been designated as something like a "Republican spear-carrier." Sheldon and Hill, *The Liberal Republicanism of John Taylor*, 54.

125. The first quotation comes from the first Franklin essay in *National Gazette*, February 16, 1793, 127. The second from March 20, 1793, 162.

126. *National Gazette*, March 20, 1793, 162.

127. Hammond, *Banks and Politics*, 123.

128. *National Gazette*, February 20, 1793.

129. Hammond, *Banks and Politics*, 124.

130. *National Review*, February 16, 1793,127.

131. *National Review*, February 16, 1793, 127.

132. "To James Madison from John Taylor, 20 June 1793," *The Papers of James Madison*, vol. 15, ed. Thomas A. Mason, Robert A. Rutland, and Jeanne K. Sisson (Charlottesville: Univ. Press of Virginia, 1985), 35.

133. "From James Madison to Thomas Jefferson, 11 August, 1793," *Papers of James Madison*, 15:52.

134. Two essays are published: the first, "Reflections on Several Subjects" on September 11, 1793 and the second, "Brief Reflections on Several Subjects" on September 14, 1793.

135. "To James Madison from John Taylor, 25 September 1793," *Papers of James Madison*, 15:123.

136. "Reflections on several Subjects," *National Gazette*, September 11, 1793, 362.

137. [John Taylor], *An Enquiry into the Principles and Tendency of Certain Public Measures* (Philadelphia, PA: Thomas Dobson, 174), 2. All subsequent editions will be located parenthetically in the text.

138. The law that established a maximum of 5-percent legal interest took effect in Virginia in 1734. It remained in effect until 1796 when the act was amended to raise the rate to 6

percent. This new rate took effect in 1797. *The Revised Code of the Laws of Virginia* (Richmond, 1819), 1:373.

139. Charles R. Geisst describes the significance of the difference between compound and simple interest to the historical debate about usury in his *Beggar Thy Neighbor: A History of Usury and Debt* (Philadelphia: Univ. of Pennsylvania Press, 2013), 16–19.

140. In this way, Taylor is hearkening back to a much earlier distinction in which a lender who charged a certain fee for the use of money was clearly engaged in usury, but where a lender whose profits were subject to risk and fluctuation was engaged in a legitimate financial transaction. See James Steven Rogers, *The Early History of the Law of Bills and Notes: A Study of the Origins of Anglo-American Commercial Law* (New York, NY: Cambridge Univ. Press, 1995), 70–1.

141. *A Definition of Parties; or the Political Effects of the Paper System Considered* (Philadelphia: Francis Bailey, April 5, 1794), 6.

142. Logan, "Excise, the favorite system of aristocrats, by which unequal and burdensome taxes are drawn from the laborious part of the community," (s.n., 1793). Logan personally circulated and delivered his broadside across western Pennsylvania in the summer of 1793.

143. Logan, *Five Letters Addressed to the Yeomanry of the United States. Containing Some Observations on the Dangerous Scheme of Governor Duer and Mr. Hamilton to Establish National Manufactories. By an American Farmer* (Philadelphia: Oswald, 1792), 8.

144. The language of the broadside is characteristic of Logan, but I discovered that his text is a verbatim repetition of passages from Joel Barlow's *Advice to the Privileged Orders, Part II*, also published in 1793. The first volume of *Advice* was printed in February 1792 and proved to be so controversial that Barlow was required to publish the second part from France, explaining in his Advertisement to the volume that the "violent attacks on the Liberty of the Press in [England]…induced [Johnson, his previous publisher] to suppress the publication of this." If we take Barlow at his word, he had completed the manuscript before his departure for France and therefore his text was written before Logan wrote his broadside. We would therefore assume that Barlow's manuscript somehow made it across the Atlantic to Logan who used it in his broadside that was published in May 1793. This assumption is challenged by Richard Buel's biography of Barlow, which asserts that "references to contemporary events, suggest that Barlow added portions to his earlier work at least through the late summer [of 1793]." Richard Buel, Jr., *Joel Barlow: American Citizen in a Revolutionary World* (Baltimore, MD: Johns Hopkins Univ. Press, 2011), 172. I cannot locate any correspondence between the two men to make clear whether Logan or Barlow is the original writer. The fact that the broadside only contains a small portion of Barlow's much longer text could indicate Barlow as the original writer, but the strenuous opposition to indirect taxation and the indictment of fiscal opacity clearly reflect Logan's voice.

145. Albertone, *National Identity*, 63. The "Introductory Note" to the Report on Manufactures in *The Papers of Alexander Hamilton*, vol. 10, ed. Harold C. Syrett (New York: Columbia Univ. Press, 1966) scrupulously documents the numerous passages that Hamilton takes and adapts from Smith. The editors concede that Hamilton references a "Physiocratic approach to the subject under discussion," but also insist that that there is nothing in Hamilton's notes to suggest that he had actually read their work, instead claiming that Hamilton's knowledge of the économistes was filtered through his reading of Smith (10:232n.127). This claim, however, underestimates how deeply Smith was himself influenced by the physiocrats, accepting many of their central premises about economic liberalism, theories of value, and scientific method. Meek declares, "It is easy to exaggerate the extent

of Smith's emancipation from Physiocratic notions. Taking the *Wealth of Nations* as a whole, Smith looks backward towards the Physiocrats almost as often as he looks forward towards Ricardo" (*Economics of Physiocracy*, 353).

146. Hamilton, "Report on the Subject of Manufactures," in *Alexander Hamilton: Writings*, 647. Further citations will be located in parenthesis.

147. Notably Hamilton ascribes this laissez-faire ideology to the physiocrats and not to Smith.

148. Smith, *Wealth of Nations*, 1:70 (I.vi.19).

149. Smith, *Wealth of Nations*, 1:70 (I.vi.20).

150. Smith, *Wealth of Nations*, 1:70 (I.vi.20).

151. Meek suggests a fundamental similarity between this Hamiltonian argument and that of Turgot who likewise "emphasized the fact that rent may be regarded as interest on the capital sunk in land" (*Economics of Physiocracy*, 357n.1).

152. Smith, *Wealth of Nations*, 2:582 (IV.vii.b.44).

153. Smith, *Wealth of Nations*, 2:582 (IV.vii.b.44).

154. See Logan, *Letters Addressed to the Yeomanry of the United States*, 9–10.

155. George Logan, *An address on the natural and social order of the world, as intended to produce universal good* (Philadelphia: Tammany Society, 1798), 4.

156. *A letter to the citizens of Pennsylvania, on the necessity of promoting agriculture, manufactures, and the useful arts* (Philadelphia, 1800), 18.

157. Hammond, *Banks and Politics*, 121.

# Chapter 3

1. Franco Moretti asserts, "Literary sociology has long insisted…on the relationship between the novel and capitalism," in *Atlas of the European Novel 1800–1900* (London: Verso Books, 1999), 16.

2. Karl Marx, *Grundrisse: Foundations of the Critique of Political Economy*, trans. Martin Nicolaus (New York: Penguin Books, 1973), 83.

3. Marx, *Grundrisse*, 83.

4. Karl Marx, *Capital*, 3 vols. trans. Ben Fowkes (New York: Penguin Books, 1990–92), 1:169. Fowkes translates the sentence "As political economists are fond of Robinson-Crusoe stories," but I follow Jacob Sider Jost who, in his "The Interest of *Crusoe*," *Essays in Criticism* 66 (July 2016): 301–19, translates "liebt" as "love" (315n1). Jost provides a reading of the traffic in economic and imaginative "interest" in Defoe's novel. According to Thomas M. Kemple, at this moment Marx is not "finding the fiction in their theory in order to expel this fiction," but is rather "analyzing the function of economic fictions in the making of economic theory" (*Reading Marx Writing: Melodrama, the Market, and the "Grundrisse"* [Stanford, CA: Stanford Univ. Press, 1995], 137).

5. Marx, *Capital*, 1:169.

6. Marx, *Capital*, 1:170.

7. Clifford Siskin proposes that the key formal feature of the novel was to "put the concept of character…into a new relationship to the 'things' ordered by system" (160) in *System: The Shaping of Modern Knowledge* (Cambridge, MA: M.I.T. Press, 2016).

8. David Harvey, *A Companion to Marx's Capital* (London: Verso, 2010), 43.

9. Bruce Robbins, "Commodity Histories," *PMLA* 120 (March 2005): 456.

10. Lukács, *The Theory of the Novel*, 56.

11. I take the term "immanence" from Lukács. The term "experience" comes from Walter Benjamin's essay, "The Storyteller," in which he specifically laments the novel's ineffectiveness to convey "experience." The novel only relays the "inexpressible meaning of life" (99) in *Illuminations*, trans. Harry Zohn (New York: Schocken Books, 2007), 83–110.

12. Frank Luther Mott, *A History of American Magazines, 1741–1850* (Cambridge: Harvard Univ. Press, 1966), 39.

13. Mott describes these as three of the four "most important magazines of this period" (*A History of American Magazine*, 30). The other is the *New-York Magazine; or Literary Repository*.

14. The phrase, "commerce of everyday life" is the title of Erin Mackie's teaching edition of selections from the *Tatler* and the *Spectator* (New York: Bedford Books, 1998).

15. Richard Squibbs, *Urban Enlightenment and the Eighteenth-Century Periodical Essay: Transatlantic Retrospects* (Basingstoke, UK: Palgrave Macmillan, 2014), 2.

16. William Rasch offers an especially clear explanation of the significance of description to complexity theory: "To simulate...the complex system, one would have to reproduce it and then include the additional information that the reproduction is meant to be a description of the former" (68). "Theories of Complexity, Complexities of Theory: Habermas, Luhmann, and the Study of Social Systems," *German Studies Review* (February 1991): 65–83.

17. *Spectator* 367, in *Spectator*, ed. Donald F. Bond, 5 vols. (Oxford: Clarendon Press, 1965), 3:380.

18. *Spectator* 367, 3:380.

19. "The Essayist 223," *Massachusetts Magazine*, October 1796, 555.

20. Samuel Johnson, *Lives of the Most Eminent English Poets*, vol. 4 (London: Printed for C. Bathurst, 1781), 363.

21. Johnson, *Rambler*, No. 184, December 21, 1751 in *Samuel Johnson: Selected Essays*, ed. David Womersley (New York: Penguin Books, 2003), 304.

22. *Rambler*, No. 184 in *Samuel Johnson*, 305.

23. "The Retailer 1," *The Columbian Magazine*, February 1788, 85.

24. "The Retailer 3," *The Columbian Magazine*, April 1788, 203.

25. "The Retailer 8," *The Columbian Magazine*, March 1789, 181.

26. "The Dreamer. No. 1," *The Massachusetts Magazine*, January 1789, 35–6.

27. *Salmagundi; or, the Whim—Whams of Launcelot Longstaff, Esq. and Others*, January 24, 1807, 3.

28. Bruce Granger, *American Essay Serials from Franklin to Irving* (Knoxville: Univ. of Tennessee Press, 1978), 3. Granger's book, now over thirty years old, offers the most comprehensive study of American periodical essays. At the time of its publication, he noted that there had been only two other studies of the American periodical form. Since Granger's book, the only significant studies are Jared Gardner's *The Rise and Fall of Early American Magazine Culture* (Urbana: Univ. of Illinois Press, 2013) and Squibb's *Urban Enlightenment*, where the final chapter offers a study of periodical essay series by Joseph Dennie. William C. Dowling's *Literary Federalism in the Age of Jefferson* likewise considers periodical essays in Dennie's *Port Folio*.

29. On the neutrality of British periodical essayists, see Bertrand A. Goldgar, *The Curse of Party: Swift's Relations with Addison and Steele* (Lincoln: Univ. of Nebraska Press, 1961);

J.A. Downie, "Periodicals and Politics in the Reign of Queen Anne," in *Serials and Their Readers 1620–1914*, ed. Robin Myers and Michael Harris (New Castle, DE: Oak Knoll Press, 1993); and Brian Cowan, "Mr. Spectator and the Coffeehouse Public Sphere," *Eighteenth-Century Studies* 37 (2004): 345–66. On the same neutrality in American writers, see Gardner, *Rise and Fall*, 31–68.

30. "The Worcester Speculator," *Worcester Magazine*, November 1787, 85. The same writer two essays later, however lambastes "neuters," or citizens who refuse to take a political position as having "no right to be ranked with rational being" (December 1787, 117).

31. "The Essayist 223," *The Massachusetts Magazine*, October 1796, 555.

32. "The Essayist 223," 556.

33. "Advertisement," *The Spirit of the Farmers' Museum, and Lay Preacher's Gazette* (Walpole: Printed for Thomas & Thomas, 1801), 313.

34. "The Retailer No. 1," 84.

35. "The Retailer No. 6," *The Columbian Magazine*, December 1788, 695.

36. "The Farrago, No. I," *The Tablet*, May 19, 1795, 1.

37. "The Farrago, No. VI," *The Tablet*, June 23, 1795, 21.

38. "The Retailer No. 6," 698–700.

39. "The Retailer No. 6," 700.

40. "The Farrago, No. VI," 21.

41. "The Trifler, No. 1," *Columbian Magazine*, December 1786, 164.

42. "The General Observer," *Massachusetts Magazine*, January 1789, 9.

43. "The Friend, No. 1" *New Haven Gazette and Connecticut Magazine*, March 1786, 42.

44. Cited in Granger, *American Essay Serials*, 116.

45. Lewis Leary, "Philip Freneau," in *Major Writers of Early American Literature*, ed. Everett Emerson (Madison: Univ. of Wisconsin Press, 1972), 249.

46. The phrase is used as the title of Lewis Leary's literary biography of Freneau, *That Rascal Freneau: A Study in Literary Failure* (New Brunswick, NJ: Rutgers Univ. Press, 1941).

47. Philip Freneau, *A Journey from Philadelphia to New-York* (Philadelphia: Francis Bailey, 1787), iii.

48. *The Miscellaneous Works of Mr. Philip Freneau Containing his Essays, and Additional Poems* (Philadelphia: Francis Bailey, 1788). This large octavo volume followed quickly on the heels of *The Poems of Philip Freneau: Written Chiefly During the Late War*. These two books and *A Journey from Philadelphia to New-York* were published by the prominent Philadelphian printer, Francis Bailey, with whom Freneau had a long association. Bailey was also the printer and publisher of *Freeman's Journal*, a weekly newspaper that ran between 1781 and 1792 to which Freneau was a frequent contributor and occasional editor between 1781–84. Subsequent quotations to the essays in this collection will be cited parenthetically in the text.

49. As we will see, as Freneau's career continues, he will attach himself to fiscal policies that repudiate tariffs, excise taxes, and duties.

50. The "Indian Priest" will ultimately emerge as another Addisonian essayist, Tomo-Cheeki.

51. Freneau would later become a member of the New York Society for Promoting the Abolition of Slavery. See Jacob Axelrad, *Philip Freneau: Champion of Democracy* (Austin: Univ. of Texas Press, 1967), 396n4.

52. The essays are originally published in *The Aurora*, but are also republished in a book volume, *Letters on Various Interesting and Important Subjects* (Philadelphia: Printed for the Author, 1799), v.

53. Burke's epithet was employed in two periodical publications in England, including Daniel Isaac Eaton's *Hog's Wash*, which he later titled, *Politics for the People, or a Salmagundy for Swine*. In Eaton's formulation, the derisive title was coupled to the work of a miscellany. See Roland Bartel, "Shelley and Burke's Swinish Multitude," *Keats-Shelley Journal* 18 (1969): 4–9.

54. Freneau, *Letters*, 42.

55. John R. Commons, "American Shoemakers, 1648-1895," *Quarterly Journal of Economics* 24 (November 1909): 46.

56. Freneau, *Letters*, 20.

57. Freneau, *Letters*, 139.

58. Unless otherwise mentioned, all citations from the *Gleaner* refer to the book volume, Judith Sargent Murray, *The Gleaner*, ed. Nina Baym (Schenectady, NY: Union College Press, 1992), and are cited parenthetically in the text. The first publication of the Gleaner letters is in *The Massachusetts Magazine* (February 1792).

59. Nina Baym, "Introduction," *The Gleaner*, x.

60. See Henry Blackstone, *Reports of Cases Argued and Determined in the Courts of Common Pleas*, 3rd ed. (London: A. Strahan, 1801): "The law of Moses is not obligatory on us. It is indeed agreeable to Christian charity and common humanity, that the rich should provide for the impotent poor; but the mode of such provision must be a positive institution" (61).

61. Kirstin Wilcox, "The Scribblings of a Plain Man and the Temerity of a Woman: Gender and Genre in Judith Sargent Murray's *The Gleaner*," *Early American Literature* 30 (1995): 127.

62. Michael T. Gilmore, "Magazines, Criticism, and Essays," *The Cambridge History of American Literature, Volume 1: 1590–1820*, ed. Sacvan Bercovitch. (New York: Cambridge Univ. Press, 1994), 560.

63. *Selected Writings of Judith Sargent Murray*, ed. Sharon M. Harris (New York: Oxford Univ. Press, 1995), xxviii and xxx.

64. Baker, *Securing the Commonwealth*, 137–38.

65. Wilcox, "The Scribblings," 126.

66. I specify Murray and her essayist because many critics have read Murray's construction of the Gleaner as combatively ironic. Edward Watts, for example, suggests that the trajectory of the series is to vanquish the masculine narrative authority of the Gleaner: Mr. Vigillius, he argues, is "the strawman of the conventional male author" (*Writing and Postcolonialism in the Early Republic* [Charlottesville: Univ. of Virginia Press, 1998], 59).

67. The deferral occasioned by the Gleaner's decision to publish his readers' letters is all the more pronounced in the original periodical publication, since his audience literally has to wait a month for the column.

68. See my *Correspondence and American Literature, 1770–1865* (New York: Cambridge Univ. Press, 2005).

69. In her *First Lady of Letters: Judith Sargent Murray and the Struggle for Female Independence* (Philadelphia: Univ. of Pennsylvania Press, 2009), Sheila Skemp proposes that the incorporation of a range of voices is confirmation of Murray's republican commitments and that the public print was no longer the prerogative of a masculine elite (229). Baym maintains that the diversity of voice represented in *The Gleaner* speaks to Murray's democratic and meritocratic agenda: she allows many to speak, but insofar as Murray orchestrates the community of participants, she clearly showcases her own artistic ingenuity (*Gleaner*, x–xi). In her essay, "The Periodical as Monitorial and Interactive Space

in Judith Sargent Murray's 'The Gleaner,'" *American Periodicals* 18 (2008), Jennifer Desiderio proposes that the inclusion of letters (and voices) from a constituency of citizens proves Murray's desire to "encourage [their] participation" (7). Wilcox is even more idealistic in her interpretation of the various voices and genres that comprise *The Gleaner*, arguing that it reveals Murray's political commitments to heterogeneity and a deliberate refusal of masculine tyranny ("The Scribblings," 123).

70. Baker, *Securing the Commonwealth*, 137.

71. See Skemp, *First Lady of Letters*, 140–57 for an extended discussion of this period in Murray's life.

72. Murray's play has a happy conclusion and all debts are paid making the slippage between charity and credit ultimately irrelevant. In other fictions, however, this obfuscation is the source of narrative drama. Consider, for example, *Charlotte Temple* in which the money loaned to Charlotte's grandfather, which originated as a charitable gift, quickly becomes a debt demanding substantial interest when the creditor wishes to possess Charlotte's mother.

73. Fichtelberg, *Critical Fictions*, 236.

74. The United States was becoming increasingly attentive to the effects of a British order passed in March 1793 that authorized these seizures. Although they had been going on for a year, news of the order was not published until almost a full year later. See Elkins and McKitrick, *The Age of Federalism*, 391.

75. Gleaner's assessment about the singular excellence of the times undergoes a fairly substantial revision between the time of the original publication in 1794 and the ultimate publication in 1798, because of her changing opinion about the French Revolution. The Gleaner describes the "struggles of the French nation" as "truly interesting," predicting that the King will "doubtless find himself embosomed in that tranquility which conscious rectitude creates." But in the later book publication, she offers corrective footnote that reads: "The Gleaner regrets, that the deplorable catastrophe, which, since the production of the above essay, closed the virtuous life of a Prince, acknowledged amiable, hath furnished so striking a proof of the ferocity of the present times" (35). However, if the regicide confirms the "ferocity of the present times," the Gleaner does not propose that it undermines the larger argument about these times as in the highest stage of improvement.

76. "The Rhapsodist, No. I," *Columbian Magazine*, August 1789, 464.

77. "The Rhapsodist, No. I," 466.

78. Gardner, *Rise and Fall*, 86.

79. Gardner, *Rise and Fall*, 86.

80. "The Rhapsodist, No. III," *Columbian Magazine*, October 1789, 598.

81. "The Rhapsodist, No. III," 598.

82. "The Rhapsodist, No. II," *Columbian Magazine*, September 1789, 537.

83. "The Rhapsodist, No. II," 538.

84. "The Rhapsodist, No. III," 597.

85. "The Man at Home, No. I," *The Weekly Magazine*, February 3, 1798, 1. The thirteen-part series is published weekly over three months (ending in late April, 1798). Further citations will be located parenthetically in the text.

86. David Hume, *An Inquiry Concerning Human Understanding*, ed. Tom L. Beauchamp (Oxford: Oxford Univ. Press, 2000), 27.

87. Hume, *An Inquiry Concerning Human Understanding*, 26.

88. When the Man at Home remarks, "Pages have been filled with ideas suggested by a broom stick," it would seem to indicate a similarity between his project and Jonathan Swift's *Meditation upon a Broom-stick* (1710). Brown's essayist also explicitly references William Cowper's "The Sofa" (1785), which likewise reveals how many stories can "spontaneously flow" from a "speculation" on a single object.

89. Brown might possibly be alluding to Pierre François Péron who was marooned on Île Amsterdam between 1792–95 and wrote an account of his experiences harvesting seal skins. His narrative, however, was not published until after Brown's own text and I have been unable to discover any references to Péron in the American press between 1795 and 1798.

90. Brown meditates on this same project in his "Henrietta Letters" (1790/92) when he pronounces that he has "conceived the design of relating every domestic incident, and accounting, every dialogue, and describing ever scene that shall occur within a certain & assynable period with the most excessive and elaborate minuteness. Relations in which no circumstance, however frivolous and inconsiderable, should be omitted, and pictures in which should be comprised every appendage" in *Collected Writings of Charles Brockden Brown: Letters and Early Epistolary Writing*, ed. Philip Barnard, Elizabeth Hewitt, and Mark Kamrath (Lanham, MD: Bucknell Univ. Press, 2013), 725.

91. Lynch, *The Economy of Character*, 43.

92. Alex Woloch, *The One vs. The Many: Minor Characters and the Space of the Protagonist in the Novel* (Princeton, NJ: Princeton Univ. Press, 2003), 13–14.

93. Woloch, *The One vs. The Many*, 19.

94. Roland Barthes, "Reality Effect," cited by Woloch, 19.

95. "The Man at Home IV," 101.

96. As Philip Barnard and Stephen Shapiro explain, Brown translates "the sketch's single character Wallace into two figures, Arthur and Wallace, and, similarly the sketch's single female object splits into Eliza Hadwin and Achsa Fielding." Headnotes to "The Man at Home. – No. XI," in *Arthur Mervyn*, ed. Shapiro and Barnard (Indianapolis, IN: Hackett Publishing, 2008), 345.

97. In their historical notes to *Ormond* (Kent, OH: Kent State Univ. Press, 1982), Sydney J. Krause and S.W. Reid say that Brown "splices in the material" (408). Paul C. Rodgers describes the inclusion as a "dubious expedient" Brown invents in a moment of imaginative deficit with the "printer breathing down his neck for fresh copy," in "Brown's *Ormond*: The Fruits of Improvisation," *American Quarterly* 26.1 (1974): 13. In his *Conspiracy and Romance* (New York, NY: Cambridge Univ. Press, 1989), Robert Levine says that the section serves as a "competing narrative, a dialogical intrusion, that challenges [an] alarmist presentation of fever" (36). Julia Stern considers the pages from "The Man at Home" to provide a "persistent metaphor for the problems plaguing early republican culture," in "The State of 'Women' in *Ormond*," *Revising Charles Brockden Brown*, 209n.23.

98. Brown, *Ormond*, 62.

99. Until very recently, scholars assumed that this series was unpublished, as it was only known because it was published in Dunlap's biography of Brown (1815) as an unfinished fragment. In 2006, Jared Gardner discovered another posthumous publication of the text in *The Ladies' Literary Cabinet* in 1822. For an extensive discussion of the differences between these texts (as well as a reprint of the 1822 version), see Gardner, "From the Periodical Archives: 'The Scribbler,'" *American Periodicals* 16.2 (2006): 219–28.

100. "The Scribbler. No. I," *Commercial Advertiser*, August 12, 1800, 2.

101. Gardner, *The Rise and Fall*, 52 and 147.

102. "The Scribbler. No. II," *Commercial Advertiser*, August 13, 1800, 2.

103. "The Scribbler. No. III," *Commercial Advertiser*, August 14, 1800, 2.

104. "The Scribbler. No. III," 2.

105. "The Scribbler. No. V," *Commercial Advertiser*, August 16, 1800, 2.

106. "The Scribbler. No. I," *The Port-Folio*, January 1809, 59.

107. "The Scribbler. No. II," *The Port-Folio*, February 1809, 163.

108. "The Scribbler. No. II," 163.

109. "The Scribbler. No V," *The Port-Folio*, July 1809, 30. In the *Monthly Magazine* the author takes the name of "Looker On" and in the *Literary Magazine* he simply goes by "C."

110. "The Scribbler. No. V," 30.

111. "The Scribbler. No. V," 32.

112. "The Scribbler. No. V," 33.

113. "The Scribbler. No. V," 30.

114. "The Scribbler. No. V," 32.

115. "The Scribbler. No. V," 34.

## Chapter 4

1. The phrase, "clumsy and obscure" is David L. Lightner's in his *Slavery and the Commerce Power: How the Struggle Against the Interstate Slave Trade Led to the Civil War* (New Haven, CT: Yale Univ. Press, 2006), 19.

2. Cited in Lightner, *Slavery and the Commerce Power*, 18. Don E. Fehrenbacher suggests there is evidence that would disprove any concerted action between New England and lower South, saying that the delegates from the lower South didn't give up their desired "requirement of a two-thirds vote for navigation acts," four of these states voting "in favor of a two-third requirement for *all* federal regulation of commerce, interstate as well as foreign" in *The Slaveholding Republic: An Account of the United States Government's Relations to Slavery* (Oxford, UK: Oxford Univ. Press, 2002), 35.

3. *Annals of the Debates in Congress*, 1st Cong. 2nd sess., Feb. 11, 1790, 1224.

4. *Annals*, Feb. 11, 1790, 1225.

5. *Annals of the Debates in Congress*, 1st Cong., 2nd sess., Feb. 12, 1790, 1240.

6. *Annals*, Feb. 12, 1790, 1241.

7. Cited in Fehrenbacher, *Slaveholding Republic*, 137.

8. *Annals*, Feb. 12, 1790, 1246.

9. *Annals*, Feb. 12, 1790, 1247.

10. *Annals of the Debates in Congress*, 1st Cong., 2nd sess., March 8, 1790, 1465.

11. See *Annals*, March 8, 1790, 1465–66. For an extensive discussion of the history of the Report see also Howard A. Ohline, "Slavery, Economics, and Congressional Politics, 1790," *The Journal of Southern History* 46 (1980): 335–60,. For a longer discussion of the importance of the print see Gould, *Barbaric Traffic*, 35–9.

12. Ohline, "Slavery, Economics, and Congressional Politics," 349.

13. Ohline, "Slavery, Economics, and Congressional Politics," 349.

14. Cited in Ohline, "Slavery, Economics, and Congressional Politics," 349–50.

15. The term, "federal consensus" is William M. Wiecek's to describe the tacit agreement that national union required the federal government to not interfere with the continuation

of slaveholding. See *The Sources of Antislavery Constitutionalism in America, 1760–1848* (Ithaca, NY: Cornell Univ. Press, 1977), 16.

16. See in particular, Eric Williams, *Capitalism & Slavery*, reprint 1994 (Chapel Hill: Univ. of North Carolina Press, 1944); Walter Johnson, *Soul by Soul: Life inside the Antebellum Slave Market* (Cambridge, MA: Harvard Univ. Press, 1999); and Edward E. Baptist, *The Half That Has Never Been Told: Slavery and the Making of American Capitalism* (New York, NY: Basic Books, 2014).

17. Jessica L. Semega, Kayla R. Fontenot, and Melissa A. Kollar, "Income and Poverty in the United States," published by U.S. Department of Commerce, Economics and Statistics Administration (September 2017), 5. https://www.census.gov/content/dam/Census/library/publications/2017/demo/P60-259.pdf

18. Jeanne Morefield, *Empires Without Imperialism: Anglo-American Decline and the Politics of Deflection* (Oxford, UK: Oxford Univ. Press, 2014), 2.

19. Thomas Jefferson to James Madison (March 6, 1796) in *The Papers of Thomas Jefferson*, 29:6.

20. See Raymond Walters, *Albert Gallatin: Jeffersonian Financier and Diplomat* (Pittsburg, PA: Univ. of Pittsburg Press), 88–94.

21. Albert Gallatin, *A Sketch of the Finances of the United States* (New York: William A. Davis, 1796), 134.

22. Gallatin, *Sketch*, 144–45.

23. Robin L. Einhorn, *American Taxation, American Slavery* (Chicago, IL: Univ. of Chicago Press, 2006), 111.

24. Gallatin, *Sketch*, 149–50.

25. Gallatin, *Sketch*, 150.

26. [March, 1783], *Journals of the Continental Congress, 1774–1789*, ed. Gaillard Hunt, 34 vols. (Washington, DC: Government Printing Office), 24:215.

27. [August, 1783], *Journals of the Continental Congress*, 24:527.

28. See "Notes of Proceedings in the Continental Congress," *The Papers of Thomas Jefferson*, ed. Julian P. Boyd (Princeton, NJ: Princeton Univ. Press, 1950), 1:320.

29. "Notes of Proceedings," 1:321.

30. "Notes of Proceedings," 1:322.

31. See Fehrenbacher, *Slaveholding Republic*, 29–33 for an extensive discussion of Constitutional Convention discussions about three-fifths compromise.

32. *The Records of the Federal Convention of 1787*, ed. Max Farrand, 3 vols. (New Haven, CT: Yale Univ. Press, 1911), 3:253. See also Ohline, "Republicanism and Slavery: Origins of the Three-Fifths Clause in the United States Constitution," *The William and Mary Quarterly* 28 (October 1971): 563–84, for a detailed account of the historical interpretations surrounding the clause. According to Ohline, the clause emerged not out of sectarian division over slavery, but as a result of negotiations over principles of representation and specifically whether the rule for representation would be fixed in the Constitution or subject to Congressional legislation. Ohline notes that "there was virtual unanimity for the principle of counting slaves" (571) and that "the actual clash was over the census and not the three-fifths clause" (579).

33. [July 11, 1787], *The Records of the Federal Convention of 1787*, 1:580.

34. *The Records of the Federal Convention*, 1:580.

35. Christopher Leslie Brown, "The origins of "legitimate commerce," in *Commercial Agriculture, the Slave Trade & Slavery in Atlantic Africa*, ed. Robin Law, Suzanne Schwartz,

and Silke Strickrodt (Suffolk, UK: Boydell & Brewer, 2013), 146. Brown argues that one reason that Benezet might have been reluctant to credit Postlethwayt was his earlier public defense of the Royal African Company (148).

36. See Gould's *Barbaric Traffic* for a longer discussion of Postethwayt (20–1 and 40–1).

37. Madeleine Dobie, *Trading Places: Colonization and Slavery in Eighteenth-century French Culture* (Ithaca, NY: Cornell Univ. Press, 2010), 14.

38. Marcel Dorigny observes that Le Mercier is the only member of the school to argue for the legitimacy of chattel slavery. See "The Question of Slavery in the Physiocratic Texts," in *Rethinking the Atlantic World*, ed. Manuela Albertone and Antonino De Francesco (New York: Palgrave Macmillan, 2009), 159–60.

39. Dobie, *Trading Places*, 222–27.

40. As quoted in Trevor Burnard and John Garrigus, *The Plantation Machine: Atlantic Capitalism in French Saint-Domingue and British Jamaica* (Philadelphia: Univ. of Pennsylvania Press, 2018), 196.

41. Michel-René Hilliard d'Auberteuil, *Considérations sur l'état present de la colonie franaise de Saint-Domingue* (Paris: Chez Grange, 1776), 133–34.

42. See Dorigny, "The Question of Slavery," 148–49. Dorigny also observes that Mirabeau was particularly critical of the racialized character of modern slavery.

43. Cited and translated by Dorigny, "The Question of Slavery," 150, 154.

44. See Dorigny, "The Question of Slavery," 153.

45. "Observations Concerning the Increase of Mankind," in *The Papers of Benjamin Franklin*, ed. Leonard W. Labaree, 37 vols. (New Haven, CT: Yale Univ. Press, 1961), 4:225.

46. See James J. McLain, *The Economic Writings of Du Pont de Nemours* (Newark: Univ. of Delaware Press, 1977), 120–22; See also Burnard and Garrigus, *The Plantation Machine*, 195–96; Dobie, *Trading Places*, 199–251; and David Allen Harvey, "Slavery on the Balance Sheet: Pierre-Samuel Du Pont de Nemours and the Physiocratic Case for Free Labor," *The Western Society for French History* 42 (2014): 75–87. Du Pont's essay begins as a review of Saint-Lambert's popular story of the heroic slave, "Ziméo."

47. Smith, *Wealth of Nations*, 387.

48. Smith, *Wealth of Nations*, 365.

49. James Ramsay, *On the Treatment and Conversion of African Slaves* (London: James Phillips, 1784), 106.

50. Noah Webster, *The Effects of Slavery* (Hartford, CT: Hudson and Goodwin, 1793), 7. Webster cites a "MSS letter from the hon. Dr. Ramsay, of Charlestown South-Carolina" as corroboration of this economic thesis.

51. For an excellent account of Hume's placement in the Atlantic economy, and its role in his articulation of *doux commerce*, see Emma Rothschild, "The Atlantic Worlds of David Hume," in *Soundings in Atlantic History*, ed. Bernard Bailyn, Patricia L. Denault (Cambridge, MA: Harvard Univ. Press), 405–50.

52. Quoted in Rothschild, "The Atlantic Worlds," 423.

53. See Hume, "Of the Populousness of Ancient Nations," in *Essays: Moral, Political, Literary*, 395.

54. Onur Ulas offers an extensive reading of Hume's "elliptical" approach to slavery in his "Between Commerce and Empire: David Hume, Colonial Slavery, and Commercial Incivility," *History of Political Thought* 39 (2018): 107–34.

55. *Annals of the Debates in Congress*, 1st Cong., 2nd sess., March 17, 1790, 1510.

56. Eric Hobsbawm, *The Age of Capital: 1848–1875* (New York, NY: Vintage Books, 1975), 170–71. Both Eugene Genovese and Elizabeth Fox-Genovese similarly insisted that North American slavery was both premodern and pre-capitalist. See Eugene Genovese, *The Political Economy of Slavery* (New York, NY: Pantheon Books, 1965) and *The World the Slaveholders Made: Two Essays in Interpretation* (New York, NY: Pantheon Books, 1969), and Elizabeth Fox-Genovese, *Fruits of Merchant Capital* (Oxford, UK: Oxford Univ. Press, 1983).

57. See Johnson's *Soul by Soul* and *River of Dark Dreams: Slavery and Empire in the Cotton Kingdom* (Cambridge, MA: Harvard Univ. Press, 2013); Baptist, *The Half Has Never Been Told*; Matthew Karp, *This Vast Southern Empire: Slaveholders at the Helm of American Foreign Policy* (Cambridge, MA: Harvard Univ. Press, 2016); and John J. Clegg, "Capitalism and Slavery," *Critical Historical Studies* (2015): 281–304. The question of productivity was also a crucial one for the highly controversial work of economists Robert William Fogel and Stanley L. Engerman in *Time on the Cross: The Economics of American Negro Slavery* (New York, NY: Norton Books, 1974). They used cliometrics to posit that slave ownership was as profitable as any other investment opportunity. As proof of this thesis, they argued that slaves worked just as efficiently as free laborers because they were given economic incentives to compel this productivity. In emphasizing pecuniary incentives, and de-emphasizing violent compulsion, *Time on the Cross* provided what many critics thought to be noxiously cheery portrait of the conditions of chattel slavery. And much of the backlash against the book focused on their de-emphasis on the subjugations peculiar to antebellum slavery. Baptist by contrast argues that physical brutality was an essential component in maximizing output from American slaves, and he details how the cotton industry's "pushing system" augmented not just the wealth of plantation owners, but the entire nation. The radical differences between these respective projects—wherein Baptist emphasizes the exceptional exploitation of slaves, while Fogel and Engerman maintain the exploitation rates as roughly commensurate to free labor—can obscure the fundamental similarity between them. Not only do they both make the case for the commensurability between slavery and capitalism, but they both stipulate the efficiency of slave labor. Also similar was the deluge of criticism both books received from both popular and academic readers.

58. Cited and translated by Dorigny, "The Question of Slavery," 156–57.

59. Adam Smith, *Lectures on Jurisprudence*, ed. R.L. Meek (Oxford: Oxford Univ. Press, 1978), 187.

60. Smith, *Lectures on Jurisprudence*, 187.

61. See Spencer J. Pack, "Slavery, Adam Smith's Economic Vision and the Invisible Hand," *History of Economic Ideas* 4 (1996): 253–69.

62. Mirabeau writes of West Indian slavery, "mais voulez-vous le borner & bientôt le render inutile? Encouragez la culture des terres dans les colonies. Vous ne le pouvez qu'en rendant les colonies florissantes" (1:148) in *L'Ami des hommes*, 3 vols. (Avignon, 1756).

63. In his essay, "Adam Smith's Theory of the Persistence of Slavery and its Abolition in Western Europe," Barry R. Weingast uses game theory to explain that even though owners might recognize that emancipation would lead to more productive labor, they would still be unwilling to free their slaves because they could not guarantee securing the labor. That is, once freed, slaves might leave and therefore owners would lose both property and labor. See https://web.stanford.edu/group/mcnollgast/cgi-bin/wordpress/wp-content/uploads/2013/10/asms-theory-of-sy.15.0725.print-version.pdf.

64. Smith, *Wealth of Nations*, 354.

65. In other words, slavery exposes what Mark Blaug calls Smith's "vulgar doctrine of the spontaneous harmony of interests," or the assumption "that decentralized atomistic competition does in some sense maximize social welfare" (60–1). *Economic Theory in Retrospect*, 5th ed. (New York, NY: Cambridge Univ. Press, 1996).

66. Jacob Viner, "Adam Smith and Laissez Faire," *Journal of Political Economy* 35 (1927): 198. Viner is focused on Smith, but we can see Smith's project of systematic order as descended from the physiocratic imperative to make economics a regularized science.

67. *Annals*, March 17, 1790, 1510.

68. *Annals*, March 17, 1790, 1510.

69. For more on early American (pre-cotton) textile industry see William R. Bagnall, *The Textile Industries of the United States*, vol. 1 (Cambridge, MA: Riverside Press, 1893).

70. Liz Bellamy, "It-Narrators and Circulation: Defining a Subgenre," in *The Secret Lives of Things: Animals, Objects, and It-narratives in Eighteenth-century England*, ed. Mark Blackwell (Lewisburg, PA: Bucknell Univ. Press, 2007), 119.

71. Bellamy, "It-Narrators and Circulation," 132.

72. Bellamy, "It-Narrators and Circulation," 133.

73. *The Tatler*, ed. Donald Frederic Bond, 3 vols. (Oxford: Clarendon Press, 1987), 2:270.

74. Bellamy, "It-Narrators and Circulation," 132.

75. Christina Lupton, *Knowing Books: The Consciousness of Mediation in Eighteenth-Century Britain* (Philadelphia: Univ. of Pennsylvania Press, 2012), 68–9.

76. Lynn Festa, "Moral Ends of 18th- and 19th-Century Object Narratives," in *The Secret Lives of Things*, 311. Both Bellamy and Festa note that the moral argument shifts as the subgenre becomes increasingly oriented towards a juvenile audience. As Festa neatly summarizes, if the early it-narrative offers a critique of a commercial world that has made people into commodities, then the Victorian it-narratives sentimentalize objects: things are not commodities, but instead "achieve apotheosis through a sentimental reunion with their most virtuous owner" (310).

77. Markman Ellis, "Suffering Things: Lapdogs, Slaves, and Counter-Sensibility," in *The Secret Lives of Things*, 105.

78. F.A. Hayek, *Law, Legislation and Liberty: Volume 1: Rules and Order* (Chicago, IL: Univ. of Chicago Press, 1973), 37. See also Emily Skarbek, "F.A. Hayek and the Early Foundations of Spontaneous Order," in *F.A. Hayek and the Modern Economy*, ed. Sandra J. Peart and David M. Levy (New York: Palgrave MacMillan, 2013), 101–18.

79. Hayek, "Lecture on a Master Mind: Dr. Bernard Mandeville," *Proceedings of the British Academy* 52 (London: Oxford Univ. Press, 1966), 129.

80. Mandeville, *The Fable of the Bees: or, Private Vices, Publick Benefits*, 5th ed. (London: J. Tonson, 1728), 412.

81. Hayek argues that this passage from *Fable* "clearly inspired Adam Smith" to his explanation of the division of labor and Smith's other it-narrative, the manufacture of the pin (Hayek, "Lecture," 134). Deidre Lynch does not identify these moments in Smith as it-narratives, but she does observe that Smith's remark, "the same guinea...[that] pays the weekly pension of one man today, may pay that of another tomorrow, and that of a third the day after" outlines a "sequence of adventures" that constitutes the plot of any number of eighteenth-century it-narratives ("Personal Effects and Sentimental Fictions," in *The Secret Lives of Things*, 73–4).

82. Festa, *Sentimental Figures of Empire* (Baltimore, MD: Johns Hopkins Univ. Press, 2006), 132.

83. Jonathan Lamb, *The Things Things Say* (Princeton, NJ: Princeton Univ. Press, 2011), 230.

84. William Fox, *An Address to the People of Great Britain, on the Propriety of Abstaining From West India Sugar and Rum*, 10th ed. (Philadelphia: Daniel Lawrence, 1792), 4. The cover of this edition includes the same lines from Cowper's "The Negro's Complaint."

85. Timothy Morton, *The Poetics of Spice* (New York, NY: Cambridge Univ. Press, 2006), 173. Carl Plasa reads Fox's pamphlet alongside other antislavery work, including Equiano's narrative, to explain how sugar eaters are associated with cannibalism in his *Slaves to Sweetness: British and Caribbean Literatures of Sugar* (Edinburgh: Edinburgh Univ. Press, 2009). See also Lawrence B. Glickman, "'Buy for the Sake of the Slave': Abolitionism and the Origins of American Consumer Activism," *American Quarterly* 56 (2004): 889–912.

86. On the use of ceramic ware in anti-slavery, see Sam Margolin, "'And Freedom to the Slave'": Antislavery Ceramics 1787–1865," *Ceramics in America* (Milwaukee: Chipstone Foundation, 2002): 81–109.

87. See especially chapter one, "The Commercial Jeremiad," in Gould's *Barbaric Traffic*.

88. Cugoano writes, "if [the west coast of Africa] was not annually ravished and laid waste, there might be a very considerable and profitable trade carried on with the Africans" (172). In *Unchained Voices*, ed. Vincent Carretta (Lexington: Univ. of Kentucky Press, 2004).

89. Henry Louis Gates, Jr., *The Signifying Monkey* (Oxford, UK: Oxford Univ. Press, 1988), 128.

90. Gould, *Barbaric Traffic*, 146.

91. Paul Gilroy, *The Black Atlantic: Modernity and Double Consciousness* (Cambridge, MA: Harvard Univ. Press, 2005), 19.

92. The conflict between these two perspectives is demonstrated by Srinivas Aravamudan's critique of Adam Potkay's "distortion" of Equiano's narrative to one that is exclusively about "spiritual and intellectual development" (*Tropicopolitans: Colonialism and Agency, 1688–1804*), 240. And then by Potkay's response that only "context that Aravamudan has no truck with is Equiano's Christianity" ("Teaching Equiano's *Interesting Narrative*," *Eighteenth-Century Studies* 34.4 [2001]: 610). Also illustrative is Andrew Kopec's essay that schematizes the "mistake" of reading Equiano's narrative exclusively as autobiography—as the story of a singular self, whether spiritual or economic. Kopec, "Collective Commerce and the Problem of Autobiography in Olaudah Equiano's *Narrative*," *The Eighteenth Century* 54.4 (2013): 461–78.

93. Katy Chiles is a notable exception to this traditional hermeneutics, opting to read Equiano's narrative not as life-writing but as a work of natural history. Chiles, *Transformable Race: Surprising Metamorphoses in the Literature of Early America* (Oxford, UK: Oxford Univ. Press, 2014).

94. Saidiya V. Hartman, *Scenes of Subjection: Terror, Slavery, and Self-making in Nineteenth-century America* (New York: Oxford Univ. Press, 1997), 5.

95. See chapter six, "Bond and Free: Contemporary Readings of Gronniosaw's *Life*" in Eve Tavor Bannet, *Transatlantic Stories and the History of Reading, 1720–1810* (New York, NY: Cambridge Univ. Press, 2011).

96. Cited in Ryan Hanley, *Beyond Slavery and Abolition: Black British Writing, c. 1770–1830* (New York, NY: Cambridge Univ. Press, 2019), 103.

97. For an excellent account of this Calvinist proslavery circle, and Gronniosaw's place in it, see Ryan Hanley, "Calvinism, Proslavery and James Albert Ukawsaw Gronniosaw," *Slavery & Abolition* 36 (2015): 360–81. Christopher Leslie Brown also discusses Selina Hastings's ambiguous location in British anti-slavery movement, observing that upon inheritance of fifty slaves from Whitefield, she doubled the number and asked that a "woman-slave may be purchased with [some of the funds], and that she may be called SELINA, after me." See also Christopher Leslie Brown, *Moral Capital: Foundations of British Abolitionism* (Chapel Hill: Univ. of North Carolina Press, 2012), 337 and J.K. Foster, *The Life and Times of Selina Countess of Huntington*, vol. 2 (London: William Edward Painter, 1840), 265–66.

98. Jennifer Harris suggests that Gronniosaw's family may have been Muslim since he was from the Borno region, which was predominately Muslim, and because the worship he describes (in which people silently "on our knees with our hands held up, observ[e] a strict silence till the sun is at a certain height" sounds very similar to the *salah*. "Seeing the Light: Re-reading James Albert Ukawsaw Gronniosaw," *English Language Notes* 42.4 (2005): 44. Gronniosaw, however, identifies his religion as polytheistic (in which "the sun, moon, and stars" were the objects of worship). All citations to Gronniosaw's text are taken from Carretta's anthology, *Unchained Voices*, and cited in the text.

99. For an extensive study of Theodorus Jacobus Frelinghuysen and his theological controversies, see James Tanis, *Dutch Calvinistic Pietism in the Middle Colonies: A Study in the Life and Theology of Theodorus Jacobus Frelinghuysen* (The Hague: Martinus Nijhoff, 1967). The biography makes no mention of either Gronniosaw or slavery.

100. Harris also observes the doubling of the scenes of worship under the two trees, but she argues that it is an example of "textual cover, a metaphorical substitution" in which Gronniosaw is using the American oak to give expression to his religious devotion under the palm ("Seeing the Light," 54).

101. Tom Wickman takes up the topic of economic illiteracy, arguing on behalf of Equiano's arithmetic skills. I agree that Gronniosaw, unlike Equiano, does not testify to his mathematical literacy, but he does demonstrate a sound understanding of commercial exchange despite his protestations. See "Arithmetic and Afro-Atlantic Pastoral Protest: The Place of (In)numeracy in Gronniosaw and Equiano," *Atlantic Studies* 8.2 (2011): 189–212.

102. Benjamin Fawcett, *A Compassionate Address to the Christian Negroes in Virginia: An Address to the Christian Negroes* (Salop, UK: Printed by F. Eddowes and F. Cotton, 1756), 8.

103. Fawcett, *A Compassionate Address*, 10.

104. On the importance of the Calico Acts to economic relations between Britain and her Atlantic colonies, see Jonathan Eacott's *Selling Empire: India in the Making of Britain and America, 1600–1830* (Chapel Hill: Univ. of North Carolina Press, 2016), 72–117.

105. We know the dates because Gronniosaw mentions that she was a "member of Mr. Allen's Meeting," and he was the pastor of a Baptist church on Petticoat Lane from January 1764 to May 1767. See Carretta, *Unchained Voices*, 57n.95.

106. Spitalfields silk weavers were instrumental to the violent eruptions and riots that ultimately resulted in the Calico Acts. See William Farrell, "Silk and Globalisation in Eighteenth-century London: Commodities, People and Connections," PhD thesis, Univ. of London (2014), 110–12.

107. W.C. Cooke, *The Handbook of Silk, Cotton, and Wool Manufactures* (London: Richard Bentley, 1843), 67–9.

108. For more on the Calico Acts and riots, see C.W. Smith, "'Calico Madams': Servants, Consumption, and the Calico Crisis," *Eighteenth-Century Life* 31 (2007): 29–55. See also the chapter on the master weaver, Simon Julins, in Zara Anishanslin's *Portrait of a Woman in Silk: Hidden Histories of the British Atlantic World* (New Haven, CT: Yale Univ. Press), 105–62.

109. Farrell, "Silk and Globalisation," 18.

110. Anishanslin, *Portrait of a Woman in Silk*, 306.

111. Frederick Burwick, *British Drama of the Industrial Revolution* (Cambridge, UK: Cambridge Univ. Press, 2015), 130.

112. The Mansfield ruling of 1772 is still three years away, which means, as was the case in New York, Gronniosaw would have reasonable fear of being resold into slavery, even as a free man living in England.

113. Maxine Berg, "Women's Work, Mechanization and the Early Phases of Industrialization in English," in *The Historical Meaning of Work*, ed. Patrick Joyce (Cambridge, UK: Cambridge Univ. Press, 1987), 64–98. Berg writes, "Women used both single and double engine looms in the 1760s, to such an extent that this was a cause of the great hostility of male weavers in 1769" (80).

114. J.H. Clapham, "The Spitalfields Acts, 1773–1824," *The Economic Journal* 26 (December 1916): 459–71.

115. H.C. Prince, "England, circa 1800," in *New Historical Geography of England*, ed. Henry Clifford Darby (Cambridge, UK: Cambridge Univ. Press, 1973), 141.

116. Gronniosaw references him as "Mr. Handbarrar," a phonetic spelling of the name. Ryan Hanley identifies him as Osgood Hanbury ("Calvinism, Proslavery," 371).

117. See Jacob M. Price, *Capital and Credit in British Overseas Trade: The View from the Chesapeake, 1700–1776* (New York, NY: Cambridge Univ. Press, 1980), 73–4.

118. George Washington to Hanburys & Lloyd, 1 June 1774, *The Papers of George Washington, Colonial Series*, vol. 10, ed. W.W. Abbot and Dorothy Twohig (Charlottesville: Univ. of Virginia Press, 1995), 81–2.

119. Gronniosaw records his name as "Henry Gurdney," but it seems almost certain he is referencing Gurney.

120. Cited in Augustus J. C. Hare, *The Gurneys of Earl* (London: George Allen, 1895), 11.

121. W.T.C. King, *History of the London Discount Market* (New York, NY: Routledge, 2006), 18. See also "The House of Overend, Gurney, and Company: Its Founders and Its Fall," *London Society*, July 8, 1866, 257.

122. "Chaff Cutters," *A Cyclopedia of Agriculture, Practical and Scientific*, vol. 1 , ed. John Chalmers Morton (London: Blackie & Son, 1875), 422.

123. In his brief death notice, Watson is referred to as "a considerable silk and stuff manufacturer, of Kidderminster." "Provincial Occurrences," *The Universal Magazine of Knowledge and Pleasure*, July 1804, 97.

124. Notably both silk and woolen markets were objects of protectionist economic policies throughout the eighteenth century.

125. Anna Mae Duane, for example, observes, "the triumphs and tragedies of his remarkable life are rendered through a narrative ledger of monetary gains and losses" (85) in "Keeping His Word: Money, Love, and Privacy in the Narrative of Venture Smith," *Venture Smith and the Business of Slavery and Freedom*, ed. James Brewer Stewart (Amherst: Univ. of Massachusetts Press, 2010).

126. Venture Smith, *A Narrative of the Life and Adventures of Venture, A Native of Africa,* in *Unchained Voices,* 382. All further citations will be located in the text.

127. Duane provides a comprehensive survey of the critics who have read "his narrative [as] tragically compromised" ("Keeping his Word," 185), noting that this dismissal has also "prevented Venture Smith's *Narrative* from getting the attention it deserves" (186). She argues that Smith's accounting project should not be read according to an American capitalist tradition, but rather a West African monetary tradition.

128. Thomas Paine, *Rights of Man,* in *Selected Writings of Thomas Paine,* ed. Ian Shapiro and Jane E. Calvert (New Haven, CT: Yale Univ. Press, 2014), 311.

129. According to a report in 1764 by the Rhode Island General Assembly (written in opposition to the renewal of the Molasses Act), the use of rum as a commodity currency began in 1723 (just before Smith's enslavement) and quickly dominated the trade. Annually almost twenty ships sailed from Rhode Island to Anomabu carrying 1800 hogsheads of rum. See Randy J. Sparks, *Where the Negroes are Masters: An Africa Port in the Era of the Slave Trade* (Cambridge, MA: Harvard Univ. Press, 2014), 164. See also James A. Rawley with Stephen D. Behrendt, *The Transatlantic Slave Trade: A History,* revised ed. (Lincoln: Univ. of Nebraska Press, 2015), 305–7.

130. Smith lived near the waterway that linked coastal Connecticut and Rhode Island to New York's Long Island, which Robert P. Forbes, David Richardson, and Chandler B. Saint identify as the "northwest corner of the Greater West Indies." See their essay, "Trust and Violence in Atlantic History," in *Venture Smith and the Business of Slavery and Freedom,* 69.

131. Forbes, Richardson, and Saint explain that the sum "indicates the commercial value of the island" ("Trust and Violence in Atlantic History," 66).

132. Barbara L. Solow, "Slavery and Colonization," in *Slavery and the Rise of the Atlantic System,* ed. Barbara L. Solow (Cambridge: Cambridge Univ. Press, 1991), 29.

133. Olaudah Equiano, *The Interesting Narrative of the Life of Olaudah Equiano* in *Unchained Voices,* 221.

134. Equiano, *The Interesting Narrative,* 221.

135. Equiano, *The Interesting Narrative,* 223.

136. On the significance of human collateral see Thomas D. Morris, "'Society is Not Marked by Punctuality in the Payment of Debts': The Chattel Mortgages of Slaves," in *Ambivalent Legacy: A Legal History of the South* (Jackson: Univ. of Mississippi Press, 1984), 147–70 and Bonnie Martin, "Slavery's Invisible Engine: Mortgaging Human Property," *The Journal of Southern History* 76.4 (November 2010): 817–66.

137. Jennifer Rae Greeson, "The Prehistory of Possessive Individualism," *PMLA* 127.4 (2012): 922.

138. Greeson, "Prehistory," 918 and 921. She borrows the word "assimilation" from William Andrews, *To Tell a Free Story: The First Century of Afro-American Autobiography, 1760–1865* (Urbana: Univ. of Illinois Press, 1986), 51–2. Although her archive is from a later period in American literary history, Katherine Adams provides an extensive analysis of this same paradoxical logic, which she terms "self-(non)possession" in her study of the necessary entailments of the American devotion to privacy and private property. See *Owning Up: Privacy, Property, and Belonging in U.S. Women's Life Writing, 1840–1890* (Oxford, UK: Oxford Univ. Press, 2009).

139. Greeson, "Prehistory," 920.

140. For an extensive study of Prentiss's life, see Kari J. Winter, "The Strange Career of Benjamin Franklin Prentiss, Antislavery Lawyer," *Vermont History* 79.2 (2011): 121–40.

141. Winter edited this new edition—and her voluminous research is almost solely responsible for our knowledge of Brinch and Prentiss. *The Blind African Slave, Or Memoirs of Boyrereau Brinch, Nicknamed Jeffrey Brace*, ed. Kari J. Winter (Madison: Univ. of Wisconsin Press, 2004).

142. Winter, "The Strange Career," 129.

143. Lynn R. Johnson, "Narrating an Indigestible Trauma: The Alimentary Grammar of Boyrereau Brinch's Middle Passage," in *Journeys of the Slave Narrative in the Early Americas*, ed. Nicole N. Aljoe and Ian Finseth (Charlottesville: Univ. of Virginia Press, 2014): 127–42. Dickson D. Bruce, Jr. makes brief mention of the narrative in his *The Origins of African American Literature, 1680–1865* (Charlottesville: Univ. of Virginia Press, 2001), 97–100.

144. Winter, "Preface," *The Blind Slave*, xi. Winter chooses to call Brinch "Jeffrey Brace," the name "he claimed for himself as a free man in the last decades of his life" (xiii). Since her focus is on biography, this decision makes a good deal of sense. I am referring to him as "Boyrereau Brinch," because my own focus is the production of him as a textual subject.

145. *The Blind Slave*, ed. Winter, 91. All subsequent citations will be to this edition of the text. The rough coordinates—as well as the later identification that the Niger River ran through the region, place the location of Brinch's birth in what is now Mali (Winter, 4).

146. Johnson, "Narrating an Indigestible Trauma," 128.

147. In the closing paragraphs of his narrative, Brinch articulates his motives for sharing his "simple narrative," and they largely follow the paradigm or earlier black Atlantic autobiographies. He provides his life story so "that all may see how poor Africans have been and perhaps now are abused by a Christian and enlightened people" and to "open[] the hearts of those who hold slaves and move them to consent to give them that freedom which they themselves enjoy" (182). He also hopes that the book's publication might be a source of small income for him.

148. This particular passage is from William Guthrie, *A New Geographical, Historical, and Commercial Grammar*, 7th ed. (London: Charles Dilly, 1782), 588. It may be, however, that both Prentiss and Brinch are taking it from Jedidiah Morse's *The American Geography*, which reprints Guthrie's sections on Africa (without attribution).

149. The only exception is when he writes that he was "bartered for old horses" (156), but even here he refuses to identify the number of horses.

150. Gilroy, *Black Atlantic*, 49.

151. Immanuel Wallerstein, *Historical Capitalism with Capitalist Civilization* (New York: Verso Books, 1983), 28–9.

## Conclusion

1. *The Financial Crisis Inquiry Report (FCIR)* (Washington, DC: U.S. Government Printing Office, 2011), xvii, 90, and 111.

2. *FCIR*, 236.

3. *FCIR*, 275.

4. *FCIR*, xi–xii.

5. "The official verdict; Postmortems on the financial crisis," *The Economist*, February 5, 2011, 98.

6. Mark S. Rzepczynski, "The Financial Crisis Inquiry Report, Authorized Edition (a review)," *Financial Analysts Journal* 7 (2012): 78–81.

7. Andrew W. Hartlage, "'Never Again,' Again: A Functional Examination of the Financial Crisis Inquiry Commission," *Michigan Law Review* 111 (April 2013): 1185.

8. *FCIR*, 414.

9. *FCIR*, 414.

10. Hammond, *Banks and Politics*, 121.

11. Jeff Madrick, "The Wall Street Leviathan," *New York Review of Books* (April 28, 2011): https://www.nybooks.com/articles/2011/04/28/wall-street-leviathan/.

12. As quoted in Dave McNary, "Martin Scorsese on 'Wolf of Wall Street,'" *Variety*, January 25, 2014): https://variety.com/2014/film/news/martin-scorsese-on-wolf-of-wall-street-i-wanted-to-make-a-ferocious-film-1201070801/.

13. Jordan Belfort, *The Wolf of Wall Street* (New York: Bantam Books, 2007), 1 and 11.

14. Michael Lewis, *The Big Short* (New York: W.W. Norton & Company, 2010), xv.

15. For a very different reading of the movie, see Clint Burnham, *Fredric Jameson and* The Wolf of Wall Street (New York: Bloomsbury Academic, 2016).

16. Leigh Claire La Berge, *Scandals and Abstraction: Financial Fiction of the Late 1980s* (Oxford: Oxford Univ. Press, 2014), 5 and 9.

17. La Berge, *Scandals and Abstraction*, 10.

18. With the exception of Michael Burry, the film renames all of the protagonists from Lewis's book. Mark Baum is therefore based on Steve Eisman, who largely serves as Lewis's protagonist.

19. Lewis, *The Big Short*, 143.

20. Lewis, *The Big Short*, 143.

21. Jameson, *Postmodernism; or, the Cultural Logic of Late Capitalism* (London: Verso, 1991), 51.

22. Jameson, "Culture and Finance Capital," *Critical Inquiry* 24 (Autumn 1997): 252. Examples of the former include La Berge whose book provides a "literary history of what happens to narrative form when too much money circulates at once" (5). See also Arne De Boever who, turning his critical eye to financial fiction written in the wake of 2008, muses that we might "need another kind of writing," because the novel is proving to be "completely irrelevant as a literary form in the era of digitized, high-frequency trading." *Finance Fictions: Realism and Psychosis in a Time of Economic Crisis* (New York, NY: Fordham Univ. Press, 2018), 18. The most impassioned case for the latter can be found in Alberto Toscano and Jeff Kinkle, *Cartographies of the Absolute* (Winchester, UK: Zero Books, 2014). Their remarkable book offers a "survey" of the many artistic works that "seem to answer the call for an aesthetic of cognitive mapping" (45). The best of this work, they propose, is capable of "representing the complex and dynamic relations intervening between the domains of production, consumption and distribution...of making the invisible visible" (56).

23. I take the term "network narrative," which has become conventional, from David Bordwell, *The Poetics of Cinema* (New York: Routledge, 2008), especially chapter 7 (pp. 189–220). Toscano and Kinkle use the term "Hyperlink cinema" (312). Some familiar examples include Steven Soderbergh's *Traffic* (2000), Paul Haggis's *Crash* (2004), and Alexandro Gonzales Iñárritu's *Babel* (2006).

24. Caroline Levine proposes that Charles Dickens's *Bleak House* is a nineteenth-century example of a network narrative and that the novel "structures the unfolding of its plot around multiple conflicting and competing webs of interconnection" (517). See *Forms: Whole, Rhythm, Hierarchy, Network* (Princeton, NJ: Princeton Univ. Press, 2015).

25. Nick Allen, "People are Smart: Adam McKay on 'The Big Short,'" *Robert Ebert Interviews* (December 14, 2015): https://www.rogerebert.com/interviews/people-are-smart-adam-mckay-on-the-big-short.

26. Deirdre McCloskey, "Storytelling in Economics," in *Narrative in Culture: The Uses of Storytelling in the Sciences, Philosophy and Literature*, ed. Christopher Nash (London: Routledge, 1990), 10.

27. G.L.S. Shackle, *Epistemics and Economics: A Critique of Economic Doctrines* (New York: Cambridge Univ. Press, 1972), 9.

28. Shackle, 10.

29. As cited in Tony Lawson, *Reorienting Economics* (Abingdon, UK: Routledge, 2003), 10.

30. Lawson, *Essays on the Nature and State of Modern Economics* (Abingdon, UK: Routledge, 2015), 13.

31. Richard Bronk, *The Romantic Economist: Imagination in Economics* (Cambridge, UK: Cambridge Univ. Press, 2009), 2.

# { WORKS CITED }

Albertone, Manuela. *National Identity and the Agrarian Republic: The Transatlantic Commerce of Ideas between America and France, 1750–1830*. Burlington, VT: Ashgate Publishing Co., 2014.

d'Alembert, Jean Le Rond. *Preliminary Discourse to the Encyclopedia of Diderot*, trans. Richard N. Schwab. Chicago, IL: Univ. of Chicago Press, 1995.

Allen, Nick. "People are Smart: Adam McKay on 'The Big Short'." *Robert Ebert Interviews* (December 14, 2015): https://www.rogerebert.com/interviews/people-are-smart-adam-mckay-on-the-big-short.

Alpers, Paul. *What Is Pastoral?* Chicago, IL: Univ. of Chicago Press, 1997.

Andrews, William. *To Tell a Free Story: The First Century of Afro-American Autobiography, 1760–1865*. Urbana: Univ. of Illinois Press, 1986.

Anishanslin, Zara. *Portrait of a Woman in Silk: Hidden Histories of the British Atlantic World*. New Haven, CT: Yale Univ. Press, 2016.

Appleby, Joyce. *Capitalism and a New Social Order: The Republican Vision of the 1790s*. New York: New York Univ. Press, 1984.

Appleby, Joyce. "Commercial Farming and the 'Agrarian Myth' in the Early Republic." *Journal of American History* 68 (1982): 833–849.

Appleby, Joyce. "The Vexed Story of American Capitalism." *Journal of the Early Republic* 21 (2001): 1–18.

d'Auberteuil, Michel-René Hilliard. *Considérations sur l'état present de la colonie franaise de Saint-Domingue*. Paris: Chez Grange, 1776.

Axelrad, Jacob. *Philip Freneau: Champion of Democracy*. Austin: Univ. of Texas Press, 1967.

Bagnall, William R. *The Textile Industries of the United States*, vol. 1. Cambridge, MA: Riverside Press, 1893.

Baier, Annette C. *A Progress of Sentiments: Reflections on Hume's Treatise*. Cambridge, MA: Harvard Univ. Press, 1991.

Baker, Jennifer Jordan. *Securing the Commonwealth: Debt, Speculation, & Writing in the Making of Early America*. Baltimore, MD: Johns Hopkins Univ. Press, 2005.

Bannet, Eve Tavor. *Transatlantic Stories and the History of Reading, 1720–1810*. New York: Cambridge Univ. Press, 2011.

Banning, Lance. *The Jeffersonian Persuasion: Evolution of a Party Ideology*. Ithaca, NY: Cornell Univ. Press, 1978.

Banning, Lance. "Jefferson Ideology Revisited: Liberal and Classical ideas in the New American Republic." *William and Mary Quarterly* 43 (January 1986): 3–19.

Beard, Charles A. *Economic Origins of Jeffersonian Democracy*. New York: Macmillan Company, 1915.

Beard, Charles A. *An Economic Interpretation of the Constitution of the United States*. New York: Macmillan Company, 1921.

Beer, Max. *An Inquiry into Physiocracy*. New York: Russell & Russell, 1939.

Behrendt, Stephen D. *The Transatlantic Slave Trade: A History*, revised ed. Lincoln: Univ. of Nebraska Press, 2015.

Belfort, Jordan. *The Wolf of Wall Street*. New York: Bantam Books, 2007.

Bellamy, Liz. "It-Narrators and Circulation: Defining a Subgenre." In *The Secret Lives of Things: Animals, Objects, and It-narratives in Eighteenth-century England*. Edited by Mark Blackwell. Lewisburg, PA: Bucknell Univ. Press, 2007.

*The Beauties of Poetry, British and American*. Worcester, MA: Mathew Carey, 1791.

Benjamin, Walter. "The Storyteller." In *Illuminations*, trans. Harry Zohn. Edited by Hannah Arendt. New York: Schocken Books, 1968.

Berg, Maxine. "Women's Work, Mechanization and the Early Phases of Industrialization in English." In *The Historical Meaning of Work*. Edited by Patrick Joyce. Cambridge, UK: Cambridge Univ. Press, 1987.

Blaug, Mark. *Economic Theory in Retrospect*, 5th edition. New York: Cambridge Univ. Press, 1996.

Bourdieu, Pierre. *The Field of Cultural Production*. New York: Columbia Univ. Press, 1993.

Bordwell, David. *The Poetics of Cinema*. New York: Routledge, 2008.

Brinch, Boyrereau. *The Blind African Slave, Or Memoirs of Boyrereau Brinch, Nicknamed Jeffrey Brace*. Edited by Kari J. Winter. Madison: Univ. of Wisconsin Press, 2004.

Bronk, Richard. *The Romantic Economist: Imagination in Economics*. Cambridge, UK: Cambridge Univ. Press, 2009.

Brown, Charles Brockden. *Collected Writings of Charles Brockden Brown: Letters an Early Epistolary Writing*. Edited by Philip Barnard, Elizabeth Hewitt, and Mark Kamrath. Lanham, MD: Bucknell Univ. Press, 2013.

Brown, Charles Brockden. "The Difference between History and Romance." *The Monthly Magazine* (April 1800): 251–53.

Brown, Charles Brockden. "The Man at Home." *The Weekly Magazine*. February–April 1798.

Brown, Charles Brockden. "The Rhapsodist." *The Columbian Magazine*. August–October 1789.

Brown, Charles Brockden. "The Scribbler." *Commercial Advertiser*. August 12–16, 1800.

Brown, Charles Brockden. "The Scribbler." *The Port-Folio*. January–July 1809.

Brown, Christopher Leslie. "Empire without America: British Plans for Africa in the Era of the American Revolution." In *Abolitionism and Imperialism in Britain, Africa, and the Atlantic*. Edited by Derek R. Peterson. Athens: Ohio Univ. Press, 2010.

Brown, Christopher Leslie. *Moral Capital: Foundations of British Abolitionism*. Chapel Hill: Univ. of North Carolina Press, 2012.

Brown, Christopher Leslie. "The origins of "legitimate commerce." In *Commercial Agriculture, the Slave Trade & Slavery in Atlantic Africa*. Edited by Robin Law, Suzanne Schwartz, and Silke Strickrodt. Suffolk, UK: Boydell & Brewer, 2013.

Buell, Lawrence. "American Pastoral Ideology Reappraised." *American Literary History* 1 (1989): 1–29.

Buel, Richard, Jr. *Joel Barlow: American Citizen in a Revolutionary World*. Baltimore, MD: Johns Hopkins Univ. Press, 2011.

Burnard, Trevor and John Garrigus. *The Plantation Machine: Atlantic Capitalism in French Saint-Domingue and British Jamaica*. Philadelphia: Univ. of Pennsylvania Press, 2018.

Burnham, Michelle. *Folded Selves: Colonial New England Writing in the World System*. Hanover, NH: Univ. Press of New England, 2007.

Burwick, Frederick. *British Drama of the Industrial Revolution*. Cambridge, UK: Cambridge Univ. Press, 2015.

Callon, Michel. "The Embeddedness of Economic Markets." In *The Laws of Markets*. Edited by Michel Callon. London: Blackwell, 1998.

Carretta, Vincent. *Phillis Wheatley: Biography of a Genius in Bondage*. Athens: Univ. of Georgia Press, 2011.

Chan, Michael D. "Alexander Hamilton on Slavery." *The Review of Politics* 66.2 (2004): 207–31.

Cheney, Paul. *Revolutionary Commerce: Globalization and the French Monarchy*. Cambridge, MA: Harvard Univ. Press, 2010.

Chernow, Ron. *Alexander Hamilton*. New York: Penguin Books, 2005.

Clapham, J.H. "The Spitalfields Acts, 1773–1824." *The Economic Journal* 26 (December 1916): 459–71.

Clegg, John J. "Capitalism and Slavery." *Critical Historical Studies* 2.2 (2015): 281–304.

Commons, John R. "American Shoemakers, 1648-1895." *Quarterly Journal of Economics* 24 (November 1909): 39–84.

Cooke, W.C. *The Handbook of Silk, Cotton, and Wool manufactures*. London: Richard Bentley, 1843.

Crèvecoeur, J. Hector St. John de. *Letters from an American Farmer and Sketches of Eighteenth-Century America*. Edited by Albert E. Stone. New York: Penguin Books, 1981.

Cugoano, Quobna Ottobah. *Thoughts and Sentiments on the Evil and Wicked Traffic of the Slavery and Commerce of the Human Species*. In *Unchained Voices: An Anthology of Black Authors in the English-Speaking World of the Eighteenth Century*. Edited by Vincent Carretta. Lexington: Univ. of Kentucky Press, 2004.

Curran, Stuart. *Poetic Form and British Romanticism*. Oxford: Oxford Univ. Press, 1986.

Davidson, Cathy. *Revolution and the Word: The Rise of the Novel in America*. Oxford: Oxford Univ. Press, 1986.

Dellinger, Walter and H. Jefferson Powell. "The Constitutionality of the Bank Bill: the Attorney General's First Constitutional Law Opinions." *Duke Law Journal* 44 (1994): 110–33.

Dobie, Madeleine. *Trading Places: Colonization and Slavery in Eighteenth-century French Culture*. Ithaca, NY: Cornell Univ. Press, 2010.

Dooley, Peter C. *The Labour Theory of Value*. New York: Routledge, 2005.

Dorigny, Marcel. "The Question of Slavery in the Physiocratic Texts." In *Rethinking the Atlantic World*. Edited by Manuela Albertone and Antonioni De Francesco. New York: Palgrave Macmillan, 2009.

Dowling, William C. *Literary Federalism in the Age of Jefferson: Joseph Dennie and the* Port Folio, *1801–1811*. Columbia: Univ. of South Carolina Press, 1999.

Du Pont, Pierre de Nemours. *De l'origine et des progress d'une science nouvelle* (1768). Paris: P. Geuthner, 1910.

Duane, Anna Mae. "Keeping His Word: Money, Love, and Privacy in the Narrative of Venture Smith." In *Venture Smith and the Business of Slavery and Freedom*. Edited by James Brewer Stewart. Amherst: Univ. of Massachusetts Press, 2010.

Eacott, Jonathan. *Selling Empire: India in the Making of Britain and America, 1600–1830*. Chapel Hill: Univ. of North Carolina Press, 2016.

Eco, Umberto. *The Limits of Interpretation*. Bloomington: Indiana Univ. Press, 1990.

Eco, Umberto. *From Tree to the Labyrinth: Historical Studies on the Sign and Interpretation*. Cambridge, MA: Harvard Univ. Press, 2014.

Edling, Max. "Hamilton and the Restoration of Public Credit." *William and Mary Quarterly*, 3rd series, 65, no. 2 (April 2007): 287–326.

Einhorn, Robin L. *American Taxation, American Slavery*. Chicago, IL: Univ. of Chicago Press, 2006.

Eisinger, Charles. "The Influence of Natural Rights and Physiocratic Doctrines on American Agrarian Thought during the Revolutionary Period." *Agricultural History* 21 (January 1947): 13–23.

Elkins, Stanley and Eric McKitrick. *The Age of Federalism: The Early American Republic, 1788–1800*. Oxford, UK: Oxford Univ. Press, 1993.

Ellis, Markman. "Suffering Things: Lapdogs, Slaves, and Counter-Sensibility." In *The Secret Lives of Things*. Edited by Mark Blackwell. Lewisburg, PA: Bucknell Univ. Press, 2007.

Empson, William. *Some Versions of Pastoral*. New York: New Directions, 1935.

Equiano, Olaudah. *The Interesting Narrative of the Life of Olaudah Equiano*. In *Unchained Voices: An Anthology of Black Authors in the English-Speaking World of the Eighteenth Century*. Edited by Vincent Carretta. Lexington: Univ. of Kentucky Press, 2004.

Farrell, William. "Silk and Globalisation in Eighteenth-century London: Commodities, People and Connections." PhD thesis, Univ. of London, 2014.

Fawcett, Benjamin. *A Compassionate Address to the Christian Negroes in Virginia*. Salop, UK: Printed by F. Eddowes and F. Cotton, 1756.

Ferguson, Robert. *Reading the Early Republic*. Cambridge: Harvard Univ. Press, 2004.

Fehrenbacher, Don E. *The Slaveholding Republic: An Account of the United States Government's Relations to Slavery*. Oxford, UK: Oxford Univ. Press, 2002.

Festa, Lynn M. "Moral Ends of 18th- and 19th-Century Object Narratives." In *The Secret Lives of Things*. Edited by Mark Blackwell. Lewisburg, PA: Bucknell Univ. Press, 2007.

Festa, Lynn M. *Sentimental Figures of Empire*. Baltimore, MD: Johns Hopkins Univ. Press, 2006.

Fichtelberg, Joseph. *Critical Fictions: Sentiment and the American Market, 178–1870*. Athens: Univ. of Georgia Press, 2003.

*The Financial Crisis Inquiry Report*. Washington, D.C.: U.S. Government Printing Office, 2011.

Forbes, Robert P., David Richardson, and Chandler B. Saint. "Trust and Violence in Atlantic History: The Economic Worlds of Venture Smith. In *Venture Smith and the Business of Slavery and Freedom*. Edited by James Brewer Stewart. Amherst: Univ. of Massachusetts Press, 2010.

Fox, William. *An Address to the People of Great Britain, on the Propriety of Abstaining From West Indian Sugar and Rum*, 10th ed. Philadelphia: Daniel Lawrence, 1792.

Freneau, Philip. *A Journey from Philadelphia to New-York*. Philadelphia: Francis Bailey, 1787.

Freneau, Philip. *Letters on Various Interesting and Important Subjects*. Philadelphia: Printed for the Author, 1799.

Freneau, Philip. *The Miscellaneous Works of Mr. Phillip Freneau Containing his Essays, and Additional Poems*. Philadelphia, PA: Francis Bailey, 1788.

Gallagher, Christopher. "The Leasowes: A History of the Landscape." *Garden History* 24, no. 2 (Winter 1996): 201–20.

Gallatin, Albert. *A Sketch of the Finances of the United States*. New York: William A. Davis, 1796.

Gardner, Jared. "From the Periodical Archives: 'The Scribbler,'" *American Periodicals* 16.2 (2006): 219–28.

Gardner, Jared. *The Rise and Fall of Early American Magazine Culture*. Urbana: Univ. of Illinois Press, 2013.

Gates, Henry Louis. *The Signifying Monkey*. Oxford, UK: Oxford Univ. Press, 1988.

Gehrke, Christian and Heinz D. Kurz. "Karl Marx on Physiocracy." *The European Journal of the History of Economic Thought* 2, no. 1 (1995): 53–90.

Gifford, Terry. *Pastoral*. New York: Routledge, 1999.

Gilmore, Michael T. "Magazines, Criticism, and Essays." *The Cambridge History of American Literature, Volume 1: 1590–1820*. Edited by Sacvan Bercovitch. New York: Cambridge Univ. Press, 1994.

Gilroy, Paul. *The Black Atlantic: Modernity and Double Consciousness*. Cambridge, MA: Harvard Univ. Press, 2005.

Gould, Philip. *Barbaric Traffic: Commerce and Antislavery in the Eighteenth-Century Atlantic World*. Cambridge: Harvard Univ. Press, 2003.

Granger, Bruce. *American Essay Serials from Franklin to Irving*. Knoxville: Univ. of Tennessee Press, 1978.

Granovetter, Mark. "Economic Action and Social Structure: The Problem of Embeddedness." *American Journal of Sociology* 91 (November 1985): 481–510.

Green, Jack P. *Evaluating Empire and Confronting Colonialism in Eighteenth-Century Britain*. Cambridge: Cambridge Univ. Press, 2013.

Greeson, Jennifer Rae. "The Prehistory of Possessive Individualism." *PMLA* 127.4 (2012): 922.

Gronniosaw, James Albert Ukawsaw. *A Narrative of the Most Remarkable Particulars*. In *Unchained Voices: An Anthology of Black Authors in the English-Speaking World of the Eighteenth Century*. Edited by Vincent Carretta. Lexington: Univ. of Kentucky Press, 2004.

Guthrie, William. *A New Geographical, Historical, and Commercial Grammar*, 7th ed. London: Charles Dilly, 1782.

Hamilton, Alexander. *Alexander Hamilton: Writings*. Edited by Joanne B. Freeman. New York: Library of America, 2001.

Hamilton, Alexander. *The Papers of Alexander Hamilton*. Edited by Harold C. Syrett. New York: Columbia Univ. Press, 1961–1987.

Hammond, Bray. *Banks and Politics in America from the Revolution to the Civil War*. Princeton, NJ: Princeton Univ. Press, 1957.

Hanley, Ryan. *Beyond Slavery and Abolition: Black British Writing, c. 1770–1830*. New York: Cambridge Univ. Press, 2019.

Hare, Augustus J. C. *The Gurneys of Earl*. London: George Allen, 1895.

Harrison, Joseph H., Jr. "*Sic et Non*: Thomas Jefferson and Internal Improvement." *Journal of the Early Republic* 17.4 (1987): 335–49.

Hartlage, Andrew W. "'Never Again,' Again: A Functional Examination of the Financial Crisis Inquiry Commission." *Michigan Law Review* 111 (April 2013): 1183–94.

Hartman, Saidiya V. *Scenes of Subjection: Terror, Slavery, and Self-making in Nineteenth-century America*. New York: Oxford Univ. Press, 1997.

Harvey, David. *A Companion to Marx's Capital*. London: Verso, 2010.

Harvey, David Allen. "Slavery on the Balance Sheet: Pierre-Samuel Dupont de Nemours and the Physiocratic Case for Free Labor." *The Western Society for French History* 42 (2014): 75–87.

Hayek, F.A. "Lecture on a Master Mind: Dr. Bernard Mandeville." In *Proceedings of the British Academy 52*. Oxford, UK: Oxford Univ. Press, 1966.

Hayek, F.A. *Law, Legislation and Liberty: Volume 1: Rules and Order*. Chicago, IL: Univ. of Chicago Press, 1973.

Hayes, Kevin J. *The Road to Monticello: The Life and Mind of Thomas Jefferson*. Oxford, UK: Oxford Univ. Press, 2008.

Heinzelman, Kurt. *The Economics of the Imagination*. Amherst: Univ. of Massachusetts Press, 1980.

Hobsbawm, Eric. *The Age of Capital: 1848–1875*. New York: Vintage Books, 1975.

Hume, David. *An Enquiry Concerning Human Understanding*. Edited by Tom L. Beauchamp. Oxford: Oxford Univ. Press, 1999.

Hume, David. *Essays: Moral, Political, and Literary*. Edited by Eugene F. Miller. Indianapolis: Liberty Classics, 1987.

Hume, David. *A Treatise of Human Nature*. Edited by David Fate Norton and Mary J. Norton. Oxford: Clarendon Press, 2011.

Jameson, Fredric. *Postmodernism; or, the Cultural Logic of Late Capitalism*. London: Verso, 1991.

Jameson, Fredric. "Culture and Finance Capital." *Critical Inquiry* 24 (1997): 246–65.

Jameson, Fredric. "Future City." *New Left Review* 21 (2003): 65–79.

Jefferson, Thomas. *Thomas Jefferson: Writings*. Edited by Merrill D. Peterson. New York: Library of America, 1984.

Jehlen, Myra. *American Incarnation: The Individual, the Nation, and the Continent*. Cambridge, MA: Harvard Univ. Press, 1986.

Johnson, Samuel. *The Lives of the Poets*. Oxford: Oxford Univ. Press, 2009.

Karp, Matthew. *This Vast Southern Empire: Slaveholders at the Helm of American Foreign Policy*. Cambridge, MA: Harvard Univ. Press, 2016.

Kemple, Thomas M. *Reading Marx Writing: Melodrama, the Market, and the "Grundrisse"*. Stanford, CA: Stanford Univ. Press, 1995.

King, W.T.C. *History of the London Discount Market*. New York: Routledge, 2006.

Knott, Stephen F. *Alexander Hamilton and the Persistence of Myth*. Lawrence: Univ. of Kansas Press, 2002.

Kopec, Andrew. "Collective Commerce and the Problem of Autobiography in Olaudah Equiano's *Narrative*." *The Eighteenth Century* 54.4 (2013): 461–78.

Kramnick, Isaac. "Republican Revision Revisited." *American Historical Review* 87 (1982): 629–64.

Kulikoff, Allan. *The Agrarian Origins of American Capitalism*. Charlottesville: Univ. of Virginia Press, 1992.

La Berge, Leigh Claire. *Scandals and Abstraction: Financial Fiction of the Late 1980s*. Oxford: Oxford Univ. Press, 2014.

Lamb, Jonathan. *The Things Things Say*. Princeton, NJ: Princeton Univ. Press, 2011.

Latour, Bruno. *Reassembling the Social: An Introduction to Actor-Network Theory*. Oxford, UK: Oxford Univ. Press, 2005.

Lawson, Tony. *Reorienting Economics*. Abingdon, UK: Routledge, 2003.

Lawson, Tony. *Essays on the Nature and State of Modern Economics*. Abingdon, UK: Routledge, 2015.

Leary, Lewis. *That Rascal Freneau: A Study in Literary Failure*. New Brunswick, NJ: Rutgers Univ. Press, 1941.

Leibiger, Stuart. *Founding Friendship: George Washington, James Madison, and the Creation of the American Republic*. Charlottesville: Univ. of Virginia Press, 2001.

Leighton, Ann. *American Gardens in the Eighteenth Century*. Amherst: Univ. of Massachusetts Press, 1976.

Levine, Robert. *Conspiracy and Romance*. New York: Cambridge Univ. Press, 1989.

Lewis, Michael. *The Big Short*. New York: W.W. Norton & Company, 2010.

Lightner, David L. *Slavery and the Commerce Power: How the Struggle Against the Interstate Slave Trade Led to the Civil War*. New Haven, CT: Yale Univ. Press, 2006.

Logan, George. *An address on the natural and social order of the world, as intended to produce universal good*. Philadelphia: Tammany Society, 1798.

Logan, George. *Five Letters Addressed to the Yeomanry of the United States. Containing Some Observations on the Dangerous Scheme of Governor Duer and Mr. Hamilton to Establish National Manufactories. By an American Farmer*. Philadelphia: Oswald, 1792.

Logan, George. *Fourteen Agricultural Experiments to Ascertain the Best Rotation of Crops*. Philadelphia: Bailey, 1797.

Logan, George. *Letters addressed to the yeomanry of the United States. By a farmer*. Philadelphia: Eleazer Oswald, 1791.

Logan, George. *Letters addressed to the Yeomanry of the United States, containing some observations on funding and banking systems*. Philadelphia: Childs and Swaine, 1793.

Loughran, Trish. *The Republic in Print: Print Culture in the Age of U.S. Nation Building, 1770–1870*. New York: Columbia Univ. Press, 2009.

Lukács, Georg. *The Theory of the Novel*. Cambridge, MA: MIT Press, 1971.

Lupton, Christina. *Knowing Books: The Consciousness of Mediation in Eighteenth-Century Britain*. Philadelphia: Univ. of Pennsylvania Press, 2012.

Lynch, Deidre Shauna. *The Economy of Character: Novels, Market Culture, and the Business of Inner Meaning*. Chicago, IL: Univ. of Chicago Press, 1998.

Maclay, William. *The Journal of William Maclay*. New York: Frederick Ugar Publishing Co., 1965.

Macleod, Duncan. "The Political Economy of John Taylor of Caroline." *Journal of American Studies* 14 (December 1980): 387–405.

Madison, James. *James Madison: Writings*. Edited by Jack N. Rakove. New York: Library of America, 1999.

Madison, James. *The Papers of James Madison*. Vol. 13. Edited by Charles F. Hobson and Robert A. Rutland. Charlottesville: Univ. of Virginia Press, 1981.

Madrick, Jeff. "The Wall Street Leviathan." *New York Review of Books* (April 28, 2011): https://www.nybooks.com/articles/2011/04/28/wall-street-leviathan/

Mandeville. *The Fable of the Bees: or, Private Vices, Publick Benefits*, 5th ed. London: J. Tonson, 1728.

Marks, Steven G. *The Information Nexus: Global Capitalism from the Renaissance to the Present*. New York: Cambridge Univ. Press, 2016.

Martin, Bonnie. "Slavery's Invisible Engine: Mortgaging Human Property." *The Journal of Southern History* 76, no. 4 (November 2010): 817–66.

Marx, Karl. *Capital*, 3 vols. trans. Ben Fowkes. New York: Penguin Books, 1990–92.

Marx, Karl. *Grundrisse: Foundations of the Critique of Political Economy*, trans. Martin Nicolaus. New York: Penguin Books, 1973.

Marx, Karl. *The Poverty of Philosophy*. New York: Penguin Books, 1995.

Marx, Karl. *Theories of Surplus Value*, trans. G.A. Bonner and Emile Burns, vol. 1. London: Lawrence & Wishart, 1951.

Marx, Leo. *The Machine in the Garden: Technology and the Pastoral Ideal in America*. Oxford: Oxford Univ. Press, 1964.

McCloskey, Deidre. "Storytelling in Economics." In *Narrative in Culture: The Uses of Storytelling in the Sciences, Philosophy and Literature*. Edited by Christopher Nash. London: Routledge, 1990.

McGuire, Robert A. *To Form a More Perfect Union: A New Economic Interpretation of the United States Constitution*. Oxford: Oxford Univ. Press, 2003.

McLain, James J. *The Economic Writings of Dupont de Nemours*. Newark: Univ. of Delaware Press, 1977.

McNamara, Robert. *Political Economy and Statesmanship*. DeKalb: Northern Illinois Univ. Press, 1998.

McNary, Dave. "Martin Scorsese on 'Wolf of Wall Street.'" *Variety*, January 25, 2014): https://variety.com/2014/film/news/martin-scorsese-on-wolf-of-wall-street-i-wanted-to-make-a-ferocious-film-1201070801/

Meek, Ronald L. *The Economics of Physiocracy: Essays and Translations*. London: George Allen & Unwin Ltd, 1962.

Mirabeau, Marquis de. *The Oeconomical Table, An Attempt towards Ascertaining and Exhibiting the Source, Progress, and Employment of Riches*. London: Printed for W. Owen, 1766.

Morefield, Jeanne. *Empires Without Imperialism: Anglo-American Decline and the Politics of Deflection*. Oxford, UK: Oxford Univ. Press, 2014.

Moretti, Franco. *Atlas of the European Novel 1800–1900*. London: Verso Books, 1999.

Morris, Thomas D. "'Society is Not Marked by Punctuality in the Payment of Debts': The Chattel Mortgages of Slaves." In *Ambivalent Legacy: A Legal History of the South*. Jackson: Univ. of Mississippi Press, 1984.

Morton, Timothy. *The Poetics of Spice: Romantic Consumerism and the Exotic*. New York: Cambridge Univ. Press, 2006.

Mott, Frank Luther. *A History of American Magazines, 1741–1850*. Cambridge, MA: Harvard Univ. Press, 1966.

Murray, Judith Sargent. *The Gleaner*. Edited by Nina Baym. Schenectady, NY: Union College Press, 1992.

Nicholson, Colin. *Writing and the Rise of Finance: Capital Satires of the Early Eighteenth Century*. Cambridge, UK: Cambridge Univ. Press, 1994.

Ohline, Howard A. "Republicanism and Slavery: Origins of the Three-Fifths Clause in the United States Constitution." *The William and Mary Quarterly* 28 (October 1971): 563–84.

Ohline, Howard A. "Slavery, Economics, and Congressional Politics, 1790." *The Journal of Southern History* 46 (1980): 335–60.

Pack, Spencer J. "Slavery, Adam Smith's Economic Vision and the Invisible Hand." *History of Economic Ideas* 4 (1996): 253–69.

Paine, Thomas. *Rights of Man*, in *Selected Writings of Thomas Paine*. Edited by Ian Shapiro and Jane E. Calvert. New Haven, CT: Yale Univ. Press, 2014.

Panagopoulos, E.P., Editor. *Alexander Hamilton's Pay Book*. Detroit: MI: Wayne State Univ. Press, 1961.

Parrington, Vernon Louis. *Main Currents in American Thought: an Interpretation of American Literature from the Beginnings to 1920*, vol.1. New York: Harcourt, Brace & World, 1927.

Patterson, Annabelle M. *Pastoral and Ideology: Virgil to Valéry*. Berkeley: Univ. of California Press, 1987.

Pocock, J.G.A. *The Machiavellian Moment: Florentine Political Thought and the Atlantic Republic Tradition*. Princeton, NJ: Princeton Univ. Press, 1975.

Pocock, J.G.A. *Politics, Language, and Time: Essays on Political Thought and History*. Chicago, IL: Univ. of Chicago Press, 1960.

Poovey, Mary. *Genres of the Credit Economy: Mediating Value in Eighteenth- and Nineteenth-Century Britain*. Chicago, IL: Univ. of Chicago Press, 2008.

Postlethwayt, Malachy. *The Universal Dictionary of Trade and Commerce*, 2 vols. London: John and Paul Knapton, 1751.

Price, Jacob M. *Capital and Credit in British Overseas Trade: The View from the Chesapeake, 1700-1776*. New York: Cambridge Univ. Press, 1980.

Price, Leah. *The Anthology and the Rise of the Novel: From Richardson to George Eliot*. Cambridge, UK: Cambridge Univ. Press, 2000.

Prince, H.C. "England, circa 1800." In *New Historical Geography of England*. Edited by Henry Clifford Darby. Cambridge, UK: Cambridge Univ. Press, 1973.

Ramsay, James. *On the Treatment and Conversion of African Slaves*. London: James Phillips, 1784.

Randolph, Edmund. "Opinion on the Constitutionality of the Bank." In *The Papers of George Washington, Presidential Series*. Edited by Jack D. Warren, Jr. Charlottesville: Univ. Press of Virginia, 1998.

Rasch, William. "Theories of Complexity, Complexities of Theory: Habermas, Luhmann, and the Study of Social Systems." *German Studies Review* 14.1 (1991): 65-83.

Rassekh, Farhad. *Four Central Theories of the Market Economy*. Abingdon, UK: Routledge, 2017.

Reagan, Ronald. "Remarks Announcing America's Economic Bill of Rights." July 3, 1987. https://www.reaganlibrary.gov/research/speeches/070387a.

Robbins, Bruce. "Commodity Histories." *PMLA* 120 (March 2005): 454-63.

Rodgers, Paul C. "Brown's *Ormond*: The Fruits of Improvisation." *American Quarterly* 26.1 (1974): 4-22.

Rogers, James Steven. *The Early History of the Law of Bills and Notes: A Study of the Origins of Anglo-American Commercial Law*. New York: Cambridge Univ. Press, 1995.

Rolt, Richard. *A New Dictionary of Trade and Commerce*. London: T. Osborne and J. Shipton, 1756.

Roosevelt, Franklin Delano. "Address at the Groundbreaking for the Thomas Jefferson Memorial." December 15, 1938, *National Archives*. https://catalog.archives.gov/id/197846.

Rothschild, Emma. "The Atlantic Worlds of David Hume." In *Soundings in Atlantic History*. Edited by Bernard Bailyn, Patricia L. Denault. Cambridge, MA: Harvard Univ. Press, 2009.

Rzepczynski, Mark S. "The Financial Crisis Inquiry Report, Authorized Edition (a review)." *Financial Analysts Journal* 7 (2012): 78-81.

Samuels, Warren J. "Adam Smith's 'History of Astronomy' Argument." *History of Economic Ideas* 15, no. 2 (2007): 53-78.

Sayre, Gordon. "The Oxymoron of American Pastoralism." *Arizona Quarterly* 69, no. 4 (Winter 2013): 1-18.

Schabas, Margaret. "Temporal Dimensions in Hume's Monetary Theory." In *David Hume's Political Economy*. Edited by Carl Wennerlind and Margaret Schabas. New York: Routledge, 2008.

Schumpeter, Joseph. *History of Economic Analysis*. New York: Oxford Univ. Press, 1986.

Shackle, G.L.S. *Epistemics and Economics: A Critique of Economic Doctrines*. New York: Cambridge Univ. Press, 1972.

Shalhope, Robert E. *John Taylor of Caroline: Pastoral Republicanism*. Columbia: Univ. of South Carolina Press, 1980.

Shalhope, Robert E. "Anticipating Americanism: An Individual Perspective on Republicanism in the Early Republic." In *Americanism: New Perspectives on the History of an Ideal*. Edited by Michael Kazin and Joseph A. McCartin. Chapel Hill: Univ. of North Carolina Press, 2006.

Shapiro, Stephen. *The Culture and Commerce of the Early American Novel: Reading the Atlantic World-System*. State College: Pennsylvania State Univ. Press, 2008.

Sharp, Granville. *An Essay on Slavery*. Burlington, NJ: West Jersey, 1778.

Sheldon, Garrett Ward and Hill, Charles William. *The Liberal Republicanism of John Taylor of Caroline*. Madison, NJ: Farleigh Dickinson Univ. Press, 2008.

Shenstone, William. "Elegy I." In *The Works, in Verse and Prose*, 3 vols. London: H. Woodfall, 1768.

Shields, David. *Oracles of Empire: Poetry, Politics, and Commerce in British America, 1690–1750*. Chicago: Chicago Univ. Press, 1990.

Shields, John C. "Phillis Wheatley's Subversion of Classical Style." *Style* 27, No. 2 (1993): 252–70.

Siskin, Clifford. *System: The Shaping of Modern Knowledge*. Cambridge, MA: M.I.T. Press, 2016.

Skemp, Sheila. *First Lady of Letters: Judith Sargent Murray and the Struggle for Female Independence*. Philadelphia: Univ. of Pennsylvania Press, 2009.

Slauter, Eric. "Revolutions in the Meaning and Study of Politics." *American Literary History* 22, no. 2 (2010): 325–40.

Sloan, Herbert E. *Principle & Interest: Thomas Jefferson and the Problem of Debt*. Charlottesville: Univ. of Virginia Press, 1995.

Smith, Adam. "The Principles which Lead and Direct Philosophical Enquiries; Illustrated by the History of Astronomy." *Essays on Philosophical Subjects*. London: T. Cadell and W. Davies, 1795.

Smith, Adam. *The Theory of Moral Sentiments*. Edited by D.D. Raphael and A.L. Macfie. Oxford: Clarendon Press, 1976.

Smith, Adam. *An Inquiry into the Nature and Causes of the Wealth of Nations* in *The Glasgow Edition of the Works of Adam Smith*, 2 vols. Oxford, UK: Clarendon Press, 1976.

Smith, Adam. *Lectures on Jurisprudence*. Edited by R.L. Meek. Oxford: Oxford Univ. Press, 1978.

Smith, Venture. *A Narrative of the Life and Adventures of Venture, a Native of Africa*. In *Unchained Voices: An Anthology of Black Authors in the English-Speaking World of the Eighteenth Century*. Edited by Vincent Carretta. Lexington: Univ. of Kentucky Press, 2004.

Solow, Barbara L. "Slavery and Colonization." In *Slavery and the Rise of the Atlantic System*. Edited by Barbara L. Solow. Cambridge: Cambridge Univ. Press, 1991.

Sparks, Randy J. *Where the Negroes are Masters: An African Port in the Era of the Slave Trade*. Cambridge, MA: Harvard Univ. Press, 2014.

Squibbs, Richard. *Urban Enlightenment and the Eighteenth-Century Periodical Essay: Transatlantic Retrospects*. Basingstoke, UK: Palgrave Macmillan, 2014.

Stern, Julia. "The State of 'Women' in *Ormond*. In *Revising Charles Brockden Brown: Culture, Politics and Sexuality in the Early Republic*. Edited by Philip Barnard, Mark Kamrath, and Stephen Shapiro. Knoxville: Univ. of Tennessee Press, 2004.

Stourzh, Gerald. *Alexander Hamilton and the Idea of Republican Government*. Stanford, CA: Stanford Univ. Press, 1970.

Sweet, Timothy. *American Georgic: Economic and Environment in Early American Literature, 1580–1864*. Philadelphia: Univ. of Pennsylvania Press, 2002.

Taylor, John. *An Enquiry into the Principles and Tendency of Certain Public Measures*. Philadelphia, PA: Thomas Dobson, 1794.

Thaler, Richard H. *Misbehaving: The Making of Behavioral Economics*. New York: Norton Books, 2015.

Tolles, Frederick B. "George Logan and the Agricultural Revolution." *Proceedings of the American Philosophical Society* 95 (1951): 589–596.

Toscano, Alberto and Jeff Kinkle. *Cartographies of the Absolute*. Winchester, UK: Zero Books, 2014.

Tracy, Count Destutt de. *A Treatise on Political Economy*, trans. Thomas Jefferson. Georgetown: Joseph Milligan 1817.

Tucker, Robert W. and David C. Hendrickson. *Empire of Liberty: The Statecraft of Thomas Jefferson*. Oxford: Oxford Univ. Press, 1990.

Vaggi, Gianni. *The Economics of François Quesnay*. Durham, NC: Duke Univ. Press, 1987.

Vardi, Liana. *The Physiocrats and the World of the Enlightenment*. New York: Cambridge Univ. Press, 2012.

Vernier, Richard. "The Fortunes of Orthodoxy: The Political Economy of Public Debt in England and America during the 1780s." In *Articulating America: Fashioning a National Political Culture in Early America*. Edited by Rebecca Starr. Lanham, MD: Rowman & Littlefield Publishers, 2000: 93–131.

Viner, Jacob. "Adam Smith and Laissez Faire." *Journal of Political Economy* 35 (1927): 198–232.

Viner, Jacob. *Essays on the Intellectual History of Economics*. Edited by Douglas A. Irwin. Princeton, NJ: Princeton Univ. Press, 1991.

Wallerstein, Immanuel. *Historical Capitalism*. New York: Verso Books, 1983.

Walters, Raymond. *Albert Gallatin: Jeffersonian Financier and Diplomat*. Pittsburg, PA: Univ. of Pittsburg Press.

Warren, Mercy Otis, *Poems, Dramatic and Miscellaneous*. Boston: I. Thomas and E.T. Andrews, 1790.

Watt, Ian. *The Rise of the Novel: Studies in Defoe, Richardson and Fielding*. Berkeley: Univ. of California Press, 1957.

Watts, Edward. *Writing and Postcolonialism in the Early Republic*. Charlottesville: Univ. of Virginia Press, 1998.

Webster, Pelatiah. *Political Essays on the Nature and Operation of Money, Public Finances and Other Subjects*. Philadelphia, PA: Joseph Crushank, 1791.

Webster, Noah. *The Effects of Slavery*. Hartford, CT: Hudson and Goodwin, 1793.

Wennerlind, Carl. "An Artificial Virue and the Oil of Commerce: A Synthetic View of Hume's Theory of Money." In *David Hume's Political Economy*. Edited by Carl Wennerlind and Margaret Schabas. New York. Routledge, 2008: 106–26.

Whatley, Thomas. *Observations on Modern Gardening*. London, UK: T. Payne, 1770.

Wheatley, Phillis. *Complete Writings*. Edited by Vincent Carretta. New York: Penguin Books, 2001.

White, Ed. "The Ends of Republicanism." *Journal of Early Republic* 30 (Summer 2010): 179–99.

Wiecek, William M. *The Sources of Antislavery Constitutionalism in America, 1760–1848*. Ithaca, NY: Cornell Univ. Press, 1977.

Wilcox, Kirstin. "The Scribblings of a Plain Man and the Temerity of a Woman: Gender and Genre in Judith Sargent Murray's *The Gleaner*." *Early American Literature* 30 (1995): 121–44.

Williams, Eric. *Capitalism and Slavery*. Chapel Hill: Univ. of North Carolina Press, 1944.

Williams, Raymond. *The Country and the City*. Oxford: Oxford Univ. Press, 1975.

Winter, Kari J. "The Strange Career of Benjamin Franklin Prentiss, Antislavery Lawyer." *Vermont History* 79, no. 2 (2011): 121–40.

Woloch, Alex. *The One vs. The Many: Minor Characters and the Space of the Protagonist in the Novel*. Princeton, NJ: Princeton Univ. Press, 2003.

Wright, Robert E. *One Nation Under Debt: Hamilton, Jefferson, and the History of What We Owe*. New York: McGraw Hill, 2008.

# { INDEX }

For the benefit of digital users, indexed terms that span two pages (e.g., 52–53) may, on occasion, appear on only one of those pages.

Printed and bound by CPI Group (UK) Ltd, Croydon, CR0 4YY